Colonial Relations

Colonial Relations offers a study of the lived history of nineteenth-century British imperialism through the lives of one extended family in North America, the Caribbean, and the United Kingdom. The prominent colonial governor James Douglas was born in 1803 in what is now Guyana, probably to a free woman of color and an itinerant Scottish father. While working in the North American fur trade, he married Amelia Connolly, the daughter of a Cree mother and an Irish-Canadian father. Adele Perry traces their family and friends over the course of the "long" nineteenth century, using careful archival research to offer an analysis of the imperial world that is at once intimate and critical, wide ranging and sharply focused. Perry engages feminist scholarship on gender and intimacy, critical analyses of colonial archives, transnational and postcolonial history, and the "new imperial history" to suggest how this period might be rethought through the experiences of one powerful family located at the British Empire's margins.

ADELE PERRY is Professor of History and Senior Fellow, St. John's College at the University of Manitoba.

Critical Perspectives on Empire

Editors

Professor Catherine Hall
University College London

Professor Mrinalini Sinha
University of Michigan

Professor Kathleen Wilson
State University of New York, Stony Brook

Critical Perspectives on Empire is a major series of ambitious, cross-disciplinary works in the emerging field of critical imperial studies. Books in the series explore the connections, exchanges, and mediations at the heart of national and global histories, the contributions of local as well as metropolitan knowledge, and the flows of people, ideas, and identities facilitated by colonial contact. To that end, the series not only offers a space for outstanding scholars working at the intersection of several disciplines to bring to wider attention the impact of their work; it also takes a leading role in reconfiguring contemporary historical and critical knowledge, of the past and of ourselves.

A full list of titles published in the series can be found at:
www.cambridge.org/cpempire

Colonial Relations

The Douglas-Connolly Family and the Nineteenth-Century Imperial World

Adele Perry

University of Manitoba

CAMBRIDGE
UNIVERSITY PRESS

CAMBRIDGE
UNIVERSITY PRESS

University Printing House, Cambridge CB2 8BS, United Kingdom

Cambridge University Press is part of the University of Cambridge.

It furthers the University's mission by disseminating knowledge in the pursuit of education, learning and research at the highest international levels of excellence.

www.cambridge.org
Information on this title: www.cambridge.org/9781107037618

© Adele Perry 2015

First published 2015

Printed in the United States of America by Sheridan Books, Inc.

A catalogue record for this publication is available from the British Library

ISBN 978-1-107-03761-8 Hardback

Contents

Illustrations

MAPS

TABLE

Acknowledgements

If twenty years ago someone had told me I would write a book in part about James Douglas, my response would have fallen somewhere between disbelieving and horrified. In the British Columbia of the 1970s and '80s that I grew up in, James Douglas was a stock figure in celebratory local histories. I came to history as a student interested in connecting feminist and socialist politics to the past, and I could not see what role stories of brave fur traders and far-sighted governors might play here. Even when critical analyses of race and empire prompted me to return to British Columbia's past with my Ph.D. dissertation and what became my first book, my priority was to excavate the history of ordinary people in the history of empire, and Douglas was not one of those.

It was in the early 2000s that I started to see different possibilities in examining the histories of local colonial elites such as the Metis family in Red River Colony, painted by artist Peter Rindisbacher around 1825 and featured on the cover of this book. The northern North American history that occurred before the last third of the nineteenth century increasingly seemed like a time of radical possibility, though certainly not equity. Studying the particular history of James Douglas, his wife, Amelia Connolly, and their family seemed a useful way of making a pointed intervention into what was a growing literature on colonial histories and geographies, and of contributing to continuing efforts to put feminist and postcolonial perspectives into dialogue. These histories also provided a way of bringing historiographies of dispossession, migration, and gender into conversation and of mapping gender, kinship, and intimacy on a close and revealing scale. What I first imagined as a modest and contained sort of research project grew in ways that I would never have predicted, and the histories of James Douglas, Amelia Connolly, and their kin have absorbed my attention for more than a decade. This book is the end result, and I am oddly sad to see it go.

I have accrued what Antoinette Burton calls archive stories on three continents and from about twenty different archives. I would like to acknowledge the help of the British Columbia Archives, and in particular

Fredericke Vespoor, David Matheson, Kelly-Ann Turkington and Diane Wardle who all helped me track down records. In Winnipeg, the Hudson's Bay Company Archives and especially James Gorton and Chris Kotecki deserve mention. A number of archivists helped make materials available long-distance, and I thank Scott Daniels of the Oregon Historical Society and Joe Winterbourne of the Fort William Historical Park for their assistance. In Georgetown I used the Walter Rodney National Archives and I would like to thank Linda Peake, Karen de Souza, and Nigel Westmaas for their advice and direction, archivist Nadia Carter and Marlene Cox and Tota Magnar from the University of Guyana for their support. The University of Manitoba's librarians were always patient with my many requests for interlibrary loans. That the United Kingdom holds many of the relevant records is a telling point, and I should thank the British Library, the National Archives of Scotland, the National Archives at Kew, the National Maritime Museum at Greenwich, and Cambridge's University Library's Rare Books Room here.

The internet can be a curse but it can also be a gift. Multi-sited and transnational research is made much more possible by the availability of historical sources online and open-access. I am grateful for the people and institutions who worked to make archival records available online. I would especially like to thank Patrick Duane and John Lutz, Jim Hendrickson, and their colleagues at the University of Victoria for making sources on nineteenth-century British Columbia, and more particularly the Colonial Office correspondence, available online at http://bcgenesis.uvic.ca/index .htm and for helping me with specific queries. I first read these records in their handwritten, microfilmed form, and am grateful that there is now a more accessible alternative. I do not know either John Lance Wilmer or Tikwis Begbie, but I am thankful for their work in making transcripts of Guyanese newspapers available online at www.vc.id.au/edg/index.html and an index of Guyanese colonists at www.vc.id.au/tb/.

If historians reject the presumption that history begins and ends within contemporary national borders, we need to follow lives and ideas along the routes they traveled. Doing so means learning new literatures and new archives, and the opportunity to learn about Guyana and the eastern Caribbean was a challenge as well as an intellectual pleasure. I also relied on the generosity and knowledge of other scholars who have worked on these histories. Charlotte Girard's 1970s and '80s scholarship on the Douglas family was in many ways work before its time, and the publications, unpublished material, and Charlotte's generous advice have been an enormous resource. John Adams's *Old Square Toes and his Lady* is an important book; I have returned to its pages regularly and appreciate John's knowledge and generosity. This is the second time that I have followed in Sylvia Van Kirk's archival footsteps, and my debts to her are substantial. The same is true for Jennifer Brown, whom I also thank for sharing unpublished material with me. Anne Lindsay helped me locate records I could not find and generously offered her research on the Connolly family to me. Nicholas Draper shared relevant files from his research on the economics of slave compensation in nineteenth-century Britain.

I have had many interlocutors and correspondents. I benefited from ongoing conversations with Laurie Bertram, Jarvis Brownlie, Diana Brydon, Antoinette Burton, Sarah Carter, Tina Mai Chen, David Churchill, Ann Curthoys, Karen Dubinsky, Ryan Eyford, Sherry Farrell Racette, Barry Ferguson, Patricia Grimshaw, Paula Hastings, Stuart C. Houston, Betsy Jameson, Esyllt Jones, Kurt Korneski, Marilyn Lake, Kiera Ladner, Mary Jane Logan McCallum, Richard Mackie, Kathryn McPherson, Erin Millions, Cecilia Morgan, Melanie Newton, Fiona Paisley, Steve Penfold, Todd Scarth, Alissa Trotz, Jane Van Roggen, Elizabeth Vibert, and Angela Wanhalla. Susan Armitage, Jean Barman, Bettina Bradbury, Sean Carleton, Gerry Friesen, Jean Friesen, and Kenton Storey all read the manuscript in its entirety, and I am especially grateful for Bettina's and Gerry's astute and careful readings. As series editor for the Critical History of Empires series, Catherine Hall has been an engaged, attentive, and (luckily) patient editor. I am responsible for whatever errors are in the pages that follow, and have been down this road enough to know that there will be some.

Research is a kind of thinking, and this is one of the reasons why I usually like to do it myself. But this project is much richer for the work of some capable research assistants: Jackie Cooney, Jarett Henderson, Jonathan Hildebrandt, Alexandre Michaud, and Karlee Sapoznik. Chris Hanna knows a great deal about the archives of nineteenth-century British Columbia, and he undertook the work with land records there. Laura Ishiguro did key work in the British archives. Krista Barclay made sense out of the footnotes, made the family tree, and helped with the images. Erin Leinberger made the maps.

All of this has been made possible by a number of institutions. I am lucky that the happenstance of academic hiring in a small country landed me at the University of Manitoba, where the university, the Department of History, and St. John's College have been unwaveringly supportive. In the middle of this project I spent the better part of a year at Clare Hall, Cambridge, and doing so changed my mind in all sorts of predictable and unpredictable ways. I am grateful for the space, community, and access to records that Clare Hall provided. For more than a decade I benefited from a Tier II Canada Research Chair in Western Canadian

Social History, and the kind of multi-cited archival research upon which this book depends was only possible because of it.

Historians write about the past, but we do so in the present and for the present. This book is about the complicated identities and relationships produced and calcified by colonialism, including the fraught histories of racialized migrants and the uneasy histories of being a settler in Indigenous space. These are my own histories and my own present. Much of my scholarly research and writing has been concerned with analyzing the vernacular experience of colonialism. I have done so alongside other scholars and in dialogue with social movements that demand a more just and sustainable way of living in Indigenous territories and among Indigenous peoples. 2012–13 was the winter we danced, and it echoes in the pages that follow.

Versions of this research were presented to audiences across Canada, England, Scotland, Australia, New Zealand, and the USA. In very different forms, parts of this research were published as "'Is Your Garden in England, Sir?': Nation, Empire, and Home in James Douglas' Archive," *History Workshop Journal*, 69:1 (Fall 2010) 1–19; "Historiography that Breaks Your Heart: Sylvia Van Kirk and the Writing of Feminist History," in Robin Jarvis Brownlie and Valerie Korinek, eds., *Finding a Way to the Heart: Feminist Writings on Aboriginal and Women's History in Canada* (Winnipeg: University of Manitoba Press, 2012) 81–97; and "James Douglas, Amelia Connolly, and the Writing of Gender and Women's History," in Catherine Carstairs and Nancy Janovecik, eds., *Feminist History: Productive Pasts and New Directions* (Vancouver: UBC Press, 2013) 23–40. I am grateful for the permission of the publishers to reprint this work here.

As someone who has both borne children and written books and found that the two experiences have almost nothing in common, I pretty much loathe the shopworn analogy between having babies and writing books. But still the babies have shaped this book, its concerns, and its arguments. The book is rooted in the presumption that the affective labors of caring for children and creating homes in contexts of inequality are highly meaningful, enormously political, and above all interesting and worthy of historical attention. As I have worked out these arguments, Peter Ives and I raised our daughter, Nell, and son, Theo, and I am grateful for all the difficult and wonderful lessons this has brought. I am also thankful for the people who have helped us do so, especially Claudia Scott and Sudesh Gupta, Thelma Randall and everyone else at Cornish Child Care.

I wrote this book in coffee shops in Winnipeg, Vancouver, Toronto, London, and Georgetown. I wrote it at a cottage in the Laurentian Mountains that my in-laws rented one summer. I wrote it in my office at

St. John's College, which began as a school for elite Indigenous children in Red River Colony. But mainly, I wrote this book at home, on the black chesterfield by the fire, while my children played, argued, and texted, and while Peter talked about global English, listened to terrible 1980s music, and tried to go rowing. All of this is also in these pages, and it could be no other way.

1   Empire, family, and archive

This book uses the story of one family to analyze the vernacular history of the imperial world over what historians call the long nineteenth century. It tracks the histories of James Douglas (1803–1877), his wife, Amelia Connolly (1812–1890), their kin, and peers in the eastern Caribbean, the United Kingdom, and various parts of North America, including the British colonies of Vancouver Island and British Columbia where Douglas would serve as governor. The story of what I call the Douglas-Connolly family (see Figure 1.1) is a complicated and at times disjointed and oblique one. Part of this story is well known to historians of Canada, and more particularly British Columbia. The story of these colonial relations is less well known to historians of empire, but their history is salutary for historians committed to critically engaging with imperialism's complicated and consequential past. This history makes clear the power and the possibility of thinking beyond accustomed definitions of empire and nation, and demonstrates the potential of re-reading empire through a critical feminist lens that connects the presumed jurisdictions of the private and the public.

I return to these points in the conclusion. I begin where historians like to, which is with the archives. In the past decade historians have explored the records produced and left by the colonial states as particular, racialized, and gendered forms of technology. In different ways, Anne Laura Stoler, Antoinette Burton, Durba Ghosh, Anjali Androkar, Julia Emberley, and Betty Joseph urge us to see archives as a terrain of colonial histories rather than simply as a source of them. Colonial archives are a technology that helped produce the world rather than a window into it.[1]

---

[1] See Antoinette Burton, ed., *Archive Stories: Facts, Fictions, and the Writing of History* (Durham, NC: Duke University Press, 2004); Antoinette Burton, *Dwelling in the Archive: Women Writing House, Home, and History in Late Colonial India* (Oxford University Press, 2003); Betty Joseph, *Reading the East India Company, 1720–1840: Colonial Currencies of Gender* (University of Chicago Press, 2003); Durba Ghosh, "Decoding the Nameless: Gender, Subjectivity, and Historical Methodologies in Reading the Archives of Colonial India," in Kathleen Wilson, ed., *A New Imperial History: Culture, Identity, Modernity,*

Douglas-Connolly Family:

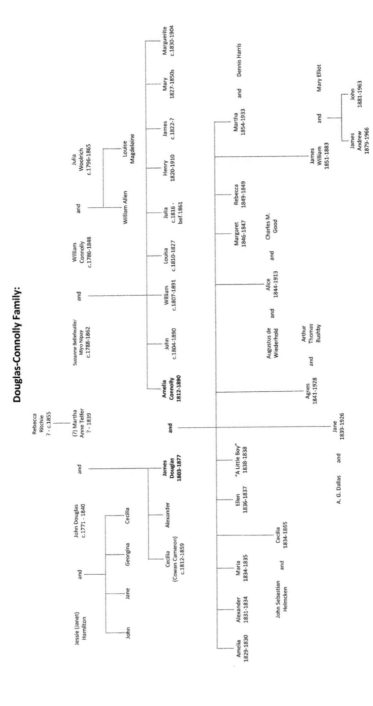

Figure 1.1 Douglas-Connolly family tree.

My analysis of the Douglas-Connolly family and the lived history of empire is based on a critical ethnographic conversation with the colonial archives. The footnotes that follow enumerate sources that are familiar to historians of imperialism, the eastern Caribbean, and western North America: the records of the British colonies of Demerara and Essequibo, Vancouver Island, and British Columbia, the papers created by the administration of slavery and abolition, the records of private fur-trade companies, especially the Hudson's Bay Company (HBC), the correspondence of missionaries and reformers, metropolitan and colonial newspapers, published travel literature and memories, a range of personal and family archives including letters and journals, and materials gathered by local historians in the late nineteenth and early twentieth century. These records are held in the archives and libraries of postcolonial Canada and Guyana, in repositories in the United States and the United Kingdom, and in the distinctly translocal space of the internet.

All of these archives are profoundly shaped by the individuals who created them, the state and private enterprises they labored on behalf of, and by the people, institutions, and societies that preserved them. These archives are multiple, scattered, and episodic. They impose a discipline on the historian who works with them. Social historians and historians of women and the colonial world have long been accustomed to reading archives "against the grain." Here I try what Stoler calls "reading along the archival grain," treating colonial archives "both as a corps of writing and as a force field that animates political energies and expertise, that pulls on some 'social facts' and converts them into qualified knowledge, that attends to some ways of knowing while repelling and refusing others."[2]

I begin with the probable time and place of James Douglas' birth, early nineteenth-century Demerara. In the 1970s and '80s, historian Charlotte Girard combed the archives of Guyana, Barbados, Canada, the Netherlands, and Great Britain for data about James Douglas' early life. She found little direct evidence, but was able to skillfully link fragments of records to produce a tentative and cautious identification of his

---

1660–1840 (Cambridge University Press, 2004); Anjali Arondekar, "Without a Trace: Sexuality and the Colonial Archive," *Journal of the History of Sexuality*, 14:1/2 (January/April 2005) 10–27; Ann Laura Stoler, "Colonial Archives and the Acts of Governance: On the Content in the Form," in Carolyn Hamilton, Verne Harris, Jane Taylor *et al.*, eds., *Refiguring the Archives* (Dordrecht: Kluwer, 2002); Julia V. Emberley, "'A Gift for Languages': Native Women and the Textual Economy of the Colonial Archives," *Cultural Critique*, 17 (1990/1) 21–50.

[2] Ann Laura Stoler, *Along the Archival Grain: Epistemic Anxieties and Colonial Common Sense* (Princeton University Press, 2009) 22.

probable mother and grandmother.[3] I have found nothing that definitively proves Girard's argument and nothing that either challenges it or provides a plausible alternative. The uncertainty about Douglas' origins is part of the history analyzed here rather than a simple impediment to it. The babies born in nineteenth-century colonial societies were a complicated problem for empire, one that was in part managed by practices of non-recognition. As Ghosh explains in her study of the family in colonial India, the archive "serviced the imperatives of the government by erasing or excluding various subjects," including "native mistresses, out-of-wedlock children, and multiple families."[4]

The colonial state in early nineteenth-century Demerara recorded ordinary people in the greatest detail when they bought property, sold property, or themselves became property through practices of slavery. I know most about Douglas' probable mother and grandmother when colonial governments regulated, taxed, or compensated them for their slaveholdings. Whatever relationships or children they or people like them had did not provoke the same kind of archival attention. British Guiana took no censuses until 1839, and there was no system of registering births until the 1860s.[5] Only a few sets of baptismal records have survived, and Georgetown's newspaper didn't report early nineteenth-century births beyond an episodic accounting of the numbers of unnamed "free coloured" and "White" boys and girls born in a given month.[6]

The personal archive does not supply all the information absent from the records kept by the state. A list of important events that Douglas kept reflected his own uncertainty about his history. "1803 June 6 Borne?" he asked himself.[7] As an adult Douglas was notoriously tight-lipped about his own background. A son-in-law recalled that "personal experiences

---

[3] Charlotte S. M. Girard, "Sir James Douglas' Mother and Grandmother," *BC Studies*, 44 (Winter 1979/1980) 25–31; Charlotte S. M. Girard, "Some Further Notes on the Douglas Family," *BC Studies*, 72 (Winter 1986/7) 3–27; Charlotte Girard, "The Guiana World of Sir James Douglas' Childhood," unpublished MS; I thank Charlotte Girard and John Adams for helping me locate this important unpublished paper. Also see W. Kaye Lamb, "Some Notes on the Douglas Family," *British Columbia Historical Quarterly*, 17:1/2 (1953) 41–51; W. Kaye Lamb, "Ancestry of Sir James Douglas, KCB (1803–1877)," British Columbia Archives (hereafter BCA), B/90/D741, Transcript.

[4] Durba Ghosh, *Sex and the Family in Colonial India: The Making of Empire* (Cambridge University Press, 2006) 253.

[5] See Dennis Arthur Brown, *The Political Economy of Fertility in the British West Indies, 1891–1921* (Kingston, Jamaica: University of West Indies, 2000) 27.

[6] See, for instance, "Monthly Return of Births in this Colony," *Esquebbo and Demerara Gazette*, May 30, 1812, accessed January 18, 2012, www.vc.id.au/edg/index.html.

[7] James Douglas, "Notes," in "Private Account," BCA, Add MSS B/90/1.

were not much talked about."[8] In 1923, one of Douglas' granddaughters asked her mother about his history. Her response was a sketchy list:

1. His mother was a Miss Ritchie.
2. Born in Lanarkshire.
3. His Father owned sugar Estates in Demerara.
4. Judge Cameron was only married once, to my Aunt, Cecilia Douglas – (she was married twice. R.B.)[9]

As either the sum total of what a daughter knew about her father or what she chose to tell her own daughter, this was scanty, unstable, and at least somewhat untrue. As in the Ngai Tahu communities of southern New Zealand studied by historian Angela Wanhalla, "stories circulated, myths abounded," and "ancestry was shadowy."[10]

All of this makes it difficult to write a standard biography of Douglas and, for not dissimilar reasons, Connolly Douglas. She was born in Cree territory in what is now northwestern Canada in 1812, and it was only an unexpected court case and some family records that put details about her parents' marriage and her birth into the colonial archive. Colonial lives like those of Douglas and Connolly Douglas force us to recalibrate our default settings for biographical research. Historian Clare Anderson has recently reminded us that we can and should tell the stories of plebeian colonial people's lives, however fragmentary our versions of them must be.[11] The necessity of working with partial and vexed archives closes down some interpretive avenues, but it opens others up. Joseph argues that "Reconciling oneself to a partial history is ultimately a call for producing a new kind of narrative."[12] While this book utilizes the analytic frame of the individual life and the family, it is not a conclusive genealogy or conventional biography. Instead, I utilize available archival evidence about one extended family to anchor an analysis of the nineteenth-century imperial world, to ground and focus these wide, wandering, and sometimes daunting histories.

---

[8] Dorothy Blakey Smith, ed., *The Reminiscences of Doctor John Sebastian Helmcken* (Vancouver: UBC Press, 1975) 140.

[9] Rose Bullen to Walter Sage, February 12, 1925, in Walter N. Sage Papers, Box 36, University of British Columbia (UBC) Archives (hereafter Sage Papers).

[10] Angela Wanhalla, *In/Visible Sight: The Mixed Descent Families of Southern New Zealand* (Edmonton: Athabasca University Press, 2010) 2.

[11] Clare Anderson, *Subaltern Lives: Biographies of Colonialism in the Indian Ocean World, 1790–1920* (Cambridge University Press, 2012) 17.

[12] Betty Joseph, "Proxies of Power: Women in the Colonial Archive," in Felicity Nussbaum, ed., *The Global Eighteenth Century* (Baltimore: Johns Hopkins University Press, 2003) 137. Also see Nupur Chaudhuri, Sherry J. Katz, and Mary Elizabeth Perry, eds., *Contesting Archives: Finding Women in the Sources* (Urbana-Champagne: University of Illinois Press, 2012).

Douglas entered the colonial archive as an unmistakable biographical subject when, in 1819, he became an unfree laborer in North America's fur trade. He surfaced occasionally in the records kept by the North West Company and more often in the records of the HBC, in the direct employ of which he would remain for more than three decades and with which he and two of his sons-in-law would remain associated for their working lives. The HBC archives are an enormous and often fastidious record of furs secured, trade goods exchanged, provisions needed, and workers and workplaces managed. Douglas became a routine presence in these records when he was appointed to a position of authority in the 1830s. From 1839 to 1858, he was the leading authority of the HBC on the Pacific coast and, as a result, a constant and formative presence in the records it left. Douglas became governor of the British colony of Vancouver Island in 1851 and of the colony of British Columbia in 1858, and in these capacities was the most powerful local representative of the British imperial state on North America's west coast. He remained as such until his retirement in 1863/4. As chief factor and governor, he was central to the making of two enormous archives of empire, and I can make no claims to comprehensive knowledge of them.

The records of the HBC and the colonial governments were mainly produced in colonial space, but with the interests and concerns of the metropole always in mind. And it was there that these records were gathered, sorted, and archived. Over the course of the twentieth century, the records of British North American colonies and the fur trade were increasingly claimed as part of the domain of *Canadian* history and relocated, literally as well as figuratively, from the space of the empire to the space of the nation. In the early twentieth century, Canada's national archive acquired copies, first in transcript and photostat and later in microform, of the Colonial Office records relating to British administration of northern North America. In 1974 the Hudson's Bay Company Archive was patriated to the Archives of Manitoba, a maneuver registered as a return of a national treasure.[13] Historians' interests made a similar sort of journey, becoming increasingly engaged with narratives of nation and region, and less engaged with imperial or oceanic frames. This book is part of a wider scholarship that aims to reconnect histories of Canada and the territories that preceded it with a critical historiography of empire.[14]

---

[13] See Jarett Henderson, "'I Am Pleased with the Lambton Loot': Arthur George Doughty and the Making of the Durham Papers," *Archivaria*, 70 (Fall 2010) 153–176; Deidre Simmons, *Keepers of the Record: The History of the Hudson's Bay Company Archives* (Montreal: McGill-Queens University Press, 2009).

[14] See Lisa Chilton, "Canada and the British Empire: A Review Essay," *Canadian Historical Review*, 89:1 (March 2008) 89–95.

The range of authors, interests, genres, and administrative regimes at play here make clear that this is not a single colonial "archive," but a polyvocal set of archives. The subjects included or excluded from these archives reflect their different priorities, interests, and optics. The records of the HBC and British colonial governments are full of men, figured as curiously separate from their lives as sons, brothers, husbands, and fathers. As an author, subject, audience, and authority, Douglas is everywhere in the archives of the HBC and of the colonial governments of Vancouver Island and British Columbia. But Douglas as a person with a history and a family is mainly absent from the formal letters, despatches, and reports. It is not that kinship and intimacy were irrelevant to this or other institutions of empire. Relations between Douglas and the male in-laws with whom he worked throughout his adult life – first his father-in-law in the HBC, then two sons-in-law in the HBC and colonial government, and finally two more sons-in-law in Vancouver Island and British Columbia's colonial governments – were key to this local colonial state. Intimate relations between male kin run subcutaneous throughout the history of the nineteenth-century empire, obscured by patriarchal naming practices that disassociated male kin from one another. These ties were not unnoticed by critics of British North American states, who deemed the colonial governments run by Douglas and other tightly knit local elites as those of the "family compact."[15] Here, I try to excavate the connections between kin and the endurance of women's connections to the families of their birth. Whenever possible I follow the practice of a number of members of the Douglas-Connolly family and use women's surnames of birth alongside their married names in an effort to trace the complicated ties that bound men and women to one another and helped to structure local states and the nineteenth-century British Empire as an aggregate.

The colonial archives imagine men in specific ways and figure women at best infrequently and in ways that obscure their histories. As Burton has argued, the official archive is gendered from the start, associated with male authority and textual records, and disassociated from women, speech, and fiction.[16] The gendered schism of record-keeping calcified

---

[15] On elsewhere in British North America, see Allan Greer, *The Patriots and the People: The Rebellion of 1837 in Rural Lower Canada* (University of Toronto Press, 1993) Chapter 7; Cecilia Morgan, "'When Bad Men Conspire, Good Men Must Unite!': Gender and Political Discourse in Upper Canada, 1820s–1830s," in Kathryn M. McPherson, Nancy Forstell, and Cecilia Morgan, eds., *Gendered Pasts: Historical Essays in Femininity and Masculinity in Canada* (Oxford University Press, 1999). That Douglas was at the center of a "family compact" was a point made from the 1860s onwards. See Chad Reimer, *Writing British Columbia History, 1784–1958* (Vancouver: University of British Columbia Press, 2009) 27.

[16] Burton, *Dwelling in the Archive*, Chapter 1.

in the North American colonial contexts when primarily oral Indigenous cultures met primarily textual European ones in charged and uneven ways. As in colonial India, Indigenous women are often tellingly nameless in fur-trade records, described only by a first name or an association with a place or a man.[17] Amelia Connolly Douglas was the daughter of one powerful man in the fur trade and then the wife of another, but her presence in the fur-trade archive was never much more than uncertain. But women and children sometimes surface in the records that desired and, at the same time, helped to constitute their presence as both tangential and unknowable. The rich historical scholarship on women and the fur trade that I draw on throughout this book would not be possible otherwise. Here, I too use the information about women found scattered throughout the fur-trade archive to piece together information about Amelia Connolly Douglas, her female kin, and the women they lived alongside. The records left by Connolly Douglas' sister, two of the family's daughters, and other female friends and kin help us situate elite colonial women within the imperial world and some of the local spaces remade within it. But this remains an archive where men speak with greater frequency, detail, and volume than do women.

I do not and cannot adequately restore Amelia Connolly Douglas to the story told here. She was recognized as the chief factor's and then the governor's wife and shared in whatever honorifics her husband accrued. Her small role in the local imperial public sphere was codified in an official archive that only rarely admitted her presence. The family's daughters were more regular participants in the public performance of empire in Vancouver Island's capital city of Victoria, and their intimate relationships and social connections were closely observed by settlers and passers-by alike. The colonial archive produced under Douglas' early administration was in part created in space that was both the family home and office of state. In the 1850s, the family's eldest daughters both assisted their father with the paperwork of governance, and Jane was recalled as Douglas' "amanuensis." This is a different iteration of the complicated politics of gender, kinship, and authorship in the nineteenth-century imperial world traced by historian Zoë Laidlaw.[18]

This pattern of voluble husbands, quiet daughters, and quieter wives reflects hierarchies and schisms between orality and literacy as well as

---

[17] Durba Ghosh, "Decoding the Nameless."

[18] Smith, ed., *The Reminiscences of Doctor John Sebastian Helmcken*, 81; Walter N. Sage, *Sir James Douglas and British Columbia* (University of Toronto Press, 1930) 339; Zoë Laidlaw, "'Aunt Anna's Report': The Buxton Women and the Aborigines Select Committee, 1835–1837," *Journal of Imperial and Commonwealth History*, 32:2 (May 2004) 1–28.

between men and women. My methodology reflects a discipline forged in the sinews of empire and nation and predicated on the colonial state's production and maintenance of the archive and the privileging of alphabetic texts. The extent to which histories of Indigenous North American societies that communicated, honed, and preserved knowledge primarily through oral and material means can be adequately addressed through this sort of lens is an enduring question worth asking again and again.[19] We might also ask whether presuming the absolute difference of Indigenous and European societies' forms of archives reifies difference and occludes the range of archival practices in both Indigenous and settler societies in nineteenth-century North America. The written archive left by settler society is far from seamless or representative. Indigenous peoples also left written archives, and this study makes use of the correspondence and memoirs created by English-speaking, Indigenous elites like Marguerite Connolly, Andrew Dominique Pambrum, Ranald MacDonald, and Cecilia Douglas Helmcken. How to describe people like these has been and continues to be a complicated question in Canada, as it is in many colonial and postcolonial societies.[20] Moving between the eastern Caribbean and northern North America, I used the terms Metis and Creole to describe people born in colonial space and tied to both local and imperial genealogies and economies. This is admittedly an imperfect way of capturing histories that were complicated in their time and remain consequential in the present.

It was after Douglas left the colonial service in 1864 that he created a significant archive of his intimate life. This reflects his attainment of secure bourgeois status, and in this sense, the association between written records, worthy and interesting stories, and class. The journals and letters Douglas wrote as an older man are not lists of furs traded and servants employed, or correspondence between different and distant levels of an imperial state, but personal documents: journals, memoirs, and the vivid and at times disarmingly intimate letters of fathers, daughters, and sons. Here the danger of becoming what Jill Lepore memorably dubs "a historian who loves too much"[21] is a real one. So is the risk of taking such material as more representative than it is even within the

---

[19] See Jennifer S. H. Brown and Elizabeth Vibert, eds., *Reading Beyond Words: Contexts for Native History*, 2nd edition (University of Toronto Press, 2003).

[20] See Chris Andersen, "'I'm Métis, What's Your Excuse?': On the Optics and Ethics of the Misrecognition of Métis in Canada," *Aboriginal Policy Studies*, 1:2 (2011) 161–165; Brenda Macdougall, "The Myth of Metis Cultural Ambivalence," in Nicole St-Onge, Carolyn Podruchny, and Brenda Macdougall, eds., *Contours of a People: Metis Family, Mobility, and History* (Vancouver: UBC Press, 2010).

[21] Jill Lepore, "*Historians Who Love too Much: Reflections on Microhistory and Biography,*" *Journal of American History*, 88:1 (2001) 129–144.

frame of one life. Douglas' private archive was overwhelmingly created in the 1860s and '70s, when he was an older, relatively wealthy man with unparalleled local influence and ample time. We cannot read the relations and subjectivities mapped in these archives backwards in time. But alongside the large and eclectic collection of papers of Douglas' son-in-law James Sebastian Helmcken and the less voluminous but still revealing diary of his other son-in-law, Arthur T. Bushby, Douglas' correspondence and journals offer a remarkable window into colonial masculinity, elite Creole-Metis life, and bourgeois domesticity. Correspondence exchanged between family members in North America and the United Kingdom later in the nineteenth century documents a different layer of bourgeois colonial life, as do the records produced by the administration of the family's estate in the twentieth century.

All of these archives reflected the societies that produced them and the ones that preserved them or were unable or uninterested in doing so. In 1888 Nicholas Darnell Davis, a colonial official and local man of letters in British Guiana, voiced the familiar *cri de coeur* of colonial peoples unable to access their own archives and write their own histories: "'Our records! Where are they?'"[22] Guyana's national archives were established in 1958. They did not fare well in the complicated and fractious years that preceded and followed Guyanese independence in 1966. In 2008, the archives were renamed the Walter Rodney National Archives after the socialist Guyanese historian assassinated in 1980. And there I read church and census records under a stern and magisterial portrait of the slain Rodney, a reminder that the work of history is always political and sometimes very dangerous. The Walter Rodney National Archives continue to inspire criticism and both local and international reform plans.[23] The history of Guyana's archives cannot be separated from its status as one of the poorest countries in the western hemisphere. The Guyanese histories mapped in this book are prised from an underfunded archive in a radically unequal world.

The archives and historiographies of Canada's westernmost province have had different colonial and postcolonial histories. British Columbia became a relatively secure settler society in the last decades of the nineteenth and the first decades of the twentieth century. Catherine Hall explains the critical role that capital H history played in justifying Britain's sense of itself as a justly imperial nation. History performed a different but not unrelated work in British Columbia, situating it within an

---

[22] N. Darnell Davis, "The Records of British Guiana," *Timehri*, new series, 2 (1888) 339–357.

[23] See, recently, "Records in the National Archives to be Digitized," *Strabroek News* (March 3, 2013), available at www.stabroeknews.com/2013/news/stories/03/03/records-in-national-archives-to-be-digitized-microfilmed/, accessed April 2, 2013.

imperial world and justifying the dominance of settler peoples within it. The professionalization of history in Canada, as Donald Wright has argued, rested in part on the exclusion of women. Mary Jane Logan McCallum has also shown how this process of professionalization was additionally predicated on the denial of authority to Indigenous scholars and writers, something that echoes uncomfortably throughout contemporary scholarly practice. These processes of professionalization dovetailed with a local history of archive and historiography building. Historian Chad Reimer has shown how the intellectual work of settler colonialism was served by a group of elite British Columbians who established a provincial archive and a local historiography with claims to professional rigor in the last decade of the nineteenth and the first decade of the twentieth century. In this sense, the creation of a local archive and historiography was critical to the location of British Columbia within what Australian historians Marilyn Lake and Henry Reynolds have called the "White Men's Countries" of the modern world.[24]

The acquisition of James Douglas' records and the celebration of his histories were central to the making of an archive and a capital H history for British Columbia. In 1923 James Douglas and Amelia Connolly Douglas' youngest child, Martha Harris Douglas, gave the Provincial Archives of British Columbia a pamphlet of addresses made to Douglas on his retirement and an odd assortment of material tokens: the trimming from Douglas' "first dress Uniform," the sash from the duffle coat he wore as HBC chief factor, and a button from his dress uniform. The archivist was deferential and grateful in response. "Needless to say," John Hosie gushed, "we treasure these possessions very much and they make a very interesting addition to the exhibition case which we have specially reserved for documents and relics of your esteemed father, Sir James Douglas."[25]

This sort of recognition reflected the secure space Douglas occupied within the aspirational historiography of regional settler colonialism. Soon after his death in 1877, he was proclaimed a "father" of British Columbia, and he held fast to that status, the namesake of schools and the subject of plaques, paintings, and commemorations. A granite obelisk erected in front of British Columbia's legislative buildings in 1881 and

[24] Catherine Hall, *Macaulay and Son: Architects of Imperial Britain* (New Haven: Yale University Press, 2012); Donald Wright, *The Professionalization of History in English Canada* (University of Toronto Press, 2005); Mary Jane Logan McCallum, "Indigenous Labor and Indigenous History," *American Indian Quarterly*, 33:4 (Fall 2009) 523–44: Reimer, *Writing British Columbia History*; Marilyn Lake and Henry Reynolds, *Drawing the Global Colour-Line: White Men's Countries and the International Challenge of Racial Equality* (Cambridge University Press, 2008).
[25] John Hosie to Dennis Harris, January 11,1923, British Columbia Provincial Archives Correspondence (hereafter BCPAC), BCA, GR 1738, Box 68, File 18.

Figure 1.2 The monument to Sir James Douglas, British Columbia Legislature, Victoria, BC.

pictured in Figure 1.2 speaks to Douglas' assigned role in modern reck-onings of British Columbia as a settler society.[26] As a fur trader, colonial governor, proverbial self-made man, and a brave pioneer, he fit nicely within expected ideas of what was a legitimate subject of local history. The first book-length biography of Douglas was published in 1908, and they continued to appear at regular intervals throughout much of the twentieth century.[27]

---

[26] See Henry J. Morgan, ed., *The Dominion Annual Register and Review, 1880–1881* (Montreal: Lovell & Son, 1882) 273.

[27] Robert Hamilton Coats and R. E. Gosnell, *Sir James Douglas: The Makers of Canada* (Toronto: Morang and Co., 1908); Sage, *Sir James Douglas and British Columbia*; Derek

But the Douglas-Connolly family could not be easily accommodated within triumphalist settler narratives. Douglas vexed his biographers. They struggled with the apparent absence of solid information about his early life. Soon after Douglas' death, Hubert Howe Bancroft, the famed historian of western America, expressed his surprise that there was so little archival material "concerning the early career of such a man."[28] Twenty years later, a local historian found it peculiar that "the first governor of the province and a citizen of great worth, leaving the impress of his individuality, his superior talents and public-spirited citizenship upon the annals of the northwest," had such an unknown early life.[29] The questions of where Douglas had been born and who his mother was were especially troubling, carrying with them the capacity to disrupt and destabilize ideals of race and of nation, and Douglas', and thus British Columbia's, place therein. Some authors avoided the question of where he had been born altogether, offering general musings about his Scottish lineage instead of the usual biographical information. Douglas' first scholarly biographer, Walter Sage, stated that Douglas had been born in Scotland.[30] This claim reflected how troubled Sage was by the possibility of Douglas being Black. In his research notes, Sage noted a report that Douglas' mother was "Creole" and dismissed it, writing "rot" in the margins. Sage's emphatic kind of abjection did not make him any less confused, and years later he would admit that Douglas was a hard subject to write a plaque about. "The real difficulty is, of course, the date and place of Douglas' birth," Sage explained in 1946.[31]

Douglas' family of birth strained available discourses of North American history, and so did the family he made with Connolly Douglas. Canadian historians could draw on romantic, longstanding narratives of the fur trade and its unique, historic, and picturesque ways. These were less available to those writing in an American idiom. Bancroft spent time in Victoria in 1878 and reported that Connolly Douglas, "though a half-breed, was a perfect lady" and her daughters charming. This he credited to Douglas, writing that "it was next to impossible for the wife

Pethick, *James Douglas: Servant of Two Empires* (Vancouver: Mitchell, 1969); Dorothy Blakey Smith, *James Douglas: Father of British Columbia* (Oxford University Press, 1971).

[28] Hubert Howe Bancroft, *The Works of Hubert Howe Bancroft: Volume XXVII, History of British Columbia, 1792–1887* (San Francisco: The History Company, 1887) 385.

[29] R. E. Gosnell, *British Columbia: A History* (Victoria (?): The Lewis Company, 1906) 340.

[30] See Coats and Gosnell, *Sir James Douglas*, 91; Sage, *Sir James Douglas*, 14.

[31] Walter N. Sage, "Workbook 1," Box 36, "BC History," Walter N. Sage to W. D. Cromarty, January 22, 1946, Box 2, File 7, both in Sage Papers.

and daughter of Sir James Douglas to be other than ladies."[32] Else-where Bancroft explained the genuine disquiet he felt at the unavoidable fact that Douglas and his peers had married Indigenous women and, worse, had Indigenous children. In his major 1884 work on the history of western America, Bancroft wrote:

I could never understand how men such as John McLoughlin, James Douglas, Ogden, Finlayson, Work, Tolmie, and the rest could endure the thought of having their name and honors descend to a degenerate posterity. Surely they were possessed of sufficient intelligence to know that by giving their children Indian or half-breed mothers, their own old Scotch, Irish, or English blood would be greatly debased, and hence that they were doing all concerned a great wrong.[33]

For Bancroft, fur traders' intimate lives made them unworthy and dis-turbing objects of historical study. Bancroft's celebratory histories of the North American west would find a place for the British colonies, but were never certain about where to place men like Douglas within them.

Popular historians of British Columbia struggled with where to situ-ate Connolly Douglas in their stories of place. She received mention in studies of her husband or in portraits of women's history, most endur-ingly in ephemeral terms that re-inscribed her status as an unknown and somehow outside history.[34] Sometimes, she was very much present, as when the Victoria branch of the Imperial Order of the Daughters of the Empire, Canada's pro-empire women's group, dubbed themselves the Lady Douglas chapter. Connolly Douglas merited a full chapter in a 1928 book on "pioneer women of Vancouver Island." This made no clear mention of her Indigenous history, but was in effect all about just that, recollecting her childhood among "the picturesque figures of the first fur traders, the Canadian voyageurs, the Indian trappers, the proud chiefs."[35]

It has been more recent histories that have emphasized Connolly Douglas' and Douglas' itinerant histories and complicated identities. The Guyanese-Canadian community has found Douglas a historical

---

[32] Hubert Howe Bancroft, *Literary Industries: A Memoir* (New York: Harper and Brothers, 1891) 286.

[33] Hubert Howe Bancroft, *History of the Northwest Coast*, Volume II (San Francisco: A. L. Bancroft and Co., 1884) 65.

[34] Marion B. Smith, "The Lady Nobody Knows," in Reginald Eyre Watters, ed., *British Columbia: A Centennial Anthology* (Toronto: McClelland and Stewart, 1958).

[35] B. A. McKelvie, *1843–1943* (n.p. [Victoria]: The Sir James and Lady Douglas Chapter of the IODE, 1943) 9; N. de Bertrand Lugrin, *The Pioneer Women of Vancouver Island, 1843–1866* (Victoria: Women's Canadian Club, 1928) 10. On the IODE, see Katie Pickles, *Female Imperialism and National Identity: The Imperial Order of the Daughters of the Empire* (Manchester University Press, 2002).

antecedent to the countless Guyanese who, since the 1960s, have migrated to the global north in general and Canada in particular. They have also worked to have him acknowledged as a historical figure in Guyana, and the handsome statue erected in Mahaica in 2008 and shown in Figure 1.3 is a clear sign of this.[36] Novelist Jane Pullinger uses Douglas and Connolly Douglas' story as a historical reference point for a fictional reckoning of the complicated pulls of race and sexuality in the postcolonial present.[37] At least two scholars have seen the Douglas-Connolly family as one of a set of families based at Fort Vancouver who well illustrate the complicated ties of nation, race, and identity in nineteenth-century North America. Historian Sylvia Van Kirk analyzed Douglas and Connolly Douglas in her critical 1980 study, and returned to the rich fabric of their lives in her later work on fur-trade elites in Victoria.[38]

Here I argue that the Douglas-Connolly family's wide-ranging and mobile histories are best registered in wide-angle and over the *longue durée*. I wrest the family, and more particularly Douglas, from the locations where they have been most understood and valued and draw out their histories in the Caribbean, the United Kingdom, in parts of North America that were later territorialized as American, and parts of North America that later became Canada. The first half of this book traces the Douglas-Connolly family in Demerara, Rupert's Land, and Oregon Territory. The last half analyzes the family mainly in British Columbia, but emphasizes their ongoing connections to a wider imperial world. This sort of approach is often dubbed a transnational one, and my analysis here is transnational in that it rejects the presumption that the modern nation-state is the best or most natural container of history. But the lives examined in this book were mainly lived in colonies, places that emphatically and by definition lacked the rights that defined nations. For this reason these histories might be better described as transimperial or, borrowing Arjun Appadurai's frame, translocal.[39]

---

[36] See "Statue of Sir James Douglas Unveiled at Mahaica Birthplace," *Strabroek News* (August 31, 2008), www.stabroeknews.com/2008/archives/08/31/statue-of-sir-james-douglas-unveiled-at-mahaica-birthplace/, accessed April 11, 2013.

[37] Kate Pullinger, *The Last Time I Saw Jane* (London: Orion, 1996). Thanks to Jeremy Mouat for this reference.

[38] Lisa Phillips, "Transitional Identities: Negotiating Social Transitions in the Pacific NW 1825–1860s," *Canadian Political Science Review*, 2:2 (2008) 21–40; Anne F. Hyde, *Empires, Nations and Families: A History of the North American West, 1800–1860* (Lincoln: University of Nebraska Press, 2011); Sylvia Van Kirk, *'Many Tender Ties': Women and Fur Trade Society, 1670–1870* (Winnipeg: Watson and Dwyer, 1980); Sylvia Van Kirk, "Tracing the Fortunes of Five Founding Families of Victoria," *BC Studies*, 115/116 (Autumn/Winter 1997/8) 148–179.

[39] Arjun Appadurai, *Modernity at Large: Cultural Dimensions of Globalization* (Minneapolis: University of Minnesota Press, 1996) 192.

Figure 1.3 Statue of James Douglas, Mahaica, Guyana, 2010.

Empire was global, but it played out in local spaces with thick and enduring histories. In early twentieth-century Victoria, Martha Douglas Harris was the most prominent local representative of what was a storied and celebrated family with diminished resources and prospects. Douglas Harris embraced the role of family representative even when it pushed at the limits of respectable middle-class womanhood. She used the surname of her birth alongside her married name, making clear that she remained a *Douglas*. Douglas Harris could also complicate the kind of racial performance that was so critical to her family and other members of the fur-trade elite. She shared her knowledge with Nellie de Bertrand Lugrin, wife of Victoria's newspaper editor and author of women's history.[40] She also worked to assert and maintain control over her family's archive and the histories tied to it. She met with Sage twice in 1923 and made her objection to his biographical research on her father unmistakably clear. "Mrs. Harris says that most of what has been written about the early life of her father is hopelessly wrong. But she is none too willing to part with the facts. She says that she has them," Sage recorded in his notes.[41]

Douglas Harris was furious when she learned that the provincial archives had allowed Sage to see some of her father's records. In 1931 she wrote a stern letter explaining that she had placed "valuable papers" in the library during the Great War under lock and key, retrieved them when she learned "that my father's letters to me had been read," but accidentally left Douglas' confidential report on colonial staff. "W. Sage had no right to see it or use that paper," she charged. Along with other members of Victoria's fur-trade elite, Douglas Harris was no fan of Bancroft, and she was horrified that Sage referenced the work of a man she considered a "*thief & a liar.*" As the provincial librarian and archivist, Hosie recognized Harris Douglas' authority over the archive and the histories that might be found therein. He returned her documents with ready and fulsome apologies. "I deeply regret the whole incident," he explained, agreeing that Bancroft had "robbed at least three of our old time families of priceless documents."[42]

It was after Douglas Harris' death that her father's private records – his letters to children at school in England, his accounts of books read and money saved, his fragmentary mentions of early life, his accounts of journey and travels – were decisively moved to British Columbia's archives.[43] In comparison to the available archives through which we might learn about Douglas' or Connolly Douglas' early life and the enormous institutional archives of the HBC and the Colonial Office, these records are rich, compelling, and detailed. But like the other sources mined in this study, these private records archives are still partial, fragmentary; a product of

---

[40] De Bertrand Lugrin, *The Pioneer Women*, 24.

[41] "Notes of a Conversation with Mrs. Dennis Harris, Daughter of Sir James Douglas," September 13, 1923, Sage Papers, Box 36.

[42] Martha Douglas Harris to John Hosie, January 17, 1931; John Hosie to Mrs. Dennis R. Harris, January 21, 1931, PPBCA, Box 68, File 18, emphasis original. Thanks to David Mattison for alerting me to this.

[43] Reimer, *Writing British Columbia History*, 122–123.

the imperial world that made them and the changed one that preserved them.

The colonial archive that makes this history of the Douglas-Connolly family and the history of the imperial world possible also occludes the knowledge a critical feminist and postcolonial scholarship seeks. The available records are weighted toward one member of the family, one location in their itinerant geography, and select aspects of their lives. This archive renders Indigenous histories at best poorly visible by treating written records as the only ones worth valuing, putting in boxes, and making available by card catalogue or search engine. A settler archive committed to a politics of Whiteness skips over or literally crosses out archival traces of a Black and, in different ways, Indigenous past. The colonial archive occludes women's histories by failing to see or value their labors, concerns, or centrality to their families and communities. It truncates the complexity and meaning of men's lives by registering their paid labor, their trade, and the relationships to states and showing much less interest in their lives as friends, husbands, and fathers. The archive is spread across multiple locations, ones that reflect distinctions between the global north and south, the national and regional mandate of archives, and the happenstance of people who made choices about what to keep and what to burn.

Taking the Douglas-Connolly family as its spine, this book is organized along topical and chronological lines. It reverses the presumed order of precedence between public and private and state and society, and begins, in each instance, with the intimate terrains of marriage, kinship, and family. The analysis starts with the imperial intimacies of early nineteenth-century Demerara and fur-trade North America before turning to the complicated histories of colonial rule and race in those places and at those times. The center of the book analyzes fur-trade North America in the middle decades of the nineteenth-century, addressing the vexed history of marriage and intimacy before turning to questions of colonial economy, race, and empire. The focus on James Douglas, Amelia Connolly Douglas, and their children sharpens over the course of the book. The final three chapters examine their lives in Vancouver Island and British Columbia, beginning with the politics of marriage before turning to governance, race, and nation in their lives and the lives of their children. It concludes by connecting the intimate histories of Douglas and Connolly Douglas' children and some of their grandchildren to questions of class, race, and nation in the modern world.

I want a history that speaks critically to the complicated present of postcolonial and settler colonial societies, to the many shattered spaces of empire. I want a history that engages meaningfully with the relentlessly gendered history of colonialism and how it has and continues to determine the fabric of our lives – Indigenous, settler, or migrant – and animate the kinds of possible futures we image and the kind of relationships we establish or fail to establish with each other and the spaces where we live. I cannot pull this kind of history whole from the colonial archive. But I can work with these records to create a history that connects people, places, and lives, and in doing so shifts our view of the imperial world and the local spaces remade by it. The Douglas-Connolly family lived in the tissues of empire, moving between the Caribbean, the United Kingdom, and northern North America. They were colonized and colonizing, White, colored, and Black, British, Scottish, and native-born, Indigenous and settler, and Roman Catholic and Protestant. They spoke English, French, Chinook Jargon, Cree, and Michif, and probably some Dutch.

But the history told here is not a story of cheerful pluralism and timeless multiculturalism, about how we were all happy then. It is a history of slavery and the racism that remained after abolition and the exploitation of the fur trade. It is very much a history of colonial rule, national states, and imperial administration. At its very core it is a history of Indigenous dispossession and settler ascendancy. This is a history of colonies and metropoles, of new nations, reworked empires, and enduring Indigenous peoples and governance. Yet this is also a history of people and their lives. The history of the Douglas-Connolly family is of women and men, wives and husbands, daughters and sons, old friends and people passing through, ties maintained and bonds misplaced and lost, sometimes temporarily and sometimes forever. This is a story about class and material relations, especially as they were lived out in local colonial spaces, ones that were hardly legible on the metropolitan stage. It is a story of local history with complex histories, and also an imperial and global one of disjointed connection and movement. Putting these colonial relations at the center of our analysis changes how we see the imperial world and the places and peoples remade by it.

2   Housekeepers and wives

Intimate relations were critical to empire in its various iterations. Domestic, familial, and sexual relations between mobile, imperial men and local women of color did particular political, economic, and social labors. They were freighted with a number of meanings, some of them local, others widely imperial, and many of them both. The lives of James Douglas, Amelia Connolly, and their friends and kin demonstrate how imperial intimacies were constituted in local terms honed to particular configurations of imperial economy and governance, and also by the connections between them. Over the course of the long nineteenth century, they lived in the eastern Caribbean, the United Kingdom, and a range of sites in northern North America, most notably Red River, Oregon, and British Columbia. In these places they crafted intimate relationships, ones that connected and in turn re-circulated the histories of Caribbean sugar, northern North American fur, and metropolitan governance and trade.

This chapter examines the Douglas-Connolly family and their peers in the first half of the nineteenth century, beginning in the eastern Caribbean and then shifting to the fur-trade territories of North America's northwest. Tracking the changing politics of intimacy in the Douglas-Connolly family sheds some light on the complicated history of colonial intimacies and their relationship to empire. Heterosexual intimacies were honed to particular colonial economies and societies, but they were also informed by and interpreted through wider discussions and insurgencies. The history of the Douglas-Connolly family's intimate relations in both Demerara and fur-trade societies was both local and translocal, revealing both particular modes of colonialism and their connections to a wider imperial world.

James Douglas was born in 1803, probably the product of a relationship that was characteristic of early nineteenth-century colonial societies dependent on plantation slavery and the Atlantic economy rooted in it. It is fairly certain that Douglas was born in Demerara. His own records identify a Scottish man named John Douglas as his father. The identity of his mother is less clear. Historian Charlotte Girard argues that Douglas' grandmother was likely a free woman of color named Rebecca Ritchie and that his mother was her daughter, Martha Ann Telfer or, less often, Telfor.[1] Given the character of the available evidence about the history of free people of color in early nineteenth-century Demerara, it is no surprise that Girard's arguments about Douglas' maternal kin are always tentative. But they are supported by available evidence, and challenged by no plausible alternatives. More important for my purposes here is what this tentative genealogy suggests about the history of intimacy and race in the nineteenth-century imperial world. Girard's cautious geneal-ogy situates Douglas' origins in the dense social relations that developed around the margins of the Atlantic slave economy and offered particular roles for itinerant White men, free women of color, the relationships they forged and the children they bore.

Telfer and Ritchie were part of a community of free women of color in urban early nineteenth-century Guyana. Like free Black communities elsewhere in the eastern Caribbean, this one was both disproportionately female and urban. In 1811, there were 1,096 free adult females of color in Demerara and Essequibo compared with only 487 males.[2] Port cities like Georgetown were located between the plantations where enslaved people produced sugar, coffee, and cotton, and the metropole, which received much of the produce and profit. (See Figure 2.1.) In the lively market economies between plantation and metropole, free women found work, opportunity, and a significant measure of independence. The free Black population became less female over time, but remained strikingly urban. In 1829, more than two-thirds of free people of color in the colonies lived in Georgetown, and 2,743 of 4,638 were female.[3]

Men like John Douglas found different sorts of opportunities in Demerara. He was a seemingly unremarkable Scottish man tied to a

---

[1] See W. Kaye Lamb, "Some Notes on the Douglas Family," *British Columbia Histori-cal Quarterly*, 17:1/2 (1953) 41–51; W. Kaye Lamb, "Ancestry of Sir James Douglas, KCB (1803–1877)," British Columbia Archives (hereafter BCA), B/90/D741, Transcript; Charlotte S. M. Girard, "Sir James Douglas' Mother and Grandmother," *BC Studies*, 44 (Winter 1979/80) 25–31; Charlotte S. M. Girard, "Some Further Notes on the Douglas Family," *BC Studies*, 72 (Winter 1986/7) 3–27.

[2] "A Return of the Population of the Colonies of Demerary & Esquibo, taken by Order of His Excellency the Governor on the 31st October and 25th," in H. W. Bentinck to Earl of Liverpool, December 26, 1811, in Colonial Office Correspondence, Demerara and Essequibo, CO 111/11, National Archives, United Kingdom (hereafter CO 111/11, NA). See Hilary McD. Beckles, "Freedom without Liberty: Free Blacks in the Barbados Slave System," in Verene A. Shepherd, ed., *Slavery without Sugar: Diversity in Caribbean Economy and Society since the 17th Century* (Gainsville, FL: University Press of Florida, 2002) 201–9.

[3] Robert H. Schomburgk, *A Description of British Guiana, Geographical and Statistical* (London: Simpkin, Marshall, and Co, 1840) 42.

Figure 2.1 E. Goodall, "View of Georgetown Guyana."

family with significant but shifting interests in sugar plantations in Demerara and neighboring Berbice and in shipping. He circulated in and around Georgetown in the early years of the nineteenth century, one amongst a larger kin network of Douglas men. Like so many of the Scottish families studied by historians Douglas Hamilton and Thomas Devine, the Douglas family's personal history and wealth were deeply tied to the imperial world, and more particularly the plantation economies of the Caribbean and the North American fur trade.[4]

   For these sorts of men, the opportunities for work and wealth that the Caribbean offered were sometimes permanent, but they were more often temporary and occurred within a distinct and relatively short phase of life. Like other Caribbean colonies marked by relatively late colonization, high proportions of African-born slaves, and small White populations, Demerara was predicated on absentee ownership. Sugar, coffee, and

[4] Douglas J. Hamilton, *Scotland, the Caribbean, and the Atlantic World, 1750–1820* (Manchester University Press, 2005); Thomas Devine, *Scotland's Empire: 1600–1815* (London: Penguin, 2003); Douglas Hamilton, "Transatlantic Ties: Scottish Migration Networks in the Caribbean, 1750–1800," in Angela McCarthy, ed., *A Global Clan: Scottish Migrant Networks and Identities since the Eighteenth Century* (London and New York: Tauris, 2006) 48–66. Also see David Alston, "'Very rapid and splendid fortunes?': Highland Scots in Berbice (Guyana) in the Early Nineteenth-Century," *The Gaelic Society of Inverness*, 8 (November 2002) 208–236.

cotton plantations were run day-to-day by managers and agents acting locally on behalf of families resident elsewhere, largely in Britain. "It may be a humiliating fact to the 125,000 inhabitants of British Guiana," someone observed later in the century, "but it is nevertheless a true one, and a fact which should never be forgotten, that the very existence of the colony, and the lives of the greater part of this population are, under Providence, in the keeping of some fifty or sixty gentlemen in Great Britain."[5]

Sojourning men made this precarious arrangement workable. It also fostered particular configurations of intimacy. There were few White women in early nineteenth-century Guyana. In 1811, the colonial government counted 1,745 adult White men in Demerara and Essequibo, and only 583 females. Even more so than in the Jamaican context studied by Christer Petley, White men were to a greater or lesser extent transient and disconnected from the usual networks of sociability and domesticity.[6] For men like John Douglas, a customary relationship with a local woman usually went alongside an instrumental role in the plantation economy or imperial state. The language that observers used to characterize this order of intimate relationships situated women of color as "housekeepers" and White men "masters" within an "establishment." These terms emphasized the hierarchy at the core of this form of imperial intimacy, and the significance of labor, and situated these households outside the sentimentalized discourse of domestic space. Travelers to nineteenth-century Demerara sketched the basic outlines. "It is usual, in these colonies," explained one in 1806, "for a person to take a negro, or more frequently a mulatto or *meflee* woman as house-keeper and companion of his bed-chamber."[7] Richard Schomburgk explained that "The least wealthy, yet to be sure rich, planters, the merchants, even Government officers, inspectors, estates' managers, and their servants are married, but usually live in concubinage with coloured people, negro or Indian women."[8]

---

[5] A Landowner, *British Guiana: Demerara after Fifteen Years of Freedom* (London: T. Bosworth, 1853) 45; B. W. Higman, *Slave Populations in the British Caribbean, 1807–1834* (Baltimore and London: Johns Hopkins University Press, 1984) 63.

[6] "A Return of the Population of the Colonies of Demerary & Esquibo"; Christer Petley, "'Legitimacy' and Social Boundaries: Free People of Colour and the Social Order in Jamaican Slave Society," *Social History*, 30:4 (November 2005) 481–489.

[7] George Pinckard, *Notes on the West Indies: written during the expedition under the command of the late General Sir Ralph Abercromby*, Volume III (London: Longman, Hurst, Rees, and Orme, 1806) 203.

[8] Walter E. Roth, ed. and trans., *Richard Schomburgk's Travels in British Guiana, 1840–1844*, Volume I (Georgetown: Daily Chronicle, 1922) 45. Also see Henry Kirke, *Twenty Five Years in British Guiana* (London: Sampson Low, Marston and Co, 1898) 45.

Relationships between sojourning White men and local women of color were regulated by a set of known conventions. Thomas St. Clair, a British military man who visited Georgetown and Mahaica in 1805 and 1806, wrote that "The first thing generally done by a European on his arrival in this country is to provide himself with a mistress from among the blacks, mulattos, or mestees." These women "perform all the duties of a wife except presiding at table, and their utility in domestic affairs, their cleanliness, and their politeness, are acknowledged by all." He was shocked at the social recognition accorded these relationships. So long as women "continue faithful and constant to the protectors by whom they are chosen, they are always countenanced and encouraged by their nearest relations and friends, who call this a lawful marriage for the time it lasts."[9] In 1807, Henry Bolingbroke offered a similar description, explaining that local customary wives "embrace all the duties of a wife, except presiding at table."[10] Here it is food and the sociability of dining that constitutes the impassable racial divide, the line that separates imperial intimacies from their presumed other, European marriage.

It was presumably in this sort of context that John Douglas established a relationship with Telfer. A detailed map of property in Demerara in 1798 owned by Britain's King George III listed a Mahaica estate as the property of "Ramsay, Telfair and Douglas."[11] But these names do not appear together in any other documents that I was able to find. That a possible relationship between Martha Ann Telfer and John Douglas went unrecorded in the archive created by Demerara's colonial state and by known church records is part of the story of this and equivalent imperial intimacies. Durba Ghosh explains how the imperial archive demonstrated its considerable political authority in part by keeping local relationships and families out of it. The children born to couples like this were their archive. Martha and John had three, and the pattern of their births speaks to the kind of transatlantic separation and reunions that characterized their relationship: two boys, Alexander and James, born in 1801 and 1803, and a daughter, Cecilia, born in 1812 after John returned from a stay in Scotland. That this was the last of the children born to them speaks to the particular temporal span of Douglas' stay in Demerara and the

---

[9] Lieut. Col. [Thomas Staunton] St. Clair, *A Soldier's Recollection of the West Indies and America with a Narrative of the Expedition to the Island of Walcherrn* (London: Richard Bentley, 1834) 114.

[10] Henry Bolingbroke, *A Voyage to the Demerary, Containing a Statistical Account of the Settlements There, And Those on The Essequebo, The Berbice, and Other Contiguous Rivers of Guyana* (Norwich: Richard Phillips, 1807) 43.

[11] Thomas Walker, *A Chart on the Coast of Guyana, Comprehending the Colonies of Berbice, Demerary & Essequebo* (London: C. G. Playter, Lewisham, Kent, 1799) 19. The map is held at the British Library, 124/40/11, Guyana 1798, Ktop CXXIV/40.

family he formed there. In 1809 he married Jessie Hamilton, a Scottish woman by whom he had four children.[12] He returned to Demerara at some point, but in 1812 traveled to Scotland, this time to stay. It was Douglas' Scottish wife, family, and life that were acknowledged as official during his life and, by his will, after his death in 1841.[13]

Intimate relationships between women of color and colonial men may have been carefully excluded from metropolitan knowledge and recognition, but within colonial spaces like Demerara they were acknowledged and regulated by known norms. These were struck within a specific social and economic space that put bourgeois local Blacks and mobile, petty bourgeois Whites into conversation and contact. In this respect, the story of these imperial intimacies is one of class as well as race. Class conditioned the kind of intimate possibilities available to White men, as Cecelia Green has recently argued.[14] It also empowered free women of color, in relative and largely local terms. It did so in part through the differential spaces accorded to enslaved women. The enslaved people who testified to colonial officials made clear the extent to which slavery empowered White men to sexually exploit enslaved women and the ways that free women located as "housekeepers" could exercise a capricious, violent, and relentlessly proximate authority over the enslaved.[15]

Even when located within a broader spectrum of intimate relationships between women of color and White men, relationships like the one seemingly forged by Douglas and Telfer complicate characterizations of a geographic economy of intimacy which positioned the Caribbean as a place of sex and England as a place of family.[16] For John Douglas, both

[12] Durba Ghosh, *Sex and the Family in Colonial India: The Making of Empire* (Cambridge University Press, 2005) 253; Girard, "Sir James Douglas' Mother and Grandmother;" Lamb, "Some Notes on the Douglas Family;" Girard, "Some Further Notes."

[13] Will of John Douglas, April 16, 1841, National Archives of Scotland, SC70/1/60, pp. 546–551. Also see Girard, "Some Further Notes," 12.

[14] Cecilia A. Green, "Hierarchies of Whiteness in the Geographies of Empire: Thomas Thistlewood and the Barretts of Jamaica," *New West Indian Guide/Nieuwe West-Indishce Gids*, 80:1/2 (2006) 4–53. Also see her "'A Civil Inconvenience'? The Vexed Question of Slave Marriage in the British West Indies," *Law and History Review*, 25:1 (2007) 1–59.

[15] See "Further Papers relating to Slaves in the West Indies (Berbice)," in House of Commons (Britain), *Papers and Correspondence Relating to New South Wales Magistrates; The West Indies; Liberated Africans; Colonial and Slave Population; Slaves; The Slave Trade; &c.*, Session February 2 to May 31 1826, Volume 16: 9, 12. On these questions in another context, see Trevor Burnard, *Mastery, Tyranny, and Desire: Thomas Thistlewood and his Slaves in the Anglo-Jamaican World* (Chapel Hill: University of North Carolina Press, 2004).

[16] Catherine Hall, *Civilizing Subjects: Metropole and Colony in the English Imagination, 1830–1867* (University of Chicago Press, 2002) 9.

Demerara and Scotland were places of family. But his two families were structurally and symbolically unequal and incomparable. Only one of his two families was acknowledged as such by law and church, recorded in the archive, and rewarded with the transmission of property. The other was customary, unofficial, and did not inherit the father's material wealth, but only the lesser and less stable commodities of his name and, for the boys at least, a metropolitan education. Anthropologist Raymond T. Smith's rubric of the West Indian "dual marriage system"[17] captures the systematized character of these arrangements, but fails to account for their fundamental spatialization and inequality.

The differential positioning of the two Douglas families was predicated on a series of overlapping relationships between gender, race, space, and life-stage. Unlike the families of the American South, the two Douglas families had, most of the time, an ocean between them. The specialization of empire sustained inequality and made it deceptively workable. As Ghosh explains in her study of nineteenth-century India, "By keeping indigenous women out of European marital and familial networks, concubinage was not a departure from the normative practice of marriage, but rather a practice that sustained the racial and gendered hierarchies of colonial societies by denying interracial relationships the public or social recognition that marriage entailed."[18] This spatialized arrangement also fit with widespread patterns of work, migration, and family for European men. Douglas went to Demerara while a young man, formed a family with a local woman that he maintained for more than a decade, before returning to Scotland to marry, have children, and live out his life there. His adult life, like those of so many European men involved in the colonial world, was played out on two spatialized and hierarchically ordered imperial stages, each with a family to fit its imperial position.

James Douglas' travels would put the imperial intimacies of the slavery-era Caribbean into direct dialogue with those of northwestern North America. (See Map 1.) After a few years of formal education in Scotland, he found work in the fur trade operating west and north of the Great Lakes. Here he entered into configurations of intimacy that were both different from and similar to the ones that had produced

---

[17] Raymond T. Smith, "Hierarchy and the Dual Marriage System in West Indian Society," in Jane Fishburne Collier and Sylvia Junko Yanagisako, eds., *Gender and Kinship: Essays toward a Unified Analysis* (Stanford University Press, 1987). Also see his *The Negro Family in British Guiana; Family, Structure, and Social Status in Two Villages* (London: Routledge and Kegan Paul, 1956); *Kinship and Class in the West Indies: A Genealogical Study of Jamaica and Guyana* (Cambridge University Press, 1988); *The Matrifocal Family: Power, Pluralism, and Politics* (New York: Routledge, 1996).

[18] Ghosh, *Sex and Family*, 9.

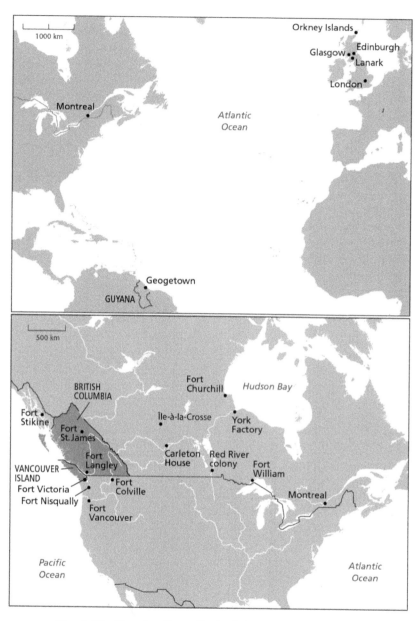

Map 1 The Douglas-Connolly family's imperial world.

him. If the intimacies of Douglas' Demerara boyhood were structured by plantation and merchant economies and the all-encompassing practice of slavery, marriage *à la façon du pays* was produced out of the particular economy of the fur trade, and more particularly its mercantilism and dependence on Indigenous economies and trade networks. Relationships between Indigenous women and the Scottish, Orcadian, French-Canadian, Hawaiian, and Iroquois men who worked in the fur trade were critical to and reflective of local iterations of imperial economy and governance in northwestern North America since the beginnings of the fur trade.[19]

By the early years of the nineteenth century, marriage *à la façon du pays* was a well-established customary mode of imperial intimacy in the fur-trade territories bordered by the Great Lakes to the east, the Pacific Ocean to the west, the Mississippi River to the south, and the tree-line to the north. The fur trade depended on independent commodity production by Indigenous peoples, and was predicated upon Indigenous trade networks that spanned the continent and well pre-dated European trade. Kinship was the central unit of community, political, and economic life in Indigenous societies. Europeans accessed Indigenous trade networks and labor by entering into dense webs of mutuality and exchange activated and maintained by the integration of men through the mechanism of marriage. Historian Brenda Macdougall explains that "No individual in a territory or community was to be without connections, so a place was made for everyone to belong."[20] Canadian-born George Nelson was

---

[19] See, for foundational histories, Sylvia Van Kirk, *'Many Tender Ties': Women and Fur Trade Society, 1670–1870* (Winnipeg: Watson and Dwyer, 1980); Jennifer S. H. Brown, *Strangers in Blood: Fur Trade Company Families in Indian Country* (Vancouver: UBC Press, 1980); and for more recent reflections, Sylvia Van Kirk, "From 'Marrying-In' to 'Marrying-Out': Changing Patterns of Aboriginal/Non-Aboriginal Marriage in Colonial Canada," *Frontiers: A Journal of Women Studies*, 23:3 (2002) 1–11; Jennifer S. H. Brown, "Partial Truths: A Closer Look at Fur-Trade Marriage," in Ted Binnema, Gerhard Ens, and R. C. McLeod, eds., *From Rupert's Land to Canada: Essays in Honour of John E. Foster* (Edmonton: University of Alberta Press, 2002) 59–80.

[20] Brenda Macdougall, *One of the Family: Metis Culture in Nineteenth-Century Northwestern Saskatchewan* (Vancouver: UBC Press, 2009) 10. Also see Robert Alexander Innes, "Multicultural Bands on the Northern Plains and the Notion of 'Tribal' Histories," in Jarvis Brownlie and Valerie Korinek, eds., *Finding a Way to the Heart: Feminist Writings on Aboriginal and Women's History in Canada* (Winnipeg: University of Manitoba Press, 2012) 122–145; Jean Friesen, "Magnificent Gifts: The Treaties of Canada and the Indians of the Northwest, 1869–1876," *Transactions of the Royal Society of Canada*, 5:1 (1986) 41–51; John L. Foster, "Wintering, the Outsider Adult Male and Ethnogenesis of the Western Plains Métis," *Prairie Forum*, 19:1 (Spring 1994) 1–13; Schuler, Monica. "Liberated Africans in Nineteenth-Century Guyana," in Brian L. Moore *et al.*, eds., *Slavery, Freedom, and Gender: The Dynamics of Caribbean Society* (Kingston, Jamaica: University of West Indies Press, 2001) 133–60.

sent into Anishinaabeg territory to trade for the XY Company in 1802. During his second winter there a senior man offered his fourteen-year-old daughter to Nelson as a wife. Nelson worried about his youth and the disapproval of his kin and peers, but agreed to marry when he realized his own success in the trade was in question. With scanty provisions and limited help, Nelson made the decision to "marry for my safety" and likely owed his relatively good returns to this decision.[21]

Fur-trade and colonial officials were impressed with the diplomatic and economic work that marriage could do. Soon after he was appointed governor of the Hudson's Bay Company (HBC) George Simpson acknowledged that marriages were essential to maintaining ties with Indigenous peoples, arguing that "Connubial alliances are the best security we can have of the goodwill of the Natives" and recommending that traders "form connections with the principal Families immediately on their arrival." Simpson considered restrictions on marriage "most baneful to the interests of the Company." Restricting marriage was "tantamount to a prohibition of forming a most important chain of connection with the Natives, so that we have solely to depend on the Indians who have no other feelings than those which interest and mercenary views create towards us." Without marriage, economic ties "never matured to attachment" and "those on whom our existence depends" remained "inveterate Enemies."[22] When HBC trader Samuel Hearne created an iconic image of the fur trade in the closing days of the eighteenth century, shown in Figure 2.2, the blue-coated British man and the Indigenous woman are as critical to the optics of empire as are the fort, the ships, and the teepees.

The imperial intimacies of the fur-trade country were regulated by known custom, just as they were in Demerara. In 1800, Daniel Harmon described the process by which his North West Company (NWC) colleague "took a Woman of this Country for a Wife or rather Concubine." Harmon explained "all the ceremonies" marking the customary marriage. "[W]hen a person is desirous of having one of the Native Daughters to live with him; he makes a present to the Parents of the Damsel, of such article as he may suppose that will best please them." If the parents accepted the gifts offered, "the Girl remains at the Fort

---

[21] George Nelson, *My First Years in the Fur Trade: The Journals of 1802–1804*, ed. Laura Peers and Theresa Schenck (Montreal: McGill-Queen's University Press, 2002) 106 and "Introduction," 8.

[22] George Simpson, "Report on Athabasca District," May 18, 1821, in George Simpson, *Journal of Occurrences in the Athabasca Department, 1820 and 1821, and Report*, ed. E. E. Rich (Toronto: Champlain Society, 1938) 392, 396.

Figure 2.2 Samuel Hearne, "A Northwest View of Prince of Wales Fort, Hudson's Bay," *c.*1797.

with her lover, and is clothed after the fashion of the Canadians, with a Shirt, short Gown, Petticoats & Leggins [*sic*] &c."[23] One child of such a marriage put greater stress on how these marriages adhered to Indigenous law. Ranald MacDonald was the son of a Chinook woman and a Scottish fur trader born in 1824 near Fort Vancouver. In his memoir, he invoked ideas of law's universality and inviolability to explain the kind of marriage his parents had. He argued that "Chinook law (custom sanctified) governed – the world over – as to any marriage, or any matter of personal contract, as marriage is." There was, he continued, "no law of any foreign country, not even of Britain, or England, or the United States, or any of such" that challenged Chinook law and, more particularly, his powerful grandfather Comcomly's interpretation of it. MacDonald figured marriage as "an institution – a sacred institution – a bringing together by God (the 'Great Spirit') which, according to the people's own local law, no man could break asunder."[24]

[23] Daniel Harmon, *Harmon's Journal, 1800–1819* (Victoria: Touchwood Editions, 2006) August 7 [8], 1800, 19.

[24] Ranald MacDonald, *The Narrative of his early life on the Columbia under the Hudson's Bay Company's regime; of his experiences in the Pacific Whale Fishery; and of his great Adventure to Japan; with a sketch of his later life on the Western Frontier, 1824–1894*, ed. William S. Lewis and Naojiro Murakami (Spokane: Eastern Washington State Historical Society, 1923) 87.

The duration of fur-trade marriages was not set. Harmon explained that if "the newly joined couple not agree, they are at full liberty to separate whenever either chooses – however no part of the property that was given to the Girls Parents will be refunded." It was this that Harmon kept in mind when he decided to marry Lisette, the daughter of a French-Canadian trader and an Indigenous, probably Secwepemc, woman. "This Day a Canadians Daughter (a Girl of about fourteen years of age) was offered me," Harmon related with a curious formality in 1805, "and after mature considering concerning the step I ought to take I finally concluded it would be best to accept of her." Harmon explained this as a response to local protocol. "[I]t is customary," he explained, "for all the Gentlemen who come in this country to remain any length of time to have a *fair* Partner, with whom they can pass away their time at least more sociably if not more agreeably than to live a lonely, solitary life, as they must do if single." Harmon accessed the prospective relationship and his participation in it on the assumption that it was negotiable and, above all, local and untransferable. He imagined his own life along the lines of John Douglas', lived in two discrete imperial spaces, each with its own customs, expectations, and intimate relationships and families. He wrote:

In case we can live in harmony together, my intentions now are to keep her as long as I remain in this uncivilized part of the world, but when I return to my native land shall endeavour to place her into the hands of some good honest Man, with whom she can pass the remainder of her Days in this Country much more agreeably, than it would be possible for her to do, were she to be taken down into the civilized world, where she would be a stranger to the People, their manners, customs & Languages.[25]

Fur-trade companies acknowledged the economic work that marriages did, but feared what families could cost the trade. Winters were long and provisions were always scarce, and food valued by newcomers especially so. Servants were usually fed and clothed by the company, and whether and under what conditions women and children attached to men who worked the trade might also expect or demand shelter and provisions rendered the terms of their connection an inevitable point of struggle. In the early years of the nineteenth century, fur-trade companies taxed marriage in an effort to keep their provisioning costs in line. In 1806, the NWC declared that "the number of women and Children in the Country

---

[25] Harmon, *Harmon's Journal*, August 7 [8], 1800, 19, October 10, [1805], 85. Also see Carolyn Podruchny, *Making the Voyageur World: Travelers and Traders in the North American Fur Trade* (University of Toronto Press, 2006) Chapter 8.

was a heavy burthen to the Concern" and resolved to "reduce by degrees the number of women maintained by the Company." They forbad men to take "any women or maid from any of the tribes of Indians now known or who may hereafter become known in this Country to live with him after the fashion of the North West." Men who violated the rule were to be fined £100, and one of the men who accompanied John Franklin's 1819–20 expedition deemed this "an excellent regulation."[26] That the fine was not applied to men who partnered with a "Daughter of a White Man after the fashion of the Country" was a measure of the extent to which ambivalence about the costs of local families was tempered by fur traders' desires to resource their own kin.[27]

In the 1820s a language newly inflected by hardening ideas of both morality and race shifted the tenor of discussions about families, costs, and benefits. Following the merger of the NWC and the HBC in 1821 and the appointment of Simpson as governor, a reconstituted HBC began cracking down on the number of women and children entitled to company resources. "[A]llmost every man in the District has a Family," Simpson would explain about the Okanagan district, "which is productive of serious injury and inconvenience on account of the great consumption of Provisions."[28] Women and children not directly tethered to men were reckoned as a military problem as well as a fiscal one. In 1821, Simpson wrote that "We understand that there are an immense number of Women and Children, supported at the different Trading Posts, some belonging to men still in the Service and others who have been left by the Fathers unprotected and a burden on the Trade." In 1822, the company called the many families living around posts "both dangerous and expensive" and asked that they be resettled in the permanent colony taking shape at the meeting of the Red and Assiniboine rivers, in what would become the Red River Colony. There the Metis would live under the guidance of Roman Catholic and Anglican clergy. The HBC continued to try to make sense of the kinfolk around the posts, asking

---

26 Robert Hood, *To The Arctic by Canoe, 1819–1821, The Journal and Paintings of Robert Hood, Midshipman with Franklin*, ed. Stuart C. Houston (Montreal: McGill-Queen's University Press, 1994) 49.

27 "Minutes of the Meetings of the North West Company at Grand Portage and Fort William, 1801–1807, With Supplementary Agreements," in W. Stewart Wallace, ed., *Documents Relating to the North West Company* (Toronto: The Champlain Society, 1934) 210–211.

28 "George Simpson's Journal, Entitled Remarks Connected with the Fur Trade in the Course of a Voyage from York Factory to Fort George and Back to York Factory 1824–25," in Frederick Merk, ed., *Fur Trade and Empire* (Cambridge, MA: Harvard University Press, 1968), April 3, 1825, 131. Also see Simpson, *Journal of Occurrences in the Athabasca Department, 1820 and 1821, and Report*, August 26, 1820, 23–4.

for "a regular statement of the women & Families maintained by each District."[29]

Persistent pecuniary concerns and occasional military ones by no means displaced imperial intimacies in this context, or even really challenged them. In the first decades of the nineteenth century, local marriages and families were a critical component of vernacular fur-trade life and the common-sense knowledges that circulated around it. Even Simpson's casual misogyny and relentless eye for the fiscal bottom-line were sometimes tempered by the recognition that marriage served important purposes in an economy premised on dense webs of mutuality forged and maintained by intimate kin ties and loyalties. Knitting newcomer men into local communities through marriage altered the terms of the men's lives and sometimes the character of Indigenous communities and identity. Lizette Hall's history of the Carrier details the many HBC men who married into the communities around Fort St. James, and the lasting imprint they made on the families, communities, and histories there.[30]

This was the intimate terrain that William Connolly entered in the earliest years of the nineteenth century. Connolly was born in Lower Canada to an Irish-Canadian family, and began working in the fur trade as a teenager. In 1803 he was working for the NWC in Rivière du Rats, Athabasca Country, and he married a fifteen-year-old Cree woman named Suzanne Bellefeuille or Miyo Nipay.[31] Miyo Nipay's marriage to Connolly was celebrated according to "the usages and customs of the Cree nation to which she belonged," which emphasized mutual consent, the approval of her family, and local repute. This relationship was negotiated outside European law and religious practice, and was preserved in the colonial archive largely because of its centrality to an 1860s legal case. As did many other men in the fur trade, Connolly married in part to enter local Indigenous economies and networks, telling his kinsmen that

---

[29] Committee of the Hudson's Bay Company to George Simpson, March 8, 1822, Committee of the Hudson's Bay Company to George Simpson, February 27, 1822, "Minutes of Council, July 1823," all in R. Harvey Fleming, ed., *Minutes of Council Northern Department of Rupert Land, 1821–31* (London: Champlain Society for the Hudson's Bay Record Society, 1940) 33, 32, 62.

[30] Lizette Hall, *The Carrier, My People* (Cloverdale, BC: Friesens Printers, 1992) 67–68.

[31] Bruce Peel, "CONNOLLY, WILLIAM," in *Dictionary of Canadian Biography*, vol. VII, University of Toronto/Université Laval, 2003, www.biographi.ca, accessed October 15, 2012; Bruce Peel, "CONNOLLY, SUZANNE," in *Dictionary of Canadian Biography*, vol. IX, University of Toronto/Université Laval, 2003, www.biographi.ca, accessed October 15, 2012; "Marguerite Connolly: The First Red River Metis Grey Nun," undated manuscript in Dossier de Sr Connolly, Srs Gris de Montreal, Mais Porv. St. Boniface Museum Collection. I thank Anne Lindsay for her help in locating this source.

he needed to marry to access Cree trade networks.[32] But the economics of the trade could not explain the twenty-eight years that Miyo Nipay and William would live together or the six children they raised to adulthood. One of them was Amelia, born at Fort Churchill or Fort Assiniboia in 1812.[33]

Fur-trade intimacies were not so much negotiated between two distinct and separate peoples as they were forged within the particular hybrid cultural and social space of this particular imperial economy. By the first decades of the nineteenth century, the officer class increasingly married daughters born to the trade. It was within this context that James Douglas married his bourgeois' or boss's daughter at Fort St. James, where Connolly was factor and Douglas a clerk. Fifteen-year-old Amelia had been engaged to another junior trader, James Murray Yale, but sometime in the winter of 1826/7 her affections or her father's calculations shifted, and an observer noted that "The only news from that quarter was 'Mr. Douglas immediately after his return from Alexandria was married to Miss Connolly' the young Lady promised to Mr. Yale."[34] Given the status of both Amelia Connolly and James Douglas, their marriage was probably celebrated among the fort's elite in the accepted style. Yet marriage à la façon du pays had no place in the official records of the fur trade. Post journals recorded the work and happenings of the fort, and were usually kept daily by the chief factor, in this case William Connolly. In the post journal of Fort St. James for Sunday, April 27, 1828 Connolly did record some routine business, but the marriage of his daughter to his favorite clerk went unmarked.[35] It was only in Douglas' private journal that the date of his and Amelia's marriage was committed to paper.[36]

By the 1820s, marriage à la façon du pays was a choice that men like Douglas made with a range of other possibilities in mind. Douglas' peers

---

[32] Justice Samuel Monk, "Connolly vs. Woolrich and Johnson et al," *Lower Canada Jurist: Collection de Decisions du Bas Canada*, Volume XI (Montreal: John Lovell, 1867) 197, 234 (hereafter Connolly vs. Woolrich).

[33] Fort Assiniboia is from Nellie de Bertrand Lugrin, *Pioneer Women of Vancouver Island, 1843–1866* (Victoria: Women's Canadian Club, 1928) 10; also Bruce McIntyre Watson, *Lives Lived West of the Divide: A Biographical Dictionary of Fur Traders Working West of the Rockies, 1793–1858* (Kelowna: Centre for Social, Spatial, and Economic Justice, 2010) 341. Her birth is sometimes also attributed to Fort Churchill. See, for instance, "Death of Lady Douglas: Another of Victoria's Earliest Pioneers Passes Away," *Colonist* (January 9, 1890).

[34] See Francis Ermatinger to Edward Ermatinger, March 5, 1829, and footnote, in Lois Halliday McDonald, ed., *Fur Trade Letters of Francis Ermatinger, Written to his brother Edward during his service with the Hudsons' Bay Company 1818–1853* (Glendale, CA: The Arthur H. Clarke Company, 1980) 90, 92.

[35] Fort St. James Post Journal, April 27, 1828, Hudson's Bay Company Archives (hereafter HBCA), B.188/a/12, Mflm 1M129.

[36] James Douglas, "Notes," James Douglas, "Private Account," BCA, Add MSS B/90/1.

carefully weighed the relative merits of different kinds of imperial intimacies and the implications they might have for their futures in a shifting
colonial world. Some stressed the pleasures and accessibility of fluid heterosexual relationships that could be renegotiated as jobs changed and
circumstances demanded. In 1829, John Tod worried that only vulgar
language could describe his relationship with a woman he described only
as "the girl who used to sing at McLeods Lake." "Why then in plain language she still continues the only companion of solitude – without her,
or some other substitute, life, in such a wretched place as this, would
be altogether insupportable."[37] Others were less concerned about violating European ideas of propriety and wrote enthusiastically about the
flexibility of fur-trade intimacies. Canadian Francis Ermatinger considered multiple connections with Indigenous women partial compensation
for poor postings and monotonous country food. "However, to coun-
terbalance the misery of Dammed Dried Salmon – with which we are
obliged to sustain a miserable existence, we have the pleasure of fine
horses, and can obtain a wife at every port, for a moderate charge, we
come to."[38]

Such remarks drew on and contributed to the wider imperial discourse that situated the intimacies of imperial life outside the legalities
and moralities of "marriage" presumed to be metropolitan and Christian. In 1827, Ermatinger explained why he wouldn't marry Cleo, his
Indigenous partner at Thompson River, or any other local woman. "Nor
do I at present mean to become attached to anyone in the country.
They are all alike, faulty in some shape or other, and to turn away one
upon vague suspicion and take another, perhaps worse, would be folly
indeed."[39] Ermatinger would later change his mind, but James Hargrave
was adamant that he would not. Hargrave's records contain evidence
of his relationships with Indigenous women, but he was clear that he
would only marry a Scottish woman. "You may yet see me with a wife,"
he explained to his mother in 1836, "but she will be one from the Old
Country."[40] By 1831, Peter Skene Ogden had at least two children by
local women, and like Ermatinger, would eventually marry an elite Metis
woman. None of this stopped him from declaring that "The Bachelors

---

[37] John Tod to Edward Ermatinger, February 14, 1829, Ermatinger Papers, Volume I,
"Letters to Edward Ermatinger from John Tod, 1826–62," HBCA, E94/1, and Transcript
(hereafter Ermatinger Papers).
[38] Francis Ermatinger to Miles Ermatinger, March 14, 1826, in McDonald, ed., *Fur Trade
Letters*, 63.
[39] Francis Ermatinger to Edward Ermatinger, December 4, 1827, in McDonald, ed., *Fur
Trade Letters*, 86.
[40] James Hargrave to Jane Melrose, July 16, 1835, in Helen E. Ross, ed., *Letters from
Rupert's Land, 1826–1840* (Montreal: McGill-Queen's University Press, 2009) 275.

Flag I have hoisted and if I ever leave it, it will not be in the H.B. Coys territories."[41] Here, marriage is wielded as a particular kind of social state, one that is associated with metropolitan society and Whiteness. Men might live with, father children by, and express genuine affection for Indigenous women and still see themselves as bachelors.

Men of this cohort who married Indigenous women did so by choice and with warm sentiments. They considered Indigenous women admirable women and worthy potential wives within the confines of dominant nineteenth-century discourse as they understood and lived it. In 1836 Archibald McDonald wrote that there were "Lots of fine young accomplished ladies" in Rupert's Land, and "Chief Factor's daughters too."[42] Harmon, who had partnered on the assumption that his relationship would not last or exist outside the cultural space of the fur trade, decided to bring his family to Canada and marry Lizette legally in 1819. He explained that his "intentions have materially changed, since the time that I first took her to live with me" and that his "conduct in this respect is different from that which has generally been pursued by the gentlemen of the North West Company."[43] Harmon's conversion was a religious one, but also a decidedly secular one based on a lived experience of intimacy which challenged his expectations of marriage, empire, and his own place in it.

For men who worked in the fur trade, questions about marriage were to some extent questions about imperial location and racial and national identity. When William Tolmie, a Scottish HBC physician, considered the question of marriage, he was sorting out the matter of where he would live out his life. In 1834 he wrote:

I feel much the want of a friend to whom I might unbosom my joys & griefs – a wife is the only being to whom one could undeservedly pour out his soul, but one with whom could be enjoyed a sweet communion of mind is not to be met with in this country & it is only when I abandon the hope and wish of laying my bones in old Scotland that I will ever think of uniting myself in the most sacred of all ties with a female of this country.

Tolmie thought that once a man had decided to settle in North America, "the sooner he takes a wife the better." He explained that married men

---

[41] Peter Skene Ogden to John McLeod, March 10, 1831, Journals and Correspondence of John McLeod, BCA, AB 40 M22K, Transcript (hereafter McLeod Correspondence).

[42] Archibald McDonald to Edward Ermatinger, January 25, 1836, in Paul C. Phillips and John W. Hakola, eds., "Family Letters of Two Oregon Fur Traders, 1828–1856," in *Frontier Omnibus* (Missoula: Montana State University Press, 1962) 33.

[43] Harmon, *Harmon's Journal*, February 28, 1819, 174.

were happier than those who lived like "a lone bachelor, & leading the sensual life, indulged in by most of the gentlemen, who live in single blessedness." It would be another sixteen years before Tolmie would himself marry Metis Jane Work in 1850 and this family would live in intimate and regular contact with the Douglas family into the twentieth century.[44]

Douglas' marriage cemented his ties to northern North America, and marked a transition from one form of imperial manhood to another. Marriage signaled a kind of rejection of the mode of imperial manhood practiced by his father – lived on two stages, with two unequally structured families – and his commitment to the economy of the fur trade and the space of northern North America. In 1827 he had given "notice of retirement."[45] "Mr. James Douglas is bent on leaving the Country," explained a colleague. "I am very sorry for it. Independent of his abilities as an Indian Trader he possesses most amiable qualities and is an accomplished Young Man."[46] In his mid-twenties, and with eight years of wage labor behind him and around £166 in savings, Douglas would have been in a good position to establish himself in a middling occupation elsewhere. But Douglas opted not to return to what was now British Guiana, nor to try his hand in the metropole that had briefly educated him. Connolly and Douglas married in April 1828, not long after Douglas received a substantial raise from £60 to £100 per year.[47]

By marrying into the fur trade, Douglas was transformed from a peripatetic wage laborer to a long-term, if not necessarily permanent, member of a local colonial society. In the fur trade, as in the Indigenous societies that helped form and were critical to maintaining it, family was critical. Jennifer Brown's *Strangers in Blood* traces how ties of kinship were woven deeply within the structure of both the NWC and the HBC, and makes clear how much occupation endogamy characterized the trade. "In the early days," recollected Douglas' contemporary, Alexander Caulfield Anderson, fur-trade officers were chosen on the basis of "strength of constitution and general probity of character" and "family influence."[48] In

---

[44] William Fraser Tolmie, *The Journals of William Fraser Tolmie, Physician and Fur Trader* (Vancouver: Mitchell Press, 1963), January 9, 1834, 261–262. Also see W. Kaye Lamb, "TOLMIE, WILLIAM FRASER," in *Dictionary of Canadian Biography*, vol. XI, University of Toronto/Université Laval, 2003, www.biographi.ca, accessed July 22, 2010.

[45] "Servants Characters & Staff Records," HBCA, A 34/1, 82.

[46] George McDougall to John McLeod, March 8, 1828, McLeod Correspondence.

[47] James Douglas, "Private Account," BCA, Add MSS B/90/1, June 1, 1827.

[48] Alexander Caulfield Anderson, "History of the Northwest Coast," HBCA E294/1, Transcript, 41; Brown, *Strangers in Blood*, especially Chapter 3.

a careful and revealing use of language, another referred to "the "patri-archal way of the HBC.""[49]

If his father-in-law used intimacies to cement trade ties with Cree com-munities, Douglas used them to locate himself with dense webs of kinship within the fur trade. Establishing ties through marriage was particularly critical for men like Douglas who had limited kin connections. For those who could not depend on an influential father or uncle or acknowledged membership in a highland Scottish clan, a well-made marriage could knit them into networks of patronage and mentoring. Hargrave consid-ered these advantages a major explanation for the persistence of fur-trade marriages in the 1830s. His peers who chose local partners were often tempted by the resources that came from giving "their hand to the daugh-ter of an Officer," though he acknowledged that others were motivated by what Hargrave called "kinder Motives."[50]

The connection to Connolly made through marriage would serve Dou-glas well. While twentieth-century biographers liked to see Douglas as a proverbial self-made man whose abstemious character, formidable work habits, and sharp mind drove his upward mobility, his contemporaries explained his meteoric rise up the fur trade ranks differently, associating it with a strategic marriage. "A C. F. [chief factor] for a father-in-law to a rising clerk nowadays is good support," Archibald McDonald opined. "James Douglas is at Vancouver & rising fast in favour."[51] When Douglas climbed further up the ranks in 1835, his peer Francis Ermatinger grum-bled more. "Douglas was promoted last year, yet we were in the country before him. And certainly my employments have been more active and much more harassing than his."[52] Correspondents emphasized the kin-ship ties that Douglas had secured through marriage, describing him as "James Douglas – Connolly's son in law."[53]

The marriage between Connolly and Douglas makes clear how the circulation of women as wives performed critical work in an economy within which ties between senior men and their juniors were key. In early nineteenth-century fur-trade correspondence, marriage is represented as a means of establishing kin ties and cementing economic relationships between men. One trader described how a colleague had "given away

[49] Louis Lootens to John Sebastian Helmcken, September 19, 1859, Helmcken Family Fonds, BCA, Add MSS 505, Volume 1, File 8.
[50] Hargrave to McTavish, June 24, 1838, *Letters from Rupert's Land*, 334.
[51] Archibald McDonald to Edward Ermatinger, February 20, 1831, in Jean Murray Cole, *This Blessed Wilderness: Archibald McDonald's Letters from the Columbia, 1822–44* (Vancouver: UBC Press, 2001) 91.
[52] Francis Ermatinger to Edward Ermatinger, March 11, 1836, in McDonald, ed., *Fur Trade Letters*, 185. Also see Francis Ermatinger to Edward Ermatinger, March 4, 1830.
[53] John Tod to Edward Ermatinger, June 29, 1836, Ermatinger Papers, Volume 1.

his daughter Margaret" to a man she had never met. The letter-writer doubted the strategy, but deemed the new husband a "fine young man" and thought that his friend was "fortunate in getting such a son in Law."[54] Senior men wielded their power to "give" women in marriage carefully, protecting this authority even when kin ties were thin. In 1837 Tod wrote to Ermatinger about the marital prospects of a "daughter said to be his" who had been raised by another family at Oxford House. Tod explained that "she is not likely to remain long single – a worthy Orkney man of the name of Kirkness in the district has been applying for her in marriage, but as the girl is still very Young I venture to interpose to defer the ceremony until such time as they heard from her father."[55]

As Ermatinger considered how best to utilize his power to "give" a reputed daughter he scarcely knew and who had been raised half a continent away, he himself was petitioning a senior man for permission to marry. After a string of relationships with different Indigenous women that earned him a reputation for callousness and violence, Ermatinger decided he needed a well-placed Metis wife to secure a father-in-law who would, as he put it, "do his best for me."[56] He spent years in an unsuccessful effort to persuade John McLoughlin, the chief factor at Fort Vancouver, to give him permission to marry his daughter Eloisa. When circumstances were right, McLoughlin granted the aging and less than reputable Ermatinger the right to marry his step-granddaughter, Catherine Sinclair. "[Y]ou may have heard of his having asked her and of her being at my Disposal," explained McLoughlin, "but as he had to be Knocking about on the plains – I would not give her." Catherine, McLoughlin explained, was "young enough to be [Ermatinger's] Daughter" and "as fine a Young Woman as I have seen in the Country and [he] need not be ashamed to take her to the Civilized World." Sinclair was the granddaughter of his wife from an earlier relationship, but still at McLoughlin's "Disposal." Given Ermatinger's track record, at least one friend was skeptical of the match, asking "How many wives in the name of goodness is he going to have?"[57]

Women, whether as prospective wives or their mothers, seem to have played secondary roles in these epistolary negotiations or at least in the archives that documented them. Sometimes men sought a woman's

---

[54] William Nourse to James Hargrave, May 1, 1840, in G. P. De T. Glazebrook, ed., *The Hargrave Correspondence, 1821–1843* (Toronto: The Champlain Society, 1838) 313.

[55] John Tod to Edward Ermatinger, July 15, 1837, Ermatinger Papers, Volume I.

[56] Francis Ermatinger to Edward Ermatinger, March 4,1830, in McDonald, ed., *Fur Trade Letters*, 133.

[57] John McLoughlin to Edward Ermatinger, February 1, 1843; R. Miles to Edward Ermatinger, August 13, 1843, Ermatinger Papers, Volume III.

approval along with that of her father. Ermatinger considered gaining "the consent of the young lady herself,"[58] a part, though a secondary one, of his failed campaign to marry Eloisa McLoughlin. Consent seems to have played little role in Harriet Vincent Gladman's first marriage, arranged by her father before she was in her teens. Letitia McTavish Hargrave, the Scottish woman Hargrave chose as his wife, committed Vincent Gladman's versions of events to paper, describing how her first husband "asked her father for her when she was 12 years old" and how she "was dragged out of her mothers room & sent away with him."[59]

Written archives also suggest some of the ways that mothers could help their daughters resist or renegotiate the terms of such marriages. Sarah Julia Ogden was an elite Metis daughter who, like Connolly Douglas, married her father's clerk. In the 1890s, Ogden McKinlay described her courtship and marriage for a local Oregon historian, and in the process, revealed much about the complicated politics of marriage in fur-trade society. "You ask me about my courtship, I never had any courting to do," she declared. Archibald McKinlay spoke to her father, Peter Skene Ogden, "about me" and received his permission to visit until Sarah was "old enough, so to speak." When she was fourteen Skene Ogden revealed the arrangement to his daughter. When she made no clear objection, he told her that the marriage was to occur, or, as Ogden McKinlay put it, that "I was to be given Mr. McKinlay." Ogden McKinlay objected, or, as she recalled, "began to think that I would rather be with my mother than be married." There was a "stall" and hard feelings on her father's part, but the girl's mother "was in my favour," thinking her daughter too young for marriage. This all came to an end when Skene Ogden made clear that he wanted his daughter married before he traveled to Canada and threatened to "leave the service" if Sarah did not agree to the match. The young woman put heavy stock in the opinion of Amelia Connolly Douglas, her godmother. "Mrs. Douglas had a long talk with me and gave great deal of advice on the subject," she recalled. With Connolly Douglas' apparent support, the couple married in 1840.[60]

The space women occupied – literally and symbolically – within fur-trade forts was limited and regulated, especially in larger forts. NWC

[58] Francis Ermatinger to Edward Ermatinger, June 1, 1837, in McDonald, ed., *Fur Trade Letters*, 199.

[59] Letitia Hargrave to Mrs. Dugald MacTavish, December 1, 1840, in Margaret Arnett MacLeod, eds., *The Letters of Letitia Hargrave* (Toronto: The Champlain Society, 1947) 82.

[60] Sarah J. McKinlay to Eva Emery Dye, January 23, 1892, Eva Emery Dye Papers, Oregon Historical Society, 1089, 2/8, 1 (hereafter Dye Papers). Also see Sarah J. McKinlay to Eva Emery Dye, December 11, 1891, Dye Papers, 1089, 2/8. Thanks to Scott Daniels for helping me access these records.

and HBC forts were both corporate and military spaces where multiple social distinctions were made manifest through space and its identification for and with certain individuals. Unmarried men lived and socialized together. "In the evening the young clerks come together to smoke in a room called Bachelor's Hall, each tells of his travels, his adventures, his fights with the Indians," reported one observer.[61] Married officers had special quarters, and chief traders and chief factors usually claimed a special apartment or even small houses within fort walls. Elite women like Connolly Douglas and her daughters lived much of their lives within these spaces. As in Demerara, it was the table rather than the bed or the nursery that served as the critical instrument of intimate racial separation. "The ladies never dined at the Table with the gentlemen," recalled a man who had visited Fort Vancouver in the 1840s.[62] Andrew Dominique Pambrum, who recalled his Fort Vancouver childhood with a critical eye, put it differently, recalling that "At no time did a woman or her children eat at the same table as her perfidious *lord*."[63]

As an older woman, Eloisa McLoughlin Rae Harvey, John McLoughlin's youngest and much-cherished daughter, remembered the explicitly gendered, and by extension racialized, separation of eating and sociability that prevailed among Fort Vancouver's elite.

The ladies who were there then lived separately in their own mess room. When my father had company, distinguished visitors & others, he entertained them in the general mess room, and not in the family mess room. The families lived separate and private entirely. Gentlemen who came trading to the Fort never saw the family. We never saw anybody.

The women sometimes saw McLoughlin's office, but never the mess room.[64] Harvey's recollection of a sequestered space for women away from the business of the fort and male spaces of sociability evokes the other female spaces in nineteenth-century households elsewhere in the imperial world like the zenana or harem. A White American

---

[61] Nellie Bowden Pipes, "Extract from Exploration of the Oregon Territory, the Californias, and the Gulf of California, Undertaken during the Years 1840, 1841, and 1842 by Eugene Duflot de Mofras," *Quarterly of the Oregon Historical Society*, 26:2 (June 1925) 155.

[62] F. W. Pettygrove, "Oregon in 1843," in "Oregon Sketches, 1878," Bank MSS P-A, Bancroft Library, University of California, Berkeley, pp. 59–68 (hereafter BL). More generally, see John A. Hussey, "The Women of Fort Vancouver," *Oregon Historical Quarterly*, 92:3 (Fall 1991) 265–308.

[63] Andrew Dominique Pambrun, *Sixty Years on the Frontier in the Pacific Northwest* (Fairfield, WA: Ye Galleon Press, 1978) 60.

[64] Eloise [Eloisa] Harvey, "Life of John McLoughlin, Governor, of the Hudson's Bay Company's Possessions on the Pacific Slope at Fort Vancouver," BL, PB 12, Mflm 12, 12–13.

schoolteacher who spent the winter of 1832/3 at Fort Vancouver recalled the patterns of sociability that accompanied dining there, and the absence of women from it. "The gentlemen of the fort were very pleasant and intelligent," he recalled, and "There was much formality at the table. Men waited on the table, and we saw little of the women, they never appearing except perhaps on Sunday or on horseback."[65]

White women who arrived in the 1830s were particularly alert to the gendered arrangement of elite social space at Fort Vancouver. Narcissa Whitman was an American missionary who visited in 1836. She expected meals to be a key site of polite heterosociability and found things otherwise. "Indeed, some of the gentlemen of the company have native wives, and have adopted the custom of the country not to allow their wives to eat with them," she explained.[66] Her husband opted to eat with the women instead, and actions like these would provoke shifts in the gendered patterns of sociability. Harvey recalled that things changed once the missionary women arrived at Fort Vancouver. "When the Missionary Ladies came it was quite different," she observed. "Then we mingled more."[67] By the early 1840s, there were three tables at Fort Vancouver, one for "Chief Factor and clerks," one for "their wives," and a third for "the American Missionaries." The sick and the Catholic Priest ate separately from them all.[68]

The mobilities and residential patterns of the fur trade reinforced the authority of husbands over wives, fragmented ties between mothers and daughters and their kinship networks, and built enduring and cross-generational communities among women who shared the social space of a given fort. Fur-trade lives were mobile ones, and wives moved with their husbands. Doing so could separate them from their kin but put them into daily conversation and community with other women in the fort. Connolly Douglas was separated from her parents and siblings when she moved to Fort Vancouver, but she built relations of care and affect with the women she met there. Ogden McKinlay would describe Connolly Douglas and McLoughlin Rae Harvey as "both great friends of mine to the last." The designation of godparent bestowed at Roman Catholic baptism was a formal recognition of these ties. Marguerite Waddin McKay

---

[65] Kate N. B. Powers, "Across the Continent Seventy Years Ago: Extracts from the Journal of John Ball of his Trip across the Rocky Mountains and his Life in Oregon, Compiled by his Daughter," *Quarterly of the Oregon Historical Society*, 3:1 (March 1902) 100.

[66] "Diaries and Journals of Narcissa Whitman, 1836," entry for September 13, 1836, www.isu.edu/~trinmich/00.ar.whitman1.html, accessed December 9, 2009.

[67] Harvey, "Life of John McLoughlin," 12–14.

[68] Edmond S. Meany, "Diary of Wilkes in the Northwest," *Washington Historical Quarterly*, 16 (1925) 219.

McLoughlin was named godmother to two of the Douglas daughters baptized at Fort Vancouver, and Maria Pambrum Barclay and Catherine McIntosh, both Metis women, stood in the same fashion to the others.[69] These ties between women, formalized by the role of godmother and rooted in shared space and lives, were meaningful and enduring, and they speak to the different kinds of social sense that bourgeois Indigenous women might make out of the particular colonial economy of the fur trade.

Since the 1980s, historians have struggled to square the evidence about Indigenous womanhood and fur-trade marriage. This question stands in for a larger one about the capacity of colonialism to radically rework gender and, more to the point, to transform matriarchal or egalitarian cultures into patriarchal ones. Many of the women who married into the late eighteenth- and nineteenth-century fur trade hailed from Plains, Subarctic, or Plateau Indigenous communities that historically accorded women a high degree of autonomy around marriage and sexuality. When they married men attached to the fur trade and raised their children within the hybrid space of the trade, they found the perimeters of womanhood significantly redrawn. Women accustomed to choosing their own partners and if and when to leave them found themselves refigured as tokens of exchange. Read in these terms, Ron Bourgeault's 1980 argument that the fur trade commodified local women through marriage just as it did the furs traded and returned to Europe at a profit packs considerable analytic weight.[70]

But these fur-trade marriages like those of Connolly and Miyo Nipay or Douglas and Connolly Douglas are not best registered as meetings between two dichotomous and wholly separate cultures. Marriage was more a mechanism through which men, including newcomers, were knitted into families, communities, and economies than a formal meeting of discrete societies bound up in the bodies of individual men and women. When Connolly and Miyo Nipay partnered, they did so within

---

[69] Sarah J. McKinlay to Mrs. Dye, January 23, 1892, Oregon Historical Society 1089, 2/8 (hereafter OHS); Harriet Duncan Munnick, ed., and Mickell de Lores Wormell Warner, trans., *Catholic Church Records of the Pacific Northwest: Vancouver, Volumes I & II, and Stellamaris Mission* (St Paul, OR: French Prairie Press, 1972) Vancouver I, 37th p, B 100; Vancouver II, 140, B 187; Vancouver II, 76, B 561; Vancouver II, 103, B 7. On godparents, see Susan Sleeper-Smith, "Women, Kin, and Catholicism: New Perspectives on the Fur Trade," *Ethnohistory*, 47:2 (Spring 2000) 423–452; Macdougall, *One of the Family*, 151–2.

[70] Ron Bourgeault, "The Indians, the Metis and the Fur Trade: Class, Sexism and Racism in the Transition from 'Communism' to Capitalism," *Studies in Political Economy*, 12 (1983) 45–79; Ron Bourgeault, "Race, Class and Gender: Colonial Domination of Indian Women," in *Socialist Studies: A Canadian Annual* 5 (1989) 87–115.

Indigenous space and according to Indigenous practice. When Douglas and his peers partnered with the daughters of senior men in the fur trade, they did so within what were, from the eighteenth century onwards, communities of long duration. These relationships were not negotiated between two cultures as much as they were made within and folded into the particular hybrid economy and society of the fur trade.

We might also recall how what Julia Emberley calls the "textual economy of the colonial archive"[71] can produce the very object it presumed, namely the disempowered Indigenous woman. Images of abject and resourceless Indigenous women are shot through the literature of nineteenth-century empire and do particular political work there. John Franklin spent winters at Cumberland House under the hospitality of Connolly and took a dim view of how traders treated their Indigenous wives, reporting that men with "Indian or half-breed wives" seemed "afraid of treating them with the tenderness or attention due to every female, lest they should themselves be despised by the Indians." "At least," he continued, "this is the only reason they assign for their neglect of those whom they make partners of their beds and mothers of their children."[72] This is not a discussion of abusive or neglectful husbands as much as it is a ritual condemnation of Indigenous societies and the men who opted to become kin to them.

It is possible to wrest a more complicated interpretation of fur-trade intimacies from the available written record. Elite fur-trade women took little responsibility for the household labors assigned to women in most European divisions of labor. "The wives here are not first rate housekeepers," wrote Whitman from Fort Vancouver in 1836. What she deemed housework was performed by male servants.[73] Visitors who commented on Metis women's absence from formal meals and sociability were equally struck by their skill and mobility as horsewomen, and their ability to move confidently through space in ways denied bourgeois European women. Whitman went riding with Marguerite Waddin McKay McLoughlin, noting that she rode "gentlemen fashion," and that this was "the universal custom of Indian women."[74] An American teacher who visited Fort

---

[71] Julia V. Emberley, "'A Gift for Languages': Native Women and the Textual Economy of the Colonial Archive," *Cultural Critique*, 17 (Winter 1990/1991) 21–50.

[72] John Franklin, *Narrative of a Journey to the Shores of the Polar Sea, in the Years 1819, 20, 21 and 22* (Edmonton: M. G. Hurtig, 1969 [1824]) 68.

[73] Narcissa Whitman to Brother Oren and Sister Nancy, October 24, 1836, in Clifford Merill Drury, ed., *First White Women over the Rockies: Diaries, Letters, and Biographical Sketches of the Six Women who Made the Overland Journey in 1836 and 1838*, Volume I (Glendale, CA: Arthur H. Clark, 1963) 108.

[74] Narcissa Whitman, September 30 1836, "Diaries and Journals of Narcissa Whitman, 1836," www.isu.edu/~trinmich/00.ar.whitman1.html, accessed 9 December 2009.

Vancouver recalled that he saw little of the women, but that "As riders they excelled."[75] Fur-trade wives might have been separated from their families of birth and lived away from the elite men of the fort, but they built sustaining ties of community within those spaces. Johnny Grant, a young Metis man sent to Fort Vancouver to winter in 1849, remembered the wives and daughters of the fort's officers spending their time in a "big communal room that served as a mess room and sitting room." He recalled it as a space that he and presumably other men were occasionally admitted to, and one of sociability and fun, the site of "many gay frolics."[76]

The written archives left by fur-trade women provide further evidence of a more complicated history of womanhood and marriage. Ogden McKinlay was not powerless in her youthful marriage, nor was the mother who supported her. Vincent Gladman, who spoke of her forced marriage at age twelve, also spoke of her ability to renegotiate the terms of her life within the framework of fur-trade marriage. After her first husband left her, she married George Gladman, an elite Metis trader. In 1840 she sported a wedding ring and made clear that her daughters could choose their own spouses. Vincent Gladman drew a clear distinction between the marriage that was forced and the one that was chosen. "She always says 'When I *was sent* with Mr. Stewart' & 'When I *went* with Mr. Gladman," reported Letitia McTavish Hargrave. This is a snippet of women's communication, one that McTavish Hargrave, a chief factor's wife and one of the very few White women in fur-trade country, felt grateful to hear. "Mrs. Gladman & I are getting very gracious, – She favoured me with her history & that of her mother before her," she reported.[77]

This was a social world of connection where women reckoned their lives in terms of the relationships that gave them meaning and satisfaction. The evaluative frames of liberal discourse could not make much sense of this, beyond the predictable sentimental gloss that accompanied descriptions of female affection and care. But even within the patriarchal and colonial confines of the trade there was room for different modes of female subjectivity. Christina McDonald McKenzie Williams was the daughter of a Metis woman and a Scottish trader. Her father, Angus, "could talk or make himself understood by all the Indians between the Cascade and the Rocky Mountains" and was remembered

[75] Powers, ed., "Across the Continent Seventy Years Ago," 100.

[76] Gerhard J. Ens, ed., *A Son of the Fur Trade: The Memoirs of Johnny Grant* (Edmonton: University of Alberta Press, 2008) 28.

[77] Letitia Hargrave to Mrs. Dugald MacTavish, December 1, 1840, in MacLeod, eds., *The Letters of Letitia Hargrave*, 83.

for being "fairly educated" and "well up in the politics of the day."
He was also "excessively fond of living the life of an aborigine, and
would much prefer to live in a tent, or lodge, than in a house built in
accordance with civilized plans."[78] Christina was raised at Fort Colville,
where she served as her father's "special companion" and interpreter.[79]
McDonald McKenzie Williams was known for her beauty and confidence. One author described her as "a splendid woman" who "always
accompanied her father, and rode a-straddle."[80] Her father boasted of
her authority, independence, and wealth. "She is well lodged and married, on her own ranch on the left bank of the Thompson River facing
the Indian Reservation. She is now a large woman, weighing over two
hundred pounds," he proudly reported.[81] Her first marriage was a typical fur-trade match – to her father's clerk. But, less typically, McDonald
McKenzie Williams inherited her husband's business on his death and
put her thick local knowledge to profitable work. In the 1920s, she recollected her challenge to gendered convention for a local historian. She
boasted of her success as a woman of capital. "I more than held my own
with them, for I was raised in the fur trade, and had been a companion
of my father so long that I knew the business thoroughly," she explained,
emphasizing that "I have made lots of money."[82]

These stories are snippets, but they are ones that disrupt the dis-
mal prognostications of Franklin and his ilk, and suggest some of the
more complicated readings of fur-trade womanhood and marriage we
might wrest from these colonial archives. McDonald McKenzie Williams
learned the trade as a child and was able to parlay her knowledge into
real wealth and local authority, and was widely admired for doing so.
Gladman survived a violent and failed marriage brokered when she was
still a child, and as a grown woman secured a more satisfactory one for
herself and created conditions under which her daughters were able to do
the same. Material culture also speaks of women's authority. Historian
Sherry Farrell Racette reminds of the power in Metis women's work,

---

[78] Garry Fuller Reese, ed., "Reminiscences of Puget Sound: Writings of Edward Huggins
as Published in Pacific Northwest Newspapers and other Locations" (unpublished MS,
Tacoma, 1984, held at Washington State Library, Olympia, WA) 119, 116.

[79] Christina McDonald McKenzie Williams, "The Daughter of Angus McDonald,"
Washington Historical Quarterly, 13 (1922) 109.

[80] Parker's Puget Sound, quoted in Hubert Howe Bancroft, "Bancroft Reference Notes
for British Columbia and Alaska, ca. 1870s–1890s," BL, BANC MSS B-C 11, Carton
1, File 3.

[81] F. W. Howay, William S. Lewis, and Jacob A. Meyers, "Angus McDonald: A Few Items
of the West," *Washington Historical Quarterly*, 8:3 (1917) 206.

[82] Williams, "The Daughter of Angus McDonald," 115.

and especially in their ability to clothe in a northern environment.[83] As in the Caribbean, women in fur-trade territory were empowered by place, their connections to it, and their knowledge of its resources. Men attached to the trade were empowered by global practices of governance and economy, but most of them were simply passing through, whether the continent or the specific territory. The interpretative sense historians can make of these marriages invariably rests on an archive that can reproduce its own brittle truths and offer only occasional glimpses of the complicated intimate history produced by colonialism in North America and elsewhere.

Imperial intimacies were both global and local. Tracking the intimate relationships of the Connolly–Douglas family and people whose lives were lived alongside them from pre-emancipation Demerara to fur-trade North America makes clear the importance of local configurations of imperialism and capitalism. Intimate relationships made between men working in the fur trade like William Connolly and Indigenous women such as Miyo Nipay were honed to and constituent of a particular configuration of colonialism. Likewise the intimate relationship of John Douglas and Martha Ritchie in Demerara during the years of slavery was structured to and animated by the needs of that colonial economy. But these were not discrete histories playing out on two separate stages. The lives of James Douglas, Amelia Connolly, and their friends and kin remind us that imperial intimacies were not lived in isolation. These were histories made by people who were born, worked for a living, moved when need and opportunity dictated, and married when it seemed expedient, appealing, or necessary. It was in local colonial spaces that a lived and uneven sort of imperial world was made and remade.

[83] Sherry Farrell Racette, "Sewing for a Living: The Commodification of Métis Women's Artistic Production," in Katie Pickles and Myra Rutherdale, eds., *Contact Zones: Aboriginal and Settler Women in Canada's Colonial Past* (Vancouver: UBC Press, 2005) 17–46.

3   Free people, servants, and states

You could buy a beaver hat in Georgetown, Demerara in 1804. You could buy various kinds: for ladies, men, children, and ones with feathers. These hats were on a long list of luxury goods that were available for purchase in a small port city of a colony dependent on the brutal economy of slavery. Many of these goods were produced elsewhere in the British imperial world: Jamaican rum, Irish linen, Indian madras and calico.[1] But the hats made of North American beaver harvested and traded by Indigenous peoples are especially germane to the histories here. There is, of course, the irony of anyone voluntarily wearing a beaver hat in a place where the average daily temperature is about 27 degrees Celsius, one that speaks to the power of this particular item to distinguish its wearer from others, including the enslaved people who were the presumed market for the "negro hats" also for sale. But beyond that there is the circulation of the products of empire not simply from periphery to metropole, but from one colonial space to another. The products of the fur trade were available in the Caribbean, and West Indian products circulated through the fur trade. In 1814, a Canadian fur trader recorded rum and molasses among the "presents" he gave to influential Indigenous men, the kind of diplomatic, intimate, and economic transactions that the fur trade was predicated on.[2] The rations that voyageurs received included loaf sugar.[3]

The beaver hats for sale in Georgetown and the sugar, molasses, and rum traded and paid as wages in the fur trade remind us of the connections between these two colonial spaces. These were not simply those of intimacy, but also of governance and race. This chapter maps some of the

---

[1] See, for instance, advertisement for James Lyon and Co., *Essequebo and Demerera Gazette* (hereafter *EDG*), September 8, 1804, www.vc.id.au/edg/index.html, accessed August 10, 2011.

[2] "Presents Given to different Chiefs, &c, &c," in Barry M. Gough, ed., *The Journal of Alexander Henry the Younger, 1799–1814* (Toronto: The Champlain Society, 1992) 747–748.

[3] Andrew Dominique Pambrum, *Sixty Years on the Frontier in the Pacific Northwest* (Fairfield, WA: Ye Galleon Press, 1978) 18.

layered workings of race, labor, and colonial rule in the first half of the nineteenth century, tying them to the layered and unstable histories of imperial governance in Guyana and fur-trade North America. Following James Douglas, Amelia Connolly Douglas, and their peers and kin alerts us to the locality and particularity of empire, and to the complicated and shifting spaces assigned to elite Creole and Metis people within it.

Empire was by definition global. But it was lived in particular places with their own thick and insurgent histories. In Guyana, colonialism was multiply layered. The colonies of Demerara, Essequibo and Berbice changed political hands six times between 1780 and 1803, a token in European conflict shuttled back and forth between Dutch, British, and to a lesser extent French power.[4] In 1803, the year of James Douglas' birth, the three colonies were returned to British control by the terms of the Treaty of Amiens. The precise parameters of imperial authority continued to shift even after British authority was clearly re-established. The two colonies of Demerara and Essequibo were united in 1813, and in 1833 they were merged with the colony of Berbice to form the single colony of British Guiana. (See Figure 3.1.)

Well after the lasting rearticulation of British authority, Guyana continued to be defined by Indigenous presence and by the histories of the Batavian Empire. As it was throughout the Americas, the assertion of European authority of any sort was premised here on the dispossession of Indigenous peoples and economies. Guyana entered the orbit of European trade and exploration at the end of the sixteenth century, and the Dutch began sugar plantations predicated on enslaved African labor in the middle years of the seventeenth. As Melanie Newton has argued, the construction of the early modern Caribbean as a space lacking in Indigenous peoples was a cultural, military, and diplomatic sleight of hand that was never wholly successful in erasing Indigenous presence.[5] This was perhaps more especially true in the mainland colonies like the Guyanas than on the islands. For all the fictions of formal documents and popular discourse, Indigenous populations were a significant part of early nineteenth-century Guyana. Indigenous peoples visited early nineteenth-century Georgetown and demanded gifts from the colonial state.[6] Where

---

[4] Linda Peake and D. Alissa Trotz, *Gender, Ethnicity, and Place: Women and Identities in Guyana* (London: Routledge, 1999) 41.

[5] See D. Graham Burnett, *Masters of All They Surveyed: Exploration, Geography, and a British El Dorado* (University of Chicago Press, 2000) 18; Melanie Newton, "Geographies of the Indigenous: Hemispheric Perspectives on the Early Modern Caribbean," paper presented at the University of Manitoba, March 23, 2012.

[6] See Bathhurst to A. General Carmichael, November 25, 1812, Colonial Office, Demerara, Esquibbo, and Berbice, CO 112/12, National Archives (hereafter NA, CO 112).

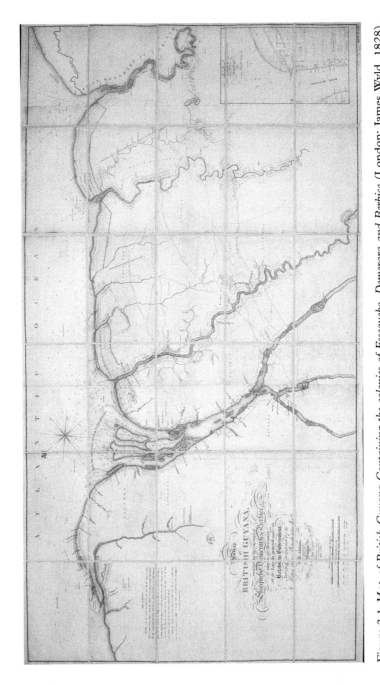

Figure 3.1 *Map of British Guyana Containing the colonies of Essequebo, Demerara and Berbice* (London: James Wyld, 1828). Plantations are numbered, and urban Georgetown is in the inset.

Indigenous peoples fit in local economies of slavery was enough of a question that the governor, writing in both Dutch and English, condemned those who would "Purchase Free Indians and keep them in their Service as Slaves." Historian Mary Noel Menezes explains that British policies for dealing with Indigenous peoples in nineteenth-century Guyana were grab-bag and inconsistent, a "conglomerate of the policy of liberal and conservative, pro- and anti-humanitarian members of the Colonial office, of sugar-minded and money-grabbing members of the Combined Court, of strong – and weak – willed Governors, of interested and uninterested officials, and of zealous missionaries."[7]

As in southern Africa and northern North America, the administration of the British imperial state was conditioned and inflected by former empires and their particular mechanics and languages of rule. In 1803, the newly appointed lieutenant governor of a colony again under British authority assured London of the "apparent reconciliation" of colonists to British rule.[8] Here, Dutch governance and nomenclature were rearticulated within the tissues of British colonial government. The practice of "winkle" or state slavery persisted long into the British period. Local administration was adjudicated by two fiscals who worked under the governor, aided by a Council of Kaizers, made up of seven members elected by "every person possessed of twenty five slaves and more."[9] The Dutch flavor of the colony could rub British colonists the wrong way. Hugh Douglas was among the twenty-one "Merchants Planters and Masters of Ships and Vessels trading to the United Kingdom of Great Britain and Ireland and to the States of America" who wrote in 1804 expressing their disappointment with the appointment of a notary public they feared to be insufficiently familiar with the English language.[10] In 1926, historian L. M. Penson argued that this particular relationship between Dutch and British administration in early nineteenth-century Demerara was critical to producing the particular constitutional status

---

[7] *EDG*, February 13, 1808, accessed October 6, 2011. Also see William Woodly [possibly misspelled] to Henry Bentinck, May 19, 1810, Colonial Office, British Guiana, CO 111/10 (hereafter CO 111); Mary Noel Menezes, *British Policy towards the Amerindians in British Guiana, 1803–1873* (Oxford: The Clarendon Press, 1977) 254–255.

[8] Robert Nicholson to Lord Hobart, November 9, 1803, CO 111, 1803 and 1804, File 4. See, on this, Bettina Bradbury, "Colonial Comparisons: Rethinking Marriage, Civilization and Nation in 19th Century White-Settler Societies," in Phillip Buckner and Daniel G. Francis, eds., *Rediscovering the British World* (University of Calgary Press, 2005), 135–158.

[9] C. Dalzell, "Observations on the Colony of Esquibo and Demerary," nd, CO 111/4.

[10] Andrew Smith *et al.* to Robert Nicholson, nd [1804], CO 111/5. See Alvin O. Thompson, *Unprofitable Servants: Crown Slaves in Berbice, Guyana, 1803–1831* (Kingston, Jamaica: University of West Indies Press, 2002).

of the "Crown Colony." This would prove a durable model of governance in a range of other contexts (including Vancouver Island) and, in Guyana, a resource in the defense of slavery in the face of abolitionist critiques.[11]

British administration of early nineteenth-century Guyana was strained, sometimes haphazard, and polyglot by necessity. Anthony Beaujon was Demerara's governor under the Dutch regime, and he was again the governor after the British re-established rule in 1803. The formal "Britishness" needed to make Beaujon an acceptable governor was arranged when his earlier residence in the British West Indies was deemed sufficient to make him a naturalized British subject.[12] Confident language about imperial possession was challenged and conditioned by pragmatic administrative decision-making that could favor men whose presence in local colonial space outweighed the fact that their claims to be British subjects were at best strained. Here, governors came and went. Within the metropolitan and bourgeois logic of the Colonial Office, Demerara was not a plum posting. It was what historian Zoë Laidlaw characterizes as a "typical early post," from which well-connected British men would predictably move on.[13] After Beaujon died in office, London made James Montgomerie, a naval brigadier who commanded the colony's troops and answered to the commander of the Leeward Fleet, governor. With its administration tightly tied to that of the navy, its colonial population focused on the coast, and its largely Indigenous interior, Demerara became a different sort of "naval colony."[14]

In early nineteenth-century Guyana, the British Empire sometimes spoke in Dutch and was sometimes administered by men on a boat or by those whose qualifications were chiefly their availability on the ground. What remained was the practice of slavery. The goods produced by the unfree labor of enslaved people of African origin gave the Guyanas their local wealth, their global significance, and their demography and politics. Guyana was what historian Barry Higman calls a "third-phase" sugar colony, one defined by its consolidation in the closing years of the eighteenth century and its striking dependence on the labor of

---

[11] L. M. Penson, "The Making of a Crown Colony: British Guiana, 1803–33," *Transactions of the Royal Historical Society*, 4th series, 9 (1926) 107–134.

[12] See correspondence in CO 111/5; M. N. Menezes, *An Annotated Bibliography of Governors' Dispatches (British Guiana), Selected Years 1781–1871 (CO 111/1(1781) – CO 384 (1781) and CO 884/1–19* (Georgetown: Department of History, University of Guyana, 1978) 4.

[13] Zoë Laidlaw, *Colonial Connections, 1815–1845: Patronage, the Information Revolution, and Colonial Government* (Manchester University Press, 2005) 24.

[14] Downing Street to James Montgomerie, June 4, 1806, CO 111/6. See Jerry Bannister, *The Rule of the Admirals: Law, Custom, and Naval Government in Newfoundland, 1699–1832* (University of Toronto Press, 2003).

Table 1 *Population, Demerara and Essequibo, 1811*

	Demerara	Essequibo	Both colonies
White adult men	1,314	431	1,745
White adult women	424	158	582
White female children	217	92	309
White male children	153	82	235
Free colored adult men	310	177	487
Free colored adult women	849	247	1,096
Free colored male children	537	196	733
Free colored female children	527	137	664
Adult enslaved men	23,021	8,463	31,384
Adult enslaved women	16,089	5,463	21,552
Enslaved male children	7,055	2,168	9,223
Enslaved female children	6,890	2,031	8,921
Total population	57,386	19,645	77,031

Source: From "A Return of the Population of the Colonies of Demerary & Esquibo, taken by Order of His Excellency the Governor on the 31st October and 25th November," in H. W. Bentinck to Earl of Liverpool, December 26, 1811, CO 111/11.

African-born slaves. Massive amounts of labor were required to transform Indigenous rainforest into plantation agriculture, and to work there afterwards. In 1810, enslaved people of African origins made up more than 90 percent of Demerara's population, and about 75 percent of these were African-born. The percentage of resident Europeans was small and became smaller as the nineteenth century wore on.[15]

Practices of colonialism invariably produced peoples and communities located between colonized and colonizing, and James Douglas' family of birth was situated among these multiple margins. His father was part of a White population that was small and getting smaller. Like many others in this community, the Douglases were Scots. They were attached to an enterprise called Douglas, Reid and Company that owned a number of plantations in Demerara and Berbice, most consistently linked to Good Hope and Belmont sugar estates in the Mahaica region to the east of Georgetown.[16] Some of the trade and commerce that the family's men

[15] B. W. Higman, *Slave Populations in the British Caribbean, 1807–1834* (Baltimore and London: Johns Hopkins University Press, 1984) 63, 76–77; "A Return of the Population of the Colonies of Demerary & Esquibo, taken by Order of His Excellency the Governor on the 31st October and 25th November," in Henry Bentinck to Earl of Liverpool, December 26, 1811, CO 111/11.
[16] See Charlotte Girard, "The Guiana World of Sir James Douglas' Childhood," unpublished MS. I thank Girard for sharing her research with me, and John Adams for helping to locate this particular manuscript. On these plantations, see William Baker, *The Local Guide Conducting to Whatever is Worthy of Notice, in the Colonies of Demerary and Essequebo* (Georgetown: Demerary, 1819) 229; James Williams, *Dutch Plantations on the Banks of*

and more particularly Hugh and Colin undertook can be traced through Georgetown's newspapers. Their work tied them to a wider imperial world. The Douglases sold salt cod from Newfoundland and regularly ran ships to Liverpool and London, sometimes armed against pirate attacks. Hugh Douglas was prominent in shipping and trade and kept a Georgetown shop. In April of 1811 he offered a long list of items for sale, material objects that spoke of local purchasing power and taste for luxury goods. The goods for sale also speak to trade networks that suggest an imperial world that extended far beyond the formal British Empire: Irish mess beef, Hyson tea, London porter, Russian sheeting, and much, much more.[17] The kinds of roles that Douglas men had in the colonial economy structured those within the colonial state. In petitions to the colonial government, Douglas men situated themselves among a constituency of engaged planters and merchants concerned about Demerara's place in a volatile Atlantic economy and British Empire.[18]

James' father, John Douglas, seems to have served a number of roles within this family enterprise and in Guyana more generally. Between 1804 and 1807, a John Douglas, sometimes spelled Douglass, was regularly reported for "returning" enslaved people who had escaped their masters. In 1803, John Douglas was the agent for the sale of the Plantation Brittania in Berbice, made up of 500 acres of what was described as "good" land, 200 acres which were cultivated buildings, and "74 Prime Negroes." He also acted on behalf of the Columbia plantation in little Courabanna, also known as Belmont, and the Good Hope plantation in Mahaica. In 1805 a John Douglas was among a long list of "Planters and Merchants of the Colonies of Demerary and Essequebo" who expressed their "respect and esteem" to an outgoing governor. In 1812, the year when Charlotte Girard thinks Douglas' father returned to Scotland with his two young sons, a John Douglas was included in the lists of those who planned to "quit" the colony.[19]

---

the Berbice and Canje Rivers in the country known since 1831 as the Colony of British Guiana and the Village Evolved from the Plantation (Georgetown: The Daily Chronicle, 1940) 151, 179; British Guiana, Report of the Titles to Land Commissioners on Claims to Land in the County of Berbice (Demerara: C. K. Jardine, 1893) 45–47.

[17] EDG, July 16, 1808, July 7, 1807, October 8, 1811, June 1, 1811, July 23, 1811, April 27, 1811, and June 15, 1811, all accessed between October 11, 2011 and January 6, 2012.

[18] See, for instance, "The Petition of the undersigned Proprietors, Merchants and Planters" to William Bentinck, NA, CO 111/7.

[19] See, for instance, "List of Runaway and Arrested Slaves," EDG, January 7, 1807, accessed April 17, 2010; October 22, 1803, accessed October 22, 2011; August 10, 1805, accessed April 17, 2010; June 6, 9, and 13, 1812, accessed January 18, 2012.

These are archival traces of people with the commonplace and almost anonymous names of a far-flung and highly mobile nineteenth-century imperial world. Unlike the Indian women studied by Durba Ghosh, European men rarely went literally nameless in the archive. Yet the widely held names of men like John Douglas – and John Taylor, a Barbados-born convicted slave trader, Canadian immigration agent, and Baptist missionary studied by historian Ryan Eyford – mean that they could be easily mistaken for or pass for another. As Kirsten McKenzie has shown, the potential for people to remake their identities in different colonial contexts was enormous and, for many, worrying.[20] It is impossible to know whether these John Douglases were one and the same man and if so, if he was the man who fathered James, Alexander, and Cecilia. The archival fragments from early nineteenth-century Guyana might describe this John Douglas, but they also might describe another man of the same name, a Scottish-born merchant or shopkeeper enumerated as living in Mahaica village in 1839 and again in 1841.[21]

The John Douglas that James identified as his father died in London in 1840. His British death certificate named him as a "West India Merchant" living in Edinburgh's fashionable Moray Place.[22] This inscribed the Caribbean on to the official record of his life, and made clear how this colonial space defined his life long after he left it and the family he had there. In 1834, John Douglas applied for compensation for property under the legislation that finalized the abolition of slavery in the British Empire. His application identifies him as absentee owner of colonial property and enslaved people, the kind that Guyana had long been organized around, and a Glasgow merchant tied to the J. T. and

---

[20] Durba Ghosh, "Decoding the Nameless: Gender, Subjectivity, and Historical Methodologies in Reading the Archives of Colonial India," in Kathleen Wilson, ed., *A New Imperial History: Culture, Identity, and Modernity in Britain and the Empire, 1660–1840* (Cambridge University Press, 2004) 297–316; Ryan Eyford, "Slave Owner, Missionary, and Colonization Agent: The Transnational Life of John Taylor, 1813–1884," in Karen Dubinsky, Adele Perry, and Henry Yu, eds., *Within and Without the Nation: Canadian History as Transnational History* (University of Toronto Press, in press); Kirsten McKenzie, *Scandal in the Colonies: Sydney and Cape Town, 1800–1850* (University of Melbourne Press, 2004).

[21] "Population of St Mary's Parrish, East Coast Demerara, 1839," AK1/2B, Folio 47, 72 and "Population of St Mary's Parrish, East Demerary," 1841, AK1, Folio 12, 66, Walter Rodney National Archives, Georgetown, Guyana (hereafter WRNA). John Douglas is listed as having died in 1841 in Mahaica village in Tikwis Begbie's remarkable "British Guiana Colonist Index," www.vc.id.au/th/bgcolonistsD.html, accessed April 24, 2011.

[22] Will of John Douglas, April 16, 1841, National Archives of Scotland, Edinburgh, SC 70/1/60. Death certificate of John Douglas, July 8,1840, copy in W. Kaye Lamb, "Ancestry of Sir James Douglas," British Columbia Archives (hereafter BCA), B/90/D74.

A. Douglas Company. He was awarded more than £12,407 compensation for 236 slaves at Good Hope, the Mahaica plantation he and his family had long been associated with. Nicholas Draper's remarkable research allows us to see that the Douglas family is as good an example as any of the economic and political work performed by slavery and slave compensation in nineteenth-century Britain.[23] The money from slave compensation was likely a component of the more than £70,000 that John Douglas' estate was valued at when he died. If some of this money came from the Caribbean, it did not return there, and would instead stay within the metropolitan space of Britain, willed to Douglas' legal family and heirs.

Free people of color were another community situated at the juncture of a local colonial society organized around slavery and global understandings of race and freedom. It is from this community that Douglas' mother likely came. The subject of free people of color in pre-emancipation Guyana has occasioned little historical interest. Historical scholarship on Guyana is overwhelmingly concerned with the years following emancipation, and more particularly the relative relationship between slavery and indenture and, sometimes by extension and sometimes de facto, the identities and social locations of Afro- and Indo-Guyanese. Yet historical studies of free people of color in other eastern Caribbean societies, particularly Barbados, make the case for their social significance, and for their significance to what Newton calls the Caribbean's "continuing entanglements with empire" and "complex racial subjectivities."[24]

Early nineteenth-century Demerara and Essequibo witnessed a consolidation of free Black identity. This was rooted in enormous population growth: between 1810 and 1830 the population of free people of color

---

[23] Slavery compensation record, British Guiana, 550, John Douglas, ID 8520. I thank Nicholas Draper for his willingness to share his valuable database on British slaveholding and compensation with me. Also see www.ucl.ac.uk/lbs/, accessed June 4, 2011, and Nicholas Draper, *The Price of Emancipation: Slave Ownership, Compensation, and British Society at the End of Slavery* (Cambridge University Press, 2010). The Douglas family is discussed on 241.

[24] Melanie J. Newton, *The Children of Africa in the Colonies: Free People of Color in Barbados in the Age of Emancipation* (Baton Rouge: Louisiana State University Press, 2008) 19. Also see Monica Schuler, "Liberated Africans in Nineteenth-Century Guyana," in Brian L. Moore *et al.*, eds., *Slavery, Freedom, and Gender: The Dynamics of Caribbean Society* (Kingston, Jamaica: University of West Indies Press, 2001) 133–160; Hilary McD. Beckles, "Freedom without Liberty: Free Blacks in the Barbados Slave System," in Verene A. Shepherd, ed., *Slavery without Sugar: Diversity in Caribbean Economy and Society since the 17th Century* (Gainsville, FL: University Press of Florida, 2002) 201–209; Pedro Welch and Richard Goodridge, *Red and Black over White: Free Coloured Women in Pre-emancipation Barbados* (Bridgetown: Carib, 2000).

in Berbice, Demerara, and Essequibo grew by about 70 percent, and easily overtook the White population.[25] Free people of color were still sometimes marked out as a distinct category of people, charged a distinct fare for the ferry from Georgetown to Mahaica, and allowed to visit public spectacles like the "Panorama of Georgetown" on some days of the week.[26] "Free man of color" was mobilized as a usable identity that could make specific demands on the local state. In 1812, the "Free Men of Colour of the Colony of Demerary" inserted themselves within the politically volatile colony whose allegiances were far from secure by submitting a petition. As "His Majesty's loyal and obedient subjects" they assured the governor "of our zeal for the success of the British arms in Europe, and throughout the world, and of our readiness, at all times, to sacrifice every thing most dear, even our lives," when called to by "our Sovereign and our country."[27]

The very term "free person of color" brought the languages of race and slavery into simultaneous play, laying bare the ways that Whiteness and Blackness and freedom and slavery helped produce and maintain one another. Italian artist Agostino Brunias created rich images that spoke to the wealth of free people of color in the late eighteenth century, and to the distinctions between them and a series of finely gradated racial others, including in his painting of a Creole woman and her Black servant shown in Figure 3.2. Metropolitan visitors could be taken aback by the extent to which free Blacks saw themselves as distinct from and superior to enslaved ones. "The free coloured population," one British traveler explained, had "a decided contempt for the slaves" even though they were only separated from them by a "smattering of education."[28] Hierarchies were complex and layered and generally not mapped in rigid spatial terms. As historian Juanita De Barros argues, early nineteenth-century Georgetown was not strictly segregated, and most groups in the city lived in most parts of it.[29]

---

[25] Higman, *Slave Populations*, 76–77.

[26] Baker, *The Local Guide Conducting to Whatever is Worthy of Notice, in the Colonies of Demerary and Essequebo* (1819) 192; Advertisement in *EDG*, July 6, 1811, accessed April 12, 2010.

[27] "Free Men of Colour of the Colony of Demerary," April 29, 1812, CO 111/12.

[28] Henry G. Dalton, *The History of British Guiana Comprising a General Description of the Colony*, Volume I (London: Brown, Green, and Longmans, 1855) 255.

[29] Juanita De Barros, *Order and Place in a Colonial City: Patterns of Struggle and Resistance in Georgetown, British Guiana, 1889–1924* (Montreal: McGill-Queen's University Press, 2003) 33. See breakdowns of neighborhoods by race in William Baker, *The Local Guide Conducting to Whatever is Worthy of Notice in the Colonies of Demerary and Essequebo, for 1821* (Georgetown: Royal Gazette, n.d. [1821]) 337; pagination added.

Figure 3.2 Agostino Brunias, "West Indian Creole Woman, with her Black Servant."

In this variegated world, the identities of slavery routinely trumped those of race per se. The Orphan Chamber was another holdover of the Dutch regime. It administered the estates of those who died intestate, a perennial problem in colonies with mobile male populations and unreliable practices for providing for locally born children. In the 1800s and 1810s, the colony's newspaper regularly published notices from the

Orphan Chamber enumerating how many White babies and free babies of color had been born in a given month, and what their sexes were. They did not count the births of enslaved people at all. There was a line separating free people of color and Whites, but the one that divided the enslaved from free was bigger, stronger, and more enduring. The colonial state was predictably preoccupied by slave resistance and its constant possibility. It was haunted by the simultaneous power and vulnerability of a regime predicated on the enslavement of the vast majority of the population. On questions of security, free people of color and White people served proximate roles. The state directed that free people of color should be counted "in the same light as Whites" in legislation regulating the ratio of free people to enslaved on plantations passed in 1805 and regularly reaffirmed thereafter. This kind of imperial calculus would not prevent the Demerara Slave Rebellion of 1823, when nearly 12,000 slaves took up arms in an action that reverberated around the imperial world.[30]

The lines that marked the division between free people of color and Whites could also be porous. Under the right circumstances free people of color could become White, or at least access the provisional privileges usually accorded to Whiteness. Reflecting on the racial particulars of Demerara, Henry Kirk argued that "The objection to the negro taint, the 'touch of the tar-brush' as it is locally called, is not as strong as in America and some of the West Indian islands." He went on to explain that

I am delighted to see any young coloured man by honest work and good behaviour raise himself to a high position amongst his fellow colonists, and many have done so. In my time there was a coloured chief justice in Barbados, a coloured solicitor-general in Trinidad, and in Demerara we have coloured gentlemen as legislators, magistrates, barristers, clergymen, mayors, and doctors, and they were treated with as much respect as White men in similar positions.

For Kirk, the limit on the upward mobility of men of color was their lack of secure metropolitan connections rather than their race per se. When "these gentry" spoke of "their family and 'home,' and sport crests, and coats-of-arms," Kirk felt compelled to laugh, "Remembering from whence they sprung."[31]

The lines separating free people of color from enslaved people were also unstable, but the risks of crossing them were different ones.

---

[30] *EDG*, May 25, 1805, accessed August 10, 2011. On the 1823 resistance, see Emilia Viotti da Costa's remarkable *Crowns of Glory, Tears of Blood: The Demerara Slave Rebellion of 1823* (Oxford University Press, 1994).

[31] Henry Kirke, *Twenty Five Years in British Guiana* (London: Sampson Low, Marston and Co., 1898) 53.

Newspaper ads warned against hiring or harboring enslaved people presenting themselves as free. In 1804, a subscriber warned people not to employ "a Mulatto Man named Sam Hacket, who endeavours to Pass as a Free Man." "A Negro Girl named Kate" was described as a Creole from Barbados with a "yellow skin" and "very good English" who might "attempt to pass as a free woman." Sally Betsey, a young and "slightly Mulatto-Woman" from Barbados, left her master in January 1812, taking "a bundle of linen" with her. "She was genteelly dressed," the advertisement explained, and "she may endeavour to pass for a free woman, under the name of Sarah Elizabeth Spencer." With her respectable dress, fair skin, and Caribbean connections, Spencer was an unstable racial subject who might subvert the distinction between enslaved and free. So was "a Negro-Woman, named Harriet, formerly the property of Mary Smith" who left her legal owner with a "Mulatto Boy-Child" named Wellington. She "speaks very good English; and no doubt will endeavour to pass for a free subject," her owner warned, threatening that the law would be "rigidly enforced" against those who might harbor this woman and her child.[32] Neither bodies nor names were reliable gauges of whether a person was enslaved or free, and this troubled a legal regime predicated on the presumed stability of a radically differentiated scheme of humanity.

This was the complicated social terrain that probably produced James Douglas' mother. Historian Charlotte Girard argues that his mother was likely Martha Ann Telfer, a free woman of color who lived in early nineteenth-century Georgetown. Here, as elsewhere in the pre-emancipation Caribbean, free people demonstrated their legal and political status in part by owning slaves. If the lives of the enslaved became most legible in the colonial archive when they were bought, enumerated as property, or manumitted as free, the lives of free people of color became most visible when they bought or sold human property or had their slaveholding regulated, taxed, or enumerated. Telfer was one on a long list of "free-coloured" people who paid their 1808 taxes for owning slaves, in her case twenty-four of them. In 1817, the British Colonial Office enumerated enslaved populations, and found that Telfer owned twenty-eight slaves. Such numbers were well above those for the average urban household in Guyana, which contained fewer than six slaves, and serves as a reliable indicator of her relative affluence. The range of occupations attributed to Telfer's slaves suggests the variety of economic activities she pursued. Her slaves included carpenters, field laborers, and hucksters (female market sellers) in addition to the expected domestic

---

[32] *EDG*, July 21 and December 29, 1804, accessed August 10, 2010; June 27, 1812, accessed January 18, 2012; May 25, 1813, accessed January 24, 2012.

workers.[33] As the slave trade was made illegal and slavery became more tightly regulated, Telfer's human property diminished numerically. In 1823, she had twenty-five slaves, in 1826 she owned seventeen, and in the next few years fifteen of those were sold. When she applied for compensation under the Slave Compensation Act, she had only one slave to her name, a tradesman for whom the British state gave her £68 8d. as compensation.[34]

Telfer's class status and social resources left other marks in the archive. She had cultural and social as well as material resources. She could write, or at least sign her name to legal documents, and was well enough known in Georgetown that an "Old Barbadian Negro Woman, named Madam" who escaped her master was identified in the newspaper as the former "property of Miss Martha Ann Telfor."[35] Historian Cassandra Pybus thinks that she may have spent some time in Glasgow.[36] Telfer died in 1839, and soon after, some of her most intimate possessions went to auction. These goods suggest her status as a well-to-do and distinctly Caribbean woman: a press, a large mahogany bedstead with bedding and curtains, a "colony-wood" bedstead, and a large mahogany sideboard.[37]

The available archive indicates that Telfer lived and worked in close connection with Rebecca Ritchie, who Girard suggests was Telfer's mother and James Douglas' grandmother. While Telfer made relatively light marks on the archive of nineteenth-century Demerara, Ritchie was harder to miss. She was not literate, and signed her documents with an X. But she knew her way around the colony's legal system, and was described as a "free coloured woman" acting in the local courts on matters of property. Ritchie bought and sold a fair bit of property herself. In 1812, she bought three town lots and sold a lot and buildings in Cummingsberg, a middle-class Georgetown neighborhood with a notable free Black population. Five years later, she bought another three lots in the same area.[38] Ritchie was not only a local subject, but a woman with economic and presumably social connections elsewhere in the British West

---

[33] *EDG*, September 25, 1810, accessed April 12, 2010; Colonial Office, "Slave Registers, 1817–1832," Demerara, entry for Martha Ann Telfer, 1817, NA, 874, T71/399; Thompson, *Unprofitable Servants*, 15; Colonial Office, "Slave Registers," Demerara, entry for Martha Ann Telfer, 1823, NA, 1388–9, T71/409.

[34] "Compensation: Registers of Claims," NA, T71/866, Claim 1366, Martha Ann Telfer.

[35] *EDG*, October 10, 1807, accessed April 11, 2011.

[36] Cassandra Pybus, email correspondence, August 17, 2011.

[37] *Royal Gazette of British Guiana*, February 11, 1840, NA, "Royal Gazette of British Guiana," CO 115/2 (hereafter CO 115). Thanks to Laura Ishiguro for this.

[38] *Royal Demerara and Berbice Gazette*, October 29, 1825, CO 115/2; *EDG*, May 16, 1812, accessed January 18, 2012; July 18, 1812, accessed April 12, 2010; Baker, *Guide to Demerara* [1821], 337; pagination added; *EDG*, September 20, 1817, accessed February 1, 2012.

Indies. Throughout the first half of the nineteenth century, she moved between Barbados, Berbice, and Demerara, following a well-worn path for free Blacks who moved from the long-established island colony to its wealthier, faster-growing mainland neighbours.[39] Kin ties and economic relations linked free and enslaved Blacks to other locations in the British West Indies, reiterating, on a smaller and otherwise different scale, some of the transatlantic connections that linked mobile colonists like the Douglases to the metropole.

As with her daughter, Ritchie's relative wealth was indicated by her slaveholdings. She owned twenty-six slaves in Demerara in 1812. Five years later, she was enumerated as owning thirty-seven slaves, twenty-two of them female, and most of them African born. While Ritchie seems to have lived mainly in Demerara, she was registered as being the absentee owner of four slaves in Barbados in 1817. After manumitting a nineteen-year-old slave, Susannah, and selling thirteen-year-old Susannah William and ten-year-old Carter John, she was left with only one slave in Barbados.[40] Her slaveholding in Demerara, in contrast, remained significant until emancipation. When she and Telfer applied for compensation for the "loss of property" wrought by abolition, she was awarded just less than £2,000 for thirty-three slaves, and another almost £200 for four slaves of Amelia Jacobs, a minor under her guardianship.[41] This was presumably the source of some of the approximately £500 that Ritchie left to James Douglas' daughters in her 1855 will.[42]

The nineteenth-century imperial world worked to devalue colonized women of color and render them invisible or at least hard to see in the archives it produced. Yet within local colonial spaces women could exercise considerable autonomy and authority. In free communities of color in the nineteenth-century Caribbean, female-headed households were the norm and marriage according to imperial law was an exception rather than a rule. Legally unmarried women could buy, sell, and own property and act on their own and others' behalf in the colony's courts.

---

[39] Newton, *The Children of Africa in the Colonies*, esp. 42.

[40] Rebecca Ritchie to John Murray, July 12, 1820, in "Petitions," 1820–1821, WRNA, A01/5; *EDG*, May 16, 1812, accessed March 6, 2010; Slave Registers, Demerara, entry for Rebecca Rithie (*sic*), 1817, NA, T71/392, 800–801; Slave Registers, Barbados, St. Michael's Parish, 1817, T71/520, 485, and 1823, T71/529, 505, available at www.ancestry.ca, accessed March 22, 2010.

[41] "Compensation: Register of Claims," NA, T71/886, Claim 1364, December 14, 1835; NA, T71/886, Claim 1365, December 14, 1835.

[42] James Douglas to James Stuart, October 7, 1868; James Douglas to Jane Dallas, June 11, 1869; both in "Private Letter Book of Sir James Douglas, Correspondence Outward, March 22, 1867–Oct. 11, 1870," British Columbia Archives, Add MSS B/40/2, Transcript (hereafter Private Letter Book, BCA).

Both Telfer and Ritchie bought and sold property and acted in the courts throughout their lives in ways that were unavailable to married women in the British and to a lesser extent French and Dutch empires. Women like Telfer and Ritchie often established relationships with White men that were located at what Pybus calls the "intimate frontiers of empire and slavery."[43] At this complicated juncture, free women drew on their legal capacity and wealth and their thick local knowledge and kin ties spread around the British West Indies. Men like John Douglas embodied the enormous structural authority and material wealth of the metropole and of patriarchal authority, but they, like men in the fur trade, were usually just passing through. Women such as Telfer and Ritchie lived their lives in the Caribbean, and however illegible they may have been to a wider imperial world, they made unmistakable marks on the colonial societies in which they lived.

These are fragmentary histories but they are also revealing ones. Carole Pateman famously argues that the civic unfreedom of women secured through marriage contract and codified by their exclusion from property ownership plays a critical role in gendered inequality, a connection that American historian Amy Dru Stanley has read through the particular idiom of slavery.[44] What happened when women did not marry according to law, and did buy, sell, and own property according to it? How did the placement of free women of color in a society ordered along a schism between free and enslaved shift the politics of gender, perhaps in ways that render it unrecognizable or at least very different? After the abolition of slavery in 1834 and the introduction of indenture in 1838, a variegated and finely wrought politics of race would replace a racialized but not strictly racial distinction between freedom and unfreedom in Guyana. But the first decades of the nineteenth century opened up particular spaces for free people of color, perhaps especially the women who constituted a substantial majority in cities like Georgetown. The imperial world functioned to render the intimate relations and identities of colonial spaces like Demerara – and also the fur trade – invisible and without rights, but within these places, complicated possibilities emerged, ones that need to be accessed on their own terms rather than simply read as the other of metropolitan thinking.

Children born in these layered social locations faced other sets of possibilities and barriers. Identities of race and legitimacy worked in ways that jibe with historian Ann Twiman's study of eighteenth-century

---

[43] Cassandra Pybus, "Tense and Tender Ties: Reflections on Lives Recovered from the Intimate Frontier of Empire and Slavery," *Life Writing*, 8:1 (2011) 5–17.

[44] Carole Pateman, *The Sexual Contract* (Stanford University Press, 1988); Amy Dru Stanley, *From Bondage to Contract: Wage Labor, Marriage, and the Market in the Age of Slave Emancipation* (Cambridge University Press, 1998).

Spanish America. Both birth and racial status, she argues, had "in-between categories" and could be possessed multiply and change over time.[45] A number of things allowed boys of color in early nineteenth-century Guyana to access a bourgeois identity and a certain kind of Whiteness. Formal schooling, especially in Britain, was critical. "If a young progeny of colored children is brought forth, these are emancipated, and mostly sent by those fathers who can afford it, at the age of three or four years, to be educated in England," wrote one observer. Metropolitan schooling here functions as a kind of acknowledgement and, as it would for the Anglo-Indian families studied by Elizabeth Buettner, a practical bridge between vernacular colonial life and imperial networks and knowledge.[46]

This was the kind of work that a metropolitan education performed for James Douglas. He and his brother Alexander may have accompanied their father on his return to Scotland in 1812. They were enrolled in the Lanark Grammar School, located at a distance from the Douglas family's residences and businesses in Glasgow and Edinburgh. At Lanark the Douglas boys received the practical, middling education that gave so many Scots the cultural capital to parlay into the daily administration of empire and a critical toehold into identities of Whiteness. Lanark Grammar School emphasized French, English, and bookkeeping, and whatever version of this curriculum Douglas received, he would invariably be described as well educated as an adult.[47] The Douglas boys were not the only mixed-race children born of empire who found themselves in this or equivalent Scottish boarding schools. Daniel Livesay points out that the migration of mixed-race children to Britain was designed to "validate and advance" those children, and ought to be studied alongside the return of Scottish men and wealth from the Caribbean.[48]

Douglas' Scottish education made him upwardly mobile within the imperial world, and offered him usable histories through which to understand and present his own location in that world. As an older man, he recalled school as a place where the lessons of masculinity were taught

[45] Ann Twiman, *Public Lives, Private Secrets: Gender, Honor, Sexuality and Illegitimacy in Colonial Spanish America* (Stanford University Press, 1999) 25.

[46] Henry Bolingbroke, *A Voyage to the Demerary, Containing a Statistical Account of the Settlements There, And Those on The Essequebo, The Berbice, and Other Contiguous Rivers of Guyana* (Norwich: Richard Phillips, 1807) 44. Also see Walter E. Roth, ed. and trans., *Richard Schomburgk's Travels in British Guiana, 1840–1844*, Volume I (Georgetown: Daily Chronicle, 1922) 45; Elizabeth Buettner, *Empire Families: Britons and Late Imperial India* (Oxford University Press, 2004).

[47] Charlotte S. M Girard, "Sir James Douglas' School Days," *BC Studies*, 35 (Autumn 1977) 57. Also see A. D. Robertson and Thomas Harvey, *Lanark Grammar School (1183–1983): The First 800 Years* (Lanark: Strathclyde Regional Council, 1983).

[48] Daniel Livesay, "Extended Families: Mixed-Race Children and Scottish Experience, 1770–1820," *International Journal of Scottish Literature*, 4 (Summer 2008) 2–3.

sternly and collectively. "You should have gone at once to a public school, and had to fight your own way with all sorts of boys," he lectured his own son, "and to get on by dint of whip and spur as I did when a boy." Douglas apparently thought this good training, and at one point urged his friends and his father to support the school when its reputation diminished.[49] His years at Lanark were important to his national and imperial identity. As part of the substantial trip that Douglas took to Britain on his retirement, he visited Lanark, noting that the houses were the same, but "The old people are all gone, and even their names are no more known in their once familiar haunts – and their very memory has perished – as it is with them so will it be with us."[50]

Both the tangible and more amorphous opportunities that colonial boys gained through their years of metropolitan schooling had some steep costs. Most obvious was early separation from their mothers, maternal kin, and, often enough, the place of their birth and early childhood. It is unlikely that Douglas ever saw his mother or Demerara again after he left for Scotland at around eight years old. The movement of bourgeois sons of color from the colony to the metropole ruptured the ties between young men and the families, communities, and places of early childhood. It was surely designed to do so, to produce a man who identified with the metropole and his paternal kin rather than local colonial space, his mother, and her people. Henry Dalton, a Georgetown physician, thought that separation from their parents early in life consigned men of color to a complicated and essentially toxic relationship with their families, the societies of their birth, and ultimately themselves:

Estranged from his parents' fostering care at an early age, he becomes forgetful or heedless of their love. The master of an ideal universe, he lives and dwells upon the fantastical creations of his brain rather than encounter the stern realities of existence. His heart is cold toward his kindred, for he has been long separated from them; his patriotism is languid, because his native land equals not in splendor and luxury the nations he has visited; generous to a fault, he is unjust to himself; eager in temperament, he is incapable of exertion; impetuous in his impulses, he is deficient in perseverance; quick of intelligence, he is slow in judgment and reasoning; not wanting physical capability, he is lazy in mental and bodily applications; humble in pretension, he is proud in spirit.

Here Dalton acknowledges the multiple registers of family, home, colony, metropole, and empire engaged when colonial children were sent to school in the United Kingdom. Dalton's is a post-emancipation text that

---

[49] James Douglas to James William Douglas, January 26, 1868; James Douglas to Mr. McGlasham, November 9, 1867; both in Private Letter Book.

[50] James Douglas, "Journal of Sir James Douglas' Trip to Europe, May 14, 1864 to May 16, 1865," BCA, B/20/1864, Transcript, 56.

stresses the enduring racial hierarchies that greeted elite people of color in Guyana. They returned home with "excellent education and polished manners," only to find their expectations disappointed by the endurance of racial thinking and hierarchy. "They found to their dismay that, in spite of high connexions, and the refinements they had acquired; they were still excluded from what was considered the 'first society,' and thus doomed to solitary seclusion, or to descent to inferior intercourse."[51]

Dalton's commentary is prescient for both the range of issues it engages and how it slides into easy racial discourses that cast Creole and Metis people as flawed, pathological, and almost tragic. These ideas are laced through nineteenth-century commentary, and they can easily over-determine historical analyses. The particularities of James Douglas' early family lay not in their blood or their bodies, but in the histories that provided the backdrop and structure for their lives. Between the re-establishment of British rule in 1803 and the abolition of slavery in 1834, the particular configuration of imperialism in Guyana produced a growing, complicated and sometimes awkward community of people who fell between the poles of enslaved Blacks and free Whites. The freedom of people like Rebecca Ritchie and Martha Ann Telfer was made real by their status as slave-owners. That Telfer, Ritchie, and women like them did not participate in British practices of marriage located them outside metropolitan discourses of female respectability and authority, but it also mitigated the incapacities that wives experienced throughout the nineteenth-century imperial world. In the lively port city of Georgetown these women were economic and legal actors. A global imperial economy drew men like John Douglas from Britain's Celtic fringe and empowered them within the Caribbean, but it did not make them stay. Mobile White men and local elite women each had their own histories and opportunities, but they were not equal or even commensurate ones. When local bourgeois sons like James Douglas were separated from their maternal kin and sent to Scotland to be educated and located within global practices of Whiteness and imperial authority, hierarchical relationships of race, nation, gender, and family were laid bare.

Douglas' life brought the thick histories of pre-emancipation Demerara into conversation with the equally thick but different racial and national politics of northwestern North America. Empire was layered here too but in different ways and to different effects. The resources of fish and fur had brought Europeans, most of them itinerant men, to northern North America for some time. In the seventeenth century, France and

---

[51] Dalton, *The History of British Guiana*, 313, 315.

Britain established formal colonies and, later, settlers and mechanics of settler rule around the St. Lawrence Valley and along the eastern coast. The territories to the north and west were formally enveloped in the politics of colonial rule by the Royal Charter of 1670, which gave the private interests of the Hudson's Bay Company (HBC) the exclusive right "to trade" on the vast territories draining into Hudson Bay. With this maneuver, Britain downloaded the work of colonial governance to a private company, an arrangement that would be maintained long after private charters fell out of fashion as instruments of empire.[52] The HBC refined the parameters of its jurisdiction following the fall of Quebec and the expansion of British North America that followed in 1763. It continued to do so as non-Indigenous American settlement and territorial control expanded along the southern margins of fur-trade country, until in 1821, it was forced to merge with its rival, the North West Company (NWC).

In the early nineteenth century, the interior of northern North America was what historical geographer Cole Harris calls "overwhelmingly native space."[53] As a form of colonization, the fur trade complicates analyses that presume that the colonization of the Americas and the Antipodes was rooted in the appropriation of land and not labor.[54] The fur trade depended profoundly on Indigenous labor and resources and was not much concerned with land per se. The trade also relied on migrant labor. Non-Indigenous people who came to work in the North American fur trade were almost entirely male, and often drawn from the fringes of an imperial and maritime world: from Scotland, the Orkneys, French Canada, and Hawaii. The connections that bound Scots merchant capitalism to the Caribbean also bound it to the North American fur trade. As in Guyana, their labor was often unfree, but the labor contracts that bound workers to companies for years at a time were of a different order than the slavery practiced in the Caribbean or elsewhere in North America.[55]

This was the colonial world that James Douglas entered as a teenager. He recalled that he "left England" in May 1819.[56] Following his brother

[52] See Edward Cavanagh, "A Company with Sovereignty and Subjects of its Own: The Case of the Hudson's Bay Company, 1670–1783," *Canadian Journal of Law and Society*, 26:1 (2011) 25–50.

[53] Cole Harris, *The Reluctant Land: Society, Space, and Environment in Canada before Confederation* (Vancouver: UBC Press, 2008) 389.

[54] See, for this argument, Patrick Wolfe, "Land, Labor, and Difference," *American Historical Review*, 106:3 (June 2011) 865–906.

[55] See Edith I. Burley, *Servants of the Honourable Company: Work, Discipline, and Conflict in the Hudson's Bay Company, 1770–1879* (Oxford University Press, 1997).

[56] James Douglas, "Private Account," BCA, Add MSS, B/90/1.

Alexander, he entered the NWC service as a clerk in that year, swearing before a Montreal notary to serve the "said Company in the Upper or North West Countries in the capacity of apprentice clerk for and during the term of six years." For this Douglas would receive £100 and "Board & Lodging Equipments & co. the same as the other Apprentice Clerks in the said trade."[57] Clerks occupied what historian Carolyn Podruchny sees as a middling position between the laboring voyageurs and the bourgeoisie. Douglas was both servant and master from the outset.[58] In the same year that he signed articles, he contracted another man, an experienced voyageur named Louis Laplante, to serve as *gouvernail* or "rudder" in the canoe traveling north and west to Fort William.[59] Work in the fur trade provided a means of class and imperial transformation for men from the cultural and geographic fringes of the imperial world or the edges of the metropole's middle class.

The fur trade was, as historian Norma Hall has shown, one node in a global labor market. Douglas' first post of Fort William was a critical entrepôt for the early nineteenth-century fur trade that tied northwestern North America to a wider maritime world. Ross Cox passed through in 1816, and he called it "the great emporium for the interior" and described it as "a metropolitan post." Cox was struck by its social rituals and by its cosmopolitanism. He found men from "England, Ireland, Scotland, France, Germany, Italy, Denmark, Sweden, Holland, Switzerland, United States of America, the Gold Coast of Africa, the Sandwich Islands, Bengal, Canada, with various tribes of Indians, and a mixed progeny of Creoles, or half-breeds."[60]

Douglas would not likely have stood out in this chunk of the nineteenth-century imperial world. His indenture contract described him as "of Scotland," but HBC employment records registered him as "West

57 North West Company Indenture, James Douglas, July 6, 1819, 2344, Fort William Historical Park. Thanks to Joe Winterbourne for help locating this. See also details for the contracts for James Douglass and Alexander Douglass in the voyageurs database at http://voyageurs.shsb.mb.ca/, accessed June 11, 2014.

58 "North West Company – Ledger," 1811–1821, F 4/32, Hudson's Bay Company Archive (hereafter HBCA), Mflm 55M8, 982 and 1031; A. Harvey Fleming, ed., *Minutes of Council Northern Department of Rupert Land, 1821–31* (Toronto: Champlain Society for the Hudson's Bay Record Society, 1940) 436–437; Carolyn Podruchny, *Making the Voyageur World: Travelers and Traders in the North American Fur Trade* (University of Toronto Press, 2006) Chapter 5.

59 North West Company Indenture Contract, Louis Laplante, 1819, HBCA, F 5/3, Mflm 5 M 13.

60 Norma J. Hall, "Northern Arc: The Significance of the Shipping Seafarers of Hudson Bay, 1508–1920," Ph.D. thesis, Memorial University of Newfoundland, 2009, Chapter 12; Ross Cox, *The Columbia River, Or scenes and adventures during a residence of six years on the western side of the Rocky Mountain*, ed. I. Stewart and Jane R. Stewart (Norman, OK: University of Oklahoma Press, 1957 [1831]) 330, 333.

Indian."[61] The *pays d'en haut* could provide a ready place for Black men seeking to escape the slave societies of the United States. The fur-trade territories of British North America also provided a practical place for members of the Caribbean middling class – both free Black and White – to relocate. Massive slave resistance, the abolitionist movement, and the British Empire's abolition first of the slave trade in 1807 and then of slavery in 1834 realigned Caribbean economies and societies. In an increasingly bifurcated world constituted by slaves and ex-slaves and a small White minority, those free Black and working White people who had run estates, kept books, and managed enterprises looked elsewhere, some of them to the growing fur-trade economies of this other part of the British Empire. As Ryan Eyford has shown, careful biographical study can help us see how the histories of these different iterations of nineteenth-century empire – slavery and abolition in the Caribbean and dispossession and settlement in the North American west – were more closely connected than historians generally assume.[62]

In 1821 Douglas was transferred west to Île-à-la-Crosse. This post was located in a region that by the mid-nineteenth century was the seat of the longstanding Metis family formation studied by historian Brenda Macdougall.[63] The fur trade was always a military as well as economic operation, and it was especially so during the years preceding and following the merger of the NWC and HBC in 1821. These were years of protracted violent conflict, and as a young man in the trade, Douglas in part proved his mettle with feats of strength, contests of will, and demonstrations of loyalty. During the long winter of 1820/1 he was listed among a group of NWC loyalists to be carefully monitored by the HBC. Along with some other NWC clerks, he was reprimanded for having a "military and hostile appearance," one that their new employers did not appreciate.[64] The duel that the then eighteen-year-old Douglas fought with HBC man Patrick Cunningham over "bodily strength" was presumably about this ongoing conflict as well as manly competition. Douglas and Cunningham's contest produced "no blood," and it was one of three duels that broke out during one month in a long winter marked by "a great deal of squabbling."[65]

[61] Entry for James Douglas, "Servants Characters & Staff Records," HBCA, A 34/1, 82.

[62] See Kenneth W. Porter, "Negroes and the Fur Trade," *Minnesota History*, 15:4 (December 1934) 421–433; Eyford, "John Taylor."

[63] Brenda Macdougall, *One of the Family: Metis Culture in Nineteenth-Century Saskatchewan* (Vancouver: UBC Press, 2010).

[64] John Clarke to George Simpson, January 1, 1821, Île-à-la-Crosse Correspondence, HBCA, B.89/b11; Resolution, April 12, 1821, Île-à-la-Crosse Correspondence, HBCA, B 89/b/2, Mflm 1M183.

[65] John Clarke to William Williams, 23 December 1821, HBCA, Île-à-la-Crosse Correspondence, B 89/b11; J. G. McTavish, "Events in the Interior during the Winter of

After the long and violent winter of the merger, Douglas committed himself to a reconceived and reorganized HBC. In 1822 Île-à-la-Crosse's chief factor, George Keith, described him as "a very sensible steady young man" and asked that he be made trader. Two years later Douglas was described as a "Fine steady active fellow good clerk & Trader, well adapted for a new country."[66] He continued to be acknowledged as an ambitious and capable young man committed to the fur trade. In 1825, he moved to the HBC's Caledonia District on the other side of the Rocky Mountains, taking up a position as clerk at Fort St. James. It was here that he came under the mentorship of chief factor William Connolly, who, like Keith, was an old NWC bourgeois with a large Indigenous family. Connolly had himself entered the fur-trade service as a clerk and was multilingual and polyglot. Born in French Canada in 1786, he described himself "a bit of an Irishman, and besides that a most devout Catholic" who was suspicious of the authority of Britain's established church.[67] In his private 1832 journal written in code, HBC governor George Simpson described Connolly as having a violent temper, and being "always tenacious of his rights privileges and dignity, disposed to magnify his own exploits and to over rate his Services."[68]

Connolly and Miyo Nipay's children were born in the complicated social location produced by early nineteenth-century fur-trade society's iteration of colonialism and its uneven conversation with global knowledges about race, identity, and privilege. This was a specific history produced by a specific society, but for all this, the history of bourgeois Metis people in northern North American fur-trade society shared significant ground with elite Creole people in the eastern Caribbean. It was certainly possible to be both bourgeois and Indigenous in the early nineteenth-century fur trade. Available languages tended to stress lived cultural experience and identity rather than fixed bodily or other characters. As historian Denise Fuchs has documented, men of Indigenous and

---

1820–21," in Gordon Charles Davidson, *The North West Company* (New York: Russell and Russell, 1918) 301–302. Douglas' brother-in-law Henry Connolly thought that the duel had been fought over sugar. See Henry Connolly, "Reminiscences of One of the Last Descendants of a Bourgeois of the North West Company," unpublished manuscript, n.d., 3; pagination added. Thanks to Jennifer S. H. Brown and Anne Lindsay for making this available to me.

66 Île-à-la-Crosse Post Journal, September 26, 1822, HBCA, B 89/a/5, Mflm 1M64; Servants Characters & Staff Records, HBCA, A 34/1, 82.

67 William Connolly to James Hargrave, February 19 1830, in G. P. De T. Glazebrook, ed., *The Hargrave Correspondence, 1821–1843* (Toronto: The Champlain Society, 1938) 2. Also see Cox, *The Columbia River*, 328.

68 George Simpson, "The 'Character Book' of George Simpson, 1932," in Glyndwr Williams, ed., *Hudson's Bay Miscellany, 1670–1870* (Winnipeg: Hudson's Bay Company Record Society, 1975) 182.

Figure 3.3 Robert Hood, "Likeness of Bois Brulé or the children of Europeans by Indian Women, February, 1820, Cumberland House, Hudson's Bay."

European origin are largely indistinguishable from Europeans in the fur-trade archive of the late eighteenth and early nineteenth century.[69] Robert Hood was a member of John Franklin's party who spent the long winter of 1819/20 at Cumberland House, where Connolly was chief factor. His painting "Likeness of Bois Brulé" is a remarkable image of three children whose fashionable European clothing marks them clearly as bourgeois and whose Cree names also mark them as clearly Indigenous. (See Figure 3.3.) As an adult, Amelia Connolly Douglas recalled being painted by one of Franklin's men, and it is certainly likely that Quatoo,

[69] Denise Fuchs, "Native Sons of Rupert's Land, 1760 to the 1860s," Ph.D. dissertation, University of Manitoba, 2000, 48–50; Denise Fuchs, "Embattled Notions: Constructions of Rupert's Land's Native Sons, 1760 to 1860," *Manitoba History*, 44 (Autumn/Winter 2002/3) 10–17.

Atatoo, and Sasasis were the same children elsewhere known as Louisa, William, and Amelia.[70]

As in Demerara, elite children of mixed origin could gain provisional access to the privileges of Whiteness by securing certain critical social markers. Again the acknowledgement and interest of their fathers was critical, especially for arranging, financing, and coordinating a formal metropolitan education requiring a trip east of the Great Lakes or across the Atlantic. Amelia's brother Henry recollected that their eldest brother, John, was sent to St. Eustache, Lower Canada, where he attended school and boarded with a family that "kept him more like a slave." Henry would instead attend school in Montreal along with other sons of NWC officers and their Indigenous wives.[71]

Gender structured the politics of mobility for elite children of mixed origin in early nineteenth-century fur-trade territories, just as it did in the Caribbean. Whatever formal education Cecilia Douglas received she received in the Demerara, and she was spared both the separation from her family and kin and the authority earned by it. Likewise fur-trade daughters might receive some formal European education to complement their Indigenous training, but in the first decades of the nineteenth century, most did so within the domestic spaces of the fort or at post schools. One of Amelia Connolly's sisters – presumably Marguerite, who later became a nun – was educated by the Congregation de Notre Dame in Montreal.[72] Amelia Connolly "was never at school," recalled a friend.[73] For elite Metis women like her, provisional access to the colonial elite was secured not through metropolitan education but through their ability to marshal less formal but no less significant signs of bourgeois European femininity: clothing, manners, and demeanor.

It is a danger to overstate the upward mobility of Metis people in the fur trade before the 1820s. The eighteenth century was hardly a space of radical racial equality: hierarchies tended to be based on lived experience inflected with ideas of culture rather than on notions of biology or blood, but they were there nonetheless. Simpson was the father of a number of

[70] Robert Hood, *To the Arctic by Canoe, 1819–1821: The Journal and Paintings of Robert Hood, Midshipman with Franklin*, ed. Stuart C. Houston (Montreal: McGill-Queen's University Press, 1994) 170. Amelia's memory is that the painter was Back, another of Franklin's men. See N. de Bertrand Lugrin, *The Pioneer Women of Vancouver Island, 1843–1866* (Victoria: The Women's Canadian Club, 1928) 10–11.

[71] Connolly, "Reminiscences," 25. More generally, see Jennifer S. H. Brown, *Strangers in Blood: Fur Trade Company Families in Indian Country* (Vancouver: UBC Press, 1980) Chapter 7; Fuchs, "Native Sons," Chapter 3.

[72] Connolly, "Reminiscences," 25.

[73] Sarah Julia [Ogden] McKinlay to Mrs. Dye, January 23, 1892, Oregon Historical Society (hereafter OHS), 1089, 2/8.

Metis children but he had little faith in them. When pressured to support formal education for Indigenous children in 1820, he used idioms of hierarchy and a loose language of race to make his point:

I have always remarked that an enlightened Indian is good for nothing; there are several of them about the Bay side and totally useless, even the half Breeds of the Country who have been educated in Canada are blackguards of the very worst description, they not only pick up the vice of the Whites upon which they improve but retain those of the Indian in their utmost extent.[74]

The ability of elite people of mixed origins to access provisional resources of imperial Whiteness was predicated on a presumed cleavage between the fur-trade elite and those called "Indians." This echoed if not replicated the situation in Demerara, where free people of color had complicated relationships to enslaved people of African descent, whom they might both own and be intimate kin to and proximate friends with. The fur trade produced Metis throughout northern North America. These communities have been the objects of sustained study and debate, with historians addressing the question of what has been dubbed "Metis ethnogenesis," asking why, and under what conditions, a durable political identity of *Metis* emerged in this one particular part of North America and only occasionally and inconsistently elsewhere in the continent.[75] However they might have defined Metis, and whether they would have located themselves within or outside its bounds, the Douglas-Connolly family and their peers made clear that it was distinct from those who lived outside the fort walls and were called, in global languages of empire, "Indians." Henry Connolly could recall his young sister Julia arming herself and announcing that she was "'Going to kill some of the Indians.'" These distinctions were not simply about descent and certainly not in any meaningful sense racial, and observers routinely noted that many "half-breeds" lived among Indians.[76] The division between "Indians" and "half-breeds" was fundamentally economic and to a lesser extent cultural, spatial, and amenable to a certain amount of fashioning by individuals, families, and communities with racial and national inflections.

[74] George Simpson to A. Colville, May 20, 1820, in Frederick Merk, ed., *Fur Trade and Empire* (Cambridge, MA: Harvard University Press, 1968) 181.
[75] See, for instance, Jennifer S. H. Brown and Jacqueline Peterson, eds., *The New People: Being and Becoming Métis in North America* (Winnipeg: University of Manitoba, 1985); Heather Devine, *The People Who Own Themselves: Aboriginal Ethnogenesis in One Canadian Family* (University of Calgary Press, 2004).
[76] Connolly, "Reminiscences," 14; John Franklin, *Narrative of a Journey to the Shores of the Polar Sea, in the Years 1819, 20, 21 and 22* (Edmonton: M. G. Hurtig, 1969 [1824]), 85.

Connolly concluded his career as an active fur trader as chief factor of Fort St. James, the headquarters of the HBC's New Caledonia District west of the Rocky Mountains. It was there that James Douglas became Connolly's favored clerk and his son-in-law. Connolly advocated for Douglas' upward mobility. After Douglas signed articles for another three years' service in 1825, Connolly made the case for his skill and potential. "Mr. Douglas's salary I conceive as inadequate to his merits," Connolly explained.

He has found six years of apprenticeship under able Masters during which period he acquired a good knowledge of the trade, of the moral character of Indians, & of the methods observed in conducting the Business, which added to a good Education, sound reason, and a frame of body and of mind able to carry him through any difficulty, qualify him in a high degree for the services of which he is engaged.[77]

Women attached to men at posts like Fort St. James were responsible for a range of productive labors that made clear how far this colonial economy was removed from nascent ideas of respectable bourgeois femininity. Writing to a trader, Simpson explained some of the labors conventionally expected of, and sometimes demanded from, fur-trade wives, explaining that it was "customary for the Ladies of this country to do all that is required in that way about the Fort" and that it was "not unreasonable to require that she works for her maintenance."[78] The trade expected women to earn their keep and it required their skills and knowledge. Another observer explained that without Indigenous women, "the men would be in a sad condition, for they are the only tailors and washerwomen in the country, and make all the mittens, moccasins, fur caps, deer-skin coats, &c, &c, worn in the land."[79]

The embodied and affective labor of bearing, rearing, and burying children dominated the adult lives of both Miyo Nipay and Connolly Douglas. Both women married in their middle teens, and went on to have the large families' characteristic of the fur-trade elite. Brown studied ninety-six families of officers between 1821 and 1850, and found that they had completed families of an average of 7.3 children. Miyo Nipay

[77] Fort St. James Post Journal, April 18, 1826, HBCA, Mflm 1M129. On the HBC in this region, see Richard Mackie, *Trading beyond the Mountains: The British Fur-Trade on the Pacific* (Vancouver: UBC Press, 1997).

[78] George Simpson to Joseph Greill, November 30, 1820, in George Simpson, *Journal of Occurrences in the Athabasca Department, 1820 and 1821, and Report*, ed. E. E. Rich (Toronto: The Champlain Society, 1938).

[79] Robert Michael Ballantyne, *Hudson Bay: Everyday Life in the Wilds of North America, 4th edition* (London: Thomas Nelson and Sons, 1886) 53.

and William Connolly raised six children to adulthood, but likely gave birth to around twelve.[80] Amelia Connolly Douglas bore her first child in 1829 when she was about seventeen and her thirteenth in 1854, when she was about forty-two. Large family sizes were sustained in spite of high levels of infant mortality. For Connolly Douglas and Douglas, infant mortality was especially high in the 1830s during their years at Fort Vancouver. Historian Gray Whaley notes that these years saw repeated and devastating epidemic disease in Oregon Territory, disease that traders and their families were never wholly isolated from.[81] Of the seven babies Connolly Douglas had between 1829 and 1839, only Jane and Cecilia survived their first few years. The list of babies who did not see their fourth year was long: Amelia, born in 1829, Alexander, born in 1831, Maria, born in 1834, Ellen, born in 1836, and, in 1838, a boy who did not live long enough to be named.[82]

The extent and regularity of the family's losses were noted by those around them. Sarah Julia Ogden McKinlay recalled meeting Amelia in June of 1833, remembering her as "the mother [of] four children but only one alive."[83] Colleagues registered Douglas as a too-often grieving parent. When Rebecca, born in March 1849, died later that year, an HBC official reported that "Poor Douglas received accounts of the death of his youngest daughter a baby about 10 months old."[84] Douglas himself described Rebecca's passing as a "misfortune" and a "death so easy and so placid, that it had no terrors for the living."[85] Parental loss was a kind of touchstone and an enduring point of connection. Douglas wrote in sympathy to a bereaved friend, explaining that "I know the bitterness of the breach death makes in a family."[86]

Mothering shaped women's days and gave meaning to their years. It was also a critical terrain of elite women's social authority within

---

[80] Brown, *Strangers in Blood*, Table 3, 154; Anne Lindsay, "Children," unpublished research on Connolly family.

[81] Gray H. Whaley, *Oregon and the Collapse of Illahee: US Empire and the Transformation of an Indigenous World, 1792–1859* (Chapel Hill: University of North Carolina Press, 2010) 91–95.

[82] From James Douglas, "Private Account," BCA, Add MSS B/90/1 and "Douglas Family Bible," in Sir James Douglas, "Journals, Notebooks and Clipping books, etc., 1835–1873," BCA, MS 0678, Mflm A00792 (hereafter Douglas, Private Account).

[83] Sarah J. McKinlay to Eve Emery Dye, January 28, 1892, OHS, 1089, 2/8.

[84] Eden Colville to George Simpson, December 7, 1849, in E. E. Rich, ed., *London Correspondence Inward from Eden Colville, 1849–1852* (London: Hudson's Bay Company Record Society, 1956) 190.

[85] James Douglas to James Hargrave, March 1, 1849, Hargrave Papers.

[86] James Douglas to James Hargrave, February 20, 1844, Library and Archives Canada, Hargrave Collection, MG 19 A21 (hereafter Hargrave Papers).

fur-trade forts. Senior women attached to officers demonstrated their status by caring for children other than their own. Scholar Julia Pollard notes that at Fort Vancouver officers' families, including the Douglases, each had at least a few wards. The McLoughlins had many more, and their son David would recall the "Many orphan Boys and Girls" who shared their home as a sign of his father's largess.[87] It was also an indication of his wife's reputation and authority. This kind of female authority paid little if any dividends on the other side of the Atlantic, and few enough to the east of the Rocky Mountains. But within the colonial world wrought by the fur trade, the work done and status enjoyed by women like Connolly Douglas was clear.

These were some of the complicated histories of race, labor, and colonial rule that surrounded Douglas' departure from the New Caledonia District in 1828. The fur trade could not function without good or at least working relationships with Indigenous peoples, relationships maintained through extensive kin ties, careful diplomacy, and, as Harris has argued, the constant threat and regular presence of staggering violence.[88] Connolly left the business of Fort St. James under Douglas' control for the summer that year, and in August Douglas had what he would much later describe as a "tumult with Indians."[89] The precise events and the actions of Douglas, his new wife, and Carrier leader Kwah are all unclear, and predictably subject to interpretation, contest, and the cleavage between European and Indigenous modes of constructing historical knowledges about memorable and difficult subjects. What is clear is that Douglas became involved in an intractable and violent conflict with Kwah and his supporters, one that Douglas' wife played a critical role in negotiating.[90]

---

[87] Juliet Pollard, "The Making of the Metis in the Pacific Northwest Fur Trade Children: Race, Class, and Gender," Ph.D. dissertation, University of British Columbia, 1990, 263; David McLoughlin to Eva Emery Dye, March 20, 1892, OHS, MS 1089, 2/9.

[88] Cole Harris, "Strategies of Power in the Cordilleran Fur Trade," in *The Resettlement of British Columbia: Essays on Colonialism and Geographical Change* (Vancouver: UBC Press, 1996).

[89] "Notes," Douglas, Private Account.

[90] See Frieda E. Klippenstein, "The Challenge of James Douglas and Carrier Chief Kwah," in Jennifer S. H. Brown and Elizabeth Vibert, eds., *Reading beyond Words: Contexts for Native History* (Peterborough, Ontario: Broadview Press, 1996) 163–192. Some useful accounts are Henry Connolly, "Reminiscences," 13; Lizette Hall, *The Carrier, My People* (Cloverdale, BC: Friesens Printers, 1992), 62–63; A. G. Morice, *The History of the Northern Interior of British Columbia, Formerly New Caledonia, 1660–1880*, 2nd edition (Toronto: William Briggs, 1904) Chapter 9; John Tod, "History of New Caledonia and the Northwest-Coast," BL, Bancroft Collection, P-C 27.

When William Connolly returned to the post, he found that the cordial relationship with local Indigenous people that the fur trade necessarily depended on had fallen apart. Connolly asked that Douglas be moved south to the Columbia District for his own safety. "Douglas's life is much exposed among these Carriers," Connolly explained, adding that "he would readily face a hundred of them, but he does not much like the idea of being assassinated."[91] Here Connolly evokes competing discourses of masculinity, situating Douglas as both the imperial man vulnerable to the physical threats of savagery and the brave man unafraid of a fair fight. That Douglas' wife and Connolly's daughter is excluded from generalizations about "Indians" is taken for granted, and it is only in Indigenous accounts and historical reinterpretations that Connolly Douglas' Indigenous knowledge and language is assigned much interpretative weight.[92]

The quotidian practices of colonialism created a particular, charged, and shifting space for local elites, just as it did in Demerara. Examining practices of race and governance in North American fur-trade territory and the eastern Caribbean makes clear how local articulations of empire bent history to their needs. In Demerara, the layered history of Dutch and British colonialism, the shape of the Atlantic maritime economy, and the gendered politics of slavery created the conditions for a distinct history of free people of color. In the fur trade, colonialism was also layered, but here with a backstory of French imperialism, the power and administrative authority of private business, and the trade's dependence on Indigenous economies, trade practices, and societies.

Tracking the histories of the Douglas-Connolly family also makes clear the connections between this distinctly northern North American story of Metis people and the fur trade and a wider imperial one. For all their differences, there were enduring connections between the history of elite Creole people in Demerara and bourgeois Metis people in the fur trade, and the family formed by Amelia Connolly Douglas and James Douglas brought these histories into direct conversation. The extent to which elite people of mixed descent and identity were identified as distinct communities with particular histories and interests came into sharpest relief when they were distinguished – and, critically, when they distinguished

---

[91] William Connolly to George Simpson, Stuarts Lake, February 27, 1829, in E. E. Rich, ed., *Simpson's 1828 Journey to the Columbia* (London: Hudson's Bay Record Society, 1947) 243.

[92] See Klippenstein, "The Challenge of James Douglas."

themselves – from colonized and enslaved people. When elite local people claimed to be distinct from Indians or slaves, they laid claim to a higher place in what was increasingly a rigidly hierarchal racial order. They mined the racial languages of the early nineteenth-century world to articulate their own ambivalent location within the connecting sinews and thick local histories of empire and rule.

4 Changing intimacies, changing empire

James Douglas and Amelia Connolly Douglas were both born to families forged in local colonial societies in the first decades of the nineteenth century. The Indigenous marriage they made in the late 1820s would be renegotiated in the following decade in response to changing circumstances of empire and intimacy. Both the marriage and its renegotiation reflected wider patterns in nineteenth-century North America. Historians have long contended that relationships between Indigenous women and newcomer men were reframed over the course of the nineteenth century. In northern North America, the process has been mapped with some precision. Sylvia Van Kirk's germinal 1980 study *"Many Tender Ties": Women and Fur-Trade Society, 1670–1870* argued that local marriages that were acknowledged and even valued began a marked decline in the middle decades of the nineteenth century, and more recent studies have largely confirmed the broad strokes of this process.[1]

Historians' conventional emphasis on decline rightly registers the seismic changes wrought by the arrival and consolidation of settler colonialism in northern North America, and the significance of intimacy and marriage to this history. But it fails to capture the complicated history of imperial intimacies across both space and time. As Jennifer S. H. Brown has recently argued, fur-trade marriages were always variable and multiple. Imperial intimacies were constituted, valued, and acknowledged in a range of ways before the middle years of the nineteenth century, and would continue to be so afterwards.

---

[1] Sylvia Van Kirk, *"Many Tender Ties": Women and Fur-Trade Society, 1670–1870* (Winnipeg: Watson and Dwyer, 1980); Jay Nelson, "'A Strange Revolution in the Manners of the Country': Aboriginal–Settler Intermarriage in Nineteenth-Century British Columbia," in John McLaren, Robert Menzies, and Dorothy E. Chunn, eds., *Regulating Lives: Historical Essays on the State, Society, the Individual and the Law* (Vancouver: UBC Press, 2002) 23–62; Sarah Carter, *Capturing Women: The Manipulation of Cultural Imagery in the Prairie West* (Montreal: McGill-Queen's University Press, 1996); Sarah Carter, *The Importance of Being Monogamous: Marriage and the Politics of Nation-Building in Western Canada to 1915* (Edmonton: Athabasca University Press, 2008).

Complicated and in some respects seemingly contradictory histories of intimacy could coexist and, perhaps, be contained within the sharply racialized terrain that came alongside northwestern North America's awkward and episodic transition to a settler society anchored in practices of sharp racial division and hierarchy. This confirms what Durba Ghosh has argued for India, namely that while the status and legitimacy accorded to imperial intimacies did decline – markedly, and for the individuals and communities involved, consequentially – over the course of the nineteenth century, they did not do so in a straightforward manner.[2]

This chapter sharpens its geographical, topical, and chronological focus and examines what the Douglas-Connolly family and their peers tell us about the complicated and contested politics of marriage in northwest North America during the middle decades of the nineteenth century. The chapter begins with two symbols of changing practices of empire in fur-trade territory in the 1820s and '30s: White wives and missionaries. It then turns to the less startling but arguably more enduring topic of elite local responses to these shifts, examining the recalibration of imperial intimacies and a legal case that offered a decisive response to shifting histories of nineteenth-century imperial intimacy. In following the Douglas-Connolly family and those around them in the middle years of the nineteenth century, this chapter maps both the challenges to and the persistence of imperial intimacies in this one colonial context. Even if on diminished terms and in particular and narrowing spaces, these marriages and families persisted, and the ways they did so prompt us to revisit expected chronologies and summaries.

As soon as intimate relationships between trader men and local women were established as an expected part of fur-trade life, they were also argued against, regulated, and doubted. As Chapter 2 showed, fur-trade families were limited by regulations that aimed to contain the numbers of women and children at posts and curtail the growth of independent Metis communities. In the letters of fur traders, and presumably in conversation between them, Indigenous women were devalued by language that excluded them from European discourses of female gentility and refinement. In the laws that episodically regulated northwestern North America and cast a tighter net over the eastern part of the continent, customary wives were generally excluded from the limited but real enough material

---

[2] Jennifer S. H. Brown, "Partial Truths: A Closer Look at Fur-Trade Marriage," in Ted Binnema, Gerhard Ens, and R. C. McLeod, eds., *From Rupert's Land to Canada: Essays in Honour of John E. Foster* (Edmonton: University of Alberta Press, 2002) 59–80; Durba Ghosh, *Sex and the Family in Colonial India: The Making of Empire* (Cambridge University Press, 2006).

and legal resources guaranteed to women acknowledged as wives. There was no golden age: fur-trade marriages were never entirely embraced by mainstream colonial discourse or those who wrote laws and enforced rules shaped by it.

But the status of imperial intimacies in northern North America did change over the course of the long nineteenth century. The 1820s and '30s in particular witnessed a linked set of economic, social, and intellectual circumstances both global and local in scope that cumulatively recalibrated the kind of imperial intimacies that had been the bedrock of colonial societies in both the Caribbean and northwestern North America. As Van Kirk noted three decades ago, these changes were represented most clearly by the bodies of missionaries and White women in fur-trade space. White women had been essentially absent from the western fur trade in the eighteenth century and the first decades of the nineteenth. Like whaling, fishing, and other forms of resource colonialism, the fur trade was predicated on the labor of Indigenous peoples and migrant men severed either temporarily or permanently from metropolitan networks of marriage, family, and kinship. As these forms of colonialism and the intimate practices they fostered came under sharper and more probing scrutiny, the HBC started to see White women as having a place in a reimagined fur trade.[3] By 1831, a fur trader described marriages with White women as "now very fashionable."[4]

George Simpson was appointed governor of the HBC in 1820, and after its merger the following year he began a wide-ranging programme of rationalization and reform. His changes to both policy and practice went alongside shifting patterns of intimacy. Here, and elsewhere, Simpson embodied many of the contradictions and complexities that characterized fur-trade imperialism. Born as an illegitimate child to a Scottish family with longstanding imperial ties, including to the Caribbean, he cut his teeth in his uncle's sugar-trading business.[5] In the fur trade, he acknowledged the fiscal and strategic utility of imperial intimacies and established local partnerships and families of his own. "Sir George Simpson had plenty of women everywhere in the interior," explained one old fur-trade servant, "whom he lived with when he went to the different places where they lived." Simpson's Indigenous sons circulated widely throughout the

---

[3] Van Kirk, *"Many Tender Ties,"* 173, 182.

[4] Archibald McDonald to Edward Ermatinger, February 20, 1831, in Jean M. Cole, *This Blessed Wilderness: Archibald McDonald's Letters from the Columbia, 1822–44* (Vancouver: UBC Press, 2001) 31.

[5] John S. Galbraith, "Simpson, Sir George," in *Dictionary of Canadian Biography*, Volume VIII, University of Toronto/Université Laval, 2003, www.biographi.ca, accessed November 9, 2010.

fur trade.[6] In 1830, this middle-aged man engaged in a different traffic in women and married his nineteen-year-old English cousin, Frances Ramsay, bringing her to York Factory. The arrival of Ramsay Simpson and another White wife in Rupert's Land was freighted with heavy and predictable meaning. The two women were carried by voyageurs over the portages,[7] replicating a curious and potent scene that was repeated the empire over when White women appeared in imperial space.

With his remarriage, Simpson became a poster-child for a self-interested, painfully racist, and calculating imperial masculinity. As governor, his example carried special symbolic weight. But his was one among a string of prominent remarriages. Amelia Connolly Douglas' father, William Connolly, had been unsatisfied with life in the fur trade for some time. In 1829 he explained: "After a residence of Twenty eight Years in the Indian Country it is not surprising that I should begin to be tired of it and in consequence to wish myself away, which I intend doing as soon as I have realized a bare competency."[8] In 1836 he married his cousin, Julia Woolrich, and the couple relocated to the outskirts of Montreal and raised two children. Connolly thus reorganized his life along the lines of the Canadian settler bourgeoisie, or as close as a man who had lived more than thirty years in fur-trade territory and had a large Indigenous family could easily do. The photograph in Figure 4.1 shows Julia Woolrich Connolly and the two children she had with William. Connolly was following the two-stage style of imperial manhood lived by John Douglas and countless others, played out on two geographic stages and with two unequal families. In a private letter, Simpson explained that Connolly's affection and sentiment had unraveled in the face of the linked phenomena of "civilization" and White women.

You would have heard of Connolly's Marriage – he was one of those who considered it a most unnatural proceeding 'to desert the mother of his children' and marry another; this is all very fine, very Sentimental and very kind-hearted

---

[6] Joseph Larocque, quoted in Justice Samuel Monk, "Connolly vs. Woolrich and Johnson et al.," *Lower Canada Jurist: Collection de Decisions du Bas Canada*, Volume XI (Montreal: John Lovell, 1867) 238 (hereafter Connolly vs. Woolrich). Also see Margaret Arnett MacLeod, eds., *The Letters of Letitia Hargrave* (Toronto: The Champlain Society, 1947) 205, fn 1.

[7] See Frances Ramsay Simpson, "Diary, British North America, 1830," in Kathryn Carter, ed., *The Small Details of Life: 20 Diaries by Women in Canada, 1830–1996* (University of Toronto Press, 2002); Sylvia Van Kirk, "Simpson, Frances Ramsay," in *Dictionary of Canadian Biography*, Volume VIII, University of Toronto/Université Laval, www.biographi.ca, accessed November 9, 2010.

[8] William Connolly to George Simpson, February 27, 1829, in E. E. Rich, ed., *Simpson's 1828 Journey to the Columbia* (London: Hudson's Bay Record Society, 1947) 244.

Figure 4.1 A portrait, likely copied from a daguerreotype, created
in Montreal of "Mrs. Connolly and her Two Children," likely Julia
Woolrich Connolly and her children, William Allen Connolly and
Louise Magdeleine.

3000 miles from the Civilized world but is lost sight of even by Friend Connolly when a proper opportunity offers.[9]

Managing structurally unequal families produced by serial partnerships remained a demanding and complicated business. In 1831, fur trader turned author Robert Cox explained the mechanics of these newly popular elite remarriages. "When a trader wishes to separate from his Indian wife he generally allows her an annuity, or gets her comfortably married to one of the voyageurs, *who, for a handsome sum, is happy to become the husband of la Dame d'un Bourgeois*." Thus "disembarrassed," the retired trader became a sought-after commodity in Montreal and Quebec society: "His arrival is quickly known, his object buzzed about." It was the White women of French Canada that Cox thought most disappointed by the process, when they realized how much they had "thrown away upon a weather-beaten, rheumatic, dog-eating, moss-chewing barbarian, whose habits were better adapted to the savage society of Indian squaws, than to that of ladies of education."[10]

Cox's account performs a telling sleight of hand by removing Indigenous women as subjects from this story of intimacy and its renegotiation. Their stake in these imperial histories was harder to erase in other colonial archives. In the 1860s, Joseph Laroque, an old, Cree-speaking NWC servant, reported on a conversation he had with Miyo Nipay about Connolly's remarriage. "*She laughed and talked about it, and said that she, Julia Woolrich, had only got her leavings*" and that her husband "'will regret it bye and bye.'" Laroque argued that given the practices of fur-trade country, Miyo Nipay would not have expected her marriage with Connolly to be binding. He also acknowledged her anger and indignation, and admitted that Connolly's second marriage "*was not over pleasing to the Indian woman*" and that "*She did scold a great deal about it, and she felt annoyed, and said he would regret it.*"[11]

But Connolly's two families were not really separate, either spatially or temporally. When he married Woolrich, Connolly renegotiated and rearranged rather than severed his longstanding relationship with Miyo Nipay and the children they shared. He continued to financially support his first wife. At first Miyo Nipay was boarded with relatives in Lower Canada, where she was known as "old Mrs. Connolly."[12] In 1840, she

---

[9] George Simpson to John G. McTavish, December 2, 1832, HBCA, B 135/c/2, Mflm 1M376.

[10] Ross Cox, *The Columbia River, Or scenes and adventures during a residence of six years on the western side of the Rocky Mountains*, ed. Edgar I. Stewart and Jane R. Stewart (Norman, OK: University of Oklahoma Press, 1957 [1831]) 362, emphasis original.

[11] Connolly vs. Woolrich, 237, 238–9, emphasis original.

[12] Connolly vs. Woolrich, 231.

and her youngest daughter, Marguerite, moved to Red River. This was timely: Red River had become an overwhelmingly Metis place, a location of community and respite as the fur-trade country to the south and east was reorganized as settler space. When Marguerite joined the Soeur Gris as a novitiate in 1845, her mother entered the convent with her.[13] After William died, Julia Woolrich would take responsibility for Miyo Nipay's expenses, and Woolrich's will specified that an annual rent be paid in the name of "Suzanne (Sauvagesse)." The will also made provision for the "enfents naturels de mon dit defunt mari," naming them as William, Henri, and Emelia. At least some of Miyo Nipay's children and grand-children, including Amelia Connolly, maintained cordial and perhaps even affectionate relationships with Woolrich.[14] This colonial family, like so many others, had complicated but often functional ways of managing the inequalities that were built deep into it.

Indigenous children had distinct experiences of these uneven and unequal rearrangements. As an old man, Metis schoolmaster Andrew Dominique Pambrum spoke to the realignments prompted by Simpson's remarriage and the arrival of Ramsay Simpson in fur-trade space. For him, Ramsay Simpson's meeting with her husband's Metis children was proof that "sin as well as murder will out." Pambrum explained:

She had not been there long when starting out one day, she met a little boy in tatters, with bare legs and cracked feet and asked him his name. "George Simpson" was his reply. Who is your father, was the next query and prompt answer was *"The Governor."* Convinced she had found a stepson, she took him to the store and dressed him up, then took him to her husband, remarking, "This is a nice smart little boy, and you must send him to school without delay." Subsequently she found others of the same noble name, a boy and two girls but claiming different mothers . . .

Pambrum's narrative puts widely circulating images of White women and colonial societies into play and then repurposes them. His characteriza-tion of Ramsay Simpson as unknowing and naïve is unconvincing given the well-known history of men, intimacy, and the imperial world that the extended Simpson family had long been involved in. Pambrum does not situate the young British woman as the heroic savior of her new husband,

[13] Marie Bonin, "The Grey Nuns and the Red River Settlement," *Manitoba History*, 11 (Spring 1986) 12–14; NA, "Marguerite Connolly: The First Red River Métis Grey Nun," undated MS in Dosier de Sr. Connolly, Srs Grise de Montreal, St. Boniface Museum Collection.

[14] Will of Dame Julia Woolrich, PP 1865–1, HBCA, PP 2109; Connolly vs. Woolrich, 245, 252. Woolrich apparently wrote to Amelia Connolly Douglas. See Marguerite Connolly to Cecilia Douglas Helmcken, May 8, 1858, Helmcken Family Fonds, British Columbia Archives, Add MSS 505, Volume 14, File 2 (hereafter Helmcken Papers, BCA).

colonial peoples, or places. He also opts not to present Ramsay Simpson as tragic, hobbled by the fragility thought inherent to bourgeois White women, by the isolation produced by her own prejudice or by her marriage to a difficult and much older man. But Pambrum disrupted usual narratives by emphasizing Ramsay Simpson's empathy and capability, noting that she "evinced no disturbance, at the discovery of the infidelity of her husband," and ensured that four of Simpson's children received educations.[15]

The sorts of struggles that White women had in fur-trade space complicated the discourses of empire and intimacy that brought them to northern North America. Letitia McTavish Hargrave did well in the fur trade, and the letters she sent to her family in Scotland allow for rich readings of the trade and its complicated social relations. Ramsay Simpson lasted only a few years in Rupert's Land before returning to England in poor physical and emotional health.[16] John Tod married a White woman whose mental health broke down quickly and dramatically in northern North America. Tod explained that "my unhappy wife has continued in a most dreadful state of mental alienation" and that he feared her "laying violent hands on either herself or her child." Unable to find anyone to nurse her at Oxford House, he arranged for his wife and child to be sent to their kin in England, and mourned "the melancholy wreck of all my prospects of domestic happiness." The racial and perhaps class lesson here was not lost on his friends. "[O]ur friend Tod," explained one, "has Married a *half Cracked Brainid [sic] Chamber Maid.*" Tod remarried Sophia Lolo, the daughter of a prominent Secwepemc and HBC man. Together they raised seven children to adulthood, and in his old age Tod would mention "my ill fated match of 1834" with little nostalgia.[17]

By 1840, the popularity of White wives had become a sort of social fact among the fur-trade elite, and so had their seeming inability to thrive in fur-trade space. In 1840, Douglas used language of the natural world to describe this. "There is a strange revolution, in the manners of the country; Indian wives were at one time the vogue, the half breed supplanted these, and now we have the lovely tender exotic torn from its parent bed, to pine and languish in the desert."[18] The idea that White

---

[15] Andrew Dominique Pambrum, *Sixty Years on the Frontier in the Pacific Northwest* (Fairfield, WA: Ye Galleon Press, 1978) 61.

[16] Van Kirk, "Simpson, Frances Ramsay."

[17] John Tod to Edward Ermatinger, July 15, 1837, W. Sinclair to Edward Ermatinger, August 1, 1835, John Tod to Edward Ermatinger, March 18, 1864, all in Ermatinger Papers.

[18] James Douglas to James Hargrave, February 26, 1840, in G. P. De T. Glazebrook, ed., *The Hargrave Correspondence, 1821–1843* (Toronto: The Champlain Society, 1838) 310.

women were "exotics" who would "pine and languish" in unfamiliar territory revived and recirculated older ideas of the inappropriateness of White women in fur-trade space.

However few in numbers White wives actually were, however capable colonial families were of accommodating unequal and multiple wives and children, and however fragmented White wives' experience in fur-trade space might have been, the arrival of White wives was a symbol of changing imperial practice. Informal standards for wifehood and womanhood were recalibrated. Archibald McDonald, another factor, explained how his Indigenous wife, Jane Klyne, was disempowered and chastened by the specter of elite fur traders rejecting their Indigenous wives in favour of White ones. McDonald boasted that "I already feel the beneficial effects of the Govr's & McTavish's marriages." Jane, he explained, "has picked up sense enough to infer from their having changed partners that the old ones were deficient in learning & that her own case may be the same when tis my turn to visit my Scottish cousins."[19] The place Metis women had in certain quarters of the fur-trade bourgeoisie was insecure by the 1830s. When Letitia McTavish and James Hargrave were courting, he explained that she should not worry about a brother in the fur trade – and, by polite implication, himself – "taking a fancy to any of the Brown Faces." He explained this as a general shift, explaining that "the days for such escapades are past: – a different tone of feeling on these matters have gradually come round, – & a young Gent[n] from Britain would as soon think of matching himself with the contemporary of his grandmother as now a [illegible] with a pure Squaw."[20]

The impact of the arrival of the handful of White women in fur-trade space was out of all proportion to their actual numbers for a reason: White women represented a wider set of shifts in thinking about intimacy, marriage, and race within this local colonial space. Protestant missionaries arrived alongside White wives, and they too represented wider shifts and kept them in motion. Empire was increasingly registered as a moral and religious and not simply economic enterprise that demanded the presence and participation of Protestant Christianity, its institutions, and representatives. Roman Catholic missionaries arrived in Red River in 1818 and the Anglican Church Missionary Society two years later. By the middle of the 1820s, Simpson was promising to bring missionaries to fur-trade posts and rightly worried that the missionaries might struggle

---

[19] Archibald McDonald to Edward Ermatinger, February 20, 1831, in Cole, ed., *This Blessed Wilderness*, 92.

[20] James Hargrave to Letitia McTavish, June 24, 1838, in Helen E. Ross, ed., *Letters from Rupert's Land, 1826–1840* (Montreal: McGill-Queen's University Press) 333–334.

Figure 4.2 Gustavas Sohon, "Fort Vancouver, at the Mouth of the Columbia River, Washington Territory, 1853."

with accepted practices of intimacy and family there. He declared that a missionary "ought to be cool and temperate in his habits and of a Mild conciliatory disposition even tempered and not too much disposed to find fault severely with any little laxity of morals he may discover at the Coy's Establishment." By morals Simpson meant marriage and family. He took care to explain that missionaries "ought to understand in the outset that nearly all the Gentlemen & Servants have Families altho' Marriage ceremonies are unknown in the Country and that it would be all in vain to attempt breaking through this uncivilized custom."[21]

The shifting politics of imperial morality, White women, and Christian missionaries came to a particular collision in Fort Vancouver in the middle of the 1830s. (Figure 4.2.) By 1835, Douglas was the chief trader and second-in-command to John McLoughlin. By then American Protestant missionaries were passing through with some regularity, and not infrequently taking issue with established practices of intimacy there. One noted "the common practice" of men "living with their families

[21] George Simpson, "George Simpson's Journal, Entitled Remarks Connected with the Fur Trade in the Course of a Voyage from York Factory to Fort George and Back to York Factory 1824–25," in Frederick Merk, ed., *Fur Trade and Empire* (Cambridge, MA: Harvard University Press, 1968) 108. For context, see Frits Pannekoek, *A Snug Little Flock: The Social Origins of the Riel Resistance, 1869–70* (Winnipeg: Watson and Dwyer, 1990).

without being married." "They do not call the women with whom they live, their wives, but their *women*," he wrote, explaining that the men knew they were "living in constant violation of divine prohibition" but were unwilling "to break off their sins by righteousness."[22]

In 1836, Herbert Beaver arrived in Fort Vancouver, the first chaplain in the HBC's Columbia District and a living symbol of a changing politics of empire in the fur trade. Beaver was another mobile subject whose biography spanned the Caribbean, the Pacific coast of North America, and the metropole. British-born and Oxford-educated, he spent the years between 1825 and 1833 in St. Lucia. In some respects, he was everything that Simpson had feared. One HBC servant recalled that Beaver "was of the fox-hunting type & soon sadly at-outs with the Dr. [McLoughlin] with the Catholics."[23] The symbolic weight of Beaver's role was reinforced by the presence of his wife, Jane, remembered as "probably the first English lady who arrived on the Coast."[24]

Beaver was quickly locked in a layered conflict with the local HBC officials over a range of issues, including the institutional recognition of Roman Catholicism within British imperial space and control over the fort school.[25] The missionary complained that the HBC provided him and his wife with country foods, inadequate servants, and unseemly accommodation including "coarse" furniture and uncarpeted rooms. McLoughlin saw Beaver's demands for the accoutrements of bourgeois domesticity as a threat to the economy and material culture of the fur trade. "I intend doing every thing to Make Mr. Beaver as comfortable as the Circumstances of the Country will Admit," he explained to London, "and I consider people ought to satisfy themselves with such things as the country affords."[26]

Questions of intimacy, family, and domesticity were laced through these struggles and merited their own space on Beaver's long list of

---

[22] Samuel Parker, *Journal of an Exploring Tour beyond the Rocky Mountains, under the Direction of the ABCFM Performed in the Years of 1835, '36, and '37* (Minneapolis: Ross and Haines, 1968 [1937]) 170.

[23] George B. Roberts, "Recollections of George B. Roberts," Bancroft Collection, Bancroft Library, University of California, Berkeley (hereafter BL), P-A 83, Mflm 2, 19.

[24] Alexander Caulfield Anderson, "History of the Northwest Coast," HBCA, E 294/148, Transcript, 48.

[25] See Stephen Woolworth, "'The School is under My Direction: The Politics of Education at Vancouver: 1835–1838," *Oregon Historical Quarterly*, 104:2 (2003) 228–251.

[26] John McLoughlin to Governor and Deputy Governor, November 16, 1836, in E. E. Rich, ed., *The Letters of John McLoughlin from Fort Vancouver to the Governor and Committee, First Series, 1825–38* (London: Hudson's Bay Company Record Society, 1941) 176.

grievances. He began his tenure with the declaration that Fort Vancouver was no worse than one might expect where there had been no "authorized minister of the Gospel; No legal marriage, no regular Baptism, no accustomed rites of Burial; Men, for the most part, not practicing, and women totally ignorant of the duties of religion."[27] As Beaver spent more time at Fort Vancouver, his critique of intimacy sharpened. With almost a decade spent in St. Lucia, he was not so surprised at the presence of relationships between women of color and White men as he was appalled by the status accorded them. It was the customary authority wielded by Connolly Douglas and even more so by McLoughlin's Indigenous wife, Marguerite Waddin McKay McLoughlin, that particularly offended Beaver's reckoning of social order and hierarchies.

Beaver argued that there was only one kind of marriage, and that failing to conform to it should merit a distinct and diminished location in the hierarchical imperial order. If people living in customary marriages had the same rights as those who had been to the church, how could "untutored minds" be "able to discriminate between the two states"? He urged the HBC to adopt a spatialized distinction between women he considered wives and those he considered concubines. This would also save his own wife from the indignity of sharing social space with Indigenous women whose relationships were unsanctioned by European custom. "If men must indulge in such unlawful connections," he explained, "they should, at least, be conducted with such outward decorum, as is usually practiced in all other countries, where there is a mixture of married persons." Beaver urged the HBC to enforce "a marked and rigid distinction between the privileges and treatment of women married to, and those of women living unmarried with men of all classes," asking that local wives be prevented from residing in company buildings, receiving rations, receiving medical attendance, and being given work or passage in company ships. He later asked that men who married according to Christian custom be granted more favorable posts.[28] Beaver wanted marriage to be deployed as a sharp and effective regulator of identity, rights, and privileges in the colonial order, to do the kind of political labor that Ann Laura Stoler has acutely analyzed in the Dutch and French Indies.[29]

---

[27] "Herbert Beaver's First Report," November 10, 1836, in Thomas E. Jesset, ed., *Reports and Letters of Herbert Beaver, 1836–1838, Chaplain to the Hudson's Bay Company and Missionary to the Indians of Fort Vancouver* (Portland: Champoeg Press, 1959) 2.

[28] Herbert Beaver to A. C. Anderson, June 17, 1837, Herbert Beaver to Governor and Committee, October 2, 1838, both in Jesset, ed., *Reports and Letters of Herbert Beaver*, 58, 57, 117–118, 166.

[29] Ann Laura Stoler, "Carnal Knowledge and Imperial Power: Gender, Race, and Morality in Colonial Asia," in Micaela di Leonardo, ed., *Gender at the Crossroads of Knowledge: Feminist Anthropology in the Postmodern Era* (Berkeley: University of California Press, 1991).

Beaver's campaigns to encourage Christian marriage met with some initial success when two HBC officers and their partners agreed to marry by Anglican custom. One of these couples was Connolly Douglas and Douglas. In February 1837 they were married by Anglican custom in the first church marriage held at Fort Vancouver.[30] Beaver's efforts to promote Christian marriage stalled thereafter. In October 1838, he wrote to HBC headquarters in London, again calling for new regulations to shore up his project:

In introducing new rules in these delicate affairs, when I see the principal house in your establishment made a common receptacle for every mistress of an officer in the service, who may take a fancy to visit the Fort, and that not only those, who may be after a manner more acknowledged as wives, but even those, who are well known to have been taken merely "pour passer le temps," there meet with a reception upon those occasions, and that they all indiscriminately mix with respectable women, and with those married to other of our officers, with whom also they are thrust, without any distinction, into society.[31]

The Christian marriages of two officers had not changed his assessment of Fort Vancouver and the status of customary relationships and Indigenous women within it.

In his letters to London, Beaver put Fort Vancouver into a mobile transimperial discourse and tried to garner metropolitan attention and support for his critique of fur-trade colonialism. This political language fell apart in local colonial space, and it did so spectacularly. McLoughlin confronted the missionary after reading one of his lengthy missives. When Beaver's response did not satisfy, McLoughlin beat the missionary in the fort's square. That this violence occurred within the limited and defined "public" space of the fort was carefully noted, as was the fact that McLaughlin struck the missionary with the man's own cane, taking Beaver's symbol of legitimate masculine authority and turning it literally on him.[32] This would have been a relatively unexceptional use of interpersonal violence in a fur-trade context where men routinely demonstrated their authority and status through physical force. But framed within the cultural logic of an imperial public sphere, the smack of the chief factor's cane on a missionary's person delivered in the public square of the fort meant something quite different. Recounting the events for a British missionary magazine, Beaver set the story within the language of slavery and abolition. Fur-trade servants, he wrote, though "free-born British

---

[30] "Fort Vancouver and Fort Victoria Register of Marriages, 1839–1860," BCA, Add MSS 520/3/4, no 1, Transcript.

[31] Herbert Beaver to Governor and Committee, 2 October 1838, in Jesset, ed., *Reports and Letters of Herbert Beaver*, 120.

[32] Herbert Beaver to Governor and Committee, March 20, 1838, in Jesset, ed., *Reports and Letters of Herbert Beaver*, 93.

subjects" were familiar with "the lash, the fetter, and the chain." Still he considered that they saw his beating as the "last greatest indignity of a coward blow put upon the servant of God."[33] This was a conflict between competing ideas of what empire ought to look like, who should rule it, and what tools they might use to do so.

McLoughlin seemed unable or unwilling to mount a defense of this very specific violation of increasingly powerful and widely circulating expectations of empire. The chief factor tried first to publicly apologize to Beaver, an act that one observer considered "humiliating himself in presence of his subordinates."[34] Beaver did not accept McLoughlin's apology, and the chief factor left Fort Vancouver on furlough, leaving Douglas in charge. Douglas maintained a working relationship with Beaver until he read the missionary's forty-one-page October 1838 report to HBC headquarters and things fell irreparably apart. It was Beaver's portrayal of fur-trade women and families that especially offended Douglas. Douglas expressed his discomfort with what the missionary had written "respecting the inmates of my dwelling." He explained that Beaver's rendition of female morality ignored historical and cultural specificity. "You might also suppose that there was a real parity in point of principle between the mothers of decent families here, and the most proflicate [sic] females of other Countries; but we cannot be so blind as to the great moral difference between willful and unconscious error."[35] Like Beaver, Douglas presumed a metropolitan audience steeped in abolitionist thought. Given his own complicated location within networks of empire, Douglas had to access these languages with caution and skill. In his letters to London, he constituted himself as a knowledgeable participant in the fur trade and a careful supporter of missionary work. Beyond references to the "inmates of my dwelling," his multiple personal investments in imperial intimacies have no clear place in this correspondence.

The arguments Douglas made had been carefully rehearsed in a thoughtful and seemingly private consideration of intimacy and marriage recorded in undated journal entries likely composed in 1837 or 1838. Here he reflects seriously on questions of gender and sexual respectability, utilizing a range of sources that likely came from Fort Vancouver's library and the newspapers and books that traveled

[33] Herbert Beaver, letter published in *Church of England Protestant Magazine*, March 1841, reprinted in R. C. Clarke, ed., "Experiences of a Chaplain at Fort Vancouver, 1836–1838," *Oregon Historical Quarterly*, 39 (March 1938) 27.

[34] Roberts, "Recollections of George B. Roberts," 19.

[35] James Douglas to Herbert Beaver, October 2, 1838, in Jesset, ed., *Reports and Letters of Herbert Beaver*, 144. Also see W. Kaye Lamb, "The James Douglas Report on the 'Beaver Affair,'" *Oregon Historical Quarterly*, 18 (March 1946) 19–28.

with men in the fur trade. He found a set of ideas about manliness, womanliness, and marriage that circulated widely around the nineteenth-century English-speaking world. He quoted Harrison's "Conjugal Felic-ity" on the topic of "Wedded Love," stating that "The flowery band that binds two willing hearts – conveys a rational sublime delight, which nothing else can give, and without which all human life were vain." He clipped and preserved an undated short essay on the "Qualities Requi-site to Make Marriage Happy" which located the husband as the critical actor within marriage. The "best husbands," he reflected, "have been most famous for their wisdom." Discretion, virtue, and good nature also mattered.[36]

In Douglas' private reckoning, both adult men and women were accorded particular roles in the making of moral marriage and domestic-ity. He included a clipping that worked to differentiate this virtuous, wise masculinity from its shallow, untrustworthy impersonators. His ideas of what made a good wife borrowed similarly from the stock of popular mid-nineteenth-century wisdom about virtuous manhood and woman-hood. He transcribed a bromide about the utility of needlework, knitting, and other domestic labors as critical to female happiness. He took care to explain that the virtue required by men was doubly so for women, whose value and worth was ultimately proved in the realm of sexuality. "Chastity is the great principle which woman is taught," he explained, and "when she had given up that principle she had given up every notion of female honour and virtue."[37]

The books and articles that Douglas could find at Fort Vancouver on marriage, manliness and womanliness, and gender would have offered him little to explain the kinds of intimate practices of either his Demer-ara childhood or his northern North American adulthood. Here there were few books or newspapers to clip from: Douglas' sources were pre-sumably oral and experiential. Whatever the sources, his argument was that marriage and sexual morality were made in particular local spaces and could not be evaluated by external standards.

The woman who is not sensible of violating any law, who lives chastely with the husband of her love, in a state approved by friends and sanctioned by immemorial custom, which she believes highly honourable, should not be reduced to the level of the disgraced creature who voluntarily plunges into promiscuous vice, sacrifices the great principle which, from infancy, she is taught to revere, & consider the

[36] "From Boswell," "Qualities Requisite to Make Marriage Happy," [1837?], Douglas, "Journals, Notebooks and Clipping Books, etc., 1835–1873," BCA, MS 0678, Mflm A00792 (hereafter Douglas, Journals).

[37] "Advice to Young Men," "Mrs. Sigourney, 'On Domestic Employments,'" and Untitled, [1837], in Douglas, Journals.

ground work of female virtue, who lives a disgrace to her friends, and an outcast from society.[38]

Here Douglas aims to recalibrate nineteenth-century discourses of female respectability by severing ideals – here of love and faithfulness – from some of their most authoritative social and cultural moorings.

Transimperial language around female chastity, manly wisdom and discretion, and thick knowledge of the imperial intimacies of the colonial world came together in two reports Douglas transmitted to London in October of 1838. His first report adopts a measured tone and seizes the language of genteel British manhood back from Beaver, using it to defend elite fur-trade families like his own. This amounted to a specific response to Beaver and in the process delineated a complex and nuanced understanding of intimacy and respectability that worked to reconcile longstanding fur-trade practice with mainstream metropolitan ideals about marital respectability. By refiguring women married by Indigenous rather than European rites as "mothers of decent families," Douglas made Beaver out as the violator of principles of morality and good taste. He took special offense at Beaver's treatment of Waddin McKay McLoughlin. She was a powerful senior woman in fur-trade society, and godmother to at least two of Douglas' children. Douglas argued that she met and excelled at different and perhaps more meaningful standards of womanly virtue. "The intrusion of Dr. McLoughlin's private affairs into a public report ... is decidedly in bad taste," he declared, "and I deeply regret that Mr. Beaver sullied those pages with unhandsome reflections upon Mrs. McLoughlin, who is deservedly respected for her numerous charities, and many excellent qualities of heart."[39] If Waddin McKay McLoughlin met a truer standard for gendered propriety, Beaver himself failed it. In a subsequent letter Douglas argued that Beaver was an untrustworthy missionary and a bad and lazy man. He was, Douglas wrote, "Dissatisfied, apparently, with the exclusive privilege of remaining here, an idle spectator, of the busy throng around him," and decided "to libel, by his discolored statements the character of every person with whom he associates." Beaver was

---

[38] "The Educated Female," n.d., in Douglas, Journals. This prefigures his October 2, 1838 letter to Beaver.

[39] James Douglas to Governor, Deputy Governor, and Committee of Hon. Hudsons Bay Co., October 5, 1838, in Jesset, ed., *Reports and Letters of Herbert Beaver*, 141; Harriet Duncan Munnick, ed., and Mickell de Lores Wormell Warner, trans., *Catholic Church Records of the Pacific Northwest: Vancouver, Volumes I & II, and Stellamaris Mission* (St Paul, OR: French Prairie Press, 1972) Vancouver I, 37th p, B 100; Vancouver II, p140, B 187.

self-interested, out to "blast reputations and procure expulsion from the service."[40]

Here was a tentative and partial defense of imperial intimacies and Indigenous women and a partial condemnation of those who disparaged them. Douglas made similar sorts of arguments in other moments and in different forums. He supported a young Metis man who found informal ways to make his objections to the intimate behavior of a White male in authority. Andrew Pambrum recalled watching "old bloat of a chief trader," presumably Frances Heron of Fort Colville, callously leave his Indigenous wife and child. "From that moment I took dislike to him," Pambrum continued, "and I never spoke to him but once on the whole trip, when he addressed me I always went out of his way, or pretended not to hear." Douglas was Pambrum's direct superior, and Pambrum thought that he "appeared to approve" of the younger man's moral approbation and means of expressing it.[41] In letters to a friend written in the early 1840s, Douglas made a clear argument for the value, pleasure, and legitimacy of imperial families like his. His argument was in part a sentimental reckoning of the pleasure of being a husband and a father. He told James Hargrave that "the wedding day is assuredly the happiest day of life," and the first-born's birth a "joy." In another letter he congratulated Hargrave on his marriage to a Scottish woman and provided an alternative reckoning of imperial intimacies at the same time. "No one rejoices more sincerely in the happiness of your domestic circle than I do," he wrote, explaining that marriage had special meaning "amid the solitude of this country where the cheerful solace of agreeable society is so seldom found."

There is indeed no living with comfort in this country until a person has forgot the great world and has his tastes and character formed on the current standard of the stage, whereon he may exhibit useful talents. To any other being less qualified the vapid monotony of an inland trading post, would be perfectly unsufferable, while habit makes it familiar to us, softened as it is by the many tender ties, which find a way to the heart.[42]

With this line, Douglas provided at least two historians with titles for their work and, more to the point, provided an alternative assessment

---

[40] James Douglas to Governor, Deputy Governor and Committee, October 18, 1838, Appendix A, in Rich, ed., *The Letters of John McLoughlin, First Series, 1825–38*, 266–7.

[41] Pambrum, *Sixty Years on the Frontier*, 39.

[42] James Douglas to James Hargrave, February 26, 1840 and James Douglas to James Hargrave, March 24, 1842, both in Glazebrook, ed., *The Hargrave Correspondence*, 381, 311.

of imperial intimacies that both acknowledged a shifting climate and challenged it on its own terms.

These affirmations of fur-trade intimacies were rooted in the conviction that Indigenous women were admirable wives and suitable objects of White men's admiration and respect. Another of Douglas' contemporaries, Charles Ross, wrote to his sister in Scotland explaining his affection for the wife with whom he raised nine children. Ross anticipated that his kin would be a doubting audience and worked to dispel their concerns. He wrote, in a long-overdue letter:

I have as yet said nothing about my wife, whence you will probably infer that I am rather ashamed of her – in this, however, you would be wrong. She is not, indeed exactly fitted to shine at the head of a nobleman's table, but she suits the sphere [in which] she has to move much better than any such toy – in short, she is a native of the country, and as to beauty quite as comely as her husband.[43]

These generous assessments of fur-trade families were rooted in a particular experience of fatherhood and marriage. At Fort Vancouver officers ate separately from their wives and families, but shared and small domestic spaces remained the norm outside of major posts. Family sizes were large for most of the officer class. Smaller posts had little room for European bourgeois practices around gender and space, and men, women, and children shared tight quarters over long winter months. McDonald wrote from his post at Fort Colville, where his wife was an effective economic partner: "Her butter cheese, ham & bacon would shine in any ordinary market & I think myself with 3000 Bushels of wheat, 1500 of Indian corn & 1000 of other grains this year would pass with your Yankees neighbours as rather a considerable sort of farmer." In 1842, he also noted the constant presence of the couple's ten children:

Were you at this moment to see them, assisted by an older brother going five years who thinks himself amazingly wise with tables, chairs, sofas, cushions, tongs, broomsticks, cats, dogs & all other imaginable things they can lay their hands on strewed around me, you would say 'twas a delightful confusion, & then exclaim "McDonald, how the deuce can you write with such a racket about you."[44]

In this context, Douglas' oft-quoted invocation of "many tender ties" should be read not simply as a description of imperial intimacies but as a specific discussion of family life in the fur trade: small buildings,

---

43 Charles Ross to Joseph Macdonald, April 24, 1843, in W. Kaye Lamb, ed., "Five Letters of Charles Ross, 1842–44," *British Columbia Historical Quarterly*, 7:2 (1943) 107.

44 Archibald McDonald to Edward Ermatinger, January 25, 1837 and March 30, 1842, in Cole, ed., *This Blessed Wilderness*, 120, 209.

large families, long winters, and the regular and sometimes pleasurable proximity of men, women, and children. It was the lived practice of being a father and a husband that kept him from making the sorts of furloughs that were a sign of elite fur traders' authority and ongoing connections to the metropole. "It is about time for me to think of taking a cruize to the civilized world, if I ever expect to enjoy that satisfaction on this side of the grave," Douglas explained in 1848. But he was daunted by the logistics of getting "a family out of this District short of a two years notice" and does not seem to have considered making the journey on his own.[45]

Within the particular imperial space of northern North America, it was these suppler and more enthusiastic perspectives on marriage and empire that prevailed. Beaver and his wife returned to England in 1839. From there he continued to criticize the fur trade in lengthy letters to the missionary and liberal humanitarian press, adding increasing doses of anti-Catholicism to his stock of rhetorical tools. He condemned Fort Vancouver as "a very strong-hold of Popery" and argued that the HBC had failed to perform as adequate representatives of Britain's empire.[46] But Beaver's attacks on the fur trade made only a modest splash in metropolitan circles. Liberal humanitarian critics of HBC rule quoted his correspondence, finding it evidence that fur traders behaved in ways "unbecoming to persons who profess the religion of the Prince of Peace."[47] But the book that Beaver had planned to write on Fort Vancouver never seems to have been published.[48] After a few years in a rural Suffolk parish, he moved on to another part of the imperial world, beginning work as an army chaplain in the Cape Colony, and dying there in 1853.[49] The changes in social practice that had delivered White wives and missionaries to fur-trade territories in the 1820s and '30s shifted the climate in the fur trade, but did not displace the sort of imperial intimacy

---

[45] James Douglas to James Hargrave, March 10, 1848, Hargrave Collection, Library and Archives Canada, MG 19 A21.

[46] "To the Editor of the Church of England Protestant Magazine," n.d., Transcript, Herbert Beaver Search File, HBCA, 1. This is likely from March 1841, as reprinted in R. C. Clarke, ed., "Experiences of a Chaplain at Fort Vancouver." Also see Nellie B. Pipes, "Indian Conditions in 1836–39," *Oregon Historical Quarterly*, 32 (December 1931) 333–342.

[47] Alexander Kennedy Isbister, *A Few Words on the Hudson's Bay Company; With a Statement of the Grievances of the Native and Half-Caste Indians, Addressed to the British Government through Their Delegates in London* (London: C. Gilpin, 1846 (?)) 19.

[48] R. C. Clarke, "Editorial Comment: Reverend Herbert Beaver," *Oregon Historical Quarterly*, 39:1 (March 1938) 73.

[49] See G. Hollis Slater, "New Light on Herbert Beaver," *British Columbia Historical Quarterly*, 6:1 (January 1942) 24–26.

practiced by Douglas, Connolly Douglas, and many others like them. At Fort Vancouver and all around North America's fur-trade territories, imperial intimacies remained the backbone of the local colonial society. The appearance of a missionary, even a loquacious and hot-tempered one with a highly attenuated register for the sexualized politics of marital respectability, did not really change that. But Beaver's complicated and fractious time at Fort Vancouver did register and contribute to a changing climate of imperial intimacies, ones to which elite Metis people found a range of ways to respond.

The Douglas-Connolly family and their peers show us how individuals, families, and communities located in the thick of colonialism could respond to its shifts. In the 1830s and '40s elite families throughout northwestern North America adapted to shifting imperial mores by renegotiating the terms of their marriages and making them consistent with British legal practice and Christian tradition. Douglas and Connolly Douglas were married by Anglican ceremony a decade into their Indigenous marriage. They were not alone. Legal, church marriages became a critical instrument separating an older from a newer kind of marriage. Church marriages became a critical cultural tool, one made possible by the arrival of both Protestant and Roman Catholic missionaries in fur-trade space.

What one observer called a "marry din" broke out in Red River in 1836. Some of the newlyweds were young people, but many were older couples recasting the character of longstanding relationships. One "Old Mr. Cook" in 1835 "stood manfully forth, and declared his intention of bringing his 35 year courtship to an early close."[50] This couple were not the only ones who recalibrated their relationship. Archibald McDonald declared that "the safest & least burthensome curse for me to pursue was to close in with the old woman tout de bon." In Red River, before the newly installed Anglican clergymen, "Archy & Jenny were joined in Holy wedlock & of course declared at full liberty to live together as man & wife, & to increase & multiply as to them might seem fit." By the time of their marriage before an Anglican missionary, Archibald and Jane had lived together for almost ten years and had four children. McDonald thought they could be an example to others and presented his course as that of a committed and affectionate partner, more subtly registering the complicated brew of racism, misogyny, and dependence that structured White men's relationship to their Indigenous partners.

---

[50] Thomas Simpson to Donald Ross, February 20, 1836, Donald Ross Papers, HBCA, MG 1, D 20, Mflm 310.

All of my colleagues are now about following the example, & it is my full conviction few of them can do better – the great mistake is in flattering themselves with a different notion too long; nothing is gained by procrastination, but much is lost by it. Some there are, as you know, who would do worse – despise, maltreat & neglect their partners when at the same time they cannot bring themselves to part with them.[51]

The records of itinerant Roman Catholic missionaries who performed marriages and baptisms at fur-trade posts throughout northwestern North America record similar weddings between couples of longstanding connection. Catholicism had a long association with French North America and played a critical role in the making of Metis communities west of the Great Lakes. Priests Modeste Demers and Francis Blanchette used relatively gentle language to describe local families and children. Marriages were described as "naturel," and this term alternated with illegitimate to describe children born to these couples. As in the Caribbean earlier in the nineteenth century, these categories were subject to change and revisions. Certainly illegitimate children could be made legitimate. In 1838, Demers married Chrisologue Pambrum and Catherine Humperville at Fort Vancouver, and "recognized as legitimate" their six children, one of whom was Andrew Dominique. James Douglas was witness to this ceremony, serving in a capacity he repeated for many other French-Canadian and Metis servants and their local families.[52]

The costs of not reorganizing relationships to better suit a changing colonial order could be steep and hard to predict. In 1843, Letitia McTavish Hargrave wrote about one of the schools that had opened up in Red River. If "the mothers are not legally married they are not allowed to see their children," she complained. McTavish Hargrave, not unlike Douglas in his response to Beaver a few years before, tried to walk the tenuous line between asserting the universal desirability of marriage and the dignity of local iterations of it and women married by it. "This may be all very right," she wrote, "but it is fearfully cruel for the poor

---

[51] Archibald McDonald to Edward Ermatinger, April 1, 1836, in Cole, ed., *Blessed Wilderness*, 110–111.

[52] Munnick, ed., and Warner, trans., *Catholic Church Records of the Pacific Northwest: Vancouver*, 1–2, 8–9, 18. Also see Susan Sleeper-Smith, *Indian Women and French Men: Rethinking Cultural Encounter in the Western Great Lakes* (Boston: University of Massachusetts Press, 2001); Jacqueline Peterson, "Many Roads to Red River: Métis Genesis in the Great Lakes Region, 1680–1815," in Jacqueline Peterson and Jennifer S. H. Brown, eds., *The New People: Being and Becoming Métis in North America* (Winnipeg: University of Manitoba Press, 1985) 37–72; Melinda Marie Jette, "'We have Almost Every Religion But Our Own': French–Indian Community Initiatives and Social Relations in French Prairie, Oregon, 1834–1837," *Oregon Historical Quarterly* 108:2 (2007) 222–245.

unfortunate mothers did not know that there was any distinction & it is only within the last few years that any one was so married." Unlike Douglas, the Scottish fur-trade wife was able to imagine a world where history might have worked out differently, and placed some of the blame on the men who had chosen to participate in this recalibration of marriage and morality. "Of course had all the fathers refused, every one woman in the country w'd have been no better than those that are represented to their own children as discreditable," McTavish Hargrave argued. Marriage had become the terrain upon which women's reputations were made and unmade in ways that would become painfully clear in scandals that marked Red River in the middle years of the nineteenth century.[53]

Ideas of appropriate and inappropriate marriage might be useful sticks to measure and discipline women, but church ceremonies never guaranteed Indigenous women a secure place within the bourgeoisie of Red River, Oregon, or the fur-trade communities spread through northwestern North America. Beaver considered Douglas and his wife one of his few Fort Vancouver success stories, and had married them "with heartfelt feelings of joy at this unexpected move in the cause of religion." But he still doubted the respectability of Connolly Douglas and her peers. Though "very respectable women in their way," Beaver thought that they were "little calculated to improve the manners of society, which will, I am decidedly of opinion never assume a higher tone, until means be found for the introduction of married females in the several classes of life, and educated accordingly."[54] Beaver was an especially stern judge, but the criteria he used were not his alone. In 1848 Robert Clouston brought his elite Indigenous wife, Jessy Ross, with him to York Factory where he was chief trader. There Clouston waged a longstanding and ultimately unsuccessful battle to receive the same amenities that his superior and his White wife enjoyed. Clouston employed the languages of class, race, and respectability to make his case.

---

[53] Letitia Hargrave to Mrs. Dugald MacTavish, September 14 [to 17], 1843, in MacLeod, ed., *The Letters of Letitia Hargrave*, 177, 178. On the Red River scandal, see Sylvia Van Kirk, "'The Reputation of a Lady': Sarah Ballenden and the Foss-Pelly Scandal," *Manitoba History*, 11 (Spring 1986) 4–11; Erika Koenig-Sheridan, "'Gentlemen, This is no Ordinary Trial': Sexual Narratives in the Trial of Reverend Corbett, Red River, 1863," in Jennifer S. H. Brown and Elizabeth Vibert, eds., *Reading beyond Words: Contexts for Native History*, 2nd edition (University of Toronto Press, 2003) 365–384; Sharron A. FitzGerald and Alicja Muszynski, "Negotiating Female Morality: Place, Ideology and Agency in Red River Colony," *Women's History Review*, 16:5 (November 2007) 661–680.

[54] Herbert Beaver to Benjamin Harrison, March 10, 1837, in Jesset, ed., *Reports and Letters of Herbert Beaver*, 35.

[F]ancy, a woman brought up as Jessy has been, obliged to live in a small room without a stove – in a place where Indians and others are constantly going out and in. [W]hy should *my wife* be so treated when other clerks have houses built for their wives and no company thrust upon them?"[55]

Jessy's class standing and the couple's willingness to embrace new marital models failed to earn them the privileges they thought it should.

The ambivalent reception that reframed intimacies could receive was presumably part of what motivated the establishment and growth of vibrant, relatively affluent, and tightly interwoven Metis communities. Some HBC officers, including Douglas' bourgeois at Île-à-la-Crosse, George Keith, returned to Scotland and the Orkneys with their Indigenous families.[56] Others went east in North America, creating smaller pockets of settlement in Canada West and around HBC North American headquarters at Lachine, Canada East. In 1842, George Gladman wrote that "there is a disposition becoming general nowadays amongst our Gentlemen West of the Rocky Mountains to establish themselves permanently" in Canada. He thought the climate tolerable and society improving. Canada's real advantage lay in its proximity and amenability for Indigenous families. Gladman wrote that most of these men "have married native Women, [and] I dare say find it more congenial to their feelings to remain there, rather than drag their families through the Continent to a new Country and new connections where the chances are they would be less happy than in their former residences."[57] It was in Red River and, to a lesser extent, Canada West, the Willamette Valley, and, after 1849, Victoria, that these particular Metis communities would make their clearest marks and establish their deepest roots in the middle years of the nineteenth century.

By arguing with missionaries when they had to, by marrying according to newly available Christian rites, and, more importantly, by creating communities where families like theirs were the norm rather than the exception, elite families like the Douglas-Connollys used the terrain of their own lives to offer a different reckoning of empire and its

---

[55] Robert Clouston to Donald Ross, September 28, 1848, Donald Ross Fonds, HBCA, MG 1, D 20, Mflm 310, Transcript (hereafter Ross Papers).

[56] Jennifer S. H. Brown, "Keith, George," in *Dictionary of Canadian Biography*, Volume VIII, University of Toronto/Université Laval, 2003, www.biographi.ca, accessed June 12, 2012. Also see Patricia A. McCormack, "Lost Women: Native Wives in Orkney and Lewis," in Sarah Carter and Patricia McCormack, eds., *Recollecting: Lives of Aboriginal Women of the Canadian Northwest and Borderlands* (Edmonton: Athabasca University Press, 2011) 61–88.

[57] George Gladman to Edward Ermatinger, August 5, 1842, Ermatinger Papers, Volume III.

history in northern North America. Some twenty years later a prominent legal case reframed and redirected this elite Metis response and resistance to a shifting politics of marriage. John was the eldest of the six children raised to adulthood by William Connolly and his Cree wife, Miyo Nipay. By 1868 John Connolly was a prominent Montreal barrister. When William Connolly died, his wife by British North American law inherited his considerable fortune. Julia Woolrich Connolly had maintained connections with her stepchildren and supported her husband's first wife. When Woolrich Connolly died, her estate was left to the two children she and Connolly had together. The six surviving Metis Connolly children were cut out of the material patrimony of their father's estate, literally and symbolically dispossessed from the material basis of class membership. The story of Connolly's will and the remarriage that preceded it are in many respects clear and decisive evidence of how the changing politics of nineteenth-century intimacy materially enriched and legally empowered White women and children at direct cost to Indigenous women and their families.

But this story also reminds us that these histories were neither simple nor uncontested, including by the very people who had the most at stake. After Woolrich died and passed her fortune on to her two children, her stepson John took the case to the Supreme Court of Lower Canada. In a Montreal courtroom in 1864, he gathered together an impressive legal team and a long roster of witnesses, including a number of old North West Company servants who had been present at his parents' 1803 wedding, a judge, and the Roman Catholic priest who had baptized his sisters. The case was high profile in its own time and has continued to attract the attention of scholars of Indigenous people, law, and Canadians alert to its implications for ongoing politics about land, law, possession, and dispossession.[58]

In this case, John Connolly used the details of his own family's life to make a point of far-reaching consequence for the overlapping history of empire and intimacy. His basic argument was this: the marriage between his father and mother was conducted according to Cree law, and since no other ceremony was available in Rivière de Rats in 1803, this law and the marriage it sanctioned was valid and binding and the children born to it legitimate. In the zero-sum game of British marriage law, William Connolly's subsequent marriage would thus be rendered bigamous and the

---

[58] See Constance Backhouse, *Petticoats and Prejudice: Women and Law in Nineteenth-Century Canada* (Toronto: Osgoode Society and the Women's Press, 1991) 11–13; Carter, *The Importance of Being Monogamous*, Chapter 4; Sidney L. Harring, *White Man's Law: Native People in Nineteenth-Century Canadian Jurisprudence* (University of Toronto Press, 1998).

children born to it illegitimate. Presiding Justice Samuel Monk's response was lengthy and thoughtful, and legal historian Sidney Harring has called it "the boldest and most creative common law decision on Indian rights in nineteenth-century Canada." Monk essentially agreed with Connolly and validated the Indigenous marriage and the six surviving children produced by it, one of whom was Amelia Connolly Douglas. This was not a small estate: Harring states that it was at the time the largest ever probated in Lower Canada.[59]

Monk's ruling was about more than this one family, its complicated history, or its considerable wealth. The key arguments in the case forced the presiding judge to grapple not only with the range of ways that societies regulate marriage, but with Indigenous legal authority within territories of northern North America claimed by the British Empire. The decision acknowledged colonial authority in some places and said it did not apply in others, recognizing the authority of Indigenous law and the limits of colonial sovereignty notwithstanding formal imperial claims. The court explained that it could not expect "Mr. Connolly to carry with him this common law of England to Rat River in his knapsack, and much less could he bring back to Lower Canada the law of repudiation in a bark canoe." At stake here were not simply questions of sovereignty but definitions of what constituted a marriage. The latter question necessarily engaged a critical one throughout the empire, namely the legality and perhaps morality of British men having two unequal and geographically distinct families. The defense argued that "the Indian woman was Connolly's concubine" and not his wife.[60] In rejecting their argument, Monk gave special weight to Miyo Nipay's residence in Lower Canada, and Connolly's acknowledgement of her as his wife within this settler space as well as within fur-trade society.[61] It was the spatialization of their relationship that ruptured the defense's efforts to present Connolly as partaking in a longstanding history of manly, imperial life lived in two stages, in two distinct geographical spaces, and with two kinds of female partners, one called a wife and one called a concubine or a woman. By taking Miyo Nipay to Lower Canada and introducing her as his wife there, William Connolly had in essence forfeited his ability to lay claim to the models of imperial manhood practiced in so many different imperial contexts.

Douglas, Connolly Douglas, and their kin followed the case closely from Victoria. They had a lot to gain from its outcome, in terms of both material wealth and the more slippery currency of social respectability. In

---

[59] Harring, *White Man's Law*, 169, 170.   [60] Connolly vs. Woolrich, 214, 236.
[61] Connolly vs. Woolrich, 199.

1864 a correspondent in Canada East asked Douglas and Connolly's son-in-law John Helmcken to tell "Mr. or Mrs. Douglas" that "John Connolly is serving the would be Mrs C. for his mother's share of the Property and with every prospect of succeeding. He has had all the monies seized in the Banks until the Law Suit is finished."[62] A few years later, Douglas wrote to their daughter Jane in Scotland that

We are now all full of the Great Connolly case. The supreme court of Canada has confer[r]ed the judgement below, which validity of Mr. Connolly's first marriage [*sic*] the second marriage was consequently null & void & Mr. Connolly's children by the valid marriage are enti[t]led as an inheritance to one half of his property and personal estate. Under this consideration Mamma will have one sixth share over valued perhaps at $50000.

Reversing the language used by Connolly in Lower Canada, Douglas' correspondence referred to Woolrich as the "2nd Mrs. Connol[l]y." The couple were pleased that the courts agreed with their reckoning of which family and wife were the primary ones. "Lady Douglas as you may suppose is delighted with the decision of the Court of Appeal," wrote Douglas to lawyers handling the case in Montreal, "and trusts that her Fathers property may be equitably divided, among his surviv[v]ing children, and will oppose every attempt to deprive them of their birth right."[63]

The implications of this case not simply for the family involved but for practices of imperial intimacy more generally were clear from the outset. In November 1867 a letter to Victoria's daily newspaper, the *Colonist*, reprinted a Canadian newspaper story on the case, making sure that the story was registered within the specific space of British Columbia, in terms that were both local and highly and pejoratively racialized.

On this coast it is no infrequent occurrence for a White man to give a few dollars, blankets, or other *iktas* to some Indian father in exchange for one of his daughters, with whom he henceforward cohabits, and who according to the usage of her tribe regards herself as his married wife.

A quickly and unequally arranged match was followed by a ruthless abandonment and remarriage. "In many of these cases," the author explained,

---

62 E. E. Armstrong to John Sebastian Helmcken, June 2, 1864, Helmcken Papers, Volume 1, File 13.

63 James Douglas to Jane Dallas, November 13, 1869; James Douglas to Alexander Cross and Alexander H. Lunn, November 2, 1869; both in "Private Letter Book of Sir James Douglas, Correspondence Outward, March 22, 1867–Oct. 11, 1870," Transcript, BCA, Add MSS B/40/2 (hereafter Private Letter Book).

the Indian is afterward turned adrift with her half blood children, and her heartless man allies himself with a pale face woman who regards *herself* as his wife and another family grows up, who according to the above righteous decision, are illegitimate children of a bigamist, and who, as well as their mother may one day find themselves penniless.

For the author of this article, the enduring point of the story was the need for White women to protect their marriages and claims to property. "To the White spinsters and widows, the decision of the Canadian Courts says, 'Look, before you leap.'"[64]

The family had a direct stake in the case's outcome saw it as a vindication of the marriages and women who had made their families. Henry Connolly, Amelia and John's brother, wrote in his memoir that "In those days there were neither Priests nor Ministers in the country, so the Whites followed the custom of the country, and these marriages have been found in our highest courts to be lawful."[65] For Douglas, the Connolly case made a larger point about justice. Writing to a Montreal correspondent, he made clear that he saw the case's favourable conclusion as a vindication of Indigenous women and their families and an indictment of the particular mode of imperial masculinity that he rejected.

John is a noble fellow and has bravely won his rights, alone and unsupported by his family; but to me the most pleasing part is, that he has vindicated his Mothers good name; and done justice to the high minded old Lady, now at rest in the peaceful grave – and worthy of a kinder husband than poor Connolly. . . . For my own part I neither want nor would accept of any thing that was Connolly's but Lady Douglas, as a matter of duty to her children wishes to file her claim to her Fathers property.[66]

Yet Douglas also wished to avoid unnecessary conflict, and perhaps even more so the publicity that would likely accompany it. The Connolly case put strains on what were by then his well-honed practices of bourgeois self-fashioning and of discretion, seemly presentations of self and principled detachment. In 1867 he acknowledged that Woolrich's children were considering appeal, but hoped that they would reconsider since Connolly Douglas preferred to avoid further litigation. As the case went on, he hired a Montreal-based lawyer to "represent Lady Douglas' interest" and made regular queries about the case. In 1870, Douglas offered to travel to Canada in the hopes of arranging a settlement. He explained that he supported a compromise, and thought that "the Connolly

---

[64] Lenex, "To Whom it May Concern," *Colonist*, November 30, 1867.

[65] Henry Connolly, "Reminiscences of One of the Last Descendants of a Bourgeois of the North West Company," unpublished manuscript, 1; pagination added.

[66] James Douglas to Mr. Armstrong, September 23, 1867, Private Letter Book.

children are not adverse to such an arrangement as would represent a fair amount of compensation for their rights." That Douglas, a man in his late sixties, was prepared to make this journey is notable given not only its length and difficulty but his own reticence about leaving Vancouver Island.[67]

There was no golden age for fur-trade marriage, and if there was a decisive moment of decline, it did not occur until the final two decades of the nineteenth century. *Connolly vs. Woolrich* again reminds us of the complicated trajectories that imperial intimacies could and did take in northern North America and the imperial world more generally. The Connolly case turned on its head the imperial legal apparatus that most often denied legal rights and inherited wealth to Indigenous families, prompting the courts to proclaim the illegitimacy of the White family and the legitimacy of the Indigenous one, to impoverish the former and bolster the wealth of the latter. It did so in 1868, well after the heyday of fur-trade intimacies is generally thought to have passed, and in the midst of a consolidation of settler imperialism expressed most clearly in the confederation of four British North American colonies as the self-governing nation-state of Canada in 1867. But the legal pluralism of Monk's decision would not characterize the new nation of Canada, nor would the vision of northern North American history that supported it. Monk's decision was upheld on appeal two years later, but subsequently settled out of court, likely in anticipation of a less favourable ruling from the Privy Council. In 1884, Quebec's courts denied the legality of Indigenous marriage, and it would be this decision that would set a long-lasting precedent.[68] It would do so in a changed political climate. Historian Sarah Carter has vividly shown that Canada's claim to the fur-trade territories west of the Great Lakes was consolidated in part through marriage policies designed to produce a male-dominated settler state.[69] Households and families forged by Indigenous women and newcomer men would persist, but they did so under different conditions and sometimes with steep costs.

Northern North America's fur trade was built on relationships and families forged between local women and newcomer men. These were challenged in the middle decades of the nineteenth century when the arrival of White women and missionaries in fur-trade spaces made new ideas about race, respectability, and empire more tangible and meaningful. A carefully observed group of elite fur traders married White women

---

[67] James Douglas to Jane Dallas, November 13, 1869; James Douglas to Thomas R. Johnson, May 18, 1869; James Douglas to Thomas R. Johnson, October 7, 1868; James Douglas to Thomas R. Johnson, May 18, 1869; James Douglas to Alexander Cross, February 11, 1870; all in Private Letter Book.
[68] Harring, *White Man's Law*, 172.   [69] Carter, *The Importance of Being Monogamous*.

and rearranged the space that their Indigenous families occupied in their lives. More elite couples probably responded as Connolly Douglas and Douglas did, recalibrating the terms of their relationship through Christian and legally recognized marriage. The complicated combination of resistance and accommodation that underwrote this path also shaped the case of *Connolly vs. Woolrich*. This 1868 case turned the usual politics of remarriage and race on their head for the individual directly involved, at least in the short term, and raised serious doubts about the political capacity of mid-nineteenth-century colonialism to radically revise imperial intimacies, or at least elite ones that could be documented to the satisfaction of a colonial archive. This would shift again in the last decades of the nineteenth century, but in the mid-century a kind of careful accommodation and cautious resistance characterized elite local responses to a shifting climate of intimacy. This is inseparable from the changing politics of governance in the fur-trade societies of the same period.

5   Local elites, governance, and authority

In 1819, James Douglas was a newly recruited clerk bound to serve the North West Company (NWC) for a term of three years. Three decades later, he was the dominant official of the west coast operations of the Hudson's Bay Company (HBC) and the de facto local colonial authority. Amelia Connolly Douglas was his wife by local rites since 1828, and by the late 1830s her roles and status were guaranteed by Protestant ritual and British law. The dramatic changes within this one family speak to the shifting histories of colonial governance on northern North America's west coast in the 1820s, '30s, and '40s, and to the critical but variable and complicated role played by intimacy and racial and national identities in making and remaking them. This history was produced within both the local colonial space of fur-trade North America and the wider imperial world. Racial and imperial hierarchies hardened following the abolition of slavery in the British Empire in 1834 and the consolidation of settler regimes in the Americas, the Antipodes, and southern Africa. These changes occurred simultaneously with the reorganization of HBC operations and the reterritorialization of parts of HBC space as American. Whether because of transimperial changes in racial thinking, a revamped practice of resource capitalism, or the increasing presence of White settlers within and nearby fur-trade territory, what it meant to be a man or a woman among the fur-trade elite shifted and sharpened in these years.

The history of the Douglas-Connolly family speaks to changing histories of local elites, governance, and authority, and to the complicated way that they were lived by people in local and highly particular colonial spaces. This chapter examines governance and authority through the lives of the Douglas-Connolly family between the merger of 1821 and the creation of the colony of Vancouver Island in 1849. It begins by tracking the changing location of elite men and women with local genealogies in fur-trade society. It then connects this history to James Douglas and his family's changing career within the fur trade. Finally, the chapter turns to liberal, humanitarian discourses on empire, tracing the work they did in the changing politics of race and within Douglas' complicated engagement with the overlapping languages of anti-slavery, Christianity, and education. As the opportunities for the Metis elites shrank, Douglas and Connolly Douglas maintained and increased their social authority, political power, and economic clout. Histories of imperial governance, like imperial intimacies, could and did take complicated trajectories in local colonial spaces.

Questions about where local elites fit within changing practices of fur-trade colonialism were inseparable from shifting histories of race. In the 1820s people who claimed or were associated with both European and Indigenous origins were increasingly registered in explicitly racial terms, ones that were bodily and reproductive, if not strictly biological or scientific. These sorts of descriptions folded in national and linguistic knowledges that registered French-speaking, Roman Catholics as a specific people with partial and conditional claims to membership within a British empire. Indigeneity complicated matters further. After spending the winter of 1819/20 at William Connolly's fort, one of John Franklin's men put it this way: "The numerous connections between the traders and the Indian women have given birth to a race called Métis or Bois Brulee's [sic] by the Canadians, and half bred by the Europeans." Robert Hood saw the evidence for this in the bodies of the people around him, describing them as having "dark hair and eyes, regular features, and intelligent countenances." A particular place in the fur-trade economy went with this particular racial lineage. "Both Canadian and English Metiss are the most useful persons in the service of the fur traders, by whom they are regularly engaged as guides and interpreters," he explained.[1]

This emphasis on the distinct economic space occupied by Metis men in the fur trade suggests the way in which changing ideas of race were tied to occupational hierarchies. As the social currency of elite Metis wives and mothers was put into question, locally born boys were increasingly excluded from the officer class of the fur trade. This shift was made tangible by the new position of apprentice postmaster developed by HBC governor George Simpson in 1831/2. This position lay somewhere between clerk and interpreter, and was the highest position to which Metis men were supposed to aspire. "Governor Simpson tells me the Company have determined to take none of these Young Men into their service," noted one observer.[2]

[1] Robert Hood, *To the Arctic by Canoe, 1819–1821: The Journal and Paintings of Robert Hood, Midshipman with Franklin*, ed. Stuart C. Houston (Montreal: McGill-Queen's University Press, 1994) 49–50.

[2] Simon Fraser to John McLoughlin, April 20, 1827, in Burt Brown Barker, ed., *The McLoughlin Empire and its Rulers: An Account of their Personal Lives, and of their*

Douglas' peers were well aware of the implications of these changes for their lives, and for those of their daughters and, more particularly, their sons. Douglas' contemporaries were mainly Scottish or Canadian born, married to elite Metis women, and to a greater or lesser extent ambivalent about the prospect of spending their adult lives in North America and the fur trade. The most brittle of racial languages could be an appealing way for these men to frame their experience and their expectations. John Tod utilized new "scientific" language to explain why Metis men, presumably including his own sons, were increasingly unable to access the category of "gentleman." "Well have you observed that all attempts to make gentlemen of them, have hitherto proved a failure – the fact is there is something radically wrong about them all as is evidently shown from Mental Science alone I mean Phrenology," he explained to a friend in 1843.[3]

Yet the intimate ties and enduring lived experience of these men could also offer them different sets of knowledge, ones that cast doubt on the veracity or at least the universality of the putatively "scientific" racism that traveled the world in books, newspapers, and conversation. In private correspondence, fur traders discussed race as a variable thing that could be remade by people and place. In 1839, Frank Ermatinger wrote to his brother in Canada West about his son, Lawrence: "Pray keep him at work and let him, if possible, be taught to read and write, and in fact let him have every chance to show his disposition, when, if he is found to be hopeless, I will bring him back here and make an Indian of him."[4] Here, race is outed as a fragile human construction dependent on individual performance, social context, material resources, and kin relationships. Archibald McDonald stressed that the process of making Metis men middle class was not simply about money or credentials, but a more complicated politics of bourgeois education and moral regulation. "All the wealth of Rupert's Land will not make a *half breed* either a good Parson, a Shining Lawyer or an able physician if left to his own discretion while young," he argued. But for all his fatherly concern and attention,

---

Parents, Relatives and Children (Glendale, CA: The Arthur H. Clark Company, 1959) 183. More generally, see Denise Fuchs, "Embattled Notions: Constructions of Rupert's Land's Native Sons, 1760 to 1860," *Manitoba History*, 44 (Autumn/Winter 2002/3) 10–17.

3 John Tod to Edward Ermatinger, March 20, 1843, Ermatinger Papers, Volume I, "Letters to Edward Ermatinger from John Tod, 1826–62," Hudson's Bay Company Archives, E 94/1, Transcript (hereafter Ermatinger Papers).

4 Francis Ermatinger to Edward Ermatinger, February 26, 1839, in Lois Halliday McDonald, ed., *Fur Trade Letters of Francis Ermatinger, Written to his Brother Edward during his Service with the Hudson's Bay Company 1818–1853* (Glendale, CA: The Arthur H. Clarke Company, 1980) 215–216.

McDonald was wracked with doubts about his children's futures, and his worries were animated by a sense of race as somehow innate. He especially fretted about his son Ranald, born to a Chinook mother in a previous relationship. The fur trader hoped that attending school in Canada West would give the boy "knowledge enough to develop what may be in him as a man." But McDonald also thought his son's possibilities limited by something he called race. "Bear in mind," he warned, "he is of a particular race."[5]

The variable and conflicting views of race that inform these discussions reflected a social world within which race could be experienced as simultaneously real, mutable, and almost capricious. Some Metis sons did become gentlemen. As in the early nineteenth-century Caribbean world of Douglas' childhood, boys of mixed descent could provisionally access the privileges of Whiteness if they had the right combination of material wealth, paternal interest, and formal education, and if they themselves were able to reliably *perform* a model of bourgeois imperial manhood. Newcomers to fur-trade society could be shocked that members of the same family could be racialized differently, and noted the centrality of the father's role in producing and managing his children's racial location. "The state of society seems shocking," wrote Letitia McTavish Hargrave in 1840. "Some people educate & make gentlemen of part of their family & leave the other savages." Her examples included John McLoughlin, who "gave 2 of his sons a regular education in England & keeps the 3rd a common Indian." To make matters more complicated, McTavish Hargrave thought that the third son was the happiest.[6]

Like the exclusion of Metis women from the cadre of elite wives, the exclusion of Metis men from the officer class of the HBC was never total. Even the pessimistic Tod recognized that George Gladman Jr., a "native" appointed chief trader in 1836, was an "exception" to racialized generalizations.[7] Into the mid-nineteenth century, Metis men with formal and especially European education were placed at the helm of posts, albeit usually small and isolated posts and in unusual circumstances. Henry Connolly rejected his father's plan for him to become a doctor and instead entered the HBC service in the predictable position of

[5] Archibald McDonald to Edward Ermatinger, April 1, 1836, in Jean Murray Cole, eds., *This Blessed Wilderness: Archibald McDonald's Letters from the Columbia, 1822–44* (Vancouver: UBC Press, 2001) 112.
[6] Letitia Hargrave to Mrs. Dugald MacTavish, December 1, 1840, in Margaret Arnett MacLeod, ed., *The Letters of Letitia Hargrave* (Toronto: The Champlain Society, 1947) 84.
[7] John Tod to Edward Ermatinger, June 29, 1836; John Tod to Edward Ermatinger, March 20, 1843; both in Ermatinger Papers, Volume I.

apprentice postmaster. By 1867, he was chief trader at Esquimaux Bay, one of the six or so "half-breeds" he reckoned had been given HBC commissions.[8] McLoughlin's son John Jr. was educated in Montreal and Paris. Along with a number of what Simpson described as "wild thoughtless young men of good education and daring character, half-breed sons of gentlemen,"[9] John Jr. spent a few years in an anti-colonial military resistance movement called the Indian Liberating Army that moved around the North American west, including spending a winter at Red River. He later returned to the fur-trade fold and was appointed clerk in charge of Fort Stikine, a small fort in Russian American territory where he was murdered by his own men in 1842.[10] Gladman, Connolly, and McLoughlin paid for their relative success with geographically isolated posts and, in the case of McLoughlin Jr., harsh judgments of their very prosaic shortcomings. But they were there.

New languages of science helped to justify hardening racial cleavages, and the circulation of new idioms of rights worked to unsettle them. Peter Pambrum argued that Metis men were being treated as "Serfs by the Company" and held to a double-standard that would be familiar to people of color around the imperial world. "Their education is as good, and conduct as correct, but conduct which in a European is overlooked, is in a native punished, and has always been the case since ever a Bois Bruille was entered the service," he complained in 1858.[11] His son Andrew worked under Douglas before becoming a teacher in Red River and an independent trader on the United States side of the border. This Pambrum recalled the history of Metis men and their exclusion from the HBC elite with a finely tuned critique, one that registered the complicated work of family and intimacy in making and remaking race in this colonial context. "It did not matter how well qualified or meritorious the individual might be, his blood kept him from promotion," he explained. He took care to point out the ironies of the intimate connections that tied the HBC elite to the Metis men they discriminated against. "Just think of the injustice of such a law, and that against their own blood," he critiqued. He described Indigenous children of White men as angry, and

---

[8] Henry Connolly, "Reminiscences of One of the Last Descendants of a Bourgeois of the North West Company," unpublished manuscript, n.d., 31; pagination added.

[9] Quoted in Jennifer S. H. Brown, *Strangers in Blood: Fur Trade Company Families in Indian Country* (Vancouver: UBC Press, 1980) 190.

[10] Appendix A, "The Murder of John McLoughlin, Junior," in E. E. Rich and William Kaye Lamb, eds., *The Letters of John McLoughlin, from Fort Vancouver to the Governor and Committee, Second Series, 1839–44* (London: Hudson's Bay Company Records Society, 1943).

[11] Peter C. Pambrum to Edward Ermatinger, June 22, 1858, Ermatinger Papers, Volume III.

appropriately so: "To this day they bear heavily the stigma and curse of their birth, for surely they are visited for the sins of their fathers being despised and even hated by their begetters."[12] Here the younger Pambrum speaks to the vexed relationships between class, race, and lineage in the fur trade, and to the dwindling opportunities for local elites in the mid-nineteenth century. He wrote of the fur trade, but he might have been describing any number of other places wrought by empire.

The opportunities for migrant men expanded as those for local elites shrank. Douglas was one such newcomer, and he firmly established his and his family's place in the elite of the fur trade and colonial governance in these years. In 1830 he left New Caledonia for the larger and more prestigious Columbia District, beginning a move that would produce multiple transformations for him and his family. Amelia remained behind at Fort St. James with her first baby for a time.[13] After the baby died, she traveled to Fort Vancouver with the brigade, making the more than 1,400 kilometer journey by canoe and horse. The chief factor and his daughter traveled in a bourgeois Metis style, with Amelia wearing embroidered leggings and moccasins "stiff with the most costly beads," "Indian boys" packing goods behind them, and a cook accompanying them.[14] The space occupied by Indigenous people within the fur trade's upper echelons may have been growing smaller, but the Douglas-Connolly family remained clearly marked by the material culture and social relations of the Metis elite.

The journey spoke both to the family's class position and to some of the ways it could be lived in clearly Indigenized ways. But Indigeneity was still a risk to be managed. Almost a hundred years later, Douglas and Connolly's daughter Martha would recollect her father's disappointment that the journey from Fort St. James to Fort Vancouver had darkened his wife's complexion and presumably reduced her perceived value in a fur-trade society where Whiteness was an increasingly powerful hallmark of status and prestige. At Fort Vancouver, Douglas had boasted that his wife was a fair woman nicknamed "Little Snowbird" by her family. When she arrived, his first response was one of racial despair: "he was disappointed because she had become so tanned during the many weeks on her voyage

---

[12] Andrew Dominique Pambrum, *Sixty Years on the Frontier in the Pacific Northwest* (Fairfield, WA: Ye Galleon Press, 1978) 69, 61.

[13] A. G. Morice, *The History of the Northern Interior of British Columbia, Formerly New Caledonia, 1660–1880*, 2nd edition (Toronto: William Briggs, 1904) 147; "Douglas Family Bible," in James Douglas, "Journals, Notebooks, and Clipping Books," BCA, MS 0678, Mflm A00792 (hereafter Douglas, Journals).

[14] N. de Bertrand Lugrin, *The Pioneer Women of Vancouver Island, 1843–1866* (Victoria: Women's Canadian Club, 1928) 14.

in the hot sun." In the next few years, Amelia re-established her reputation for fairness. A visitor described her as a "half-breed from Hudson Bay" and "the lightest woman" at Fort Vancouver.[15] Sarah Julia Ogden McKinlay was Connolly Douglas' goddaughter, and she acknowledged the older woman's fair complexion without reducing her to it or some other flat racial caricature. Ogden McKinlay recalled meeting Amelia in 1833, recalling her as "nice looking quite stout but rather short, very pale," and was "a very kind hearted person."[16]

Douglas' transfer to the major entrepôt of Fort Vancouver gave him a wider canvas upon which to develop the model of bourgeois imperial manliness that would serve him so well in the decades that followed. Fort Vancouver was under the looming authority of chief factor John McLoughlin. Like Douglas' two previous bourgeois, McLoughlin was an old NWC man with an Indigenous family. The fort he supervised was in essence a village, with thirty buildings within the fort walls and another fifty or more outside, and extensive orchards and fields. To one French observer, Fort Vancouver looked like a large European farm, and this is certainly the impression given in Gustavus Sohon's 1853 drawing shown in Figure 4.2. But it was situated in what was undeniably an Indigenous and Pacific world, with most servants "married to Indian wives."[17] The community was polyglot and polyvocal. A visiting linguist found "five languages are spoken by about five hundred persons, namely, the English, the Canadian French, the Chinook, the Cree, and the Hawaiian."[18] An American observer described the village outside the fort walls as home to "a mongrel race, consisting of English, French, Canadians, Indians of different nations, and half breeds, all in the employ of the company."[19]

For all of this American visitors still registered Fort Vancouver's cultivated and almost metropolitan appearance. In 1836, Narcissa Whitman, a visiting American missionary, described the fort as distinct from the

[15] Lugrin, *The Pioneer Women*, 14; Kate N. B. Powers, "Across the Continent Seventy Years Ago: Extracts from the Journal of John Ball of his Trip across the Rocky Mountains and his Life in Oregon, Compiled by his Daughter," *Quarterly of the Oregon Historical Society*, 3:1 (March 1902) 144.

[16] Sarah J. McKinlay to Eva Emery Dye, January 23, 1892, Oregon Historical Society (hereafter OHS), 1089, 2/8.

[17] Nellie Bowden Pipes, "Extract from Exploration of the Oregon Territory, the Californias, and the Gulf of California, Undertaken during the Years 1840, 1841, and 1842 by Eugene Duflot de Mofras," *Quarterly of the Oregon Historical Society*, 26:2 (June 1925) 155, 154.

[18] Horatio Hale, *An International Idiom: A Manual of the Oregon Trade Language or "Chinook Jargon"* (London: Whittaker and Co., 1890) 19.

[19] Joel Palmer, "Journal of Travels over the Rocky Mountains, 1845–6," in Rueben Gold Thwaites, ed., *Early Western Travels, 1748–1846*, Volume XXX (Cleveland, OH: Arthur H. Clark, 1906) 2010.

surrounding territory, for her a welcoming space in a disconcertingly foreign land. "What a delightful place this is; what a contrast to the rough, barren sand plains, through which we had so recently passed," she wrote. Whitman was asked to go walking with Amelia Connolly Douglas and Marguerite Waddin McKay McLoughlin, and the elite Metis women showed her a rich physical environment bearing witness to global conversations and bourgeois aspirations. "Here we find fruit of every description, apples, peaches, grapes, pears, plums, and fig trees in abundance; also cucumbers, melons, beans, peas, beets, cabbage, tomatoes and every kind of vegetable too numerous to be mentioned," she wrote. "Every part is very neat and tastefully arranged, with fine walks, lined on each side with strawberry vines. At the opposite end of the garden is a good summer house covered with grape vines" grown from seeds brought from London.[20]

Fort Vancouver was a hub for a colonial economy organized around trade. If Fort William tied northern North America to Europe and Georgetown tied the Caribbean to Europe, Fort Vancouver linked North America to Hawaii, Russia, and China, and linked the Pacific, Atlantic, and Circumpolar iterations of the imperial world. Each spring, HBC ships arrived "laden with coarse woolens, cloths, baizes, and blankets; hardware and cutlery; cotton clothes, calicoes, and cotton handkerchiefs; tea, sugar, coffee and cocoa; rice, tobacco, soap, beads, guns, powder, lead, rum, wine, brandy, gin, and playing cards; boots, shoes, and ready-made clothing, &c; also, every description of sea stores, canvas, cordage, paints, oils, chains and chain cables, anchors, &c." Outgoing goods included "a cargo of lumber to the Sandwich Islands, or of flour and goods to the Russians at Sitka or Kamskatka," and later the furs collected at Fort Vancouver, eventually shipped to England.[21]

Douglas' appointment as clerk of this major post was a sign of his upward mobility, and at Vancouver he continued to impress his masters. In 1830 McLoughlin wrote that Douglas and the two other clerks were "kept constantly employed from day light to eleven at night."[22] In the same year, the HBC's records described Douglas as a "Steady respectable man tolerable education good Clerk & Trader, superior to many of his

---

[20] Narcissa Whitman, September 12, 1836, in "Diaries and Journals of Narcissa Whitman, 1836," www.isu.edu/~trinmich/00.ar.whitman1.html, accessed December 9, 2009.

[21] John Forsyth and W. A. Slacum, "Slacum's Report on Oregon, 1836–7," *Quarterly of the Oregon Historical Society*, 13:2 (June 1912) 186–187.

[22] John McLoughlin to HBC, November 24, 1830, Correspondence, Columbia District, HBC Archives (hereafter HBCA), 1830, B 223/b/6.

class, looks to promotion wh. confidence."[23] In 1832, Simpson privately recorded his impression of Douglas: "A stout powerful active Man of good conduct and respectable abilities: tolerably well Educated, expresses himself clearly on paper, understands our Counting House business and is an excellent Trader." Simpson thought Douglas well qualified for any posts requiring "bodily exertion, firmness of mind, and exercise of Sound judgment."[24] The governor predicted that Douglas would likely be promoted, and in 1835 he was, being made chief trader at Fort Vancouver and attending the HBC's annual council meeting at Red River. Within another four years Douglas could be described as "the acting man in the depot."[25] In 1840 he was appointed chief factor, making him the HBC's leading official on the Pacific coast before he was forty years old.

Fur-trade authority of the sort exercised by Douglas rested on the material authority of the mercantile trade backed by a particular version of the colonial state. These were exercised with a benevolent sort of paternalism and a brutal kind of force. As historian Tina Loo has argued, the fur trade operated on a "club-law" that wove interpersonal violence into relationships of authority between men. Cole Harris has argued that the fur trade depended on a carefully orchestrated practice of terror in the absence of an effective sovereign colonial authority in the Cordillera. Fear was part of what kept Indigenous people from compromising the trade and profits of Europeans, and what kept them trading when there were other options.[26] McLoughlin considered force a necessary tool for controlling labor in this colonial context:

It is true, in the civilised world when a man refuses his Duty you may dismiss him, and replace him with another. In this country we cannot do it, but do our work with the people we have, as we cannot replace them, it therefore leaves us no alternative, but to make them do their duty.[27]

[23] HBCA, Servants Characters & Staff Records, A 34/1, 82.

[24] "The 'Character Book' of George Simpson, 1932," in Glyndwr Williams, ed., Hudson's Bay Miscellany, 1670–1870 (Winnipeg: Hudson's Bay Company Record Society, 1975) 204–205; Margaret A. Ormsby, "Douglas, Sir James," in Dictionary of Canadian Biography, Volume X, University of Toronto/Université Laval, 2003, www.biographi.ca, accessed June 9, 2008; Bruce McIntyre Watson, Lives Lived West of the Divide: A Biographical Dictionary of Fur Traders Working West of the Rockies, 1793–1858, Volume I (Kelowna: Centre for Social, Spatial, and Economic Justice, 2010) 340–341.

[25] Archibald McDonald to Edward Ermatinger, February 1, 1839, in Cole, ed., This Blessed Wilderness, 135.

[26] Tina Loo, Making Law, Order, and Authority in British Columbia, 1821–1871 (University of Toronto Press, 1994) Chapter 2; Cole Harris, "Strategies of Power in the Cordilleran Fur-Trade," in The Resettlement of British Columbia: Essays on Colonialism and Geographical Change (Vancouver: UBC Press, 1997).

[27] John McLoughlin to Governor, October 26, 1837, in E. E. Rich, ed., The Letters of John McLoughlin, from Fort Vancouver to the Governor and Committee, First Series, 1825–38 (London: Hudson's Bay Record Society, 1941) 193.

This kind of authority was supported and reinforced by the structure of the HBC. Andrew Pambrum explained that "Each Chief Factor could verily say, 'I am lord of all I survey,' because he was lord, lawmaker, sheriff and hangman of the district."[28]

Within the contained spaces of the fur trade, physical violence could be a predictable and known quantity, meted out in careful measure and by men in authority or those delegated by them. Regularized violence was punctuated by more spectacular and less controlled acts, as when Frank Ermatinger ordered the tip of "an Indian's" ear cut off because he had "run off with his woman" or when an HBC doctor "emasculated" an "Indian" who "used to dress himself up as a female and go on board the Vessels and offer himself to the Sailors."[29] The fear that the fur-trade masters inspired left lasting impressions on those who were the intended audience for these displays of violence and fury. Ranald MacDonald recalled being afraid of only two people: his father and McLoughlin.[30] Andrew Pambrum also grew up at Fort Vancouver, and the image of McLoughlin disciplining his men stayed with him into old age. He recalled:

Methinks I see Dr. McLoughlin standing on his gallery and in his stentorian voice, face distorted with rage, call a man's name. The wretch, at sound of his name turns pale and in vain efforts to surmise the cause, approached, hat under his arm and trembling with fear, and the probabilities are that he gets a good sound caning.[31]

Like his mentor, Douglas earned a reputation as a stern and demanding bourgeois. One man reflected on his time at Fort Vancouver with the comment that "both the Dr. [McLoughlin] & Douglas were disciplinarians & their success was largely owing to that."[32] Roderick Finlayson also used the word disciplinarian to describe Douglas, explaining that he allowed "no one to impose upon him."[33] Like McLoughlin, Douglas used fear as a critical instrument in colonial labor relations, one whose simple utility outweighed the liberal ideals of justice that he is better remembered for. Historian Edith Burley argues that Douglas thought that seamen's obedience to their officers flowed from fear since sailors

---

[28] Pambrum, *Sixty Years on the Frontier*, 20.

[29] John McLoughlin to Governor, January 17, 1837 and John McLoughlin to George Simpson, March 16, 1831, in Rich, ed., *The Letters of John McLoughlin, First Series*, 185, 227.

[30] Ranald MacDonald to Eva Emery Dye, July 24, 1892, OHS, MS 1089, 2/5.

[31] Pambrum, *Sixty Years on the Frontier*, 20.

[32] George Roberts to Mrs. F. F. Victor, June 23, 1879," in George B. Roberts, "Letters to Mrs. F. F. Victor, 1878–83," *Oregon Historical Quarterly*, 63: 2/3 (June–September 1962) 216.

[33] Roderick Finlayson, "The History of Vancouver Island and the NorthWest Coast," Victoria, 1878, Bancroft Manuscript, PC 15, Bancroft Library, University of California Berkeley (hereafter BL), 78.

were indifferent to "'upright principle.'" The records Burley examined are littered with complaints about the excessive discipline of Douglas and the men directly under him.[34] Simpson's assessment of Douglas included the codicil that he was "furiously violent when roused."[35]

Violence structured relations among men in the fur trade and paternalism legitimated it. Douglas was known as a fearsome master but also as a kind man. Johnny Grant's father thought working under Douglas would discipline his difficult son. The young Grant was afraid of being sent to a man who might be "worse than father," but found Douglas kinder than he had expected. Grant was not the only young person who bore witness to Douglas' gentleness. He "was at heart a kind and genial man, loved and respected by all who knew him," explained a woman who grew up at Fort Victoria. She recalled Douglas as especially kind to children, a man who "never passed by without a cheery word and a pat on the head."[36]

When Douglas became chief factor he also became the effective local colonial authority. The jurisdiction that he ruled on behalf of the HBC was layered, shifting, and, in the 1840s, diminishing in geographic terms. The United States had long been interested in the territory between the Rockies and the west coast, and its territorial designs were buoyed by new claims to "manifest destiny," a doctrine of dispossession that gave special rights to the United States to claim contiguous territory.[37] Also at issue was the extent to which the HBC's particular brand of colonialism could exist within a newly ambitious settler America. HBC rule was dependent on Indigenous commodity production, wage labor, and kin ties and premised on monopoly powers and the British Empire that granted them and defended their right to hold. The American brand of settler colonialism being refined in the 1830s and '40s was of a different order: committed to Indigenous dispossession and the resettlement of agriculturalists living in nuclear families. Indigenous peoples and other models of empire could not easily be incorporated. HBC and American settler colonialism could not easily coexist.

American expansion was registered as a threat not only to the interests of the HBC, but to the survival of the communities that depended

---

[34] Edith I. Burley, *Servants of the Honourable Company: Work, Discipline, and Conflict in the Hudson's Bay Company, 1770–1879* (Oxford University Press, 1997) 177, 204–206, 209–210, 238.

[35] "The 'Character Book' of George Simpson, 1832," 205.

[36] Gerhard J. Ens, ed., *A Son of the Fur Trade: The Memoirs of Johnny Grant* (Edmonton: University of Alberta Press, 2008) 22, 28; "Fort Victoria in Pioneer Days, 70 Years Ago," recalled by Mrs. J. C. [Finlayson] Keith, *The Daily Province* (Vancouver) January 24, 1925.

[37] Robert J. Miller, "American Indians, the Doctrine of Discovery, and Manifest Destiny," *Wyoming Law Review*, 11:2 (2011) 329–348.

on it. The rumor that "every man who has an Indian wife ought to be driven out of the Country, and that the half breeds should not be allowed to hold lands" understandably terrified what McLoughlin referred to as "the Americans and Canadians who have half-breed families." Douglas defended a particularly British mode of fur-trade imperialism, placing his loyalties to Indigenous people above those to the American newcomers. He wrote to Simpson: "No people can be more prejudiced and national than the Americans in this country, a fact so evident to my mind, that I am more suspicious of their designs, than of the wild natives of the forests."[38] He was suspicious of what he described as a "restless, intriguing and unprincipled American population." The American newcomers had no working relationships with, knowledge of, or affection for the Indigenous people they found themselves among. "There exists no sympathy between the two races, nothing in their feelings or manners runs in harmony, there is consequently a complete absence of those useful ties which produce unit of purpose, and the absorbing spirit of participation in a country," he explained to a colleague on the other side of the Rocky Mountains.[39] Douglas was disappointed at how easily the British Empire was abandoned in the face of an aggressive American alternative. "While the American Party are pouring petition after petition into the hands of their government and keeping the national feelings alive, by a system of ceaseless agitation, we are doing nothing," he reported in 1845. "British feeling is dying away so much, that Englishmen, in the Willamette, are either afraid or ashamed to own their country."[40]

In 1846, the Oregon Treaty redrew the boundary between British and American interests on the Pacific and reterritorialized the land lying between the forty-second and forty-ninth parallel as American. This was one of many imperial sleights of hand that redrew nineteenth-century political geographies, including the one that made Demerara British in 1803. In both places, the rebranding of empire produced layered and complicated histories for those who lived their lives in spaces that were always more than colored parts on maps. In Oregon and Washington territories, small French-speaking, Roman Catholic Metis settlements

---

[38] John McLoughlin to Hudson's Bay Company, March 28, 1845; James Douglas to George Simpson, April 4, 1845; both in E. E. Rich, ed., *The Letters of John McLoughlin, from Fort Vancouver to the Governor and Committee, Third Series, 1844–46* (London: Hudson's Bay Record Society, 1944) 73, 190.

[39] James Douglas to James Hargrave, February 10, 1845, Library and Archives Canada, Hargrave Collection, MG 19 A21 (hereafter Hargrave Papers).

[40] James Douglas to George Simpson, March 5, 1845, in Rich, ed., *The Letters of John McLoughlin, Third Series*, 180.

remained as testaments to the history and complexity of Indigeneity and empire on North America's Pacific.[41]

The HBC redefined its geographic scope when it shifted the location of its Pacific operations northward to Vancouver Island. As Daniel Clayton has shown, Vancouver Island had been the site of wide-ranging colonial trade, knowledges, and conflict for a century. Sustained trade between Europeans and Indigenous people began in the 1770s with Spanish ships exchanging trade goods for Nuu'chal'nulth sea otter pelts. In 1778, British explorer James Cook passed the east coast of Vancouver Island, and the territory was irrevocably placed within the orbit of British imperial politics and aspirations.[42] Five principal nations – Russia, the United States, France, Spain, and Britain – continued to compete over the trade in sea otter pelts which were sold on the Canton market. British influence was solidified in the early nineteenth century, and in 1843, Douglas established a new fort on the island, choosing the location for its perceived compatibility with European agricultural practice. He dubbed this place Camousack, signifying "beads of necklaces" in Cree, a "language with which he was fairly familiar."[43] After some indecision the location was predictably renamed after the ruling British queen and the imprint of Britain in northwestern North America was casually but clearly reasserted.

For Douglas, this relocation represented a loss, a reminder of what he called "the cession of the Columbia to a Foreign Power." In 1845 he described the move from Fort Vancouver to Fort Victoria as a forced one, a kind of exile: "It appears probable that we will be obliged to leave the Columbia and to withdraw to Vancouvers Island, to rusticate, among the savages there."[44] Within a short time Victoria was very much Douglas' fort. When he, Connolly Douglas, and their family of four daughters took up residence there they acquired a literal and symbolic role at the helm

---

[41] See Melinda Marie Jette, "'We Have Almost Every Religion But Our Own': French–Indian Community Initiatives and Social Relations in French Prairie, Oregon, 1834–1837," *Oregon Historical Quarterly* 108:2 (2007) 222–245; Jean Barman, "Taking Everyday People Seriously: How French Canadians Saved British Columbia for Canada," 2007, www.sfu.ca/humanities-institute-old/Taking%20Everyday%20People%20Seriously.pdf, accessed June 27, 2012.

[42] Daniel Clayton, *Islands of Truth: The Imperial Fashioning of Vancouver Island* (Vancouver: UBC Press, 2000).

[43] James Douglas to John McLoughlin, July 12, 1842, copy enclosed in Great Britain, Colonial Office, Vancouver Island, CO 305/1, http://bcgenesis.uvic.ca, accessed September 7, 2013; James Robert Anderson, "Notes and Comments on Early Days and Events in British Columbia, Washington and Oregon, Including an Account of sundry happenings in San Francisco; being the Memoirs of James Robert Anderson, Written by himself," BCA, MS 1912, Box 9, Transcript, 149.

[44] James Douglas to James Hargrave, March 24, 1847, Hargrave Papers.

of a rearranged British Pacific. Like Fort Vancouver, Fort Victoria was in essence a palisaded village, a militarized commercial space that spoke to the blunt material aspirations and colonial authority of the private fur-trade company. The fort had residential buildings for various categories of employees, and warehouses, a blacksmiths' shop, a bakery, and a belfry at the center with a bell that was rung for rising, meals, work, and for Christian service on Sunday. The fort walls distinguished who and what belonged to the HBC, what did not, and what was at its margins. Outside the fort were the cabins of HBC servants and their Indigenous families, many of them local, unlike the mainly Metis women married to HBC officers.[45]

Fort Victoria was a built testament to both the powers of the British Empire and its desire to remake the lived experience of the diverse spaces it awkwardly and sometimes violently claimed. The fort's gates, watchmen, and bastions spoke to empire, and so, over time, did the land. The cultivation of gardens served as particularly potent symbols of empire, tangible reminders of its capacity to rearrange and repurpose space. James Robert Anderson was sent from Fort Alexandria to Fort Victoria to attend school and, like many fur-trade children sent to a major post for schooling, was placed in the care of the chief factor and his family, in this case James Douglas and Amelia Connolly Douglas. Anderson recalled the fort's garden "redolent with the perfume of mignonette, stock and wallflower and gay with echoltsia, mallow, hollyhock, marigold, candytuft, sweet William and others of the old-fashioned flowers." He also remembered the peas, turnips, carrots, cabbage, potatoes, and onions, and especially the apple trees. These were grown from seeds sent from trees at Fort Vancouver, which had in turn been grown from seeds brought from England. Anderson recalled being given an apple by "kind, motherly Mrs. Douglas." The apple was "a great favour" and Anderson soon learned to appreciate its strange taste. He also experienced Connolly Douglas as a fine hostess. Anderson recalled a memorable picnic and the "lurid happiness of that delightful day," and another picnic given by Douglas and his wife in honor of the arrival of a new British ship, one characterized by "lavish hospitality in the dispensation of wines and spirits for which the Company was so justly celebrated."[46]

In Fort Victoria Douglas' authority relied on a racialized bourgeois identity, and his performance of it makes clear how complicated these

[45] See Anderson, "Notes and Comments on Early Days and Events in British Columbia," 153–154; James Deans to Mr. Monleith, May 12, 1878, in James Deans, "Settlement of Vancouver Island," BL, Bancroft MS, P-C 9, Mflm 1, 1–2.
[46] Anderson, "Notes and Comments," 152–153, 181.

identities could be in this and other parts of the nineteenth-century imperial world. Douglas had an obviously Indigenous family and was widely known to be of Caribbean birth and some iteration of Black. Simpson's "character book" described him as a "Scotch West Indian."[47] Tod, who began working with Douglas in 1834, wrote that he was "a native of the West Indies" whose "mother was a creole," though he also mistook Douglas' place of birth as Jamaica.[48] In the early 1840s Letitia McTavish Hargrave referred to Douglas as "*a mulatto* son of *the* renowned Mr Douglass of Glas^{ow}."[49] Observers also read Douglas through mobile languages of the British Empire and a particularly pliant language of Scottishness. A French man disinclined to credit the HBC with much identified Douglas as an intelligent and young "Scotchman."[50] This was the national identity that Douglas seems to have most often claimed for himself.

The more authority Douglas exercised the less he was read through the available racial optics. One American visitor to Fort Vancouver described him as "a shrewd & intelligent gentleman about 40 years of age tall & good looking with a florid complexion & black hair."[51] John Sebastian Helmcken, Douglas' future son-in-law, recalled meeting him in 1849, remembering him as a "dark-complecioned man – with rather scanty hair, but not too scanty – muscular – broad-shouldered – with powerful legs a little bowed – common to strong men; in fact he was a splendid specimen of a man."[52]

Whatever Douglas' colleagues made of his bourgeois sort of Blackness and ongoing kin ties to the Caribbean, they did not seem to make very much of them. In Rupert's Land and Oregon Territory, the primary racial and economic cleavages were between Indigenous and Europeans, broadly defined. Anxieties about racial mixture focused on people of mixed European and Indigenous descent, and where they might and might not fit within the economy of the fur trade. In this context, Douglas' iteration of Blackness did not merit much attention, disapproval, or surprise. He was able to access and make use of symbols of a racialized bourgeois respectability that were increasingly closed off to the

---

47 Simpson, "The 'Character Book'", 74.
48 John Tod, "History of New Caledonia and the Northwest-Coast," 1878, BL, Transcript, 46.
49 Letitia Hargrave to Mrs. Dugald Mactavish, 5 December 1842, in Macleod, ed., *The Letters of Letitia Hargrave*, 132, emphasis original.
50 De Mofras, in Pipes, "Extract from Exploration of the Oregon Territory," 157.
51 Edmond S. Meany, ed., "Diary of Wilkes in the Northwest," *Washington Historical Quarterly*, 16 (1925) 221.
52 Dorothy Blakey Smith, ed., *The Reminiscences of Doctor John Sebastian Helmcken* (Vancouver: UBC Press, 1975) 81 (hereafter Helmcken, *Reminiscences*).

Metis men he had long worked with and was related to through marriage. By the second third of the nineteenth century, he had an assured grasp on the privileges of Whiteness.

Douglas' connections to the Caribbean may not have been readily visible or of much interest to his observers, but his ties to Guyana left traces in the archive. He paid a bill for Miss C. Douglas, presumably his teenaged sister Cecilia, in 1830, and he covered her and her husband's expenses in the 1840s. In 1846, Cecilia wrote to the HBC, explaining her plans to return to the West Indies and that "My Brother Mr. James Douglas has authorized you to pay me annually the sum of thirty pounds to meet the expense of educating my Daughter." A year later, Douglas paid a bill in Demerara for an "A. Douglas," presumably his brother Alexander. Douglas was a dutiful older brother who used his resources to support his younger siblings who remained in the Caribbean, echoing the circumstances analyzed by historian Elizabeth Vibert in her study of siblings and transatlantic intimacy.[53]

There was no doubt where Douglas was situated or situated himself in the complicated racial schema of the fur trade. In his private papers, he explained "Indians" as a racial other that was located on a lower station in stadial theories of human and racial development. In 1840, he located Indigenous people within a global schema of racialized humanity, one that divided people into categories of civilization and savagery or barbarianism:

The North-American Indians, like all barbarians, possess a body of traditional history, or perhaps more properly speaking a patched medley of absurd fables interwoven with real events; some of these traditions I have collected, as they exhibit the unaided workings of the human mind, and illustrate the moral and social feelings of man in the earliest stages of ~~human life~~ savage life, when the untutored reason, darkened by ignorance is overcome by the fierce impulses of the passions, and the mere animal instincts given for the support and preservation of life hold absolute sway.[54]

Here Douglas wholly detaches himself from the people he describes, studies, and ultimately disparages. This reflects a radical sort of distancing from his own much-loved family and the people with whom he had

---

[53] Cecilia Cameron to Governor and Committee, March 19, 1846, HBCA A 10/21, folio 182, Mflm 71; James Douglas, "Private Account," BCA, Add MSS B/90/1; Elizabeth Vibert, "Writing 'Home': Sibling Intimacy and Mobility in a Scottish Colonial Memoir," in Antoinette Burton and Tony Ballantyne, eds., *Moving Subjects: Gender, Mobility, and Intimacy in the Age of Global Empire* (Chicago: University of Illinois Press, 2009) 67–88.

[54] James Douglas, "Journal of J. Douglas, 1840-1," HBCA E 243/6, Transcript, 81, crossing out in the original.

labored and lived since his teens. An adult life lived with and alongside Indigenous peoples did not prevent him from consciously adopting a dichotomous reckoning of humanity – first writing "human life," and then modifying it to "savage life" – and always placing himself firmly on one side of it.

Douglas remade himself within knowledges of race, and also those of class. The chief resources with which he seems to have entered the fur trade were the cultural capital of his Scottish lineage and his formal education. In the fur trade he found material wealth. In 1825, he began to keep detailed records of his annual salary, his debts, and his savings, subjecting his personal finances to the same kind of account-keeping that he performed for the HBC. This indicated the kind of prudent subjectivity critical to ideals of nineteenth-century bourgeois masculinity, and it also documented the growing personal wealth that backed it up. Douglas' wealth grew during his years at Fort Vancouver, and by 1839, he had more than £1,400 saved. He became a man of modest and regular charity. Beginning in 1830 he recorded modest donations made to a range of good causes, including the Catholic Church and the Bible Society, as part of his personal accounting. A few years later he began a separate "Charity Account" where he noted the small donations he made to individuals, churches, or to Fort Vancouver's Orphan Fund.[55]

Douglas entered middle age a relatively secure man in material terms. His location amongst the fur trade's elite was indicated by his status in the quasi-military organization, by his material resources, and by the resources and status accorded to his family. These included servants, a critical measure of class the transimperial world over, but with particular meaning in the fur trade. At Fort Vancouver, the officers shared a head servant, cooks, and waiters who kept the elite's "bed rooms and Halls in order." Douglas had another servant, a Canadian named Charifel. There, and in Fort Victoria, keeping the fort remained primarily the work of servants rather than wives. "An Indian woman came to wash and scrub, but even those who were well-to-do must cook and sweep, nurse and care for their children," Helmcken recalled. The "general work of the establishment" was the responsibility of HBC servants. These included a Kanaka man who cooked meals for the officers' mess.[56]

Women and girls demonstrated elite status in gendered terms. When Connolly Douglas relocated to Fort Nisqually for the summer in the

[55] James Douglas, "Private Account," BCA, Add MSS B/90/1, n.p. (hereafter Douglas, Private Account).

[56] "Social History of Victoria," Colonist, 50th anniversary supplement, December 13, 1908; Helmcken, Reminiscences, 282.

interests of her children's health, she traveled with two or three servants. The servants, the fact that the HBC clerk at Nisqually gave up his room for her, and her mode of travel all marked Connolly Douglas as an elite woman. "[S]he didn't come up in a canoe. Oh no!," remembered the clerk, Edward Huggins. "One of the steamers brought her." He remembered "Mrs. D." as a good-looking woman who "treated me very kindly."[57] At Fort Victoria, the teenage Douglas daughters wielded their access to and knowledge of female fashion over other members of the Metis elite. When Charlotte Eliza Anderson arrived there to attend school, she was dressed in a loose print gown, moccasins, and a "poke bonnet." "These were all pronounced by the Douglas girls as being quite out of fashion and a gown, or as we were told to call it, a dress, was made with a point in front and small straw bonnet obtained from the Sale Shop," Anderson's brother recalled.[58]

Douglas and Connolly Douglas' household and the arrangements that kept it spoke to their location within the fur trade's elite. At first at Fort Vancouver the family lived in intimate proximity to other officers' families, under "the same roof with only a partition between."[59] At Fort Victoria, increased status meant increasingly separate domestic space that gestured to if never quite met metropolitan norms for bourgeois domesticity. The photograph of Fort Victoria's interior in Figure 5.1 shows the residence of the chief factor to the left, and the bachelors' quarters and school dormitory to the right. The Douglas family's residence within the fort walls – recalled by one witness as "the largest house inside the stockade"[60] – marked their class status and distinguished them from the men who lived in the bachelors' quarters, the schoolchildren, and even the English chaplain and his wife, whose residences all were located in one long building. Fur-trade patterns of domesticity persisted for the family's first years at Fort Victoria. Spaces of home were spaces of work, and relations of family were relations of labor and of colonial administration. The space where Douglas worked was "partly an office and partly domestic" and Cecilia "assisted her father in clerical work, correspondence and so forth" and was, as her husband recalled, "in fact a private secretary."[61] The family lived mainly within the fort. It was within its walls that "poor little Rebecca Douglas" died in

---

[57] Edward Huggins to Eva Emery Dye, February 8, 1904, Edward Huggins, "Huggins Letters Outward 1899–1906 to Mrs. Eva Emery Dye, Joseph Huntsman," typescript (n.p., n.d.). Thanks to the Tacoma Public Library for making this available.

[58] Anderson, "Notes and Comments on Early Days and Events," 160.

[59] Ranald MacDonald to Mrs. E. E. Dye, July 24, 1892, Eve Emery Dye Papers, OHS, MS 1089, 2/5 (hereafter Dye Papers).

[60] Keith, "Fort Victoria in Pioneer Days."   [61] Helmcken, *Reminiscences*, 81.

Figure 5.1 Interior of Fort Victoria.

1849,[62] and where James William, Douglas and Connolly Douglas' only son to survive past early childhood, was born in 1851.

Here, as at Fort Vancouver, elite girls lived spatially limited lives shaped by expectations of bourgeois femininity, military practices, and presumptions of Indigenous threat. As an old woman, the chief trader's daughter, Jane Finlayson Keith, recalled the crisis provoked by her one childhood escape from the fort. Her father carried her to the platform atop the stockade to give her a "first glimpse of the outside world and the sea." Jane later ran away when the fort's keeper's back was turned, and "a hue and cry was raised within the fort and a successful search made for her." Fearsome ideas of an Indigenous other, one distinguished from the Indigenous people within the fort, were critical to keeping this child in her literal place. Here the presumed Indigenous other was "King Frizee," the name that traders and settlers used to refer to local Lekwungun leader Chee-ah-thluc, and to the men who followed him. Jane was told that

---

[62] Roderick Finlayson, "Fort Victoria Journal," entry for November 11, 1849, http://fortvictoriajournal.ca/, accessed July 15, 2012.

"if she ventured forth again from the protection of the stockade walls King Frizee might catch her."[63]

At both Fort Vancouver and Fort Victoria, Douglas used the mess as a space of teaching and socialization for the men under him. Former clerk George Roberts recalled Douglas using his own wardrobe to ensure that a guest was "presentable" at Fort Vancouver's mess. There Douglas schooled the men in a kind of bourgeois masculinity with global aspirations and distinct local meanings. "The decanters and fine English glass set off the table & made it look I suppose superb to those who had come across the country with hardly the commonest necessities," recalled Roberts. He recognized that Douglas' conduct and demeanor were designed to provoke emulation and do special disciplinary work. "I've often smiled at Douglas's behavior to teach us, honest Douglas, who had not been accustomed to show much outward respect to any one – his excessive politeness would extort a little in that way from them in return," he recalled.[64] Fort Victoria's mess hall was a similarly masculine, privileged, and instructional space. The British missionary was the only married man who did not dine in the mess, and meals "were served in military style at the mess table over which Mr Douglas presided."[65]

Cultures of reading went alongside those of manly dress, decorum, and manners. Douglas himself read seriously, and inventories of his books made in 1829 suggest that his effort to acquaint himself with a wider British imperial world anchored in European history was well underway even then. Then in his mid-twenties, he owned a forty-five-volume set of "The British Classics," a wide range of British newspapers and periodicals, seven volumes of Smollett's *Continuation of the History of England,* Buchan's *Domestic Medicine,* a French dictionary, a guide to grammar, and a grammar exercise book.[66] As Douglas aged and rose up the ranks, he shared the specific knowledge and general culture he gained from books. Helmcken remembered him sitting at the head of a table of more than twenty men and saying grace. After the meal he toasted "the Queen" and the junior officers left the table. The senior men then smoked and Douglas led them in a closely regulated conversation. "I was informed

[63] Keith, "Fort Victoria in Pioneer Days." On Chee-ah-thluc, see John Sutton Lutz, *Makúk: A New History of Aboriginal-White Relations* (Vancouver: UBC Press, 2008) Chapter 4.

[64] George B. Roberts, "Recollections of George B. Roberts," Bancroft Collection, BL, P-A 83, Mflm 2, 73.

[65] "Social History of Victoria," *Colonist,* December 13, 1908; Helmcken, *Reminiscences,* 283.

[66] "Inventory of My Effects Aug. 29th 1829," Douglas, Private Account.

that no frivolous conversation was ever allowed at table," recalled Douglas' son-in-law, "but that Mr. Douglas as a rule came primed with some intellectual or scientific subject, and thus he educated his clerks."[67]

Douglas' self-fashioning was not simply about accumulating material wealth, political authority, or raw status. It was also a cultural project that aimed to cultivate a sort of Christian, learned, and civic-minded subjectivity and reconcile it with the very different image of manly authority that went with the role of the fur-trade master. Recalibrating the class languages mapped by Leonore Davidoff and Catherine Hall in *Family Fortunes* to the very different context of the North American fur trade is a necessarily complicated project, one that was eased by the supple language of liberal humanitarianism. Historians such as Hall, Zoë Laidlaw, Alan Lester, and Elizabeth Elbourne have all traced the emergence of a liberal humanitarian thought that did not critique empire as much as it criticized *how* and *why* it was implemented. This sort of argument was critical to the abolition of slavery in the Caribbean, including in British Guiana, and to the attempted reform of settler colonialism in the Canadas and the Antipodes.[68] In the fur trade, liberal humanitarianism provided critics like Herbert Beaver with an expressive language with which to challenge the HBC's right and capacity to rule on Britain's behalf. From within the tissue of the HBC, Douglas made the liberal humanitarian thought that circulated around the imperial world his awkward and decisively colonial own and, in doing so, remade it.

In a private journal entry likely written at Fort Vancouver in 1837 or 1838, Douglas laid out his goals as a colonizer. He did so as a man newly remarried by Anglican ceremony and soon to be made chief factor. From this location he wrote down his four priorities for what he called "the place":

> The moral preservation of the place.
> Abolition of slavery within our limits.
> Lay down a principle & act upon it with confidence.
> To build a Church of Christ in this place.[69]

---

[67] Helmcken, *Reminiscences*, 284.

[68] Leonore Davidoff and Catherine Hall, *Family Fortunes: Men and Women of the English Middle Class, 1780–1850* (University of Chicago Press, 1987); Elizabeth Elbourne, "The Sin of the Settler: The 1835–36 Select Committee on Aborigines and Debates over Virtue and Conquest in the Early Nineteenth-Century British White Settler Empire," *Journal of Colonialism and Colonial History*, 4:3 (Winter 2003); Alan Lester, *Imperial Networks: Creating Identities in Nineteenth-Century South Africa and Britain* (London: Routledge, 2001); Catherine Hall, *Civilising Subjects: Metropole and Colony in the English Imagination 1830–1867* (University of Chicago Press, 2002).

[69] Douglas, Private Account.

Here was a set of goals that would not have been out of place in an abolitionist pamphlet, a newspaper article denouncing settler avarice, a magic lantern show documenting the supposed savagery of Indigenous peoples, or in any number of other pieces of popular culture from the imperial world of the 1830s or 1840s. In the lives of the Douglas-Connolly family and their friends, the ideals that circulated through the imperial world were thus brought to unevenly coexist with the quotidian imperial practice of the fur trade, including unfree labor, routinized violence, and imbrication with Indigenous societies, intimate connections, and social relations.

The "moral preservation" of Fort Vancouver was Douglas' first stated goal. The term moral was a capacious one in the nineteenth-century imperial world. It was associated with a number of things, including temperance. In the fur trade, liquor was a routine item of trade and exchange. It was also a critical part of conventional labor relations, demanded as part of men's daily labors and special celebrations. In the mid-1820s the HBC urged that "the use of Spirituous Liquors be gradually discontinued,"[70] but liquor continued to lubricate the fur trade in multiple ways. In the middle decades of the nineteenth century, the fur trade's use of liquor was increasingly challenged by a discourse that registered alcohol as something that exploited Indigenous people and cheapened those who traded with them and ruled them. As historian Jan Noel has shown, the temperance movement appeared but met an ambivalent reception in Red River Colony.[71] Further west, Douglas acknowledged the danger and destruction caused by liquor without committing himself or his administration to temperance. He gestured to the morality of temperance, but argued that liquor could not be eliminated. He explained that temperance, perhaps like free labor, was unsustainable within the particular colonial context of the fur trade. In 1846, he wrote to a newspaper serving Oregon's growing settler population that the liquor trade continued in spite of his opposition. If "my wishes could influence the community, there would never be a drunkard in Oregon," he declared.[72] Douglas' modest drinking was itself a statement. "I roomed in the same building & messed at the same table with Douglas & McLoughlin for years," recalled Roberts, and "I never saw anything but wine used."[73]

---

[70] "Minutes of Council, July 1824," in R. Harvey Fleming, ed., *Minutes of Council Northern Department of Rupert Land, 1821–31* (London: Champlain Society for the Hudson's Bay Record Society, 1940) 90.

[71] Jan Noel, *Canada Dry: Temperance Crusades before Confederation* (University of Toronto Press, 1995) Chapters 13–15.

[72] James Douglas, letter to *Oregon Spectator*, June 11, 1846.

[73] Roberts to Mrs. F. F. Victor, [no day] May 1879, in Roberts, "Letters to Mrs. F. F. Victor, 1878–83," 214.

The term "moral preservation" was also associated with the regulation and formal education of children. As it had for Douglas and other boys of color from the Caribbean, a European, British, or Canadian education could confer on Metis children some critical markers and resources in a complicated and sometimes unfriendly imperial world. In the 1830s and '40s fur traders knew that the cards were increasingly stacked against their children, and they fretted over how best to secure them a decent life in a world that was increasingly inhospitable to Indigenous people, including the traders' children. "Taking us altogether we are men of extraordinary ideas; a set of selfish drones, incapable of entertaining liberal or correct notions of human life," wrote Archibald McDonald from Fort Colville in 1832. "Our great password is a *handsome provision for our children.*"[74] Fur traders had long sent their children, and more especially their boys, across the Atlantic or east of the Great Lakes, and this strategy took on new urgency from the 1820s onward. Charles Ross considered his nine children "growing wild around me without proper education or example" his chief regret about a life lived in Fort McLoughlin. Later he would find the money to send three children, including one daughter, to England, but worried that he might never see them again.[75]

Establishing schools within fur-trade space was another critical piece of this project. The HBC had mixed results with earlier efforts to encourage the establishment of post schools, and they returned to this in the 1820s as part of the wider transition that followed the merger. Formal schooling, defined in explicitly imperial terms, became a critical part of efforts to recalibrate the HBC's particular form of imperial practice. The Council of the Northern Department argued that providing formal education for Metis children was a means of avoiding the expense and danger of supporting "a numerous population of this description in an uneducated and Savage Condition." It called for the creation of residential schools for both boys and girls at Red River, and demanded that men at the posts act as teachers and missionaries for their own Indigenous families. The regulations of 1827 asked that

As a preparative to Education that the mother and children be always addressed and habituated to converse in the vernacular dialect (whether English or French) of the Father and that he be encouraged to devote part of his leisure hours to

---

74 Archibald McDonald to Edward Ermatinger, April 1, 1836, in Cole, ed., *This Blessed Wilderness*, 112, emphasis original.
75 Charles Ross to Mrs. Joseph Macdonald, April 24, 1843, and Charles Ross to Donald Ross, January 10, 1844, in W. Kaye Lamb, ed., "Five Letters of Charles Ross, 1842–44," *British Columbia Historical Quarterly*, 7:2 (1943) 108, 111.

teach the Children their A.B.C. Catechism, together with such further elementary instruction as time and other circumstances may permit.[76]

    This sort of schooling was about remaking the social selves of adult women as well as children. At Fort Vancouver, elite men made a number of complicated arrangements for schooling their daughters, and in some case their wives and prospective wives. American missionary Narcissa Whitman spent the winter of 1836/7 at Fort Vancouver while her husband built a mission station at Walla Walla. She told her family that McLoughlin "has put his daughter in my care and wishes me to hear her recitations."[77] Douglas prompted his friend Tolmie to ask an American missionary family if they would accept Tolmie's prospective wife, Jane Work, as a boarder and pupil. Tolmie felt that "she would derive lasting benefit from a residence in your amiable family," one he valued especially for their missionary work among "the poor benighted natives."[78] Amelia Connolly Douglas received lessons from Douglas and from two American missionary women. "[S]he was never at school only what she got from husband and in 1835 Mrs Whiteman [sic] and Spalding kept a little school, and gave her lessons while they were there and that was all the schooling she got," recalled Sarah Julia Ogden McKinlay.[79]

    The fort school established at Vancouver represented a different set of imperial logics. In 1832 McLoughlin began a school "for the Good of the Native children in this Quarter."[80] Its first teacher was an itinerant American, followed by an assortment of HBC employees and Protestant missionaries who taught boys and girls English, grammar, and arithmetic, supervised their labor in the garden, and sometimes offered religious instruction. By 1837, there were around sixty students. Within a few years, the school had a dubious reputation. Despite "all their reformation & Christian improvement at the great Fort Vancouver, the young eleves are in a deplorable condition," McDonald explained. "The character of that Seminary is most extraordinary."[81]

---

[76] Brown, *Strangers in Blood*, 166; Minutes of Council, March 8, 1822 and July 1827, in Fleming, ed., *Minutes of Council*, 33–34, 230–231.

[77] "Diaries and Journals of Narcissa Whitman, 1836," www.isu.edu/~trinmich/00. ar.whitman1.html, accessed December 9, 2009.

[78] William Fraser Tolmie to Sir, n.d. [1838], in William Fraser Tolmie, *The Journals of William Fraser Tolmie, Physician and Fur Trader* (Vancouver: Mitchell Press, 1963) 332.

[79] Sarah J. McKinlay to Mrs. Dye, January 23, 1892, OHS 1089, 2/8, Dye Papers.

[80] John McLoughlin to Edward Ermatinger, February 1, 1836, Edward Ermatinger Papers, Volume III, HBCA, Transcript, E 94/3, 238.

[81] Francis Ermatinger to Edward Ermatinger, March 16, 1837, in McDonald, ed., *Fur Trade Letters of Francis Ermatinger*, 195; Archibald McDonald to Edward Ermatinger, January 25, 1837, in Cole, ed., *This Blessed Wilderness*, 121. See Stephen Woolworth,

Concerns about Fort Vancouver's school were in part gendered. To the dismay of at least one missionary, boys and girls were educated together and received a similar emphasis on manual, agricultural labor.[82] The school's apparent lack of interest in modeling ideals of bourgeois gender norms meant that it failed to live up to some of the core goals of colonial education. Its mandate was shaken further in the late 1830s when Douglas discovered that the American schoolmaster was "in the habit of taking advantage of the female part of his pupils." The disgraced teacher was flogged "in the most public manner twice." Frank Ermatinger declared that even this punishment was "not half severe enough for the villain. He ought to have been shot." As Juliet Pollard has shown, this crisis brought co-education to a close and ushered in a new emphasis on gendered propriety at Fort Vancouver.[83]

Douglas continued to try to build what he called a "respectable English school" for "children belonging to officers in the Company's service" at Fort Vancouver. In 1844 he had secured Simpson's support and was canvassing officers to pay part of the salaries of a "teacher and Governess."[84] As with marriage and intimacy, hybrid iteration emerged in the breach between rigid transimperial ideals and local circumstances. In 1845, Roman Catholic nuns were educating the girls at Fort Vancouver, and demonstrating, according to Douglas, "a surpassing degree of address, in the management of children."[85]

In these years Douglas parted company with the many Metis families who chose Roman Catholic education for their girls. In 1849 his family with Connolly Douglas "consisted of four daughters, yet of tender ages." The three eldest were placed at a school in Oregon City, a settler town that had grown in anticipation of the American takeover. There

"'The School is Under My Direction': The Politics of Education at Fort Vancouver, 1836–1838," *Oregon Historical Quarterly*, 104:2 (Summer 2003) 228–251.

[82] Herbert Beaver to A. C. Anderson, June 17, 1837, in Thomas E. Jesset, ed., *Reports and Letters of Herbert Beaver, 1836–1838, Chaplain to the Hudson's Bay Company and Missionary to the Indians of Fort Vancouver* (Portland: Champoeg Press, 1959) 56.

[83] Francis Ermatinger to Edward Ermatinger, February 26, 1839, in McDonald, ed., *Fur Trade Letters of Francis Ermatinger*, 215–216; Juliet Pollard, "The Making of the Metis in the Pacific North West: Fur Trade Children: Race, Class and Gender," unpublished Ph.D. thesis, University of British Columbia, 1990, 299–300.

[84] James Douglas to James M. Yale, November 4, 1844, and "Extracts of Sir George Simpson's Letter," enclosed, J. M. Yale, Correspondence, BCA, Transcript, BCA, MS 0182.

[85] James Douglas to George Simpson, March 5, 1845, in E. E. Rich, ed., *The Letters of John McLoughlin, from Fort Vancouver to the Governor and Committee, Third Series, 1844–46* (London: Hudson's Bay Company Record Society, 1944) 184.

fourteen-year-old Cecilia, ten-year-old Jane, and eight-year-old Agnes boarded with what Douglas called "a very respectable American Lady who is remarkably kind and attentive." In the local newspaper, Mrs. M. N. Thorton advertised that her "Female School" offered "everything usually comprised in a thorough English education" along with plain and ornamental needlework, drawing, and painting. "Strict attention will be given, not only to the intellectual improvement of the pupils, but also to their morals and manners," the school promised. It was the latter that impressed Douglas. He thought the cost of the school moderate, the system of education "sound and practical," and that his daughters benefited from exposure to the institutional framework of a bourgeois, colonial femininity that was not available at the fort. "They also enjoy the advantage of having a church and a most estimable Clergyman, Sabbath Schools, temperance and Juvenile Societies for the relief of the poor, and other aids which have an important influence in forming the character, and training children to virtue and usefulness," he explained.[86] In a climate where metropolitan education was increasingly seen as a necessary predicate to bourgeois life, Douglas was satisfied with, or perhaps defensive about, sending his daughters to a small school for girls in Oregon City. This could have reflected a number of factors, including the flexibility of his cultural strategies, Amelia's desire to keep her children close to home, and a patriarchal calculus of a father of girls.

The Douglas girls would continue to be educated close to home after the family relocated to Fort Victoria. Plans for a fort school that made separate provision for boys and girls at the new HBC Pacific headquarters were there from the start. But it was an Oblate priest who offered the first formal education at Fort Victoria, operating what was described as a "promising School, composed of the Wives and Children of the Companys Canadian Servants."[87] This would be gradually supplanted by the kind of school that Douglas had long requested, with separate provision for girls and for boys and no provisions for wives. In 1848, the HBC hired Cambridge-educated Robert Staines and his wife, Emma, for the job, rushing Staines to enter holy orders so he could serve Fort Victoria as chaplain as well. The school Staines and his wife commenced in 1849 was made up almost entirely of elite Metis students; in some

---

[86] James Douglas to Donald Ross, March 8, 1849, Ross Papers, File 39, Mflm 309; "Female School," *Oregon Spectator*, August 5, 1847.

[87] James Douglas to the Governor, Deputy Governor, and Committee, October 27, 1849, in Hartwell Bowsfield, ed., *Fort Victoria Letters, 1846–51* (Winnipeg: Hudson's Bay Company Record Society, 1979) 59.

cases their families were resident at the fort, while other students were sent there to board.[88]

Like Beaver before him, Staines provoked mixed responses from the fur-trade community he was sent to instruct and minister to. His class patina did not sit well with the fur-trade elite. Finlayson recalled him "as a man full of frill, as we say & liked display, kept a servant."[89] Another HBC man remarked that Staines would have made a better "Parish lawyer" instead of a "parish priest."[90] Predictably, Staines reckoned his place in Fort Victoria very differently. He wrote to his uncle in 1852:

> There is the school, the ministry, the Colony, my neighbours, strangers, English & Americans, the natives, helping Emma to make the bed, sending one of my pupils with an Indian servant to try to get meat for the day, trading venison, partridges, salmon, mats, blankets, berries, &c, &c, &c., with Indians, cutting up a deer, or a quarter of beef, or a sheep, teaching the Indians how to cook it, occasionally coming into the kitchen to see that all is going on right, preparing and mixing ingredients for soup, gardening, including fencing.[91]

Here Staines emphasizes the difference of colonial life, the multiple demands of his role as schoolmaster and missionary, and the disruption of expected gender roles and divisions of labor.

The work that Emma Staines did as schoolmistress took on particular meaning because of her status as the reputed "first English Lady" in the territory.[92] The female elite at Fort Victoria were overwhelmingly Indigenous, most of them born to as well as married into fur-trade families. Henry James Warre traveled undercover with a British team investigating newly expanded American territorial claims. He both admired and was confused by the Indigenous women and French-Canadian rituals of sociability he found at Fort Victoria in 1845. The men were given a

---

[88] See G. Hollis Slater, "Rev. Robert John Staines: Pioneer Priest, Pedagogue, and Political Agitator," *British Columbia Historical Quarterly*, 19:4 (October 1950) 187–240, and the list of students in James Robert Anderson, "Notes and Comments on Early Days and Events in British Columbia, Washington and Oregon, Including an Account of sundry happenings in San Francisco; being the Memoirs of James Robert Anderson, Written by himself," BCA, MS 1912, Box 9, Transcript, 158; Aurelia Manson, "Reminiscences and Recollections of School Days," April 1928, BCA, Add MSS EE M31, Transcript.

[89] Roderick Finlayson, "The History of Vancouver Island and the NorthWest Coast," BL, Bancroft MS, PC 15, 52.

[90] James Cooper, "Maritime Matters on the North West Coast and Affairs of the Hudson's Bay Company in early Times," BL, Bancroft MS, PC 6, 7–8.

[91] Robert Staines to Uncle Boys, July 6, 1852, in Thomas Boys to Earl of Desart, October 11, 1852, CO 305/3, http://bcgenesis.uvic.ca, accessed August 30, 2013.

[92] Alexander Caulfield Anderson, "History of the Northwest Coast," HBCA, E 294/1, Transcript, 48–49. On the Anderson family, see Nancy Marguerite Anderson, *The Pathfinder: A. C. Anderson's Journey in the West* (Victoria: Heritage House, 2011).

day off and a ball was held in honor of the visit, and visitors enjoyed "the gay and festive scene" of forty people dancing reels to the tune of a violin until past midnight. "Such an assemblage of Women I never saw, they were all Indian Women & dressed a l'European," Warre reported, deeming this "very good fun" and leaving the sketch of his dance partner shown in Figure 5.2.[93]

Emma Staines' status within this social world was predicated on small continuous acts separating her from the elite Indigenous women who lived within the fort. Her arrival demanded a shift in the physical space of the fort and the meanings it conveyed. She demanded to know "where the streets were," and the traders "put down what we could for her to walk on." Emma Staines established her distance from the elite Metis women at the fort, including Connolly Douglas. Helmcken recalled that she and "Mrs. Staines did not chum at all – there being too much uppishness about the latter, she being the great woman."[94] For Staines, as for White women engaged in the work of empire elsewhere, creating and maintaining a distinction between White women and elite women of color was a critical, demanding, and never complete or stable project.

But it was Emma Staines' work as a teacher of children that impressed her observers. "Mrs. Staines was a much more energetic person, she it was who really kept the school going and in spite of many undoubtedly adverse circumstances managed comparatively most creditably," remembered Anderson. Part of what she taught was the subtleties of imperial femininity. "I can see her now in my mind's eye, with a row of curls down each side of her angular face," Anderson continued, "by no means unprepossessing however, spare figure, clad in black a lady undoubtedly, and when walking out holding up her skirts on each side and ordering the girls to follow her example."[95] Emma Staines "really was the best schoolmistress ever seen since in Victoria," Helmcken reminisced a half-century later.[96]

If Douglas' first goal for Fort Vancouver was a project of moral preservation tethered to hybrid and local visions of temperance and formal education, his second goal was the seemingly more direct one of abolition. But applying this goal provides another example of how local colonial practice reworked the ideas that circulated through transnational circuits. The languages of slavery and anti-slavery were everywhere in

[93] Madeline Major-Frégeau, ed., *Overland to Oregon in 1845: Impressions of a Journey across North America by H. J. Warre* (Ottawa: Public Archives of Canada, 1976) 108.
[94] Helmcken, *Reminiscences*, 82, 120.
[95] Anderson, "Notes and Comments on Early Days and Events in British Columbia, Washington and Oregon," 159.
[96] Helmcken, *Reminiscences*, 144.

Figure 5.2 Henry James Warre, "My Partner at a Grand Ball Given at Fort Victoria, October 6th 1845."

the nineteenth-century imperial world, offering a powerful critique of the slave economies, societies, and politics, including those of what was by 1831 territorialized as British Guiana. Men who worked in the fur trade connected Indigenous and fur-trade practices of unfreedom to the transimperial language of slavery and abolition. Some noted the legislation that finally brought British slavery to a legal end and compensated owners like Douglas' mother, grandmother, and father. "You will see that Negro Slavery in the West Indies has received its death blow, to the tune of 'Twenty Million Sterling compensation,'" wrote one trader to another in 1831.[97]

Slavery was not just about another colonial "there" but also about the "here" of northern North America. Forms of unfreedom were shot through the fur trade. Enslaved Africans labored in fur-trade settlements, but most enslaved people were Indigenous. Some Indigenous North American societies, including those of the west coast, practiced forms of human unfreedom, often ones closely tied to warfare and military conflict and to a lesser extent to trade, and always profoundly gendered. At Fort Vancouver, McLoughlin tended to write about slavery as one of the many Indigenous practices that the fur trade was compelled by circumstance to accommodate. When escalating American criticism that preceded the takeover of HBC territory forced him to explain his policies around slavery, he stated that he aimed to discourage it in a piecemeal fashion. He informed slaveholders that "it is very improper to keep their fellow beings in Slavery," purchased and freed individual slaves, sought opportunities to "make them work, & pay them as other Indians when possible." But McLoughlin admitted that they were unable to "prevent Indians having Slaves," and had failed to "make the Servants Wives send their slaves away."[98]

It was Herbert Beaver, the Anglican missionary who escalated Fort Vancouver's integration into transimperial discourses on marriage and respectability, who also gave new and pressing weight to global languages of slavery and freedom. He read slavery here as he did intimacy: through eyes shaped by his own history in the Caribbean and a transimperial language of empire, its brutalities, and the challenges this posed to a secure British identity. "I have seen more real slavery in the short time

---

[97] Thomas Simpson to Ronald Ross, December 13, 1833, Ross Papers, File 200, Mflm 311.

[98] John McLoughlin to Captain Miners, September 8, 1830, Correspondence, Columbia District, HBCA, 1830, B 223/b/6; John McLoughlin to William Miller, March 24, 1845, in E. E. Rich, ed., *The Letters of John McLoughlin, Third Series, 1844–46*, 271, 275. Generally, see Leland Donald, *Aboriginal Slavery and the Northwest Coast of North America* (Berkeley: University of California Press, 1997); Brett Rushford, *Bonds of Alliance: Indigenous and Atlantic Slaveries in New France* (Chapel Hill: University of North Carolina Press, 2012); Jacqueline Peterson, "Many Roads to Red River: Métis Genesis in the Great Lakes Region, 1680–1815," in Jacqueline Peterson and Jennifer S. H. Brown, eds., *The New People: Being and Becoming Métis in North America* (Winnipeg: University of Manitoba Press, 1985) 37–72.

I have been here, than in the eight years and a half I was in the West Indies," the missionary wrote to London. Beaver drew attention to the same practices of bodily violence that abolitionists critiqued in the Caribbean. He argued that discipline at Fort Vancouver was enforced "by the use of the lash and the cutlass, supported by the presence of the pistol." He saw many kinds of unfreedom at Fort Vancouver, all of them cruel rebukes to his vision of what the British Empire should and might be. American critics of HBC rule used a different language, one that connected HBC monopoly and slavery, seeing them both as practices that invalidated British moral authority and claims to Oregon.[99]

At Fort Vancouver, Douglas tried to walk a course between these multiple languages of abolition and longstanding local practices of unfreedom. He distinguished his policy from that of McLoughlin, taking care to acknowledge the nobility of abolition and associating himself with it, writing that he was anxious to suppress "the traffic of slaves." Yet Douglas did not commit himself unequivocally to abolition. Writing to London, he explained that the "state of feeling among the Natives of this river, precludes every prospect of the immediate extinction of slavery." He proposed "the exertion of moral influence alone" amongst Indigenous peoples. With those whom he dubbed "our own people" – a grouping that would have included Indigenous employees and many families – Douglas leaned on the language of free-born British men and the HBC's juridical claims to be able to enforce it. It was within this political space that Douglas denounced slavery as contrary to law. He promised that this two-pronged policy of moral suasion would "greatly mitigate the evils of slavery," if not end it altogether.[100] He also made prosaic attempts to intervene in practices of unfreedom. A few years later, he would record the goods he spent "to ransom a slave," counting this as one of his charitable expenses.[101]

As he did with marriage, Douglas worked to reconcile global imperial discourses on slavery with local practices. By tying his administration to the promise of anti-slavery politics within the context of the fur trade, he associated himself with the liberal, humanitarian visions of empire that circulated around the imperial world. Within the particular context of

[99] Herbert Beaver to Benjamin Harrison, November 15, 1836, in Jesset, ed., *Reports and Letters of Herbert Beaver*, 21; Forsyth and Slacum, "Slacum's Report on Oregon, 1836–7," 188.

[100] James Douglas to Hudson's Bay Company, October 18, 1838, in E. E. Rich, ed., *The Letters of John McLoughlin, from Fort Vancouver to the Governor and Committee, First Series, 1825–38* (London: Hudson's Bay Company Record Society, 1941) 237, 238; "Editor's Note to Beaver's First Letter to Benjamin Harrison," in Jesset, ed., *Reports and Letters of Herbert Beaver*, n.p.

[101] Douglas, Private Account, September 11, 1840.

1830s and '40s Oregon, his cautious abolitionism was also couched in terms that situated British imperialism in a kind of superior opposition to American encroachment. Using the high-octane language of British race, nation, and anti-slavery within the ambivalent context of a fur-trade fort also gave Douglas another means to associate his own stock with an increasingly racialized fur trade, and to distance himself from the proximate Americans and, in a different way, from the Metis community that his marriage made him a member of.

Douglas' insertion of himself and his rule within liberal optics of empire was reinforced by his third goal, which was to "Lay down a principle & act upon it with confidence." To invoke the category of "principle" was to modify fur-trade practices of governance and decision-making which were notoriously pragmatic, improvised, and venal. When he promised principle, Douglas aligned his governance with a transimperial dialogue that asked that empire be motivated by *higher* callings. His additional commitment to act upon those principles with what he described as confidence repackaged *ancien régime* and Indigenous modes of fur-trade authority with the values of a nineteenth-century liberal imperial world.

The last promise that Douglas made to himself was "To build a Church of Christ in this place." Christianity was not a new pursuit for him. Since entering the fur trade he had himself been a faithful Christian and worked to bring formal Christian observance to the commercial and colonial spaces of the fur trade. At Île-à-la-Crosse it was the multilingual, twenty-year-old Douglas who led services in a largely French-speaking fort. His factor had found "an old French Prayer Book" and "resolved to read a few prayers in that language to the people of the Estate." Keith explained that "In consequence Mr. Douglas being well versed in the French Language and possessing a clear and distinct pronunciation was good enough to officiate and read a part of the French Litany and several Prayers, during which the greatest propriety and decorum was observed."[102]

Douglas would continue to do this kind of religious work at Fort Vancouver, developing a flexible Christianity that spoke English, French, and Chinook Jargon, and moved easily between Roman Catholic and Protestant iterations. He also read the Bible on board ship, though he was willing to overcome "religious scruples" and order the crew to work on Sunday.[103] He and William Fraser Tolmie, a newly arrived physician from Scotland, started a "sort of Sunday School for Indians of all ages" at Fort Vancouver, aiming "to teach them a prayer in their own language." In these years the family took little account of the presumed

[102] Île-à-la-Crosse Post Journal, October 31, 1824, HBCA 89/a, Mflm 1M64.
[103] Douglas, "Journal of J. Douglas, 1840–1," 21.

distinction between Protestantism and Roman Catholicism and associated itself informally and formally with the faith of Connolly Douglas and her kin. Beaver was perplexed and offended that Douglas, a professed Protestant, led Roman Catholic services to "the Frenchmen in their own language."[104] Certainly the Douglas-Connolly family challenge presumptions about the solvency of schisms between Roman Catholics and Protestants, and French and English speakers in nineteenth-century British North America. They remained marked as both Francophones and Anglophones and Roman Catholic and Protestant. Douglas and Connolly Douglas had been married by Anglican ceremony, but at least three of their children were baptized as Roman Catholics.[105]

At Fort Victoria, Douglas' brand of Christianity continued to be adaptable and local, straying far outside the institutional moorings that his metropolitan correspondents considered most important. After 1848, the schoolteacher and missionary held services in the vernacular space of the fort, as had Douglas before him. "The services were carried out at the Mess Room of the Fort, which was made to serve for about every purpose," remembered chief trader Roderick Finlayson.[106] "It is true that no Church or Chapel has been built," Douglas' superiors acknowledged in 1852.[107] Like his promised morality and abolition, the church that Douglas helped to build and the kind of Christianity he practiced looked little like anything easily recognizable as such across the Atlantic.

The fur trade was remade in the decades that followed the merger of 1821. Tracking these changes through the history of James Douglas, Amelia Connolly Douglas, and their family and kin suggests the power of these historical changes and the complicated and uneven trajectory they took. As many Indigenous men were squeezed out of the fur trade's elite, the authority held by James Douglas and the status extended to his family increased, whether measured in formal titles and jurisdictions or the less

[104] Herbert Beaver to Benjamin Harrison, March 19, 1838, in Jesset, ed., *Reports and Letters of Herbert Beaver*, 84, 74. Also see Eloise Harvey, "Life of John McLoughlin, Governor, of the Hudson's Bay Company's Possessions on the Pacific Slope at Fort Vancouver," 1878, BL, Bancroft Collection, PB 12, Mflm 2, 10–11.

[105] These were Jeanne (Jane), Marguerite (Margaret), and Rebecca. See Harriet Duncan Munnick, ed., and Mickell de Lores Wormell Warner, trans., *Catholic Church Records of the Pacific NorthWest: Vancouver, Volumes I and II and Stellamaris Mission* (St. Paul, OR: French Prairie Press, 1972) Vancouver I, 37th P B100; Vancouver II, 76, B561; Vancouver II, 40, 187; Vancouver II, 103, B7.

[106] Roderick Finlayson, "The History of Vancouver Island and the NorthWest Coast," BL, Bancroft Manuscript, PC 15, 53. Also see James Douglas to Archibald Barclay, May 27, 1853, "Sir James Douglas' Correspondence Book, 1850–1855," HBCA, Transcript, E 243/9.

[107] A. Colville to John Packington, December 1, 1852, CO 305/3, http://bcgenesis. uvic.ca, accessed August 30, 2013.

stable currencies of homes and servants. Liberal humanitarian discourse provided a useful way for Douglas to engage transimperial languages within the particular colonial spaces of fur-trade country. The extent to which ideals of morality, abolition, and Christianity were remade in the thick colonial histories of the fur trade reminds us of both the limits and the power of these discourses to shape local colonial societies, whether the one where Douglas was born or the one where he labored, married, fathered, and came to rule.

Empire changed in northern North America in the second half of the nineteenth century, and so did the intimacies that helped produce and maintain it. The relationships, households, and families formed by newcomer men and Indigenous women that worried and sustained the fur trade in the middle decades of the nineteenth century came to vex and confound the settler colonial and national projects that were created in what had been fur-trade and Indigenous space.[1] But as Angela Wanhalla's and Jean Barman's research makes clear, marriages between newcomer men and local women persisted within northern North American settler societies on both sides of the Rocky Mountains.[2] Some imperial intimacies even prospered within the revamped and reordered colonial societies that seemingly denied and often denigrated their existence. The family of James Douglas and Amelia Connolly Douglas is an example *par excellence* of the complicated trajectory that imperial intimacies could sometimes take within the fledgling settler societies of nineteenth-century northern North America.

This chapter examines the politics of intimacy in the Douglas-Connolly family during and following Douglas' years as governor of the British colonies of Vancouver Island and British Columbia. Douglas' political

[1] See Carol J. Williams, *Framing the West: Race, Gender, and the Photographic Frontier in the Pacific Northwest* (Oxford University Press, 2003); Jean Barman, "Aboriginal Women on the Streets of Victoria: Rethinking Transgressive Sexuality during the Colonial Encounter," in Katie Pickles and Myra Rutherdale, eds., *Contact Zones: Aboriginal and Settler Women in Canada's Colonial Past* (Vancouver: UBC Press, 2005) 205–227; Adele Perry, *On the Edge of Empire: Gender, Race, and the Making of British Columbia, 1849–1871* (University of Toronto Press, 2001); Sarah Carter, *Capturing Women: The Manipulation of Cultural Imagery in Canada's Prairie West* (Montreal: McGill-Queen's University Press, 1997); Sheila McManus, *The Line which Separates: Gender, Race, and the Making of the Alberta–Montana Borderlands* (Edmonton: University of Alberta Press, 2005).
[2] Angela Wanhalla, "Women 'Living across the Line': Intermarriage on the Canadian Prairies and Southern New Zealand, 1870–1900," *Ethnohistory*, 55:1 (Winter 2008) 29–49; Jean Barman, "Invisible Women: Aboriginal Mothers and Mixed-Race Daughters in Rural Pioneer British Columbia," in Ruth Sandwell, ed., *Beyond the City Limits: Rural History in British Columbia* (Vancouver: UBC Press, 2000) 159–179.

power and social influence, the family's wealth and status, and the shifting interests and technologies of colonial states mean that these histories can be parsed with some precision and detail. Births, marriages, and deaths that were of little interest to the colonial state in Demerara or to the creators of early nineteenth-century fur-trade records came under the sustained scrutiny of various states. Shifting practices of communication and shifting class locations combined to produce a different sort of private archive. Some members of the Douglas-Connolly family wrote letters, kept diaries and journals, and some of these were preserved. Family histories that had been unknown, uninteresting, or unspeakable became points of pride, or at least record.

In this chapter I capitalize on these archives and narrow my focus to the immediate family of Douglas and Connolly Douglas almost exclusively. I begin with their Victoria house, some of the meanings it held, the labors required to keep it, and the roles it played. I then turn to Douglas and Connolly Douglas' marriage and the political work it did and did not do in settler Victoria. Finally, I examine some of the ways in which power and care circulated within the family and household, analyzing relations of affect and authority between husbands and wives, and parents, grandparents, and children. The histories mapped here remind us of the pervasive authority of nineteenth-century ideals about the appropriate roles for women, men, and children, and about how they were bent and remade in local colonial contexts. Practices of gender and family became important tools through which this particular colonial family laid a powerful sort of claim to the empire that had produced them.

In the 1830s Douglas and Connolly Douglas had renegotiated the legal and religious terms of their relationship in response to the changing colonial context in fur-trade North America. As the fur-trade Pacific was redefined as a kind of settler space under Douglas' authority in the 1850s, they revamped their domestic space. When Douglas was appointed governor of Vancouver Island in 1851, the family moved out of the fort into their first home that would be legible as such within sentimental metropolitan discourse. When the governor, his wife, and their five children moved into a private house in Victoria's James Bay neighbourhood, they confirmed the connection between bourgeois domestic space and imperial authority. Domestic space was a key terrain for the simultaneous performance of colonial governance, gender, and domesticity throughout the British Empire. As Bruce Curtis has shown, Lord Durham's "suite" was critical to his particular brand of political theater in mid-nineteenth-century Canada. Charlotte Macdonald has likewise discussed how domesticity was central to the kind of imperial authority mobilized by George Selwyn, first Bishop of Aotearoa/New Zealand, and his wife,

Sarah.[3] Unlike the Selwyns or the Durhams, the Douglas family did not reconstitute their domestic space in unfamiliar social terrain. Like their intimate relationship, their house was a localized product of thick histories that included but never simply reproduced mainstream, bourgeois imperial norms and expectations.

The Douglas' Victoria house was a tangible sign of the family's wealth and power, one that took care to articulate its ties to the metropole. But it was also a marker of Douglas' decision to live out his life within northwestern North America. In 1851, he wrote to an old fur-trade friend: "I have now almost abandoned the hope of being able to return to the civilized world and begin to think seriously of settling in this country." By this he meant Victoria, newly reorganized as a provisional and aspiring settler space. Here was the tentative but meaningful infrastructure of settler colonialism, with Indigenous territory divided into saleable lots under control of the Crown. "I have lately purchased a bit of land in this neighbourhood and have laid the foundation of the first private house in the Town of Victoria," Douglas went on to report, admitting that it would cost a "great deal of money" but be a "refuge in time of need."[4] The house cost £1,000 to build from local logs, and the same to fit it out with imported British furnishing. These included two cushioned mahogany armchairs "made in England and shipped out to Victoria by sailing vessel round the Horn."[5] It was "considered to be a very grand affair and the most up-to-date house in the Colony."[6] Surrounded by "a large old fashioned garden with borders of flowers and enclosing squares of fruit trees & vegetables,"[7] the Douglas house kept its ground

3 Bruce Curtis, "The 'Most Splendid Pageant Ever Seen': Grandeur, the Domestic, and Condescension in Lord Durham's Political Theatre," *Canadian Historical Review*, 89:1 (March 2008) 55–88. Also see Mark Francis, *Governors and Settlers: Images of Authority in the British Colonies, 1820–60* (London: Macmillan, 1992); Ian Radforth, *Royal Spectacle: The 1860 Visit of the Prince of Wales to Canada and the United States* (University of Toronto Press, 2004); Charlotte Macdonald, "Between Religion and Empire: Sarah Selwyn's Aotearoa/New Zealand, Eton and Lichfield, England, *c*.1840s–1900," *Journal of the Canadian Historical Association*, 19:2 (2008) 43–75.

4 James Douglas to James Hargrave, January 23, 1851, Library and Archives Canada, Hargrave Collection, MG 19 A21.

5 Margaret Orsmby, "Introduction," in Hartwell Bowsfield, ed., *Fort Victoria Letters, 1846–1851* (Winnipeg: Hudson's Bay Company Record Society, 1979) LXXXVII; Dorothy Blakey Smith, ed., *The Reminiscences of Doctor John Sebastian Helmcken* (Vancouver: UBC Press, 1975) 119, and fn. 2 (hereafter Helmcken, *Reminiscences*); "Fort Victoria in Pioneer Days, 70 Years Ago" recalled by Mrs. J. C. [Finlayson] Keith, *The Daily Province* (Vancouver) January 24, 1925.

6 James Robert Anderson, "Notes and Comments on Early Days and Events in British Columbia, Washington and Oregon, Including an Account of sundry happenings in San Francisco; being the Memoirs of James Robert Anderson, Written by himself," British Columbia Archives (hereafter BCA), MS 1912, Box 9, 181.

7 Sophia Cracroft in Dorothy Blakey Smith, ed., *Lady Franklin Visits the Pacific Northwest: Being Extracts from the Letters of Miss Sophia Cracroft, Sir John Franklin's Niece,*

Figure 6.1 The Douglas home, Victoria. On the veranda are Amelia Connolly Douglas and her brother, probably Henry Connolly.

as the colonial city grew around it. (See Figure 6.1.) Martha, the family's last child, was born there in 1854. The house and its gardens would continue to impress. "The Governor has a *very* nice garden with gravel walks w:h looked quite *clean!*," enthused a British woman new to the colony in 1858. "He gave us some roses, heart[s] eases &c. & some *splendid* Apples."[8]

In these years the house and gardens required Connolly Douglas' labor and were the site of much of her and her children's lives. Newly mobile and powerful ideas about the sacred character of domestic space and women's and children's place within it gave meaning and weight to the longstanding association of elite women and children with spaces set aside from the business of the fur trade and, more profoundly, from the people and spaces around it. In 1868, Douglas reported that his wife

from February to April 1861 and April to July 1870 (Victoria: Provincial Archives of British Columbia Memoire, No. 11, 1974) 24 (hereafter Smith, ed., *Lady Franklin Visits*).

[8] Mary Moody to Dearest Mother, December 25, 1858, Mary Susanna[h] (Hawks) Moody, "Correspondence Outward," BCA, Add MSS 60, Transcript, emphasis original.

seldom left the house and garden.[9] Martha Douglas recalled the family's garden with affection and made clear how her childhood movements were contained within its limits. "As children we were not allowed out of these boundaries unless accompanied or riding or driving," she recalled.[10] Adults, horses, or carts needed to stand between the Douglas children and the "public" space of what had become a small colonial city. The substance of women's and children's lives was contained within this domestic space. Adult men had less at stake in it. They could and did move between the world of home, the local colonial society of Victoria, and a wider continental and transimperial world that could be accessed by letters, through newspapers, and by travel across the mountains, down the west coast, or, less frequently, by lengthy and complicated journeys to the metropole.

Douglas' role in the household reflected the complicated location of husbands and fathers within bourgeois households and the practices of local colonial rule. As a number of historians have argued, mid-nineteenth-century discourses on appropriate bourgeois family life gave a greater role to men as both husbands and fathers than easy iterations of "separate spheres" often assume. Douglas paid attention to household work and expenses, keeping track of the family's purchases of food and household goods.[11] He had an abiding interest in the produce of the family's ample gardens, and his personal correspondence is punctuated by remarks about the year's pears, apples, or strawberries.

But Douglas' domestic presence was limited by more than the expected conventions of bourgeois gender norms in the 1850s and '60s. As chief factor and then governor of two colonies, one at a significant distance, he was certainly absent from home for substantial periods of time.[12] It was after his retirement that he became more present within and more observant of the James Bay household, gardens, and the people within them.

---

9 James Douglas to Miss [Jane] Douglas, July 13, 1868, "Private Letter Book of Sir James Douglas, Correspondence Outward, March 22, 1867–Oct. 11, 1870," BCA, Add MSS B/40/2, Transcript (hereafter Private Letter Book).

10 Martha Harris, "Reminiscences of her Early Life in Victoria, Including Notable Victoria Families," in Martha (Douglas) Harris Collection, Diaries, etc., BCA, Add MSS 2789, Box 1, File 12, 1.

11 See clippings in "British Columbia – Governor (Douglas), Correspondence Outward (Miscellaneous Letters), 30 November 1859–8 December 1863," BCA, C/AB/10.4/2 (hereafter Douglas Correspondence, 1859–1863). On men and "separate spheres," see John Tosh, *A Man's Place: Masculinity and the Middle-Class Home in Victorian England* (New Haven and London: Yale University Press 1999); Lynne Marks, "Railing, Tattling, General Rumour and Common Fame: Speech, Gossip, Gender and Church Regulation in Upper Canada," *Canadian Historical Review*, 81:3 (September 2000) 380–402.

12 See the Fort Victoria journals, 1846–1850, http://fortvictoriajournal.ca/, accessed July 25, 2012, for a daily account that includes Douglas' comings and goings.

"[F]or the truth is there is no busier man than me," he wrote in 1870. He liked the outdoor work, and complained that it was "confinement, writing and all desk work that wearies disconcerts and quite unhinges me."[13]

The unpaid labor of wives and daughters allowed this domestic world to function. Helmcken recalled that Connolly Douglas in these years was a "very active woman, energetic and industrious."[14] She was still busy two decades later. In 1873, Douglas reported to Martha: "Mamma busy getting things put to rights."[15] A jaundiced British observer thought that the two grown-up Douglas daughters living at home in the early 1860s took advantage of their mother's labor, reporting that the daughters "make her do all the domestic work, while they sit in the Drawing room doing nothing."[16] Family archives offer a different picture, speaking to other children's awareness of and appreciation for Connolly Douglas' household labor. "I suppose you have made all your jams and jellies by this time. I wish I was there to help you," wrote an adult Jane to her mother in the summer of 1861.[17] The gardens, the fruit trees, and the poultry that surrounded the James Bay house all commanded Connolly Douglas' attention and care. A rare surviving note offers thanks for a gift of chickens, and explains that "I am really very proud of my fowls, and take great interest in their management" and offers apples in exchange. The apple trees were grown from the seeds originally sent from England to Fort Vancouver and then to Victoria, a sign of global connections.[18]

Maintaining the house and producing food were domestic labors that Connolly Douglas performed with pleasure and an eye to cementing relations of kin and friendship. Fresh food was a material sign of care and affect. Connolly Douglas and Cecilia sent Douglas a basket of vegetables, turkey, and fresh butter when the business of rule took him away from Victoria.[19] "Mamma is now busy with preparations for Christmas,"

[13] James Douglas to Jane Dallas, May 5, 1870, Private Letter Book.
[14] Helmcken, *Reminiscences,* 120
[15] James Douglas to Martha Douglas, August 13, 1872, in James Douglas, "Letters to Martha Douglas," October 30, 1871 to May 27, 1874, Transcript, BCA B/40/4A (hereafter Letters to Martha).
[16] Sam Anderson to my dearest Janet, April 14, 1860, Samuel Anderson Papers, Correspondence, 1859–1862, WA MSS s-1292, Box 1, Folders 17–20, Beinecke Rare Book and Manuscript Library, Yale University, New Haven, CT, Transcript. Thanks to Eva Wrightson for her assistance in accessing this.
[17] Jane Dallas to Amelia Douglas, August 9, 1861, Helmcken Family Fonds, BCA, Add MSS 505, Volume 14, File 9, Transcript (hereafter Helmcken Papers).
[18] Amelia Douglas to Mrs. Pritchard, undated, Private Letter Book; Anderson, "Notes and Comments," 153.
[19] James Douglas to Cecilia Douglas Helmcken, April 29, [1860], Helmcken Papers, Volume 14, File 2.

explained Douglas in 1872. "Turkies and no end of fouls [*sic*] are being slaughtered, and as for cakes, mince meat, puddings &c their number is Legion." A granddaughter, a son-in-law, and six friends would be joining them, and the meal was served by a man who left his farm for the purpose.[20]

Like bourgeois households around the imperial world, the Douglas-Connollys' practices of domesticity were predicated upon the paid labor of servants. In 1857, daughter Cecilia reported her mother's complaint that it was hard for one person to manage the rooms and basins.[21] A decade or so later twelve-year-old Martha Douglas "ordered" a man named Edward to bring her lunch.[22] Servants worked the garden as well as the house. A "very skilful old man named Thomas" laid out the Douglas gardens and others tended them. By the late 1860s Douglas was ambivalent about the cost of household labor. "I am remodelling my establishment," he explained, reducing household staff and replacing the gardener with "hired men" in the interests of not "keeping a regular staff of idle drones."[23]

The ways that race structured relations of household labor in this family changed alongside histories of colonialism, migration, and labor within the local context of Victoria. In the 1850s and for much of the 1860s domestic workers were almost all Indigenous. "Indians performed all manual labor," reminisced a settler who had grown up in Victoria.[24] As a married woman Cecilia Douglas Helmcken relied on an Indigenous man and later a married couple for assistance. "Of course the most of the work had to be done by self and wife," her husband would explain, "but the Indians were very useful for chopping wood, carrying water, and doing odd jobs."[25] This local practice of domestic labor shared much in common with others around the imperial world, and reminds us of the limits of analyses of North American colonialism that implicitly or explicitly presume its exceptionality. Here Indigenous labor was appropriated and incorporated within the households of the local elite.

---

[20] James Douglas to Martha Douglas, December 21, 1872, Letters to Martha.

[21] Cecilia Helmcken to Jane Tolmie, March 17, 1857, Helmcken Papers, Volume 14, File 2, Transcript.

[22] Martha Douglas, Diary, February 24, 1867, 51.

[23] Harris, "Reminiscences," 1; James Douglas to Jane Dallas, March 9, 1868, Private Letter Book.

[24] Edgar Fawcett, *Some Reminiscences of Old Victoria* (Toronto: William Briggs, 1912) 84; "Social History of Victoria," *Colonist*, 50th anniversary supplement, December 13, 1908. On Indigenous people and wage labor in nineteenth-century British Columbia more generally, see John Sutton Lutz, *Makúk: A New History of Aboriginal–White Relations* (Vancouver: UBC Press, 2008) especially Chapter 6.

[25] Helmcken, *Reminiscences*, 127, 130.

In the later 1860s, patterns of dispossession and trans-Pacific labor migration meant that Chinese men came to replace Indigenous men and women in elite Victoria households. The 1871 census found a Chinese man, almost certainly a servant, living in the Douglas household and a few years later they had Ang, described as a "most useful man." Ang and other Chinese male servants did household labor that elsewhere was considered women's work, including polishing door handles and stoves in manners deemed satisfactory or not.[26] In 1881, the widowed Connolly Douglas shared her house with a widowed daughter, a married daughter and her husband, and a total of five grandchildren. They had three servants: Ah One, a forty-year-old cook, Ah Soa, a sixteen-year-old gardener, and Jessie Catherine, an eighteen-year-old nurse.[27]

The Douglas house was a family residence and a space of agricultural production. It was also a space of sociability for a wider social network. At its core were kin and friends of long duration, many of them elite families connected to the fur trade. As the numbers of settlers in and around Victoria increased following the Fraser River gold rush and the creation of the mainland colony of British Columbia in 1858, this circle expanded to include selected newcomers. This was a distinctly domestic sort of sociability, but not one that reflected a straightforward embrace of the bourgeois ideology of "separate spheres" as much as it was a recalibration of older fur-trade practices to the demands of the settler society emerging around them.

Within the space of the household Connolly Douglas loomed large. She was part of dinner parties "en famille." "Mrs. Douglas came to dinner," reported a British guest in 1859: "Seems a good old sole soul."[28] Connolly Douglas played games popular in mid-nineteenth-century middling circles with family and friends, enjoying bataille and receiving a gift of a backgammon board from Douglas in 1866.[29] The impression she left on children and grandchildren was especially vivid. "We had a jolly Christmas dinner," reported a granddaughter in 1868. "Uncle Cameron and all our family dined with Grandmamma we had so much turkey and chicken we could not eat any plum pudding."[30]

---

[26] Entry for Jas. Douglas, 2091, "Victoria Municipal Census of 1871," www.vihistory.ca, accessed July 23, 2012; James Douglas to Martha Douglas, May 6, 1873; James Douglas to Martha Douglas, March 5, 1873, Letters to Martha.

[27] Canadian Census of 1881, family 466, www.vihistory.ca, accessed July 10, 2009.

[28] Dorothy Blakey Smith, ed., "The Journal of Arthur Thomas Bushby, 1858–1859," *British Columbia Historical Quarterly*, 11 (1957/8) 131.

[29] Martha Douglas, Diary, January 3, 1866, BCA, E/B/H24A, Transcript, 1.

[30] Aimee Helmcken to Jane Dallas Douglas, February 14, 1868, Helmcken Papers, Volume 1, File 17.

Figure 6.2 "Composite" portrait of Amelia Connolly Douglas and James Douglas, with their daughter Martha Douglas Harris' artwork embellishing the image.

Her children and grandchildren recalled Connolly Douglas with admiration and love. Martha Douglas Harris created the portrait of her parents shown in Figure 6.2, merging two separately composed portraits and adding affectionate and naturalistic illustrations. "My Mother was of course my first love," Martha Douglas Harris explained.[31] Connolly Douglas offered children and grandchildren knowledge as well as affection. In 1901, Douglas Harris published a small book that carefully recounted her mother's teaching without clearly naming the "Folk Lore of Cree Indians" as such. "As a little girl I used to listen to these legends with the greatest delight," she recalled, explaining to her audience that these legends were best expressed in the "quaint songs and sweet voice that told them."[32] In the middle of the twentieth century Martha's and Cecilia's own children recalled their grandmother's energy, kindness, and her careful transmission of oral tradition. "She wasn't at all frail," they explained, recalling that the children "always went to say good-night to Granny before we went to bed – we looked forward to it; she told such wonderful stories, mostly Indian legends."[33] The archival fragments left by children and grandchildren recall Connolly Douglas as a competent woman who loved and was loved in return, and whose Indigenous knowledge was both a resource and a pleasure.

Connolly Douglas' intimate bonds stretched beyond her immediate family to include elite Metis families who had settled in Victoria after long years in the fur trade. As Sylvia Van Kirk has shown, by mid-century, the Works, Tolmies, Finlaysons, and Tods shared thick personal histories and dense and multiple points of connection.[34] Connolly Douglas' most active ties of friendship were to elite Metis families who had had thick mutual histories made up of roughly equivalent genealogies, and, more

---

[31] Douglas Harris, "Reminiscences," 2.

[32] Martha Harris Douglas, *History and Folklore of the Cowichan Indians* (Victoria: Colonist Printing and Publishing, 1901) n.p., 7–8, 121.

[33] From a "conversation" with James Chichester Harris and "Cecilia's granddaughter" from April 1957, in Marion B. Smith, "The Lady Nobody Knows," in Reginald Eyre Watters, ed., *British Columbia: A Centennial Anthology* (Toronto: McClelland and Steward, 1958) 480–481. Also see K. A. Finlay, "*A Woman's Place*": *Art and the Role of Women in the Cultural Formation of Victoria, BC 1850s–1920s* (Victoria: Maltwood Art Museum and Gallery, 2004) 108.

[34] Sylvia Van Kirk, "Tracing the Fortunes of Five Founding Families of Victoria," *BC Studies*, 115/116 (Autumn/Winter 1997/8) 148–179; Sylvia Van Kirk, "Colonised Lives: The Native Wives and Daughters of Five Founding Families of Victoria," in Alan Drost and Jane Samson, eds., *Pacific Empire: Essays in Honour of Glyndwr Williams* (Melbourne University Press, 1997) 215–236; Sylvia Van Kirk, "A Transnational Family in the Pacific North West: Reflecting on Race and Gender in Women's History," in Elizabeth Jameson and Shelia McManus, eds., *One Step over the Line: Toward a History of Women in the North American Wests* (Edmonton: University of Alberta Press, 2008) 81–93.

to the point, a long shared experience of cramped quarters within fort walls, long journeys, and itinerant lives stretched over North America and sometimes beyond. Connolly Douglas and an adult daughter spent at least one day "paying visits" to Josette Work and her married daughter and granddaughter in 1873.[35] "Mrs. Work and my Mother were the most loving friends," Martha recalled, remembering her as "Such a loving friend, so true and sympathetic, and stood by my dear Mother on many sad occasions."[36] This intimate and multigenerational community of fur-trade women was what Peter Pambrum's daughter Maria missed. She stayed in Oregon, and wrote wistfully to Cecilia Douglas Helmcken in Victoria: "I am unable to express the pleasure I feel in hearing from my Dear friend I feel as if I could put on my Bonnet and run over to see you but my heart saddens when I perceive that happiness is beyond my reach."[37]

Care for vulnerable and needy bodies – the birthing, the newly born, the ill, and the dead – marked these ties of kin and friendship. Amelia "nursed" Cecilia before she died following childbirth.[38] Twice Connolly Douglas went to stay with her daughter Alice in New Westminster when she had a new baby, and it was only Douglas' opposition to her traveling in winter that prevented her from making the same trip to be with Agnes and her newborn.[39] Martha remembered her mother being resolutely in command of the care given to the dead. "I can see the scene now, my Mother taking charge and putting the servants to work and performing the last sacred offices for the dead. No strange hands touched our dead," she proudly recalled.[40] Relations of care extended beyond immediate family. Mrs. Tod came to help Cecilia when her babies were young, and Amelia too went to friends in times of illness, childbirth, and death. "Mamma goes out very seldom," wrote Douglas in 1873, but "she went the other day to call on Mrs. Work, who has not been well lately."[41]

Connolly Douglas sometimes moved beyond the circle of elite Metis families to make connections with settlers who arrived in Victoria from the late 1850s onward. A White woman who grew up in Victoria recalled playing in the Douglas' yard and her mother and Connolly Douglas "chatting on the verandah."[42] Relations of sociability were anchored in

---

[35] James Douglas to Martha Douglas, October 24, 1873, Letters to Martha.

[36] Martha (Douglas) Harris, "Reminiscences," 3.

[37] Maria Barclay to Cecilia Helmcken, n.d., Helmcken Papers, Volume 14, File 2.

[38] Helmcken, *Reminiscences*, 214–215.

[39] Martha Douglas, Diary, September 18, 1866, 34 and June 18, 1867, 63; James Douglas to Agnes Bushby, December 30 [no year], Private Letter Book.

[40] Harris, "Reminiscences," 1–2.

[41] James Douglas to Martha Douglas, May 6, 1873, Letters to Martha.

[42] Susan Crease, "Personal Recollections," Crease Family Papers, BCA, Add MSS 55, Box 13, File 3/2–4, 214–215.

the generosity and mutual obligations of care. "She was very kind to outsiders," recalled Helmcken about his mother-in-law in the 1850s, "visited them when ill, and in fact nursed them more or less." Connolly Douglas making one newcomer woman "kneel down at the bedside" during childbirth was long remembered for its efficacy.[43] The informal social ties forged with newcomers in the early years of colonial Vancouver Island would diminish in the early 1860s, or at least become less legible in the colonial archive. That they did so suggests the complicated work that the Douglas Connolly marriage performed during and after the years of Douglas' governorship.

In the past two decades feminist historians of empire have shown how marriages were key to the making, maintenance, and sometimes unmaking of empire in its various iterations. Douglas and Connolly Douglas' marriage was struck within the particular colonial context of the fur trade and persisted in a revamped colonial order, showing how intimate ties that were constituent to one articulation of empire could be selectively incorporated into new configurations of governance, settlement, and rule. Connolly Douglas was the chief trader's wife, the chief factor's wife, the governor's wife, the Lady to his Sir, and finally the grieving widow of a celebrated local hero. The authority of this marriage and Connolly Douglas' place in it were not seriously compromised by the history of their relationship or by Connolly Douglas' unavoidable Indigeneity. The alterity of the governor's marriage was instead registered in the less stable but still real currencies of social authority, spatialization, and status. In settler Victoria, Connolly Douglas' wifehood was cautiously exercised, carefully monitored, and sternly evaluated. This was especially the case at the height of Douglas' political authority in the late 1850s and early 1860s.

By most standards, the recalibration of intimacy that Connolly Douglas and Douglas undertook alongside other elite Metis couples in the 1830s worked. Douglas became chief factor and then governor, and there was no real doubt that his was a marriage by the terms that so often invalidated imperial intimacies. When Douglas was granted positions and titles, Connolly Douglas accrued the honorifics usually accorded to wives. A handed-down account of the dinner at the Douglas home in recognition of Douglas' being named to the Order of the Bath upon his retirement from the colonial service has Matthew Begbie, the colony's justice, raising a toast "To our esteemed hostess, Lady Douglas," described as "the wife of the Governor of British Columbia, and the first lady in the land."[44] When Douglas died in 1877, Amelia was recognized as

---

[43] Helmcken, *Reminiscences*, 118.

[44] N. de Bertrand Lugrin, *The Pioneer Women of Vancouver Island, 1843–1866* (Victoria: Women's Canadian Club, 1928) 23.

his grieving widow.[45] The local newspaper noted the particular durability of their marriage, writing that Douglas and Connolly Douglas had been "married fifty years."[46] The solemnity of their marriage was both acknowledged and empowered by formal legal codes and less formal names and practices.

The titular and formal recognition the Douglas marriage received did not save it from being an enduring matter of interest, comment, and discussion in settler Victoria. Some observers accorded the governor's mixed-race marriage positive meaning and explanatory value. In 1862 Malcolm Cameron, an improving Canadian politician who was no fan of the governor, told a Montreal audience that Douglas "had read deeply, studied human nature profoundly, and had succeeded in winning the confidence of the Indian tribes, had married a half-breed, a fine, sensible, and intelligent woman, he had a beautiful and excellent family, and himself practised a noble hospitality."[47] A British naval officer whose father had known Douglas turned the story of his marriage into a cookie-cutter colonial romance, writing in 1909 that Douglas' wife "was herself an Indian princess, and his saviour from death at the hands of her people." "Here lay his romance," John Moresby intoned, reworking the story of Douglas' 1828 conflict with Kwah at Fort St. James to include "a horde of maddened Indians" and "like Pochahantas herself, an Indian girl, the daughter of a chief" who "lived to share his honours" and, as Moresby explained, "to become Lady Douglas, wife of the Governor and Commander-in-Chief of British Columbia."[48]

The marriage could stand for colonial romance, and also for a particularly British practice of North American imperialism. As the United States consolidated its authority over Oregon and Washington territories to the south of British Columbia, this would increasingly seem noteworthy. Caroline Leighton, an American woman who passed through Victoria, argued that Douglas' decision to marry Connolly Douglas by Christian rite and British law was a policy choice of sorts, one imbedded in a set of aesthetic and political decisions that separated British and American practices of empire. Douglas "lives at Victoria in a simple, unpretending

---

[45] See, for instance, "Memorial of Condolence to Lady Douglas on the death of her husband, 1877," in James Douglas, "Miscellaneous Honours," BCA, Add MSS 112, File 5; "The Death of Sir James Douglas," *Colonist*, August 4, 1877.

[46] "Reminiscences of the Late Sir James Douglas," *Colonist*, August 8, 1877.

[47] Malcolm Cameron, *Lecture Delivered by the Hon. Malcolm Cameron to the Young Men's Mutual Improvement Association* (Quebec: G. E. Desbartes, 1865) 14; Margaret Coleman, "Cameron, Malcolm," in *Dictionary of Canadian Biography*, Volume X, University of Toronto/Université Laval, 2003, www.biographi.ca, accessed July 28, 2012.

[48] Admiral John Moresby, *Two Admirals: Admiral of the Fleet Sir Fairfax Moresby, GCB, KMT, DCL (1786–1877) and his Son, John Moresby* (London: John Murray, 1909) 122.

way," she reported. "It was made a law in British Columbia, that no White man should live with an Indian woman as wife, without marrying her. He set the example himself, by marrying one of the half-breed Indian women."[49] Leighton was wrong: there were no laws demanding marriage. There was, as Renisa Mawani and others have shown, an array of extra-legal tools worked to criminalize or more subtly pathologize relationships forged across purported racial lines. But Leighton's characterization did gesture to some enduring differences about the work marriage and race did in American and British territory, most clearly symbolized by the presence of laws preventing marriage across perceived racial lines to the south of the border, and none to the north of it.[50] By associating national, imperial, and legal cultures and presenting British Columbia as a different and more admirable form of North American colonialism, Leighton anticipated an ideological maneuver that would become a well-worn and highly usable feature of settler Canadian discourse and identity.

These readings of the governor's marriage give weight to Damon Salesa's analysis of the complicated politics of racial crossing around the nineteenth-century British Empire. "Racial crossing was not only ground for discursive contests," he argues, "but an illustration of the unevenness and particularity of how discourses circulated and were distrusted."[51] We might explain the endurance and authority of the Douglas marriage by a chain of extraordinary circumstances, most notably Douglas' political authority as governor, the family's considerable wealth, and the fickle choices of a far-away and a not very interested imperial government. But perhaps we do not need to search for a tidy explanation as much as we need to nuance the narrative we tell about race and respectability in the nineteenth-century imperial world. The Douglas-Connolly family was unusual, but hardly *sui generis*. It was one node in a wider network of bourgeois Metis peoples whose histories and wealth were associated with the fur trade but who persisted in the settler societies of Victoria, Red River, and in smaller numbers in the Canadas and Scotland. Local histories and geographies of empire both produced these families and framed how they were understood long after models of

---

[49] Caroline C. Leighton, "Diary of Caroline C. Leighton, December 1868," in *Life at Puget Sound, with Sketches of Travel in Washington Territory, British Columbia, Oregon & California* (Boston, MA: Lee and Sheppard, 1884) 76.

[50] Renisa Mawani, *Colonial Proximities: Crossracial Encounters and Judicial Truths in British Columbia, 1871–1921* (Vancouver: UBC Press, 2009); Jean Barman, "What a Difference a Border Makes: Aboriginal Racial Inter-Mixture in the Pacific Northwest," *Journal of the West*, 38:3 (July 1999) 14–24; Peggy Pascoe, *What Comes Naturally: Miscegenation Law and the Making of Race in America* (Oxford University Press, 1991).

[51] Damon Ieremia Salesa, *Racial Crossings: Race, Intermarriage, and the Victorian British Empire* (Oxford University Press, 2011) 236.

governance and economic practices ceased to define the territories they operated in.

Newcomers attracted by the promises of gold rushes or settlement associated elite Metis marriages with the particular histories and practices of the fur trade, and consigned this to an earlier time and a different model of colonialism. But these gestures could not and did not wholly retool the discourses through which non-Indigenous observers read and accessed marriages like that of Douglas and Connolly Douglas. Around the imperial world, the middle decades of the nineteenth century witnessed a hardening and proliferation of languages that subtly and unsubtly derided and caricatured relationships made across perceived racial lines. In the local context of Vancouver Island and British Columbia, Indigenous dispossession and imperial repossession was ongoing, ever present, palpable, and far from secure. Douglas' marriage was a readily available and reliable weapon in the hands of some of his critics. Powerful discourses about the capacity of imperial intimacies to strip men of their racial and civilizational authority were put into play when a working-class British woman complained about Vancouver Island's administration in 1854. Douglas' long residence in North America and his Indigenous wife were to her indications of poor and disreputable government. The governor, she wrote,

has been in the Company out here ever since he was a boy about 15 years of age and now he is a man upwards of 60 now – so you may say he has been all his life among the North American Indians and has got one of them for a wife. So how can it be expected that he can know anything at all about governing one of England's last Colony's in North America.[52]

This was the sort of pliant racial thinking that could be accessed by people with very different locations in imperial hierarchies. A decade later, a visiting naval officer, Edmund Hope Verney, wrote home to his father, a man well connected to improving metropolitan circles. Verney complained that Douglas conversed openly with a man who lived in "open adultery with an Australian woman," arguing that "this was all very well in the days of the Hudson's Bay company, when they encouraged their servants to co-habit with native women to keep up trade, but now it shocks refined people," including, presumably, Verney. He was offended by Douglas' willingness to acknowledge people whose intimate lives stretched bourgeois metropolitan standards, and by everything that Douglas' wife represented, embodied, and spoke. "Mrs. Douglas is a

[52] Annie Deans to My dear Brother and Sister, February 29, 1854, Annie Deans Correspondence, BCA, E/13/D343.

good creature, but utterly ignorant: she has no language, but jabbers french or english or Indian, as she is half Indian, half English, and a French Canadian by birth," Verney explained. He thought Vancouver Island deserved a different governor, one with "enlightened feelings and ideas, and a lady for his wife."[53]

These racial and gendered languages were powerful ones that could produce effects the opposite of those intended. In 1863 the New Westminster newspaper critiqued Douglas' postal policies, one of a handful of enduring issues guaranteed to raise settler ire. This time, the newspaper made its point by linking Douglas and his family with the specter of savagery and one of the hoariest and best-traveled of imperial tropes, the harem:

Complaint, remonstrance and agitation seem alike to have lost their effect upon the thick skin of our model autocrat, who, snugly ensconced in his harem at James' Bay during ten or eleven months in the year, complacently folds his arm, and employs a savage delight in witnessing, from his island retreat, the agonizing contortions of the poor, helpless victims of his tyranny.[54]

But putting a more decorous version of well-worn ideas about marriage, gender, and race into a newspaper column prompted opposition rather than applause. Readers took special umbrage at the suggestion that Douglas was anything other than a model man, husband, and father. Journalists responded by comparing harems to ladies' compartments on ships, and by arguing that the newspaper had "never been prostituted as a medium for attacking any man's private character or domestic arrangements." While admittedly "severe enough upon Mr. Douglas politically, in his public capacity," the paper felt compelled to state that they had "ever expressed the highest estimation of his private character and worth as a gentleman, a husband and a father."[55]

Rather than critiquing who she was, others attacked Connolly Douglas' performance of elite femininity, focusing on what she did or failed to do. In the 1860s observers routinely noted her absence from what they reckoned as "society." The settler society that developed in Victoria was symbolized by a string of predictable markers in imperial and political histories: the building of a legislative building, the operation of courts, trials, and the law, and the proclamation of a far-away imperial government. It was substantiated and regulated by a modest calendar of balls, banquets, theater, and the like. These events and occasions did the

---

[53] Edmund Hope Verney to Harry Verney, July 20, 1862, in Allan Pritchard, ed., *Vancouver Island Letters of Edmund Hope Verney, 1862–1865* (Vancouver: UBC Press, 1996) 75.
[54] "The Postal Department," *British Columbian*, January 21, 1863.
[55] "Harem," *British Columbian*, January 24, 1863.

sort of critical but never clearly defined work that historian Penny Russell argues was performed by manners in colonial Australia.[56] If there was any doubt about how these events regulated social inclusion and exclusion, protracted struggles over the right of African-American settlers to sit in the "dress circle" of the theatre, and where they chose in Protestant churches confirmed it.[57]

Where the governor and his wife fit within this settler elite was complicated and, in important ways, insecure. Douglas was governor, and the presumed social as well as political leader. But he and his wife were also routinely absent from the social events that were key to constituting and legitimating this authority. Douglas' archive is rich in notes begging off invitations for himself and, more often, his wife. In 1863, Douglas agreed to have dinner with a naval officer, but explained that "Mrs. Douglas prays you to excuse her non-appearance on that occasion, as she is not very well at present, and seldom, even when in good health, ventures so far from home."[58]

The female social authority usually accorded to elite wives and mothers was instead delegated to younger female kin. The Douglas daughters sometimes acted as escorts and hostesses and Douglas' Guyanese niece, Cecilia Eliza Cowan Cameron, was given important duties and responsibilities within the household. Douglas had paid for her schooling near Cologne, Germany in 1846,[59] and five years later put her presumably genteel training to use when Cowan Cameron came to live in the Douglas family home in Victoria and was invested with social and moral authority over it. Douglas "brought a niece with him to instruct him and his wife and daughters in the ways of the fashionable world, of which she was supposed to be a habituée," Verney explained with typical derision.[60] Helmcken recalled Cowan Cameron's role as a more familial one. He remembered the cousin assisting in his courtship with Douglas' second-eldest daughter, noting that it was Cowan Cameron who "played propriety."[61] Cowan Cameron's role in the Douglas household persisted after her marriage in the late 1850s to W. A. G. Young, colonial secretary

[56] Penny Russell, *Savage or Civilised? Manners in Colonial Australia* (Sydney: New South Books, 2010).

[57] Crawford Killian, *Go Do Some Great Thing: The Black Pioneers of British Columbia* (Vancouver: Douglas and McIntyre, 1978) Chapter 5.

[58] James Douglas to Admiral Kingcome, August 11, 1863, Victoria Correspondence Book, 1859–1864, HBCA, E 243/10, Transcript.

[59] Cecilia Cameron to Hudson's Bay Company, March 19, 1846, HBCA, A 10/21.

[60] Edmund Hope Verney to Harry Verney, July 20, 1862, in Pritchard, ed., *Vancouver Island Letters*, 74. Also see Anderson, "Notes and Comments on Early Days and Events in British Columbia, Washington and Oregon," 282–283.

[61] Helmcken, *Reminiscences*, 120.

of both Vancouver Island and British Columbia, and one of Douglas' trusted underlings. Verney wrote that by "virtue of Mrs. Douglas being a half-breed, and her daughters quarter-breeds, Mrs. Young considers herself, and is considered by many, the leading lady in the island."[62] The Youngs helped the Douglas daughters when Jane Franklin and her traveling companion, Sophia Cracroft, visited Victoria, planning and helping to host the lunch the British visitors had with Connolly Douglas "in place of paying her a formal visit."[63]

Members of the transimperial elite who reported on Victoria in the 1850s and '60s often noted that Connolly Douglas did not take on the social and political performances expected of the wives of men holding colonial office and associated this failure with her identity as an Indigenous woman. George Hills was appointed bishop of the new Anglican diocese, and in 1860 he explained that "Mr. Douglas' wife is a half caste between Indian & Canadian. She seldom appears but is I understand an amicable person."[64] Cracroft saw a similar connection between Indigeneity, its meanings, and feminine sociability. "Have I explained that her mother was an Indian woman, & that she keeps very much (far too much) in the background." Cracroft was willing to credit the governor's wife with some core womanly virtues, but not with the desirable and expected commodity of bourgeois female authority. "She has a gentle, simple & kindly manner which is quite pleasing," she conceded, "but she takes no lead whatever in her family."[65]

These sorts of comments were made chiefly by British newcomers, and they are best read like other colonial archives, as productive rather than reflective of the worlds they represented. Remarks about Connolly Douglas' absence did not record a rigidly racialized settler society defined through the exclusion of women of color and local intimacies as much as they worked to bring it into fuller realization. To describe Connolly Douglas as absent required an unwillingness or inability to see Victoria's elite Metis community and its constituent events, including the weddings that Connolly Douglas attended along with her husband and daughters.[66]

---

[62] Edmund Hope Verney to Harry Verney, July 20, 1862, in Pritchard, ed., *The Vancouver Island Letters*, 74–5; James E. Hendrickson, "Young, Sir William Alexander George," in *Dictionary of Canadian Biography*, Volume XI, University of Toronto/Université Laval, 2003, www.biographi.ca, accessed September 2, 2010.

[63] Smith, ed., *Lady Franklin Visits*, 22.

[64] George Hills, "Bishop Hills Journal, 1 January–25 June 1860," Archives of the Ecclesiastical Province of British Columbia, University of British Columbia, Vancouver Theological School, January 6, 1860, Transcript, 4.

[65] Smith, ed., *Lady Franklin Visits*, 22–24.

[66] James Douglas to Martha Douglas, October 6, 1873, Letters to Martha; Douglas Harris, "Reminiscences," 8.

It also required a revealing unwillingness to acknowledge the roles that Connolly Douglas did serve within the parts of settler Victoria's public sphere that were open to bourgeois women. Connolly Douglas may have been a modest participant in settler Victoria's public sphere, but she was there. She was the official "patroness" of Victoria's Female Aid Association in 1864 and appeared at a church opening with a married daughter a year later.[67] Along with her family, she attended an Anglican church where a private rented pew made clear the family's elite status. In September 1873 Douglas reported that "she has attended Divine service for the last three Sundays. She loves the House of god to sing his praises and to hear the glad tidings of salvation."[68]

Connolly Douglas' public persona grew following her husband's retirement from colonial service. She was an active force in the Female Infirmary for the Sick and Destitute of All Denominations,[69] doing the kind of charitable work that was considered appropriate for bourgeois women elsewhere in British North America. She participated in some of the social events that were expected of wives of colonial officials. Vancouver Island's new governor and his daughters paid Amelia a visit in 1866, leaving a gift of a pheasant feather for the family's youngest child.[70] In the same year, Connolly Douglas went to the first ball given by incoming British Columbia governor, Frederick Seymour. In 1876, she attended a dinner with the visiting Canadian governor general and his wife, and a ball marking the same.[71] When Jane Franklin returned to Victoria in 1870, her niece was surprised that Connolly Douglas invited their party, which included the current governor, inside. "She was very cordial, & I am sure much pleased to see my Aunt, & vexed that Sir James was out," Cracroft explained.[72]

Widowhood brought further growth in Connolly Douglas' public persona. For her, as for many women in British North America, widowhood was a time of relative independence and engagement in a wider social world. The portrait in Figure 6.3 shows her in the full

[67] "Female Aid Association," *Colonist*, March 26, 1864; Helmcken, *Reminiscences*, 214–215.

[68] Fawcett, *Some Reminiscences of Old Victoria*, 150; James Douglas to Martha Douglas, September 16, 1873, Letters to Martha.

[69] Christ Church Cathedral, Victoria, Journal, Proceedings of the Ladies' Committee re the restoration of the Parish Church and Cathedral, 1869–1871, 1876–1885, "Christ Church Cathedral Collection," BCA, Add MSS 520, Box 1, Folder 7. Also see Helmcken, *Reminiscences*, 214.

[70] Martha Douglas, "Diary, January 1 1866–April 3, 1869," BCA, E/B/H24A, Transcript, October 16, 1866, 36 (hereafter Martha Douglas, Diary).

[71] "The Ball at the Government House," *Colonist*, December 13, 1866; "Grand Ball at Government House," *Colonist*, September 19, 1876; "His Excellency's Programme," *Colonist*, August 16, 1876; "At Home," *Colonist*, August 22, 1876.

[72] Smith, ed., *Lady Franklin Visits*, 118.

Figure 6.3 Amelia Connolly Douglas in widow's weeds.

regalia of nineteenth-century middle-class widowhood. In these years she was one of six "lady patronesses" of the ball held to benefit the British Columbia Benevolent Society, was engaged in the work of the Christ Church Cathedral women's group, and, after her family left that church, became active in their new church, serving as the regular president of fairs held by "Ladies of the Reformed Episcopal Church."[73] As a widow Connolly Douglas came into her own as a hostess. What became known as "Lady Douglas' grounds" was the site of church fetes and what was deemed a "brilliant reception" in 1887.[74] When she died in 1890 the newspaper celebrated her "unvarying kindness and her unostentatious Christian charity ministering to thousands."[75]

That Connolly Douglas' role in settler Victoria seemingly expanded following her husband's retirement and then death likely reflects something about the internal economies of their relationship as well as the codes of respectable bourgeois womanhood. That she was an elite Indigenous woman and that their marriage was first sanctified by fur-trade custom structured the sorts of political meanings their marriage could and did carry in settler Victoria. But this was not the only set of histories that shaped their marriage or how it was evaluated. Comments about Connolly Douglas' absence from Victoria's society are too simple, and like so much of colonial discourse, helped constitute what they purported to merely describe.

The domestic and family life of the Douglas-Connolly family is only occasionally visible in the newspapers that recorded the activities of Victoria's modest public sphere. It is more visible in the private records left by White and elite Metis people, and a central concern of the private archive that Douglas created in the 1860s and '70s. Affection, approval, and disapproval circulate unevenly through the letters sent and received and journals kept and preserved. Expectations for nineteenth-century bourgeois gendered roles were often repeated and sometimes enforced. At other times, ideals of appropriate roles for girls and boys and mothers and fathers were reworked and recast. Douglas died in 1877, leaving a will that both reaffirmed the authority and material power of the British Empire's particular flavour of patriarchy and selectively and tellingly modified it.

---

73 "A Charity Ball," *Colonist*, November 16, 1879; "Proceedings of the Ladies' Committee re the Restoration of the Parish Church and Cathedral, 1869–71, 1876–85," BCA, Add MSS 520, Box 1, Folder 7; "Grand Fancy Fair," *Colonist*, October 2, 1879; "Ladies Bazaar," *Colonist*, March 21, 1881.

74 "The RE. Garden Fete," *Colonist*, June 14, 1887; "Ball," *Colonist*, January 29, 1887.

75 "Death of Lady Douglas: Another of Victoria's Earliest Pioneers Passes Away," *Colonist*, January 9, 1890.

Connolly Douglas may have been an ephemeral presence in the public life of settler Victoria, but she was a vivid presence in the letters her husband wrote to friends and family. Douglas described his wife with a combination of exasperation and love. He chided her for the interest she took in poultry. "The chickens, now fill her mind with anxious cares, and we all look grave and appear to sympathize, if mishaps occur. To laugh, would be a a [*sic*] serious offence," he wrote to their youngest daughter.[76] Douglas thought his wife was overly concerned with her own health and her ego too easily bruised. "I may tell you in confidence," he wrote to another daughter, "that Mammas health is not so bad as she thinks: – but you must be careful not to say so to her for she will be deeply offended if you do."[77] Douglas also wrote about Amelia with affection. He described a wedding party they had attended, Connolly Douglas in a fawn silk dress, a white and blue shawl and bonnet. "Mama looked wonderfully youthful for a Lady of 62," wrote a seventy-year-old Douglas.[78] An earlier literature stressed the economic dependencies between newcomer men and Indigenous women in the fur trade. Here it is the complicated currencies of affect that sustain and animate a relationship of more than forty years' duration and where relations between husband and wife are negotiated in part through their shared responsibility for children and grandchildren.

But this was never only about immediate family. In these years the house in James Bay was often home to an extended family. Douglas' sister and her family and later adult children, spouses, and grandchildren shared domestic space with the immediate family. The family reckoned kinship in flexible ways that made room for relations by marriage. When his daughters married, Douglas knitted their spouses into his reckoning of kin, calling his three favoured sons-in-law "sons," employing no distinction between children by marriage or by birth.

Like marriage, relations between adults, children, and grandchildren were other critical points of intimate connection lived at the juncture of global ideas and local articulations of empire. Douglas and Connolly Douglas lived with and cared for children all of their adult lives. They raised their six surviving children and played a significant role in the childhoods of at least seven grandchildren. After Cecilia Douglas Helmcken died in childbirth in 1864, her three children were a regular presence at their grandparents' home and were in essence raised alongside the two youngest Douglas children. Martha, the youngest Douglas

[76] James Douglas to Martha Douglas, April 15, 1874, Letters to Martha.
[77] James Douglas to Jane Dallas, February 22, 1869; Private Letter Book.
[78] James Douglas to Martha Douglas, October 6, 1873, Letters to Martha.

daughter, remained in the family home after her marriage. Two of her sisters returned to James Bay with their children when death or separation made them lone mothers. Alice Douglas Good brought her children to live at her parents' house after her marriage fell apart, and Douglas and Connolly Douglas were pleased she did. "It is so delightful to find oneself at home again with the dear Parents," Alice wrote, "they received me so kindly – I found our darling Mother at the door in tears & felt as tho' I could forever hug & kiss her."[79] When her sister Agnes Douglas Bushby was widowed a decade later, she made a similar move.

If cultural precedence and continuity can explain some of the Douglas-Connolly family's configuration in these years, it cannot explain much. The maintenance of strong ties between grandparents and grandchildren and matrilocal patterns of residence are all part of Cree, Metis, and Afro-Caribbean kinship practices.[80] But the Douglas-Connolly extended family, shown at home in Figure 6.4, was not simply a straightforward continuation of tradition. Douglas may have spent his early childhood among his mother's extended kin, but he was separated from them at a tender age. Connolly Douglas lived with her parents and siblings in Indigenous territory until the early years of her marriage, but she did so within the particular culture of the fur-trade fort and likely far away from her maternal kin. The extended family household that Connolly Douglas and Douglas maintained from the 1860s to the 1890s was thus not a seamless maintenance of any one tradition as much as an amalgamation and reinvention of multiple traditions in a very different colonial context.

A practice of family and kinship that emphasized active and frequent residential ties between adult children and parents and between grandchildren and grandparents conflicted with the sorts of mobilities expected of elite bourgeois children in the second half of the nineteenth century. Douglas wanted his children to be members of a transimperial elite, and this required extended stays in the metropole, but he also wanted them to stay near home. He pushed his children to leave Victoria and mourned their absence and worried about them when they did so. It was in the years between the youngest children's departures and the return of adult

---

[79] "Sister Alice," in James Douglas to Martha Douglas, January 24, 1872, James Douglas to Martha Douglas, May 1, 1873, Letters to Martha.

[80] See, on patterns of matrifocality and extended kin in the Caribbean, Raymond T. Smith, *The Matrifocal Family: Power, Pluralism, and Politics* (New York: Routledge, 1996). On Cree–Metis kinship, see Jennifer S. H. Brown, "Women as Centre and Symbol in the Emergence of Metis Communities," *Canadian Journal of Native Studies*, 1 (1983) 39–86.

Figure 6.4 Amelia Connolly Douglas, children, grandchildren, and great-grandchildren.

daughters that he was most bereft. "My own House is now almost a solitude," he explained in 1862, with one "little daughter" at home and a son far away.[81]

For all this anxiety, Douglas knew that the demands of transimperial parenting exacted their stiffest emotional costs from his wife. To have few children at home was "a privation which Mrs. Douglas feels with even more sensibility than myself."[82] Connolly Douglas certainly cherished her children's proximity and worried about their distance. The prospect of a married daughter returning home was a comfort to a woman "who is always delighted to see her daughters near her." Children far from home were a source of multiple anxieties. Connolly Douglas worried that Jane Douglas Dallas' Scottish home would catch fire.[83] She worried about the risks of travel, of strangers, and of climate when her youngest daughter

---

[81] James Douglas to Arthur Bushby, November 24, 1862, James Douglas, "Letters," BCA, Mflm 246A (hereafter Douglas, Letters).

[82] James Douglas to Arthur Bushby, November 24, 1862, Douglas, Letters.

[83] James Douglas to James William Douglas, February 4, 1869; James Douglas to Jane Douglas Dallas, October 19, no year [1868], Private Letter Book.

was sent to England for schooling. When Martha left home her mother had "a burst of incontrollable grief" and sobbed and called for her child. In 1872, Douglas both acknowledged and derided his wife's anxieties about England and the risks it held for their daughter:

Mamma is very well & has a cry now & then about her dear Martha. She is afraid people won't take good care of her, that she won't keep herself warm, in short that the cold climate of England will be the destruction of her health: – then there is the risk of travelling by rail, of being upset in boats & of foundering at seas, in ships & being buried deep, deep, deep under the dark green waves; all these things cause her endless disquiet...[84]

For all of Douglas' sarcasm, the anxieties that Connolly Douglas felt when children moved to the metropole were hardly inexplicable. Within this particular family and the local colonial elite more generally, children routinely went away and never returned. The core promise of metropolitan education was social mobility and transformation, one predicated on a radical spatial separation between elite colonial children and their maternal kin and the spaces of their birth and early years. Douglas was himself one of those children, and his own history made Connolly Douglas' "endless disquiet" about children far from home entirely explicable.

The shared but profoundly unequal terrain of parenting shaped how Douglas and Connolly Douglas responded to their children and grandchildren and structured their own intimate relationship. Douglas sometimes referred to his wife as Mrs. and later Lady Douglas, but more often as Mamma, placing her identity as a mother above that of a wife or individual with a given name. He could be awed by the strength of Connolly Douglas' maternal feelings, such as when his wife received a photograph of a child far from home. "What a scene ensured on unfolding the precious gem," he wrote. "Mamma was in exstacies [sic], kissing it...as if you had been here yourself to receive her endearments, and after a time went off in a burst of tears." For Douglas, this was evidence of the ferocity of maternal affect: "Oh the depth of a mothers love, who but a mother can conceive its power and intensity."[85]

The flip-side of Douglas' admiration of his wife's maternal feelings was a predictable and misogynistic sort of distrust and recrimination. He was confident about his wife's ability to raise girls but thought her affectionate mothering had failed their only son to survive infancy. "James is still a sad disorderly boy," he explained in 1868. He credited this to the fact

[84] James Douglas to Martha Douglas, August 13, 1872; James Douglas to Martha Douglas, February 12, 1872, Letters to Martha.
[85] James Douglas to Martha Douglas, January 24, 1872, Letters to Martha.

that the teenager "was never before taught habits of order & regularity." Douglas was relieved that his son was now under the jurisdiction of his eldest sister and hoped that Jane's "training" would impart the habits that their mother had presumably failed to. When Douglas' niece bore a son, he used his own family as a cautionary story that illustrated the dangers of affectionate mothering. The baby would naturally be "a great pet," and if "Mamma is not very wise and careful," he would "become a thoroughly spoilt young gentleman, just as my own James was by his doting Mamma."[86]

For all his criticism of his wife's gentle ways with children, Douglas himself opposed adults' managing children through physical force and blunt authority. This was a rejection of accepted practice in much of the formal schooling around the imperial world and of practices of discipline within the fur trade. In letters, Douglas urged James William's teachers to earn his son's respect and compliance rather than demand it. He wrote that the "success of his future training will be greatly influenced by the kind feeling with [sic] he may entertain for his Teachers, whether in fact he regards them in the character of friends or oppressors."[87] Douglas might threaten James Helmcken, a mischievous grandson, "with the ropes end" but he was disinclined to follow through. When the boy smashed a dozen panes of glass "by way of amusement," the punishment was "no gift on Xmas day." Douglas declared that "Master Jimy is certainly a pickle & requires looking after,"[88] but the sort of "looking after" Douglas himself offered rejected the violence that was so critical to the fur trade and his own practice within it.

The stories of fathers, grandfathers, and children in this archive suggest some of the ways that practices of fatherhood were lived and perhaps redefined in this particular bourgeois context. It is unlikely that Douglas took responsibility for much of the daily care of his own children, especially the older ones raised when he held demanding positions in the fur trade and colonial service. As a retired man with a considerable income and a flexible schedule, he was an engaged, affectionate, and controlling presence in the lives of his younger children and nearby grandchildren. He spent time riding and walking with them, and paid close attention to their development, manners, and potential. The noise and chaos that children brought to the household still held the power to surprise. He found his grandson Harry Good loud and his granddaughter Helen Good

[86] James Douglas to Jane Douglas Dallas, December 2, 1868; James Douglas to Edith Cameron Doughty, October 22, 1869, Private Letter Book.
[87] James Douglas to Henry Doughty, April 30, 1862, Douglas Correspondence, 1859–1863.
[88] James Douglas to James William Douglas, February 4, 1869, Private Letter Book.

bright but restless. "It is impossible to keep her quiet, for ten minutes together even in my stern presence," he reported.[89]

Douglas' paternal affection was animated by enduring memories of the seven children who died as babies or young children. Had this family been a community or nation, its rate of infant mortality would be roughly comparable to that of the contemporary poor Brazilian families studied by Nancy Scheper-Hughes in her haunting *Death without Weeping*.[90] The loss of children was a familiar experience but it remained an enduring sorrow. In his late fifties Douglas still recalled theirs as a "family of 13."[91] "God knows what a sore trial it is, for a Parent to lose a beloved child," he wrote to a niece who had lost a baby. He thought there was no greater trial of Christian faith: "the truest Christian may in that hour stand in need of grace to keep down the feelings of the rebellious heart, and that he may learn submission to Him, who knoweth what is best for us."[92]

Douglas cherished his living children, but never without conditions or reservations. His parental love was inseparable from his moral approval and its inevitable companion, disapproval. "I love my children dearly and nothing can be more gratifying than to hear of their good qualities and virtuous deportment," he happily explained to a daughter about whom he had received glowing reports.[93] In common with people around the nineteenth-century imperial world, he employed a definition of good and virtuous deportment that was relentlessly gendered and a repository for transimperial bourgeois ideals of what made a good man and a good woman.

As a wealthy family's only son to survive early childhood, James William was saddled with a particularly weighty set of gendered expectations. In the 1860s and '70s Douglas made clear that his son was expected to live up to what was by then his highly cultivated practice of bourgeois, imperial masculinity. This meant rejecting some of the sorts of violence that were critical to the fur trade and, Douglas acknowledged, to his family's history. Douglas admitted that theirs was a lineage "all times more famous for strength of arm, than for sharp words." But he expected a different future for his son, and was horrified when he received reports of a teenaged James William fighting at school. "My son must cultivate

---

[89] James Douglas to Martha Douglas, November 17, 1873, Letters to Martha; James Douglas to Alexander Dallas, January 3, 1870, Letters to Martha.

[90] James Douglas, "Private Account," BCA, Add MSS B/90/1; "Douglas Family Bible," James Douglas, "Journals, Notebooks and Clipping Bbooks, etc., 1835–1873," BCA, MS 0678, Mflm A00792; Nancy Scheper-Hughes, *Death without Weeping: The Violence of Everyday Life in Brazil* (Berkeley: University of California Press, 1993).

[91] James Douglas to Mr. Langmore, n.d. [1862], Douglas Correspondence, 1859–1863.

[92] James Douglas to Edith Cameron Doughty, October 18, 1869, Private Letter Book.

[93] James Douglas to Martha Douglas, February 28, 1874, Letters to Martha.

a kind and generous disposition and scorn to *bully* little boys," he wrote. This kind of masculine subjectivity that Douglas sketched out had distinctly political points of reference that connected interactions between schoolboys to principles of oppression and tyranny. "Tyranny is hateful in every form; the strong should never oppress the weak," he lectured.[94] Historians have shown how expectations of bourgeois masculinity shifted over the course of the nineteenth century, and Douglas' transition from fearsome fur-trade master to gentle and controlling father map this shift on a small and precise scale.

The sort of manly persona Douglas imagined for his son was also rooted in an embrace of prudence and morality, one that worked to solidify the family's stakes in the imperial world. In a letter Douglas urged his son to "keep out of evil company; and to shun vicious and degrading courses." He wanted his son to exercise special caution given the family's particular economic location. "I have no wish to see James a fast young man, indulging in expensive habits, and squandering away the little means I may have given him in folly and idleness," Douglas wrote in 1868.[95] Douglas urged hard work and industry, and saw these in gendered terms. He stressed "Vigorous and steady application," and argued that "Early difficulties must be met in a manful spirit."[96] When the teenaged James William pawned the watch his father had given him and the gold chain his mother had offered as "a parting token of her love," Douglas was deeply hurt and disappointed.[97] It would not be the last time that James William would disappoint his father.

It is predictable that Douglas had different expectations for his daughters. This was especially true for the family's youngest child, Martha, born and raised at a time when the family was most able to access mobile ideals of respectable femininity that reshaped womanhood around the imperial world. Douglas made clear that he expected Martha to be a "lady" of a distinctly imperial and bourgeois sort. Martha took these lessons to heart. When she was thirteen she chastised her friend for making faces at a boy who had hurled a rock at them, since "it is not nice for young ladies, to be falling out with little street boys, who are always disposed to be rude."[98] Douglas was ready to remind Martha when she

---

[94] James Douglas to Alexander Dallas, October 12, 1869; James Douglas to James William Douglas, November 1, 1867, Private Letter Book.

[95] James Douglas to James William Douglas, November 7, 1868; James Douglas to Alexander Dallas, June 8, 1868, Private Letter Book.

[96] James Douglas to James William Douglas, March 16, 1867, "Correspondence – J. Douglas & Other Papers, 1839–1867," HBCA, E 243/13.

[97] James Douglas to James William Douglas, June 15, 1868, Private Letter Book.

[98] Martha Douglas, Diary, March 21, 1866, 13–14.

appeared to forget the many and complicated lessons of polite bourgeois womanhood. He corrected her for mentioning her "weary *legs*" in a letter, suggesting "would it not be nicer to say, weary *limbs*" and noting that she spoke more harshly about a cleric "than a lady ought to do." He requested that Martha defer to the teachers at her English ladies' school on how to speak, write, and act. "I wish you to be, in all respects, lady-like, both in speech and manner," he explained, adding that "A lady never uses slang phrases, which are essentially vulgar, and to me unbearable."[99]

The sort of feminine subjectivity that Douglas had in mind for his daughter was not simply restrictive. He also worked to make Martha educated, engaged, and worldly. She was the family's youngest daughter, raised during Douglas' retirement and the object of his special admiration and cultivation. When she was eleven, she began to keep a diary, writing that "This exercise will be useful in teaching me to express my ideas, and to write with ease and familiarity," and that she would "not be so busy or indolent as to neglect this means of improvement." When she lost interest, her father took over for her and admonished the intended author, writing "Miss Douglas has, for several months past, been remiss with her Journal; for which she is now very sorry, and will I hope be more attentive to this duty hereafter, and strive to entertain her readers, with useful as well as entertaining remarks." He went on to offer a model accounting of the day: "She rode to Belmont today with her Papa – the weather bright and warm at intervals – Calm."[100] Being James Douglas' bright, cherished, and cultivated daughter could not have been easy. Martha was regulated but she was also appreciated and valued by her family. As an older teenager she was encouraged to bring her skills, ideas, and judgment to her parents' home. She arranged flowers, "copied" in her father's library, and made decisions about what land to buy and what to sell. "So you do not fancy a land purchase at Cadboro Bay notwithstanding the beauties of the site?" Douglas asked her in 1872. "You are probably right in that decision."[101]

In treating his youngest daughter as an economic actor capable of making decisions about the ultimate commodity of nineteenth-century settler colonialism – land – Douglas reworked the usual ideas of elite womanhood. He could admire other women who were independent economic actors in their own right and hope that his daughters might emulate them. In the 1870s he shared a stage-coach ride with Christina McDonald McKenzie Williams, the daughter of an old fur-trade colleague. The

---

[99] James Douglas to Martha Douglas, November 13, 1872, James Douglas to Martha Douglas, October 10, 1873, Letters to Martha.

[100] Martha Douglas, Diary, undated, and November 30, 1867.

[101] James Douglas to Martha Douglas, October 17, 1872, Letters to Martha.

widowed Metis woman impressed him with her wealth, authority, and other charms. "I was Widow McKenzie with two children," she elsewhere explained, recalling that Douglas "gave me great credit for doing business even when left alone & said he only wished his daughter do the same."[102] Douglas was aware that his expectations for his daughters challenged or at least significantly reworked the most available bourgeois gender conventions. He bid Martha to "remember you are to be my learned daughter, the veritable Blue-stocking of the family, & at the same time endowed with a meek & gentle spirit." The stern warning that followed – "I shall be satisfied with nothing less" – made clear that Martha's accomplishments were also always his.[103]

Martha may have been a particular object of Douglas' hope, attention, and paternal labor, but he generally regarded his daughters with satisfaction and his one surviving son as a worry and a disappointment. In the late 1860s he evaluated his life and made plans for its end. He was proud that his daughters "are *all healthy, well to do and* ~~respectable~~." His decision to omit his one surviving son from this satisfied assessment is notable, as is his decision to invoke and then score out the ideologically weighty term "respectable." He concluded with the hope that his daughters would find Christ, and offered a sort of paternal benediction: "My daughters have been crowned with blessings, and are all that I could wish them."[104]

Legal and cultural presumptions of the authority of husbands over wives, the precedence of sons over daughters, relations by blood over those by marriage, and male over female lines were both confirmed and modified by the will that Douglas left. Durba Ghosh calls wills "telling reproductive biographies."[105] Douglas' will revealed no partially acknowledged children or relationships, but it did give material weight to the economy of intimacy within his family and community and confirmed that the authority to do so was his alone. Douglas died a wealthy man. His will, first drawn up in 1872 and revised regularly until his death in 1877, made modest gifts to churches and missionary organizations and distributed the bulk of his wealth amongst his kin. How it did so reflected a kind of sentimental patriarchy, one selectively reworked to reflect local histories of kinship and emotion.

[102] Christina McDonald McKenzie Williams, "The Daughter of Angus McDonald," *Washington Historical Quarterly*, 13 (1922) 115–116; Christina Williams to Eva Emery Dye, February 10, 1904, Oregon Historical Society, MSS 1089, 2/15, 2.

[103] James Douglas to Martha Douglas, February 12, 1872, Letters to Martha.

[104] James Douglas to my dearest Child [Jane Dallas Douglas?], October 14, 1868, Private Letter Book.

[105] Durba Ghosh, *Sex and the Family in Colonial India: The Making of Empire* (Cambridge University Press, 2006) 137.

This bourgeois family, like most of those studied by Bettina Bradbury in Montreal, had little interest in a narrow sort of primogeniture and instead divided resources amongst daughters, sons, and the surviving spouse.[106] Douglas' will stretched beyond the immediate family to acknowledge certain extended kin. The descendants of his sister Cecilia who received cash were the only kin outside the immediate family to do so. But most of his wealth went to his children. The Douglas daughters inherited both cash and land. His married daughters and the children of his deceased daughter received $12,000 in cash each, and the unmarried Martha $20,000. Each also received substantial real estate, chosen with care. For Martha, there was a town lot and 319 rural acres she was to live off until she was twenty-five, and then own in full. Agnes and Jane received equal shares in another rural property, and Alice two town lots to be held in trust. After the death of their mother, two expensive pieces of Victoria real estate would be divided among the five daughters. The lots of Fairfield Farm, a major piece of Douglas property at the edge of Victoria, were divided precisely amongst the daughters and their heirs.[107]

While distributing wealth amongst female kin, Douglas' will also acknowledged his one surviving son as the family's presumed and ultimate heir. James William was given an annual income of £3,060 per year and substantial residual rights, including to the expensive and highly symbolic property of the "House, garden and premises at James Bay." As much as the will codified the transmission of wealth from father to son, it also took extraordinary measures to limit James William's control over family resources, especially during his mother's lifetime. Douglas' will created a trust and appointed as trustees three sons-in-law – John Sebastian Helmcken, Alexander Grant Dallas, and Arthur Bushby – paying them $4,000 for their trouble. It was only after Bushby died that Douglas' will was modified to make its primary heir, by then a man in his mid-twenties, a trustee.[108] When Douglas had first drawn up the will, James William was arguably too young to take on the responsibility of administering and inheriting his father's estate. But there was more at stake in Douglas' unwillingness to give his son control over the estate that would eventually be his. Dallas thought that Douglas had intended his son to be a trustee and that the lawyer had made a "sad blunder" in specifying otherwise. It was only after receiving information that prompted a response about James William being likely to "out run the Constable"

---

[106] Bettina Bradbury, *Wife to Widow: Lives, Laws, and Politics in Nineteenth-Century Montreal* (Vancouver: UBC Press, 2011) 169.

[107] Will of James Douglas, January 4, 1872, BCA, GR 1806, 2–3 (hereafter Douglas Will).

[108] Douglas Will, 6, 17, and Codicil 2, January 1876, Douglas Will, 19.

that Dallas decided that his father-in-law's choice of trustees was fully intentional.[109]

In his will Douglas struggled to reconcile dominant gender conventions with his opinions, experiences, and sentiments concerning his daughters as well as his son. Martha was the only unmarried daughter when he planned the dissolution of his property. The marriage prospects of Martha and her brother were both the subject of some interest within the family and elite Victoria more generally.[110] When some of the land intended for Martha was sold, a codicil was added granting her another $5,000 "for her own use" free from the debts of "any husband she may marry."[111] Four years later she had become engaged, and the family took legal measures to ensure the application of the limited provisions modifying the strict patriarchy of British common law and acknowledging married women's control over property that had been passed in the province of British Columbia. When Martha became engaged, the family drafted a special "marriage settlement" that evoked the authority of British Columbia's 1870 Married Women's Property Act and stipulated that Martha be able to administer her considerable income "as if she were a feme [sic] sole" even after her marriage. Material resources and family support were hereby deployed to limit and contain the blunt instrument of patriarchal marriage.[112]

When it came to Douglas' wife, his will invoked the full weight of the British Empire's expectations about marriage, property, and gender. The will left Amelia no money or real estate and made her a dependent with rights of use and limited authority to participate in decision-making. Amelia was named as "dear wife" and given the right to "use occupy and enjoy the plate, linen, furniture, carriages horses, and all other goods, chattels and effects which may be in or upon my house and Premises at James Bay." James William's income from the trust was specified, but Amelia's was to be determined by the trustees, who were instructed to pay her whatever money "she may require for her own use." Connolly Douglas was, the will declared, a "dependent of his estate for the remainder of her life." The will did give her a few ways to make

---

[109] Alexander Grant Dallas to John Sebastian Helmcken, November 2, 1877, Helmcken Papers, Volume 2, File 4; Alexander Grant Dallas to John Sebastian Helmcken, November 15, 1878, Helmcken Papers, Volume 2, File 5; Alexander Grant Dallas to John Sebastian Helmcken, February 22, 1878, Helmcken Papers, Volume 2, File 5.

[110] Dallas to Helmcken, February 22, 1878.

[111] Codicil, dated June 23, 1874, Douglas Will, 18.

[112] "Marriage Settlement: Martha Douglas and Dennis Reginald Harris, to John S. Helmcken and James William Douglas," March 14, 1878, Helmcken Papers, Volume 2, File 49. On the law, see Chris Clarkson, *Domestic Reforms, Political Visions and Family Regulation in British Columbia, 1862–1940* (Vancouver: UBC Press, 2007).

decisions about her immediate surroundings and the lives of her children. It specified that the estate's property could be divided and rented only with her approval, stipulated that the estate pay for Martha's education "as my said Wife shall think necessary," and recognized Amelia as a "Guardian of my infant children" alongside her sons-in-law. Connolly Douglas was "dear" but ultimately and indisputably dependent upon the money and decision-making of her son and sons-in-law, even after her husband's death. Between Douglas' death in 1877 and Amelia's in 1890, the Douglas estate was administered by a paid estate agent, and he doled out money monthly, directly paid Amelia's bills, or gave James William money to do so.[113]

The will was designed to safeguard Connolly Douglas' interests without giving her any substantial authority over them. The results were predictably contradictory, as they were with so many social regulations instituted in a presumed effort to "protect" women or Indigenous people. Dallas worried that the widow's allowance "is one that *might be* abused" and expressed his concern about how the division of property might work in a transimperial family that was, by 1877, spread widely around the Anglophone world. "I quite understand Sir James leaving property to his daughters only after Lady Douglas' death, but *undivided* lots among five people who may be scattered over the world is a complication," he opined. Dallas stated that he had no desire to displace his mother-in-law, remarking that "I also sincerely hope Lady Douglas may long live to be a Centre at James Bay for all to cling to." But his own interests in a simple inheritance for his wife were clear enough, and he was unsurprised and almost pleased when the sisters began to fight among themselves about the properties they had been left. "I am not at all surprised at the split at James Bay," he wrote to Helmcken. "I should have been surprised if it had *not* happened. Three families of angels would not hold together long."[114]

The Douglas-Connolly family was forged and lived within empire and reflected both the power and the limits of some of its most cherished ideals and enduring practices. The household they lived in from the 1850s onward was a concrete symbol of the family's wealth and authority within a local colonial society, one sustained by unequal divisions of labor and authority and mobile notions of bourgeois domesticity. The marriage at

---

[113] Douglas Will, 3–5, 17; "Trustees of the Estate of Sir James Douglas, Deceased, Journal," August 1877–July 31, 1891," BCA, Department of Provincial Secretary, MS 1344, Mflm A-7.

[114] Alexander Grant Dallas to John Sebastian Helmcken, November 2, 1877, Helmcken Papers, Volume 2, File 4; Alexander Grant Dallas to John Sebastian Helmcken, November 15, 1878, Helmcken Papers, Volume 2, File 5.

the core of this household did complicated political and social work in the settler society that grew up around them and under their authority in the 1850s, '60s, and '70s. The status of the marriage and Connolly Douglas' role as wife within it were fundamentally secure, and their alterity was marked in informal but still powerful social and spatial ways. The bourgeois Metis community that provided the context for the governor's marriage also provided Connolly Douglas with a rich and sustaining social life, one that was hardly registered in the usual mediums of local and transimperial colonial discourse and, by extension, in the colonial archives. That history is more legible in the private archive of kin and friends, one that also allows us to track the work of emergent bourgeois gender norms within this particular imperial context. In the Douglas-Connolly family, ideals of genteel femininity and masculinity were both reinforced and reworked: the family found ways to accommodate bright and defiant daughters, but struggled to make sense of their struggling son. Ideals about the privacy and dependency of women, even in their widowhood, remained powerful here as they were throughout so much of the imperial world.

In the latter half of the nineteenth century, the northwestern North American territories where Douglas, Connolly Douglas, and their immediate family lived witnessed social and political change on a seismic scale. The settler regimes that for some time had defined British North America east of the Great Lakes increasingly shaped the territory to the west of it. The boundaries between British and American territories west of the Rocky Mountains were redrawn. Britain established Vancouver Island as a colony in 1849, and almost a decade later the first of a string of gold rushes brought in a substantial non-Indigenous population and provoked the creation of the mainland colony of British Columbia. For all the change it brought, the settler population remained much, much smaller than the Indigenous population, and it would continue to be so for another half-century. Confederation in 1867 had made Canada a nation-state, but one clearly articulated within the framework of the British Empire. Canada's claims to nationhood were in part substantiated when it transformed the Indigenous and fur-trade territories to its west into colonies of its own. With the full and active support of the Colonial Office, British Columbia joined Canada as a province in 1871. This was one part of a wider transformation of the territories lying between the Great Lakes and the Pacific coast. The military resistance of Indigenous peoples in 1869/70 in Red River and in 1885 in the Northwest reshaped but did not halt the modern apparatus of settler imperialism which followed: the "numbered" treaties between First Nations and the Crown starting in 1871, the dispossession of the Red River Metis, the Indian Act passed in 1876, the creation of a carceral reserve system and the systematic removal of Indigenous children in what became known as the residential school system, and the increased racialization of federal immigration policy with the 1885 Chinese Immigration Act.

The Douglas-Connolly family lived these changes immediately and at a number of locations within these layered histories of colonies, nations, and metropoles. This chapter draws on the rich archive produced by and in response to Douglas' governorship of the colonies of Vancouver

Island and British Columbia to analyze the family's multiple roles in the colonization of northwestern North America in the second half of the nineteenth century. It begins with Douglas' appointment as governor and some parts of his administration. I then turn to how Douglas' governorship was evaluated and understood locally and within a wider transimperial sphere. The chapter then analyzes the family's complicated racial performances and entanglements with Caribbean, Indigenous, and metropolitan identities and networks in the latter half of the century. Members of the Douglas-Connolly family were often very much colonizers, sometimes of the highest and most consequential order. Sometimes they were also colonized though rarely in uncomplicated ways. The family's multiple and simultaneous locations remind us how complicated the relations and identities of imperialism were in lived history, local colonial space, and real time.

In 1849, Vancouver Island was made a colony of Britain under terms that reflected imperial precedents and local insurgencies. Britain had lost its claims to Oregon and formally colonizing the territory to its north promised to assert Britain's relevance to this particular venue of the imperial game.[1] The Hudson's Bay Company (HBC) was again made the de facto colonial state. In exchange for seven shillings a year and a promise to undertake the work of colonization, the HBC was named the "true and absolute lords and proprietors" of Vancouver Island for a ten-year period. Vancouver Island's colony was based on the "old colonial system" that prevailed in the West Indies, with an appointed governor and executive council, and an elected assembly. The system of land tenure was modeled loosely on the ideas of Edward Gibbon Wakefield. Wakefield had a kind of rock star status in 1830s and '40s imperial circles. His arguments about how best to re-create what was, to his mind, the best of British society – stable, hierarchical, heteronormative, and agricultural – had a particular impact on New Zealand. They also helped shape Vancouver Island's early colonial policy. Here, land was to be sold for £1 an acre and large landowners were required to sponsor the immigration of five married couples or six single men.[2]

---

[1] J. H. Pelly to Sir [Earl Grey], March 4, 1848, Colonial Office Correspondence, Vancouver Island, 305/1, http://bcgenesis.uvic.ca, accessed September 8, 2013 (hereafter CO 305).

[2] James Hendrickson, "Introduction," *Journals of the Colonial Legislatures of the Colonies of Vancouver Island and British Columbia, 1851–1871* (Victoria: Provincial Archives of British Columbia, 1980), Volume IV, xxvi. Also see Jack Little, "The Foundations of Government," in Hugh J. M. Johnson, ed., *The Pacific Province* (Vancouver: Douglas and McIntyre, 1996); Richard Mackie, "The Colonization of Vancouver Island, 1849–1858," *BC Studies*, 96 (Winter 1992/3) 3–40; Jeremy Mouat, "Situating Vancouver Island in the British World, 1846–49," *BC Studies*, 145 (Spring 2005) 5–30.

The HBC plainly hoped that the authority Douglas held as chief factor would be redoubled with his appointment as governor. HBC officials recommended him to the Colonial Office on the grounds of "his experience in the country, & the interest he took in the colony" and took care to mention that he was a "gentleman" and "a man of property."[3] In the midst of sharp critiques of Britain's willingness to concede the work of colonial governance to a self-interested commercial enterprise, the Colonial Office opted to make a conventional appointment by naming Richard Blanshard as governor. Blanshard had the sort of "imperial career" explained by David Lambert and Alan Lester, having been educated at Cambridge, spent time in the Caribbean, and served in the British army in India. Like so many other colonial officials, his first appointment was facilitated by ties of affinity and patronage and found him dispatched to a distant and less than prestigious colony.[4] He was promised a thousand acres of land in the colony but no salary. He accepted this unconventional arrangement in the hope that the land would become valuable and that his "services would be considered by Her Majesty's Government afterwards."[5]

Blanshard arrived at Fort Victoria in June of 1850. Douglas was reportedly "taken by surprise" by his appearance. The new governor landed "under a salute of guns" from both the ship and the fort and took up his commission,[6] but his embodiment of local imperial authority faltered thereafter. Like Beaver before him, Blanshard was vexed by the domestic comforts provided him. There had been no separate house built, and the new Governor apparently turned down Douglas' offer to "lodge him in his own house" and opted to stay aboard the naval ship he had arrived in. More broadly, Blanshard was offended that the authority of the HBC as an organization and of Douglas as an individual so plainly exceeded

[3] Eden Colville to George Simpson, December 7, 1849, in E. E. Rich, ed., *London Correspondence Inward from Eden Colville, 1849–1852* (London: Hudson's Bay Company Record Society, 1956) 186–187; J. H Pelly to Earl Grey, September 13, 1848, CO 305/1, http://bcgenesis.uvic.ca, accessed September 29, 2011. Also see Stephen Royle, *Company, Crown, and Colony: The Hudson's Bay Company and Territorial Endeavour in Western Canada* (London: Macmillan, 2011).

[4] David Lambert and Alan Lester, eds., *Colonial Lives across the British Empire: Imperial Careering in the Long Nineteenth Century* (Cambridge University Press, 2006); James E. Hendrickson, "Blanshard, Richard," in *Dictionary of Canadian Biography*, Volume XII, University of Toronto/Université Laval, 2003, www.biographi.ca, accessed October 31, 2012; Zoë Laidlaw, *Colonial Connections, 1815–1845: Patronage, the Information Revolution, and Colonial Government* (Manchester University Press, 2005) Chapter 2.

[5] Great Britain, *Report from the Select Committee on the Hudson's Bay Company; Together with the Proceedings of the Committee, Minutes of Evidence, Appendix and Index* (London: House of Commons, 1857) 288.

[6] Commander C. R. Johnson to Sir, June 21, 1850, Sir Phipps Hornby Papers, National Maritime Museum, London (hereafter NMM), PH1/3/5.

that of the British imperial government as an institution and himself as its chosen representative. Less than a year passed before he submitted his resignation. It took a predictable nine months for the Colonial Office's reply to reach him, and during that time Blanshard allied himself firmly with critics of HBC rule. John Sebastian Helmcken remembered him as a "gentleman," with a "rather military carriage and military moustache" who was disappointed by the fact that "Mr. Douglas had all the power and all the men." Helmcken thought Blanshard's conviction that "Douglas plotted in order to displace him and be Governor himself and so threw difficulties and unpleasantness in his way" was far from wrong.[7]

If Blanshard's appointment was a symbol of Britain's commitment to bringing Vancouver Island in line with mid-century expectations of colonial governance, it also showed how this commitment – with these expectations – broke down and was remade in local colonial space. Without Colonial Office permission, Blanshard left his post and returned to England. He never received the thousand acres of land, and the Colonial Office made him pay for his return passage. A few years later, he enumerated the cards stacked against him in Vancouver Island: he had insufficient personal means to live without a salary, no preparations had been made for his arrival, he and his servant were compelled to live in an empty store room in the fort, he was forced to purchase provisions at inflated HBC prices, and he had to travel for "several days in an open canoe." More than that, Vancouver Island's colonial subjects were almost all Indigenous or allied to the HBC and, to his mind, thus either ungovernable or somehow unrecognizable. "There was not any materials to build with scarcely any inhabitants except the Indian tribes and the Hudson's Bay Comp'ny servants," he explained.[8]

The May 1851 appointment of Douglas as governor and vice-admiral of Vancouver Island confirmed that vernacular and customary practices of imperial rule could prevail over official metropolitan ones. News of the appointment did not reach Douglas until late October of 1851.[9] His appointment and the way it was carried out again signaled how

[7] Dorothy Blakey Smith, ed., *The Reminiscences of Doctor John Sebastian Helmcken* (Vancouver: UBC Press, 1975) 118–119 (hereafter Helmcken, *Reminiscences*). Also see James Robert Anderson, "Notes and Comments on Early Days and Events in British Columbia, Washington and Oregon, Including an Account of sundry happenings in San Francisco; being the Memoirs of James Robert Anderson, Written by himself," British Columbia Archives, MS 1912, Box 9, 157.

[8] Richard Blanshard to Earl Grey, January 1852, CO 305/3, http://bcgenesis.uvic.ca, accessed September 8, 2013.

[9] Margaret A. Ormsby, "Douglas, Sir James," in *Dictionary of Canadian Biography*, Volume X, University of Toronto/Université Laval, 2003, www.biographi.ca, acces June 9, 2008.

metropolitan reckonings of empire were disciplined to local iterations of it. Much like the Dutch nationals entrusted with British rule in the Guyana of his childhood, Douglas' greatest qualification for governor was that he was *there* when *there* was literally and metaphorically beyond the metropole's reach.

As governor, Douglas was a creole sort of colonizer. He retained his role as chief factor for the HBC, becoming what one biographer enduringly termed a "servant of two empires."[10] During a time when new languages of self-government and democracy were reshaping British settler colonies west of the Great Lakes, Douglas demonstrated little enthusiasm even for the limited sort of settler self-government that Britain expected of Vancouver Island. He opined that "the best form of government, if attainable, is that of a wise and good despotism."[11] He declared himself to be "utterly averse to universal suffrage, or making population the basis of representation."[12] The elected assembly of Vancouver Island would not meet until 1856, and even then it was a ramshackle business. The Colonial Office worried about Douglas' vernacular ways of government, but they mainly approved of the results that it produced. "Governor Douglas does not exhibit any want of determination, when he has made up his mind to a course of proceeding," wrote one staffer in an 1854 note.[13]

The non-Indigenous population remained very small. In 1855, Douglas reported on what he called the "White" population of Vancouver Island, a category he defined to include people of a select range of Indigenous identities, including Kanaka, Haudenosaunee, and Metis. There were 232 of these people at Victoria and a total of 774 within the colony of Vancouver Island. The population was disproportionately male and strikingly youthful. Almost half were children, and nobody was older than sixty. Of the 416 persons over the age of twenty, only 109 were women.[14] This settler population lived amongst a substantially larger Indigenous population. When Douglas enumerated the "Indian Population" of Vancouver Island in 1856, he counted a total of 25,873 people, including the 700 Songhees or Lekwungun people resident in and around the city of Victoria.[15]

---

[10] Derek Pethick, *James Douglas: Servant of Two Empires* (Vancouver: Mitchell Books, 1969).

[11] Quoted in Ormsby, "Douglas," n.p.

[12] James Douglas to Henry Labouchere, May 22, 1856, CO 305/7, http://bcgenesis.uvic.ca, accessed September 29, 2012.

[13] Hendrickson, "Introduction," xxviii; Arthur Johnstone Blackwood, June 9, 1854, in James Douglas to Newcastle, March 13, 1854, CO 305/5, http://bcgenesis.uvic.ca, accessed September 29, 2012.

[14] W. Kaye Lamb, ed., "The Census of Vancouver Island, 1855," *British Columbia Historical Quarterly*, 4 (1940) 51–52.

[15] "Indian Population Vancouver's Island, 1856," in James Douglas to Henry Labouchere, October 20, 1856, CO 305/7, http:/bcgenesis.uvic.ca, accessed October 23, 2013.

The scope of Britain's colonial project and Douglas' authority within it expanded and was redefined in 1858. Knowledge of gold on the mainland adjacent to Vancouver Island brought new attention and a substantial non-Indigenous population arriving via American territory to the south. The new migrants were almost all men. Many of them were armed and had the complicated itineraries that characterized nineteenth-century Pacific gold rushes. Douglas did not wait to receive official permission to proclaim British jurisdiction over the gold fields. "The torrent of immigration is setting in with impetuous force, and to keep pace with the extraordinary circumstances of the times; and to maintain the authority of the Laws, I have been compelled to assume an unusual amount of responsibility," he explained to London, seeking approval for actions he had already taken.[16] The rituals of the colonial state followed after it had begun to act. "The ceremonies of swearing in the Governor & reading the various proclamations went off most admirably & his Excellency was very well received," reported the admiral of the Royal Navy's ship the *Ganges*.[17]

Some ten years earlier, Douglas had been appointed governor of Vancouver Island some six months before he was made aware of it. Now he began to assert British authority long before the Colonial Office declared him governor of a new colony of British Columbia and gave him temporary emergency powers to legislate by proclamation alone. In May 1859 Britain terminated the HBC's grant to the island, made Vancouver Island a Crown Colony under its direct control, and streamlined the two colonies' baroque constitutional apparatus. Douglas began to receive a salary as governor, but was required to sever his formal connection with the HBC.[18]

The gold rush promised to remake the two colonies and reconfirmed some of the salient limits on this remaking. Victoria's population swelled during the heat of the Fraser River gold rush, reportedly reaching about 20,000 people, and again in response to the Cariboo gold rush of 1862. It shrunk thereafter, hovering at about 6,000 in 1864, and 3,630 in 1871.[19] But the transformations wrought by the arrival of a sizeable non-Indigenous population would endure, however much the gold rush

[16] Hendrickson, "Introduction," xxxiv; James Douglas to Lord Stanley, July 26, 1858, CO 305/9, http://bcgenesis.uvic.ca, accessed August 29, 2013. More generally, see Daniel Marshall, "Mapping the New El Dorado: The Fraser River Gold Rush and the Appropriation of Native Space," in Ted Binnema and Susan Neylan, eds., *New Histories for Old: Changing Perspectives on Canada's Native Pasts* (Vancouver: UBC Press, 2007).

[17] Admiral Baynes to Sir, December 4, 1858, Sir Julian Stafford Corbett Papers, NMM, CBT/29/S.

[18] Hendrickson, "Introduction," xxxii; Ormsby, "Douglas."

[19] Vancouver Island, *Blue Books and Statistics, &c., 1865*, BCA, Mflm 625-A; Municipal Census of Victoria, http://vihistory.ca/content/census/1871/census1871.php?show=y, accessed October 8, 2013.

population differed from the usual imperial expectations of what British settlers ought to look like, and however quickly it diminished. Douglas remained firm in his conviction that this group of settlers were not worthy of the kind of self-government being granted to settlers in the Antipodes and the Canadas. In 1861, he suggested that London keep in mind that the mainland colony lacked the class and national credentials necessary to govern themselves, and that the Colonial Office respectfully dismiss the demands of settlers asking for "Representative Institutions . . . a form of Government similar to that existing in Australia, and the Eastern British North American Provinces."[20]

A chain of imperial happenstance and a more enduring set of local conditions worked to make Douglas the governor of two separate British colonies. For the mid-nineteenth-century British Empire this was not a conventional arrangement and Douglas was not a conventional choice for governor. As Zoë Laidlaw explains, by this time the colonial service was a professionalized business, knitted together through metropolitan ties of kin and patronage and accessed through metropolitan experiences and credentials. Historian Julie Evans has used colonial governor Edward Eyre as the frame for a rich critical analysis that sits at the juncture of transnational, colonial, and biographical history.[21] We can do this with Douglas as well, but the histories his career as governor maps are necessarily very different.

Historians of British Columbia have analyzed Douglas' dealings with Indigenous peoples in some detail, finding similarities and differences between his policies, the policies of other parts of British North America and around the British Empire, and those of the colonial and provincial governments that would follow. Particularly key here are the fourteen land "purchases" or "conveyances" that Douglas negotiated with Vancouver Island First Nations between 1850 and 1854. These documents are all similar, a few pages of text promising modest material goods, small amounts of cash, and reserve lands in exchange for title to the lands of a specific Indigenous community. Cole Harris argues that what have become known as the "Vancouver Island treaties" were adaptive, polyglot, and practical documents. They reflected Colonial Office advice and transimperial precedence, most notably from New Zealand, but were

---

[20] James Douglas to the Duke of Newcastle, January 2, 1861, in Colonial Office, British Columbia Correspondence, CO 60/10, http://bcgenesis.uvic.ca, accessed September 29, 2012 (hereafter CO 60).

[21] Laidlaw, *Colonial Connections*; Julie Evans, "Biography and Global History: Reflections on Examining Colonial Governance through the Life of Edward Eyre," in Desley Deacon, Penny Russell, and Angela Woollacott, eds., *Transnational Ties: Australian Lives in the World* (Canberra: ANU EPress, 2009); Julie Evans, *Edward Eyre: Race and Colonial Governance* (Dunedin: Otago University Press, 2005).

also created out of Douglas' reading of shifting local politics and the best way of securing British interests within them.[22] Late in the twentieth century, courts declared these treaties in the full sense of Canadian law, folding them into a long history of treaty-making that was codified by the 1763 Royal Proclamation passed by King George III, which articulated Britain's claim to northern North America and stipulated that Indigenous title be extinguished through treaty before settlement. The Vancouver Island treaties serve as a salutary reminder that the considered and often bellicose denial of Indigenous title that characterized British Columbia's colonial and provincial governments for the next century might have been otherwise.

Douglas' governance was polyvocal and adaptive, forged from a number of imperial precedents and a great deal of lived practice. He saw Indigenous people as worthy candidates for a kind of imperial citizenship based on wage labor, landownership, and participation in a romantic image of British justice. In 1854, he wrote to London, explaining his policy of enforcing the "Laws of England" only in the "sacred ground" of colonial settlements and that he considered Indigenous people and their wage labor "exceedingly useful to the Colonists."[23] When settlers in Victoria argued for the eviction of Indigenous people from urban space, he conceded that the "presence of those Indians so near the Town is a public inconvenience," but was unwilling to commit to a rigid racialization of space, explaining that "their violent removal would be neither just nor politic."[24]

Douglas' reckoning of Indigenous peoples was variegated, particular, and variable. He reworked the usual mid-nineteenth-century language of racial mixture, writing about the "half-Whites" he enlisted as kinds of marshals in the early 1850s.[25] Douglas' land policy accorded Indigenous people the signal right of liberal citizenship – the right to own land, and, more particular in the context of settler colonialism, the capacity

[22] Cole Harris, *Making Native Space: Colonialism, Resistance, and Reserves in British Columbia* (Vancouver: UBC Press, 2002) Chapter 2. Also see Wilson Duff, "The Fort Victoria Treaties," *BC Studies*, 3 (Fall 1969) 3–57; Hamar Foster, "Letting Go the Bone: The Idea of Indian Title in British Columbia, 1849–1927," in Hamar Foster and John McLaren, eds., *Essays in the History of Canadian Law: British Columbia and the Yukon* (Toronto: Osgoode Society, 1995) 28–86; Raymond Frogner, "'Innocent Legal Fictions': Archival Convention and the North Saanich Treaty of 1852," *Archivaria*, 70 (Fall 2010) 45–94.

[23] Herman Merivale, October 1, [1854], note with James Douglas to Newcastle, July 28, 1853, CO 305/4, http://bcgenesis.uvic.ca, accessed September 29, 2012.

[24] James Douglas, February 8, 1859, in James Hendrickson, ed., *Journals of the Colonial Legislatures of the Colonies of Vancouver Island and British Columbia*, 72.

[25] James Douglas to John Packington, January 21, 1853, CO 305/4, http://bcgenesis. uvic.ca, accessed October 22, 2013.

to pre-empt it.[26] Writing to the metropole in 1859, he made clear that he considered Indigenous people rational and economically autonomous subjects within the conventions of liberal thinking. He explained how he would implement his newly expanded jurisdiction over the mainland, arguing that Indigenous peoples "should in all respects be treated as rational beings, capable of acting and thinking for themselves."[27] A few years later he wrote to British philanthropist Angela Burdett-Coutts, arguing that Indigenous peoples required careful colonial tutelage but were "not destitute of all the qualities which lend dignity to character" and were "fully capable" of supporting themselves "by their own labour."[28]

These arguments both invoked a typical nineteenth-century sort of liberalism and tried to modify some of the more schematic racial thinking it could both justify and produce.[29] Douglas' kind of liberalism was variable, uneven, and extended to different people at some times and not others. Against the grain of much settler thought, he was willing to accord certain rights of liberal citizenship to Indigenous peoples under certain circumstances and not others. He folded some non-White migrants into discourses of British settler rights and situated others outside its promises. Mifflin Winstar Gibbs recalled the "warm welcome" that he and the roughly eight hundred other African Americans who migrated to Victoria in 1858 received from the governor as "cheering," a harbinger of "the benefits of constitutional liberty."[30] The Pioneer Rifle Company was a volunteer militia of Black men established in 1861 and colloquially known as the African Rifles, shown parading below a British flag in Figure 7.1. When two hundred of what the local newspaper called "the *elite* of our coloured population" met to celebrate Emancipation Day in Victoria, there were speeches, sermons, and dancing at the "Hall of the African Rifles."[31] The sobriquet of "Pioneer" suggests how languages of

---

[26] See Paul Tennant, *Aboriginal Peoples and Politics: The Indian Land Question in British Columbia, 1849–1989* (Vancouver: UBC Press, 1990) Chapter 3; Robert E. Cail, *Land, Man, and the Law: The Disposal of Crown Lands in British Columbia, 1871–1913* (Vancouver: UBC Press, 1974) 177–178.

[27] James Douglas to Edward Bulwer Lytton, March 14, 1859, 4800, CO 60/4, http://bcgensis.uvic.ca, accessed July 7, 2013.

[28] James Douglas to Angela Burdett-Coutts, August 25, 1861, British Columbia – Governor (Douglas), Correspondence Outward (miscellaneous letters), November 30, 1859–December 8, 1863, BCA, c/AB/10.4/2 (hereafter Douglas Outward Correspondence).

[29] See Uday Singh Mehta, *Liberalism in Empire: A Study in Nineteenth-Century British Liberal Thought* (University of Chicago Press, 1999); Charles W. Mills, *The Racial Contract* (Ithaca and London: Cornell University Press, 1997).

[30] Mifflin Winstar Gibbs, *Shadow and Light: An Autobiography with Reminiscences of the Last and Present Century* (Washington, DC: n.p., 1902) 59.

[31] "Emancipation Day," *Colonist*, August 2, 1861. Also see Crawford Killan, *Go Do Some Great Thing: The Black Pioneers of British Columbia* (Vancouver: Douglas and McIntyre, 1978) Chapter 7; Natasha I. Henry, *Emancipation Day: Celebrating Freedom in Canada* (Toronto: Dundurn, 2010) Chapter 9.

Figure 7.1 Victoria's Pioneer Rifle Corps, also known as the Coloured Regiment or the African Rifles.

settlement and exploration could be accessed by Black newcomers. The muskets that Douglas' government provided to the African Rifles were a tangible symbol of the governor's willingness to accord Black people the rights of colonizers. The governor who replaced Douglas thought the militia's formation improper, and they were disbanded and replaced by White volunteers.[32] Douglas did not include Chinese migrants in these symbolic gestures. When 2,000 arrived, he explained that "They are certainly not a desirable class of people, as a permanent population, but are for the present useful as labourers and consumers."[33]

Douglas' seeming ability to rule Indigenous peoples and spaces earned him praise from non-Indigenous observers on both sides of the Atlantic. Under-Secretary for the Colonies, Herman Merivale, saw Douglas as a good example of the efficacy of fur-trade colonialism compared with the vagaries of settler governments and the relentless violence of American

[32] Edgar Fawcett, *Some Reminiscences of Old Victoria* (Toronto: William Briggs, 1912) 219

[33] James Douglas to the Duke of Newcastle, April 23, 1860, CO 60/8, http://bcgenesis.uvic.ca, accessed April 24, 2014.

colonialism. "For my own part I believe that whatever their demerits, the Co. have one merit, viz. that of *systematic* dealing with the natives," something he contrasted to the "mere caprice of ordinary settlers." He credited the HBC with absence of "the fearful massacres & fightings" that marked American territory.[34] Douglas' adroit use of Indigenous and fur-trade practices of governance was routinely noted. Naval officer Richard Mayne recalled him diffusing a conflict with well-worn and distinctly Indigenous rituals of generosity and sustenance. Douglas instructed his men not to arm the bastion of the fort against Indigenous men but instead to "Give them a little bread and treacle."[35] Here Douglas made use of Indigenous practices of generosity and gift-giving, delivered through the particularly imperial medium of Caribbean treacle. Another missionary recalled Douglas' diplomatic tools as biscuits and molasses,[36] but the point was the same: the political power of generosity, and the symbolic and material work of Caribbean sugar in this very different imperial context.

This was a distinctly imperial sort of paternalism and it was registered as such. Gilbert Sproat, a local entrepreneur, amateur ethnographer, and colonial official, described Douglas as "the great White Chief of the Indians."[37] When Douglas died, *The Times* explained that the "Indian population had great confidence in Sir James, and looked upon him as their principal chief and their best friend."[38] Edward Cridge came to Vancouver Island as an HBC chaplain, and he became Douglas' friend and later his clergyman. Cridge explained that "Douglas treated the Indians with the affection of a father" and that this "coupled with his justice & fairness gave him unbounded influence with them."[39] Another Anglican missionary, John Good, argued that Douglas' fatherly interactions with Indigenous people were the greatest evidence of his authority and character. "But to witness still nobler characteristics of this great, good man, one needed to see him addressing a body of unsophisticated savages in the light of a patriarch, and father inculcating principles of morality, and

---

[34] Herman Merivale, October 1, [1854], in James Douglas to Newcastle, July 28, 1853, CO 305/4, http://bcgenesis.uvic.ca, accessed September 29, 2012.

[35] Richard Charles Mayne, *Four Years in British Columbia and Vancouver Island* (Toronto: S. R. Publishers, 1969 [London: John Murray, 1862]) 54.

[36] John B. Good, "British Columbia," May 1878, BL, P-C 19, Mflm 3, 11.

[37] G. M. Sproat, "James Douglas," typescript in "BC History – James Douglas," Box 35, File 34, Walter N. Sage Papers, University of British Columbia (UBC) Archives and Special Collections (hereafter Sage Papers).

[38] "British Columbia," *The Times* (London), September 12, 1877.

[39] Edward Cridge, "Characteristics of James Douglas," Bancroft Collection, P-C 8, Mflm 1, Bancroft Library, University of California at Berkeley (hereafter BL), 2 (hereafter BL).

good government, and exhibiting by word and deed those innumerable principles of truth and justice."[40]

This paternalism was thought to serve Douglas well in his interactions with plebeian settlers as well as with Indigenous people. Observers thought that it was Douglas' paternalism that guaranteed his authority with the itinerant gold miners whose arrival en masse in 1858 promised to both make a settler colony possible by delivering a non-Indigenous population and unmake it by destabilizing its claims to Britishness. Cridge recalled some ten thousand polyglot miners arriving in Victoria in 1858, and that Douglas "conferred with them as a father and a friend."[41] Mayne agreed. He wrote that "Few men could perhaps have been selected better adapted for dealing with the strange, heterogeneous population of Victoria than Mr. Douglas."[42] Sometimes these assessments slid into a more generic sort of hyperbole. Douglas, recalled an old settler, was "beloved and reverenced by all who had the honour of knowing him intimately," a man "with the frame of a Hercules, the heart of a child and the intellect of a Beaconsfield."[43]

By describing Douglas as a kind of worthy patriarch, these observers imagined relations of empire in terms of kin, age, and authority, and in doing so worked to naturalize relationships that were historical and volatile, constituted and lived in particular colonial spaces. Transforming Douglas-the-colonizer into Douglas-the-father went alongside the acknowledgement and celebration of his use of force. The governor who was lauded for his polyvocality and his paternalism was also recalled for his willingness to wield decisive and brutal force. Douglas "knew when and how to use bread and treacle, he also knew when to draw the sword, and what is more, how to use it," explained one.[44] Two years into his governorship of Vancouver Island, Douglas explained his strategy for both acknowledging Indigenous law and enforcing colonial law. "I consider it unwise, and something beyond the power of Government, to restrain the exercise of their natural rights, out of the limits of the settlements," he explained. "I think it advisable to teach the natives that the settlements are sacred ground, and must not be polluted with innocent

---

[40] Good, "British Columbia," 10–11. Also John Booth Good, "The Utmost Bounds of the West: Pioneer jottings of forty years missionary reminiscences of the Out West Pacific Coast AD 1861–AD 1900," Anglican Church of Canada, Diocese of New Westminster/Ecclesiastical Province of British Columbia Archives, Vancouver School of Theology, PSA 52, File 9, 50–52 (hereafter DNW/EPBCA).

[41] Cridge, "Characteristics of James Douglas," 2.

[42] Mayne, *Four Years in British Columbia and Vancouver Island*, 55.

[43] Benjamin William Pearse, "Early Settlement of Vancouver Island, 1900," BCA, Add MSS E/B/P31, BCA, Transcript, 19.

[44] "Our Letter from Victoria, VI," *Daily Alta Californian* (San Francisco) June 21, 1864.

blood."[45] When Douglas thought that the "sacred grounds" of colonial settlements had been violated, he responded with speed and authority. Helmcken remembered his father-in-law as a "cold brave man" under such circumstances.[46] A missionary who remembered Douglas relying on bread and treacle also recalled how the governor put men to death in an effort to scare their fellows.

In the teeth of the entire assembled body of armed savages consisting of hundreds of infuriated, determined men, [he] honourably arrested the evil doer and had him hung publicly before all of the friends of the culprit, thereby satisfying justice and infusing a wholesome terror among the well-known body of treacherous inhabitants of that isolated district.[47]

As governor, Douglas was many things. What he called "wholesome terror" punctuated his paternalism, underlay his diplomacy, and structured his capacity and his reliance on Indigenous and fur-trade idioms of governance. His spectacular imperial violence does not cancel out his belief that Indigenous people had a legitimate and valuable place in settler society, his conviction that they were rational peoples who deserved British justice and some (but certainly not all) of the rights offered by the settler state, or his uneven recognition of the Indigenous title and his engagement in practices of treaty-making. Certainly these views separated Douglas from his more bellicose contemporaries and from almost all of the colonial and provincial officials who followed him. But these views did not mean that Douglas was not a colonizer, and one who was remarkably skilled at mobilizing the necessary resources to preserve imperial interests as he perceived them.

Douglas' devastating efficacy was made most clear when he employed the techniques of rule that have become known as "gunboat diplomacy." Historian Kenton Scott Storey points out that there were only two years between 1854 and 1862 when Douglas did not evict from Victoria the Indigenous peoples hailing from the Northern Coast.[48] These routine actions provided the background for the more radical removal of northern Indigenous people from Victoria amidst a devastating smallpox epidemic in 1862. The people who Douglas had often defended as valuable wage-earners, traders, and rights-bearers were sent up the coast, their homes

---

[45] James Douglas to the Duke of Newcastle, July 28, 1853, 9499, CO 305/4, http://bcgenesis.uvic.ca, accessed September 29, 2012.
[46] Helmcken, *Reminiscences*, 130.   [47] Good, "British Columbia," 11.
[48] Barry Gough, *Gunboat Diplomacy: British Maritime Authority and Northwest Coast Indians, 1846–1890* (Vancouver: UBC Press, 1984); Kenton Scott Storey, "'What Will They Say in England?': Violence, Anxiety, and the Press in Nineteenth Century New Zealand and Vancouver Island," *Journal of the Canadian Historical Association*, 20:2 (2009) 28–59.

set alight, and their return thwarted by legal and extra-legal maneuvers of Victoria's municipal government. Here was the full weight of the colonial state at its most plainly destructive, self-interested, and unconcerned with Indigenous lives.

This iteration of the local colonial state had been there all along. Douglas' commitments to legal pluralism and a liberal sort of imperial citizenship were always underwritten by judicial and extra-judicial violence, and a confidence in imperial military power and the fear it inspired and was designed to. In 1853, he explained that "War was carried to their own doors last winter and they are sensible that we can at any moment repeat the experiment, and march a force into any part of their country, and that it is in our power to harass and annoy them in a thousand ways."[49] American administrators were impressed with Douglas' ability to terrify Indigenous people with the symbols and tools of a martial and racial empire. In 1878, the mayor of a nearby American town declared himself "a great admirer" of Douglas who considered the governor a "great statesman." This American recalled "a vessel with 14 British flags at the Fore, telling the Indians that in a war of races they had a war with all the White man."[50] Douglas was a governor able to use long experience with Indigenous and fur-trade diplomacy. He believed that Indigenous people were deserving of a certain kind of colonial citizenship. But this did not discount his role as a head of an embattled colonial state committed to asserting its authority over Indigenous peoples and lands. The hangings, the evictions, and the gunboats left no doubt about this.

The criticisms leveled against Douglas' administration cannot be spliced along the predictable lines of colony and metropole. Supporters argued that Douglas was uniquely equipped to govern a fractious, multicultural colony where the Indigenous population greatly outnumbered the settler one. He was lauded and celebrated for his supposedly efficacious management of Indigenous peoples and for running two colonial governments on the cheap. He was also criticized for his actions and policies, especially for his autocratic governance, his tendency to favor the island colony, his glaringly obvious patronage, and his restrictive land policies. Douglas was also criticized for who he was. Critics distrusted his marriage and his long association with the HBC. They also doubted whether a man who had lived his life almost entirely outside

---

[49] James Douglas to Archibald Barclay, March 21, 1853, "Sir James Douglas' Correspondence Book, 1850–1855," Hudson's Bay Company Archives, E 243/9, Transcript (hereafter HBCA and Douglas Correspondence, 1850–1855).

[50] Elwood Evans, "John M. Swan & the Olympia Club Conversazione," BL, P-B 15, Mflm 3, 13.

the metropole could reliably rule on behalf of it. All of these evaluations circulated around Vancouver Island, British Columbia, adjacent American territories, and the metropole. They shaped Douglas' appointment as governor, shaped his thirteen years in office, and set the course for his retirement in 1863/4.

Douglas' appointment as governor was invested with larger meanings about colonialism in North America. In the face of critiques of Britain's willingness to invest a private trading company with colonial authority, the Colonial Office defended the HBC in general and Douglas in particular as effective colonizers. They continued to find Douglas an effective governor, albeit one without the administrative skills they thought governors ought to possess. Colonial Office staff asked that he number his paragraphs, and Douglas himself apologized for his "ignorance of the prescribed forms" and worried that his dockets were made out incorrectly.[51] In 1858 the newly arrived Admiral Baynes reported that Douglas was a "man of strong natural sense" who was "quite suited to the emergency of the moment," though one who would do better "assisted by a good Colonial Secretary."[52] It was Secretary of State Edward Bulwer Lytton who appointed Douglas governor of British Columbia as well, and he would remain ambivalent about this choice. In 1860 Lytton would refer to Douglas as "a mere jobber,"[53] an accidental and situational kind of governor rather than the professional sort. It was only Douglas' perceived capacity to rule Indigenous people that inspired his shaky confidence. In retrospect, Lytton reported that "he appointed Gov. Douglas on account of his great influence with the Indians yet he received his dispatches with reserve."[54]

People who doubted London's decision to put a private company in charge of a colony saw the appointment of Douglas as governor of Vancouver Island as a powerful breach of principles of liberal government they thought ought to be a cornerstone of appropriate colonial practice. A self-described group of "independent colonists" wrote expressing their "unfeigned surprise and deep concern" that Vancouver Island's government has been "committed to a chief factor of the Hudson's Bay Company."[55] These men found some support in transimperial circles.

---

[51] Herman Merivale, note, January 29, 1853, in James Douglas to John Packington, November 11, 1852, CO 305/3; James Douglas to the Duke of Newcastle, February 28, 1854, CO 305/5, both in http://bcgenesis.uvic.ca, accessed April 14, 2014.

[52] Admiral Baynes to Sir, November 17, 1858, Stafford Papers, NMM, CBT/29/s.

[53] Edward Bulwer Lytton, April 4, [1860], note in James Douglas to Edward Bulwer Lytton, February 9, 1859, CO 305/10, http://bcgenesis.uvic.ca, accessed April 14, 2014.

[54] Hills, Journal, August 21, 1863, 129.

[55] Undated letter in Britain, *Report of the Select Committee*, 293.

Rear Admiral Fairfax Moresby, stationed at Esquimalt in the early 1850s, explained that "the attempt to Colonize Vancouver by a Company with exclusive rights of Trade, is incompatible with the free & liberal reception of an Emigrant Community." He predicted "difficulties & embarrassment must be the result."[56]

The sort of difficulties and embarrassments that Moresby predicted arrived in 1854 when Douglas appointed his brother-in-law David Cameron chief justice of Vancouver Island. Cameron was the first man to act in this position. As governors, both Blanshard and Douglas had previously exercised judicial authority, and Douglas in particular was willing to handle legal matters, including capital cases, in local and pragmatic ways and make no recourse to whatever provisions for long-distance justice were available. The extent to which Vancouver Island operated outside normative standards of the rule of law concerned both local and metropolitan observers.[57] The appointment of Cameron did little to allay fears that Vancouver Island's government was despotic and capricious. Cameron was married to Douglas' sister Cecilia, and they were newly arrived from Georgetown and living with the Douglas-Connolly family in Victoria. Soon after Cameron's appointment, a "deputation of respectable colonists" began to organize, arguing that the chief justice had "only arrived six months since from Demerara," that the "community know nothing whatever, of his previous career," and that "he is brotherinlaw of Gov. Douglass [sic] who appointed him."[58] The self-styled "independent colonists" found a spokesperson in missionary and schoolteacher Robert Staines, dismissed by Douglas as "a violent party man... prudent neither in his conduct, nor associations." Staines set out to bring these grievances to a British audience, but his life and the documents he carried were both lost when the ship that carried them went down.[59] The argument continued, and when the Select Committee on the Hudson's Bay Company heard witnesses in England in 1857, a former colonist argued that Cameron was trained as a draper, that he had worked as the superintendent of a sugar estate in Guiana before

---

[56] Fairfax Moresby to Sir, 7 July 1851, enclosed in J. Parker to Frederick Peel, 28 November 1851 CO 305/3, http://bcgenesis.uvic.ca, accessed September 8, 2013.

[57] See Hamar Foster, "Long-Distance Justice: The Criminal Jurisdiction of Canadian Courts West of the Canadas, 1763–1859," *American Journal of Legal History*, 34:1 (January 1990) esp. 43–47.

[58] "The Vancouver Island Resolutions, relative to Judge Cameron, &c," *Pioneer and Democrat* (Washington Territory) August 5, 1854.

[59] James Douglas to George Grey, December 11, 1854, CO 305/5, http://bcgenesis.uvic.ca, accessed September 29, 2012; James Cooper, "Maritime Matters on the North West Coast and Affairs of the Hudson's Bay Company in Early Times," BL, P-C 6, Mflm 1, 9–10.

he ran into financial trouble, and that he had no qualifications for the position of chief justice beyond "the interest of his brother-in-law, the Governor."[60]

Cameron's appointment became a critical flashpoint that circulated around Vancouver Island, nearby American territories, and in England. It carried a set of potent racialized, spatialized, and gendered meanings about the HBC in general and Douglas in particular. An American newspaper reported:

> You must first be informed that a certain Mr. David Cameron, who had not long since arrived from Demerara, and who is fortunately for him, married to the sister of the sapient head of our favored government, has lately been clothed by his brother-in-law with the ermine. The colonists objected to the appointment, and presented a remonstrance to Mr. Douglass [sic] on the subject; he, however, treated this manifestation of public opinion with contempt, and so ignorant is he of the power of the people's voice, that this servant to a company of fur traders – this man over whom the sun of civilization has not dawned these thirty years, and who, does not, perchance know a windmill from a spinning-jinney, and who is bound by the ties of sympathy and affection more closely to the savage than the White man – had the assumption to treat with scorn, and the folly to answer with falsehood, a deputation of respectable colonists who waited on him with the written expression of a great portion of the inhabitants, disapproving of the measure.[61]

Here Cameron's appointment is a signal of Douglas' Caribbean connections, his long association with the HBC, and his affection for Indigenous peoples and spaces. This was not the only article to see the appointment as evidence that Douglas practiced a hybrid, Indigenized, and feminized sort of governance. Another satirized that Cameron was "judge supreme – judge over all, judge in every thing, judge in Queen's bench, equity, common pleas, chancery, judge in cotton prints, glass beads, blankets, rum and tobacco, and in short, a complete *factotum*" whose support lay with a string of racialized and gendered others: "Company's clerks, Canadians, Kanackers, Ethiopians and Eunichs [sic]."[62] The Colonial Office listened to critiques of Cameron's appointment, but they took reassurance from Douglas' response that there were no trained lawyers in Vancouver Island for him to appoint and defense of Cameron's "manly and fearless conduct, in the administration of Justice." It was also noted that Douglas

---

[60] Testimony of James Cooper, in Great Britain, *Report from the Select Committee on the Hudson's Bay Company*, 200; George P. Martin to Charles Frederick, October 16, 1854, enclosed in W. A. B. Hamilton to Herman Merivale, January 27, 1855, CO 305/6, http://bcgenesis.uvic.ca, accessed August 29, 2013.

[61] "The Vancouver Island Resolutions, relative to Judge Cameron, &c," *Pioneer and Democrat* (Olympia, Washington Territory) August 5, 1854.

[62] Olny O'Hallaron, Letter, *Pioneer and Democrat*, September 23, 1854.

had disclosed Cameron's lack of training and kinship to London before the appointment.[63]

The Colonial Office was not without reservations about Douglas' government. Historian James Hendrickson has documented London's concern with Douglas' administrative practices, his handling of the 1859 San Juan dispute or the Pig War, and most of all with his spending.[64] In 1857, a knowledgeable observer could confidentially report to a British parliamentary committee that he considered Douglas "an excellent Governor" and that "the Colonial Office had a great opinion of him from all that I have heard."[65] Misgivings about Douglas' administration accrued over the following years, but in 1861 Colonial Office staff still took a kind of relieved satisfaction in his government. This was a distant colony and one that didn't command much interest in the metropole, and they were relieved that Douglas seemed willing to rule it. One staffer explained that "The public has always seemed to me fortunate in obtaining at this remote and inaccessible settlement, so far out of the reach of much control from home, a Governor of so much self-reliance and practical ability."[66]

American, Canadian, and especially British newcomers to Vancouver Island continued to find Douglas a curious departure from their ideals of what and who a governor should be. Mary Hawks Moody was the wife of the military commander sent to cement Britain's claims to the newly created colony of British Columbia. She found Douglas disconcerting, and plainly hoped that he would be replaced, perhaps by her own husband, Richard. "I had a visit from the Gov:r today," she reported in September of 1859. "I don't get over his formal politeness at all. He certainly is not 'the right man in the right place.' I do wish they wd send us another or make Richard Gov:r; I sh:d not object to that!!!!"[67] The Anglican bishop who arrived in Victoria early in 1860 described Douglas as naïve, and thought this reflected a life lived outside metropolitan space. George

---

[63] Herman Merivale, note dated March 22, 1855, and James Douglas to Archibald Barclay, November 3, 1854, Douglas Correspondence, 1850–1855; James Douglas to George Grey, December 11, 1854, CO 305/5; notes in response to Edward E. Langford to Duke of Newcastle, May 21, 1862, CO 305/19, both at http://bcgenesis.uvic.ca, accessed April 14, 2014.

[64] James E. Hendrickson, "The Retirement of Governor James Douglas: The View from the Colonial Office," unpublished paper, 1984. I am grateful to James Hendrickson for making this paper available to me.

[65] Testimony of Edward Ellis, *Report from the Select Committee on the Hudson's Bay Company*, 350.

[66] Thomas Frederick Elliot, June 11, [1861], note enclosed in James Douglas to Newcastle, January 2, 1861, CO 60/10, http://bcgenesis.uvic.ca, accessed September 29, 2012.

[67] Mary Moody to Mamma, March 21, 1859, "Mary Moody Outward Correspondence," 27.

Hills reported that the governor was duped by suave metropolitans and the letters of introduction they carried. "I think the Governor does not understand characters," he intoned. "His appointments have been of persons subservient to himself & not men of independent feeling & high intelligence." This, Hills explained, could be accounted for "partly to his never having lived in England or in any civilized community."[68]

Observers like these struggled with what to make of Douglas. Sophia Cracroft, Jane Franklin's niece and traveling companion, appreciated Douglas' intelligence and wide reading. But acknowledging this destabilized the presumed dichotomy between metropolitan and colonial people and confused her deeply. How could a man who had lived his life in colonial places and amongst Indigenous people be so capable and knowledgeable?

All people speak with great admiration of the Governor's intellect – and a remarkable man he must be to be thus fit to govern a colony. He left England or rather Scotland as a boy of 15 in the Hudson B. Cos Service, in which he has risen through the usual grades, and has acquired not merely immense local information, but general also, by reading. He has read enormously we are told & is in fact a self educated man, to a point very seldom attained. His manner is singular, and you see in it the traces of long residence in an unsettled country, where the White men are rare & the Indians many. There is gravity & a something besides which some might & do mistake for pomposity, but which is the result of long service in the H.B.Cos service under the above circumstances . . . His family is a very respectable one (from Lanarkshire) – he is the nephew of Sir Niel [Neill] Douglas, – has one nephew in the 11th Hussars. The wonder is that having never been in England or in fact out of the Hudson Bay Territories all his life, he should appear to so much advantage, and should be in any degree fit for his position.[69]

Cracroft was careful to locate Douglas within elite Scottish kin networks and a transimperial circle and made no mention of whatever knowledge she may have had about Douglas' Caribbean history. But none of this was enough, and Cracroft left Vancouver Island both impressed and deeply perplexed by its governor.

Hawks Moody, Cracroft, and Hills were participants in and contributors to what historians have called an imperial network that moved ideas, practices, and people around the nineteenth-century British Empire. Personal correspondence was a critical medium in this traffic, as were the

[68] George Hills, "Journal," December 26, 1861, DNW/EPBC, 168–9, Transcript (hereafter Hills, Journal).

[69] Cracroft, in Dorothy Blakey Smith, ed., *Lady Franklin Visits the Pacific Northwest: Being Extracts from the Letters of Miss Sophia Cracroft, Sir John Franklin's Niece, from February to April 1861 and April to July 1870* (Victoria: Provincial Archives of British Columbia Memoire, No. 11, 1974) 64–65.

putatively private letters intended for wide circulation and sometimes publication. In the summer of 1862 a naval officer began something of a campaign to circulate knowledge of Douglas' shortcomings in England. Edmund Hope Verney was well connected to "improving" metropolitan circles, and this was the intended audience of his argument that Vancouver Island needed a different governor than Douglas. "I think that the sooner the governor is relieved, the better; with every good intention, he is I think a great drag on the place," he explained. Verney followed with a letter that he admitted to be full of "a great deal of scandal, abuse, &c," one offered in an attempt to encourage his father to "help us to get a better governor, we want a man who will raise the standard of excellence in religion, in morals, in dinners, servants, gardens, houses, dress, manners and customs."[70]

For Verney, as for Hills, Douglas' failings reflected a life made and lived in colonial spaces.

Considering his great disadvantages governor Douglas is a wonderful man, but he has no pretension to be a high-minded, superior gentleman; he is very pompous and ridiculous, and always cruizes about in uniform, with a bombadier [sic] of Engineer lashed on a cavalry sword following in his wake: this solemn procession of two may be seen parading Victoria every evening.

Douglas' embrace of the symbols, clothing, and language of imperial authority made him especially laughable, sad, and absurd. Verney and Hills both found the modest parties that Douglas gave at his home made the same point.

[On] the Queen's birthday he gave a state dinner, and put on all the gold lace he could muster: he proposed the Queen's health in a penny-a-liner speech, and three times three: you may guess what a preposterously ridiculous farce it was, when I tell you we were only eleven at table, and all burst out laughing when we ought to have cheered.[71]

The bishop similarly found the Douglas-Connolly family's lack of metropolitan knowledge both startling and hilarious. Hills explained that the family had not known where the well-dressed servant who accompanied him to a dinner party should eat. Eventually they consulted Douglas' English secretary "who informed them that the other gentleman was the Bishops Servant that it was customary to bring a servant on such occasions & that he would wait on table & be quite content in the kitchen."[72]

[70] Edmund Hope Verney to Harry Verney, July 2, 1862; Edmund Hope Verney to Harry Verney, July 20, 1862, both in Allan Pritchard, ed., *Vancouver Island Letters of Edmund Hope Verney, 1862–1865* (Vancouver: UBC Press, 1996) 71–72, 76.
[71] Edmund Hope Verney to Harry Verney, August 2, 1862, 71–72.
[72] Hills, Journal, August 8, 1861, 131.

This sort of cultural cringe went alongside a critique of Douglas' well-known practices of patronage. For both settlers and newcomers, the governor's willingness to reward friends and kin with posts within the colonial administration was a sure indication of his poor government. "It is generally stated," reported Verney, "that all roads are led through the property of the governor or some of his relations, for each of whom he appears to have found a snug berth." Verney expanded his point further, explaining that

the colonies provide for the Governor, his three daughters and his niece: in addition to this the Attorney-General's wife is more distantly related to him: now, can you wonder that people complain that the colonies are governed by a family clique, who know that in these civilized days, their reign cannot last long, and are feathering their nests as fast as they can?[73]

Verney struggled to find the right words to describe Vancouver Island's government, declaring that the "government here is not Yankee certainly, but it is not English: it is a Hudson Bay government, mean, petty, slovenly."[74] While the gloss here was a distinctly disapproving and metropolitan one, the substance of Verney's argument was not much different from what circulated in meetings of independent settlers or in the pages of local newspapers. A few years before, a local newspaper explained that the new colony of British Columbia needed representative government, by which they meant White male suffrage.

If a Legislature is so necessary to throw open to the world the vast resources of the *terra incognita* the *Times* talks about, then obtain a parliament of the good old-fashioned sort, patterned after the Imperial type, and not after the hermaphrodite institutions of such barbarian communities as Ceylon, or such half-unknown places as British Guiana.[75]

By early in 1863 these concerns had become the Colonial Office's own. A delegation of disgruntled settlers from British Columbia visited the Colonial Office in January, and by March the Duke of Newcastle wrote to Douglas explaining that two new governors would be appointed in his place.[76] In June the Anglican bishop George Hills traveled from Victoria to London, and with him came the critiques of Douglas that had long circulated around the informal public sphere. The bishop found the Colonial Office staff notably uninformed about the two colonies, and relished how this made him a special sort of interlocutor. He met with

---

[73] Verney to Verney, July 2, 1862, 72; Verney to Verney, July 20, 1862, 75.
[74] Edmund Hope Verney to Harry Verney, July 16, 1862, 82.
[75] "British Columbia Legislature," *Colonist*, October 17, 1860.
[76] See Hendrickson, "The Retirement."

Chichester Fortescue, Under-Secretary for the Colonies and defended Douglas' appointment of his sons-in-law to positions in the colonial government, arguing that the governor had not abused his office to acquire land and wealth. For Hills, the issue was not what Douglas had done, but who he was. He explained that "The Governor was a fine specimen of a loyal Englishman, but never having seen a Dock, or a Railway he could not be up to the day, but of his integrity there could be no doubt." As a colonial person, Douglas lacked "confidence in his own experience." Fortescue questioned Hills at length about the governor, asking about his questionable appointments, his choice of capitals, and the money spent on road-building. Fortescue concluded that there ought to be two governors and "that this arrangement wd be carried out at once." The under-secretary wondered "what wd become of Gov. Douglas" and Hills replied: "I said he would probably visit Europe & then come & end his days in Vancouver."[77]

Hills' predictions turned out to be mainly true. Douglas retired as governor of Vancouver Island in 1863 and as governor of British Columbia the following year. Arthur Kennedy, a career colonial servant who had worked in Sierra Leone, Hong Kong, Queensland, and Western Australia, was appointed governor of the Island colony. In British Columbia, Douglas was replaced by Frederick Seymour, who had worked in Van Diemen's Land, Antigua, Nevis, and British Honduras. Both Kennedy and Seymour were men who fit neatly within Laidlaw's portrait of typical mid-nineteenth-century Colonial Office appointments. Lytton commented on the traits that made Seymour a good fit for the job, explaining that he was a "highly cultivated & decided man, but quick & retired, distinguished at Oxford."[78]

In Victoria, Douglas and his friends told a triumphalist narrative that stressed the dignity of his retirement and the benefits and honours he accrued from it. Douglas explained that the retirement was in "perfect accordance" with his "wishes and personal convenience" and argued that "during the whole course of my service I have experienced nothing but kindness from Her Majesty's Government."[79] The pension he received was meaningful recognition. "The Queen, god bless her, has granted me a ~~life~~ pension for life of L500 a year," he wrote to his half-sister Jane in Paris; "this I value as a recognition of my services perhaps as much as for the money – part."[80] The story of a loyal and valued governor

---

[77] Hills, Journal, June 26, 1863, 109, 111.   [78] Hills, Journal, August 21, 1863, 129.

[79] James Douglas to Colonel Hawkins, November 23, 1863, "Victoria Correspondence Book, 1859–1864," HBCA, E 243/10.

[80] James Douglas to Miss [Jane] Douglas, December 15, 1866, in James Douglas, Correspondence Outward, Dec. 15, 1866 to March 16, 1867, BCA, B/40/3, Transcript

and a grateful monarch became the one that locals told. "Honoured by the Queen, valued by her Government, beloved by the people, be they British or foreign, known and respected from Bering straits to Cape Horn, looked upon and admired as one of nature's noblemen, he rallies around him friends innumerable. This is not retirement, but elysium," explained one newspaper.[81] Especially critical to these celebratory accounts was Douglas being named Knight Commander of the Order of the Bath. His friends and family were pleased that he would now be known as Sir. "I am so glad dear Papa is Sir James now," one daughter wrote to another.[82] One of Douglas' old fur-trade cronies commented that this title was more valuable and meaningful than a hereditary one. To be named to the Order of the Bath was "a distinction which though not hereditary conveys with it in the English estimation a degree of honor far in advance of that implied by a simple knighthood."[83] This nuance was mainly lost on those around Douglas, and the claim that he had been knighted was made regularly and sometimes escalated to him having been "Knighted by Queen Victoria's own hand."[84]

The events that marked the end of Douglas' career as governor spoke to tensions between different iterations of empire. The formal dinner held at Victoria's theatre was described as a "glorious and brilliant affair," with the dress circle and boxes "filled with ladies." If Douglas' wife attended the dinner the local newspapers made no mention of it. They did mention the speeches and toasts from local representatives of state, including Douglas' son-in-law Helmcken, his brother-in-law Cameron, and his niece's husband, W. A. G. Young. In the ceremony, the predictable symbols of a martial empire – flags, toasts to the army, navy, and the royal family – were performed alongside enduring local issues, including contentious relations between Vancouver Island and British Columbia – roads and mail service.[85]

As an older woman Martha Douglas Harris would recall "a far more interesting and less formal ceremony" held at the family home, where "Mr. Douglas sat at the side of the table and his wife held her customary

(hereafter Douglas Correspondence, 1866–1867); "Papers relating to Order of the Bath, 1858, 1863," in James Douglas, "Papers," BCA, Add MSS 1112, File 6.

81 "Evening Express," March 10, 1864, in Martha (Douglas) Harris Collection, BCA, Add MSS 2789, File 19.

82 Jane Dallas to Cecilia Helmcken, n.d. [1864?], in Helmcken Family Fonds, BCA, Add MSS 505, Volume 14, Transcript (hereafter Helmcken Papers).

83 Alexander Caulfield Anderson, "History of the Northwest Coast," HBCA, Transcript, E 294/1, 30.

84 F. W. Howay, William S. Lewis, and Jacob A. Meyers, "Angus McDonald: A Few Items of the West," *Washington Historical Quarterly*, 8:3 (1917) 229.

85 "Grand Banquet to Sir James Douglas," *Colonist*, March 11, 1864. Also see "Address on the Occasion of Retirement by Civil Servants of the Colony, 1864," BCA, Add MSS 1112, File 8.

place at the head" and where "our esteemed hostess, Lady Douglas" was toasted and acknowledged as "the wife of the Governor of British Columbia, and the first lady in the land."[86] This version resituates Douglas' being named to the Order of the Bath in time, and more profoundly, in social and domestic space. Here it is not the honorifics of a distant empire or the public celebrations of a colonial sphere, but an intimate affair in the family home where the presence of Connolly Douglas was acknowledged and celebrated. This story reflects the local, creole sort of governor that Douglas was, removes his political career from the overwrought public space of settler Victoria, and resituates it within the intimate space of home, most of all, in the presence and full recognition of his wife.

Douglas called his retirement trip to England, Scotland, and Europe in 1864 and 1865 "a return home after so long an absence."[87] In doing so he invoked the presumption that metropole was "home" and the colony "away," the former assumed to be superior and original and the latter flawed and derivative. But Douglas' life, and even his administration of the colonies of Vancouver Island and British Columbia, made clear how labored and fragile this distinction was. His was a life lived in a series of colonial spaces and as a governor he was lauded for his capacity to work and speak in colonial vernaculars. Douglas was also the effective head of a local colonial state committed to an ongoing, visceral, and violent process of Indigenous dispossession. Historians of colonial societies, including those of Vancouver Island and British Columbia, have long acknowledged the complicated and layered histories of empire *in situ*. Historians of empire, as Antoinette Burton and Jean Allman explain, have offered different analyses that emphasize "the power and hegemony of the imperial state."[88] Histories of empire would be better able to speak to complicated postcolonial and settler colonial presents if they more thoroughly recognized how the imperial world was made in complicated and ongoing conversations with local peoples, places, and their thick and abiding histories.

Between Douglas' appointment as governor in 1851 and Connolly Douglas' death in 1890, the racial and national languages and connections engaged by the family and used to interpret them shifted but never

---

[86] N. de Bertrand Lugrin, *The Pioneer Women of Vancouver Island, 1843–1866* (Victoria: Women's Canadian Club, 1928) 22–23. This was based on Martha Douglas Harris' recollections: from "Mrs. Harris' recollections of her mother, and stories heard at her mother's knee, this account has largely been written." (24).

[87] James Douglas, "Journal of Sir James Douglas' Trip to Europe, May 14, 1864 to May 16, 1865," Transcript, BCA, B/20/1864, January 27, 1865, 157–158 (hereafter Douglas Journal).

[88] Antoinette Burton and Jean Allman, "Gender, Colonialism, and Feminist Collaboration," *Radical History Review*, 101 (Spring 2008) 200.

disappeared, lost their authority, or were wholly replaced. This confirms American historian Martha Hodes' argument that race has both a "mercurial nature" and an "abiding power."[89] It also prompts us to acknowledge that in the nineteenth-century imperial world race was local and irrecoverably tied to place and to the distinct histories contained therein. In the latter half of the nineteenth century, the Douglas-Connolly family's story also reminds us of the critical role played by class and material power, and by gender, kinship, and the significance of individual performance – including of sociability, manners, and the body, but also the more ephemeral terrain of character – in making and remaking race in different lives and different places.

Observers in Victoria explained the governor's wife and the challenge her identity posed by locating her outside local space and current time. Her particular kind of Indigeneity was usually ascribed to Red River. This was not a straightforward description of Connolly Douglas' origins – she may have been born near Red River, but she never lived for any amount of time there – but a more general association of her with the elite Metis peoples associated with the fur trade in general and Red River Colony in particular. In 1858, a Canadian passing through the colony described Douglas' wife as "a lady from Red River Settlement."[90] In 1850s and '60s Victoria, the association of Connolly Douglas with Red River drew its shelf life from its capacity to disassociate her and her family from the Indigenous peoples who surrounded them on Vancouver Island. A hopeful gold miner who passed through Victoria and paid a de rigueur visit to Douglas in 1862 wrote about drinking to "the health and happiness of the Governor, his wife and family," and noted that "We did not see the Governor's wife. I understand she is a red river Indian, but not a woman of much colour." That this author did not see Connolly Douglas did not stop him from offering an assessment of her race and what it meant. In doing so he accorded her the class status that came with the term "lady" and situated her with the thick Metis histories of Red River. This geographic distancing relied on the distinction Europeans had for some time made between coastal and plains Indigenous people, one that, as historian Elizabeth Vibert has shown, accorded plains people with a set of martial and moral virtues.[91]

[89] Martha Hodes, "The Mercurial Nature and Abiding Power of Race: A Transnational Family Story," *American Historical Review*, 108:1 (February 2003) 64–118.
[90] C. C. Gardiner, "To The Fraser River Mines in 1858," ed. Robie L. Reid, *British Columbia Historical Quarterly*, 1:1 (October 1937) 253.
[91] John Emmerson, *Voyages, Travels, & Adventures by John Emmerson of Wolsingham* (Durham, UK: Wm. Ainsley, 1865) 34–35; Elizabeth Vibert, *Traders' Tales: Narratives of Cultural Encounter in the Columbia Plateau* (Norman, OK: University of Oklahoma

To locate the governor's wife within the geographic space of Red River disassociated her from local Indigenous peoples and linked her to the fur trade, understood as a particular temporal space that was antecedent to the pressing present of British Columbia's emergent settler regime. It also allowed observers to access romantic and picturesque traditions of imagining the fur trade and its traditions. Writing in the late nineteenth century, one Protestant missionary made clear that he considered the marriages between newcomer men and Indigenous women in the fur trade wholly distinct from those occurring around him. "In olden days the Hudson Bay was encouraged to form communities with the natives from motives of policy and were in effect married," he explained. He did not extend this respect to the imperial intimacies forged in settler British Columbia, explaining that these were made "without any kind of sanction and the offspring consequent upon such cohabitation have grown up with out any kind of sanctities of home life."[92]

However observers might dislocate Connolly Douglas' Indigeneity both geographically and temporally, it could not or would not be disappeared altogether. The governor's wife was a kind of Indigenous woman, and the governor himself had a tenuous connection to Britishness. Connolly Douglas' Indigeneity and Douglas' lack of secure metropolitan credentials were readily available and effective discursive tools. In the context of mid-nineteenth-century Victoria they clearly trumped Blackness, or at least the variety of it that Douglas embodied. As Douglas accrued credentials, authority, and wealth, his Blackness no longer became a topic of polite discussion, and became submerged in coy and thinly allusive terms. Thus one author noted that "A gentleman of large property, reported to be of Mulatto origin, is married to a half-breed Indian."[93] Douglas might be explained as a "dark-complecioned man,"[94] but it was not the languages of Blackness that circulated around settler Victoria that observers called upon when they described the governor.

For more than a decade in a critical period of Vancouver Island and British Columbia's history, Douglas was the most politically powerful and among the wealthiest men there, and he would retain this material wealth and cultural authority after his retirement. He managed the tensions produced by this particular collision of identities and relationships

---

Press, 1997) esp. Chapter 7; Elizabeth Vibert, "The Contours of Everyday Life: Food and Identity in the Plateau Fur Trade," in Carolyn Podruchny and Laura Peers, eds., *Gathering Places: Aboriginal and Fur-Trade Histories* (Vancouver: UBC Press, 2010).
92 Good, "British Columbia," 102.
93 Matthew Macfie, *Vancouver Island and British Columbia: Their History, Resources, and Prospects* (London: Longman, Green, Longman, Roberts, and Green, 1865) 379.
94 Helmcken, *Reminiscences*, 81.

in a number of ways. Most obviously, he used his considerable wealth and political authority to insulate himself and his family from the worst excesses of racial thinking. He also undertook a highly demanding racial and gendered performance. This was in part an embodied one. Douglas took care with his clothing. In 1869, although notoriously tight-fisted, he shelled out for a new wardrobe – including a morning coat, a suit, and twelve pairs of kid gloves – that associated him with the metropole's particular kind of bourgeois respectability and privilege. Making his order to a London tailor, Douglas asked that "the material and finish be of the very best description and sutiable [sic] in style to a staid elderly gentlemen [sic] of Three score and five, who is yet, however very particular about the fit and appearance of his clothes."[95]

This performance was also one of character and demeanor. Occasionally the archive yields up the story of an unguarded and personable Douglas. Christina Macdonald McKenzie Williams recalled him as "a very jolly, companionable man – a great ladies' man." She remembered a long stage-coach ride where Douglas brought her drinks, held her hand, and admired her capabilities.[96] More often contemporaries described Douglas as hyper-competent, stern, unyielding, and constantly concerned with his own reputation and dignity. Americans in particular liked to narrate stories of the governor walking around Victoria preceded by a uniformed and armed Scotsman, or keeping visitors at a physical distance even if it meant depriving them of the warmth of a fire on a cold winter day. "There was much ceremony," recalled one American observer. "Douglas himself was the greatest man to stand on dignity you ever saw."[97]

Those who knew Douglas well also tended to remember him as overly formal and officious. A colleague's daughter recalled that he "was much impressed with the dignity of his own high office and somewhat pompous in manner on state and ceremonial occasions."[98] Helmcken was Douglas' son-in-law. The two men worked together for almost three decades and relied on one another for domestic and household support, especially after Helmcken became a single father. For all of these points of intimate connection, Helmcken recalled that Douglas was "not humorous – never

95 James Douglas to Mstrs. Olliver and Brown, June 2, 1869, Private Letter Book.
96 Christina McDonald McKenzie Williams, "The Daughter of Angus McDonald," *Washington Historical Quarterly*, 13 (1922) 116–115.
97 Elwood Evans in "John M. Swan & the Olympia Club Conversazione," Bancroft Collection, P-B 15, Mflm 3, BL, 12; John M. Swan, "The Colonisation around Puget Sound," Bancroft MS, BL, P-B 21, Mflm 3.
98 Mrs. J. C. Keith, "Fort Victoria in Pioneer Days, 70 Years Ago," *Daily Province* (Vancouver) January 24, 1925. Also see Barry M. Gough, "Sir James Douglas as Seen by his contemporaries, a preliminary list," *BC Studies*, 44 (Winter 1979) 32–40.

joked – always staid and decorous" and noted that "personal experiences were not much talked about, excepting when the Chief Factors and Chief Traders happened to collect in Victoria or strangers asked questions."[99] In 1870 John Tod included himself and Douglas in a group of four who were "the last of old fur traders."[100] By then Tod and Douglas had known each other for four decades, and their working lives and families were knitted together at multiple intersections. Still Tod found Douglas distant and self-absorbed. "I had a long chat the other day with our friend Douglas (now Sir James) ever still and formal as in time past qualities which, from long habit he could not now lay aside, if he would, and probably ought not, if he could," Tod reported. A year later, Tod explained that Douglas was stout and healthy but isolated and self-absorbed. "Yet old age has evidently wrought a perceptible change in his, once powerful, mind, which seems now entirely absorbed in its self." Despite his undeniable wealth, Douglas was "as eager and grasping after money as ever" and sometimes "seized with gloomy apprehensions of dying a beggar at last." Tod explained that his old friend was "old, crafty, and selfish" and, as a direct result, isolated.[101]

Douglas struggled when the strangers did ask questions about who he was. On a French omnibus in 1865, he was politely asked about where he lived. His reply stressed his "curious" history, his long time in North America, and his new recognition that the presumed distinction between "home" and "away" did not apply to him:

My history is a rather curious one. I left England, on leaving school and have never returned to it till now – After an absence of 40 years – Described the Colonies – all much interested – Reflection on a return home after so long an absence – more painful than agreeable – the fact of nature remains the same, but every thing else is changed. I was advised of these changes, deaths and departures were duly reported, but it was only upon my return that I felt the stern reality. Before then I saw only the image of home as I left it, peopled with those who were dear to me – indelibly photographed as it were upon the mind. The vision is now dispelled and the past with its delusive hopes, has forever vanished.[102]

Douglas' life challenged readily available narratives about nations and empires. Sometimes he might challenge them, but more often, he opted

[99] Helmcken, *Reminiscences*, 140.
[100] John Tod to Edward Ermatinger, March 22, 1870, Ermatinger Papers, Volume I, HBCA, E 94/1, Transcript, 185 (hereafter Ermatinger Papers).
[101] John Tod to Edward Ermatinger, May 20, 1868, Ermatinger Papers, Volume II, 166; John Tod to Edward Ermatinger, November 12, 1868, Ermatinger Papers, Volume II, 170; John Tod to Edward Ermatinger, March 22, 1870, Ermatinger Papers, Volume II, 185–186.
[102] Douglas, Journal, January 27, 1865, 157–158.

Figure 7.2 James Douglas, 1876.

simply to not discuss his life. "My father was a very modest man and never could understand why people were so curious," explained Martha Douglas Harris to an inquiring biographer in 1923, asking that the limited information she was willing to provide not be published.[103]

It is easy to read Douglas' self-fashioning as a calculated attempt to "pass," in the American lexicon. But that is too simple, partly because Douglas never really passed. As poet and cultural critic Wayde Compton notes, Douglas never confirmed or denied his Blackness.[104] He also both formally and informally associated himself and his administration with Victoria's Black community. When Franklin and Cracroft came to town, Douglas arranged for them to stay at the best local boarding house, kept

103 Walter Sage, "Notes of a Conversation with Mrs. Dennis Harris," September 13, 1923, Sage Papers, Box 36.
104 Wayde Compton, 'JD,' *Bluesprint: Black British Columbian Literature and Orature* (Vancouver: Arsenal Pulp Press, 2001) 272.

by the Moses family. "They are probably one generation if not farther from the pure Negro, & Mr. Moses calls himself an Englishman, which of course he is politically & therefore justly," Cracroft explained.[105] Discourses of passing cannot account for Douglas' clear and public connection to the self-identified Black community in and around Victoria and are also predicated upon a highly distinctive post-Civil War American reckoning of Blackness. Douglas lived nineteenth-century Blackness in different circumstances and on different terms. In Victoria, as in Oregon Territory, Black/White hierarchies were not the sole or main racial cleavage. The amount of social latitude accorded to the mixed-descent elite had certainly shrunk over the course of the nineteenth century, but it had not, as the history of the Douglas-Connolly family surely indicates, disappeared altogether. Self-invention and re-invention were made possible by a far-flung empire tied together with limited communication networks.[106] It was in this context that a man born into the complicated location of free people of color and married into an elite Metis family, or at least an especially careful and diligent one who was repeatedly in the right place at the right time, could serve as the highest representative of the British Empire in a northern North American colony.

The family's British identities and connections were cultivated and celebrated. Douglas donated money to the St. Andrew's Society.[107] In settler Victoria the family was usually described as Scottish, and less often English or Irish. Douglas was said to be the descendant of various storied Scots, including "Black Douglas."[108] These vernacular attributions were given official weight in official censuses taken at the end of the colonial period and in British Columbia's early days as a Canadian province. In 1870, a local census enumerated the entire Douglas-Connolly family as "White," and a later one listed Connolly's background as "Irish."[109]

The scholarship on the "British world" has made clear how amenable discourses of Britishness were to highly localized and colloquial performances. Douglas' life both exemplified this and demonstrated some of the limits to these vernacular and hybrid sorts of Britishness. The trip

[105] Smith, ed., *Lady Franklin Visits*, 6.
[106] See Martha Hodes, *The Sea Captain's Wife: A True Story of Love, Race and War in the Nineteenth Century* (New York: Norton, 2006) 231; Kirsten McKenzie, *Scandal in the Colonies: Sydney and Cape Town, 1820–1850* (University of Melbourne Press, 2004); Donald B. Smith, *Honore Jaxon: Prairie Visionary* (Regina: Coteau Books, 2007).
[107] James Douglas to Mr. Burns, November 29, 1868, Private Letter Book.
[108] See, for instance, R. E. Gosnell, *A History: British Columbia* ([Victoria]: Lewis Publishing, 1906) 192.
[109] Vancouver Island Census of 1870, Record 1871: 2091; Canadian Census of 1881, family 466, http://vihistory.ca, accessed July 10, 2009.

that he made to England, Scotland, and Europe in 1864 and 1865 was an opportunity to rearticulate his British identity and reactivate and in some cases create kin ties. "Sir James Douglas will return to England in a week or ten days, after an absence of fifty years," reported Verney. "I hardly think he will remain long in England, as he will find himself such a stranger, and so utterly lost in the crowd."[110] It was a long trip of slightly more than a year's duration that took Douglas close to the locations of his childhood. He traveled via the West Indies, visiting plantations in Jamaica and the British colonial officials in San Domingo and St. Thomas. It was there that Douglas observed a "bevy of Creole Ladies" who spoke "in a peculiar, drawling style of English" and conversed with a "wonderfully intelligent, *woman like* child" on her way to England for school.[111]

Douglas' trip would take him first to England. In London he visited the standard metropolitan attractions: Parliament, Westminster Abbey, the National Gallery, Madam Tussaud's "wax works," Regent's Park, and the British Museum, which he found a "wonderful place." Later he would attend meetings of the British Association for the Advancement of Science, remarking that "No one can be more sensible than I am of the benefits to be derived from the extension of Science." He would go to France, Switzerland, Germany, Italy, and Spain, visiting major sites and friends and making careful observations. In December of 1864 he made an argument for "the principal of naturalism," or that the "best social state" was a limited one committed to guaranteeing "public peace" and based in the recognition that "Liberty of conscience and of worship is an inherent right possessed by every man, and must be guaranteed and protected." Douglas may have become committed to a certain kind of liberalism, but not to democracy. In April 1865 he returned to England, and there he explained that "Representative Governments cannot be carried on without recourse directly or indirectly to bribery and corrupting influences."[112]

This was a trip by a retiring colonial servant making himself directly acquainted with the offices of empire he had long corresponded with and reported to but had little direct contact with. Douglas met Frederick Rogers and other Colonial Office officials, but had "Difficulty in finding

---

[110] Edmond Hope Verney to Harry Verney, May 2, 1864, in Pritchard, ed., *Vancouver Island Letters*, 202.

[111] James Douglas, "Journal of Sir James Douglas' Trip to Europe, May 14, 1864 to May 16, 1865," BCA, B/20/1864, Transcript, June 9, 1864, 21–23; June 13, 1964, 24; June 16, 1864, 27 (hereafter Douglas Travel Journal).

[112] Douglas Travel Journal, July 25, 1864, 45–46; September 16, 1864, 66; December 31, 1864, 134–135; May 1, 1865, 220.

Sir. Ed. Lytton." He dined with Edward Cardwell, Secretary of State for the Colonies. Cardwell's Scottish wife inquired if he knew "Mrs. Douglas of Douglas' park – or Archibald of Glenart – or Tom of Dunlop – or John Douglas." Douglas was proud that he "knew them all." He also advised Cardwell on colonial policies, urging him not to "deviate from the Indian policy" established under Douglas. This advice would not be heeded as subsequent governments undid critical components of Douglas' regime, but at the time, the old governor was pleased with and grateful for Cardwell's thanks and recognition.[113] In these meetings Douglas asserted his own location in circuits of imperial governance and his authoritative knowledge of colonial places and peoples.

Douglas' time in Scotland was spent with an eye to reacquainting himself with the landscape of his childhood and re-establishing ties with his father's kinfolk. He met with Douglases in Edinburgh, Glasgow, and Inchmarten, tracing complicated lines of connection but not always explaining his own relation to them. He visited Lanark, noting that it had grown in size, and that "The old people are all gone, and even their names are no more known in their once familiar haunts –, and their very memory has perished – as it is with them so will it be with us." He had repeated meetings and meals with his sister Jane, born to his father's Scottish marriage, an unmarried woman living in Paris.[114] It was in a letter to Jane that he would explain his interest in remaining near "my peaceful home."[115]

It was the mechanism of marriage that provided the most active and reliable metropolitan ties for Douglas. The extended family of son-in-law Arthur Bushby was important here, as were the families of the men who married Douglas' nieces Edith and Rebecca. Alexander Grant Dallas was Berbice-born and had a long history of colonial careering before he came to Vancouver Island with the HBC and married Douglas' second eldest daughter, Jane. In 1862 Jane Douglas Dallas was living in London, and she missed home and kin terribly. "I feel so lonely sometimes & as tears wont come I can only wring my hands & stretch out my arms towards home," she explained. In letters to her sister Cecilia, she stressed the fundamental difference of metropolitan society. "It is so different from Victoria you know," she explained, stating that a friend's return to Victoria was no surprise given that "everything is in such a different style

[113] Douglas Travel Journal, June 29, 1864, 35; July 4, 1864, 37; June 30, 1865, 36; July 20, 1864, 43–44; April 26, 1865, 219; May 1, 1865, 219, 220.
[114] Douglas Travel Journal, August 26, 1864, 56; December 5, 1864, 118; December 6, 1864, 118; December 8, 1864, 120–121; December 11, 1864, 122.
[115] James Douglas to Jane Douglas, July 13, 1868, Private Letter Book.

to what she has been accustomed." Domestic servants were different, clothing was different, and configurations of class were different. Douglas Dallas assessed the streetscape of mid-nineteenth-century Britain with a critical eye for class politics and urban poverty. She wrote to her sister Victoria about the fashions being different from "our country," about her in-laws' many domestic servants, and about donkeys and carts that resembled the ones her family had before only seen in the pages of *Punch*. She sent greetings to "my poor Indian boy" and struggled with the embodied urban poverty of London. "It is quite dreadful to sit at a window in town to see the miserable beggars & deformed people that pass by," she explained.[116]

At her in-laws' home in Inverness and in London, Douglas Dallas had access to metropolitan knowledge, networks, and material culture. "Both my mother & sisterinlaw are so kind as they can be to me," she explained. She took up opportunities to transform her embodied self, "overhauling my teeth" with daily visits to the dentist. She had a careful eye for fashion, noting that "crimson & scarlet cloaks are all the rage right now" and using her new knowledge to correct her sisters' use of the words "ball dresses" and "evening dresses."[117] In London, the Dallases were well connected and busy. They rode around Hyde Park, visited the "new Exhibition building," had their photographs taken at a studio, toured the National Gallery, and called on naval and Colonial Office officials. This was about accessing metropolitan cultural authority, but it was also about remaking colonial networks anew in metropolitan space. Dallas was a regular presence at the HBC's London headquarters. He and Douglas Dallas dined regularly with Angela Burdett-Coutts, who had endowed the Anglican Church's work in British Columbia, and spent time with Douglas-Connolly kin, including the Doughty, Bushby, and Cameron families.[118]

Dallas and Douglas Dallas relocated permanently to Scotland in 1864, keeping an estate at Dunain and sometimes a residence in London. They raised nine children, and their prosperous Scottish home served as a stable metropolitan base for the Douglas-Connolly family in the metropole. James Douglas' and Dallas' ongoing differences about questions of the

---

[116] Jane Dallas to Cecilia Helmcken, July 20, 1861, Helmcken Papers, Volume 14, File 9; Jane Dallas to Cecilia Helmcken, January 20, 1862, Helmcken Papers, Volume 14, File 9, Transcript; Jane Dallas to Cecilia Helmcken, July 5, [1861], Helmcken Papers, Volume 14, File 9.

[117] Jane Dallas to Cecilia Helmcken, October 19, [1861]; Jane Dallas to Cecilia Helmcken, October 19, [1861]; Jane Dallas to Agnes Bushby, October 17, 1861, all Helmcken Papers, Volume 14, File 9, Transcript.

[118] Alexander Grant Dallas, Journal, 1862, HBCA E 36/2.

HBC, land, and colonial governance did not seem to seriously limit the relations between the two households or two men. Dallas and Douglas Dallas hosted Douglas during his retirement trip, and it was there that he had one of his most heartfelt reunions. In August 1864 he arrived at the Dunain house:

> on enquiring at the door of the house, she recognized my voice, and I heard her exclaim Oh my own dear papa she rushed to the door and threw herself into my arms – overcome by my emotions I could hardly speak either to her or Dallas, but made up for my silence by a hearty and prolonged shake of the hand. I cannot express the joy I felt on this happy occasion.

When Douglas said goodbye to Jane and her children a few weeks later he found it "impossible to repress the painful feeling, that it may be for the last time," but "kept these sad feelings strictly confined to my own breast."[119] When a friend visited the Dallas' Scottish estate in 1885, he found Jane stouter, but otherwise "little altered," in "fine" surroundings, and interested in news of "old friends and the Island home she still loves."[120] Douglas Dallas had been born a colonial daughter in Fort Vancouver in 1839, and lived her adult life as a secure member of a provincial British bourgeoisie. Her children had different if no less imperial identities and experiences. In the middle of the twentieth century, a daughter born in Scotland recollected: "I, alas, have never seen the beautiful Country or the 'Rockies' as I was married to a soldier and most of our life we were roaming about India, Kashmir, and South Africa."[121]

In a range of ways, Caribbean, Metis, and British histories complicated and contextualized the Douglas-Connolly family's claims to Britishness. Children remained a powerful archive. As John Adams suggests, given names held particular meaning in the family.[122] Given names situated children within lineages and carried itinerant histories from place to place. The Douglas-Connolly children's names placed them within both their maternal and paternal lineages and within Guyanese, Scottish, and

---

[119] Douglas Travel Journal, August 8, 1864, 50; August 24, 1864, 54–55. See W. Kaye Lamb, "Dallas, Alexander Grant," in *Dictionary of Canadian Biography*, Volume XI, University of Toronto/Université Laval, 2003, www.biographi.ca, accessed January 9, 2013.

[120] J. D. Pemberton to John Sebastian Helmcken, November 22, 1884, Helmcken Papers, Volume 2, File 11.

[121] [Cecilia A. Rickards], "Recollections from Various Sources of the Life of My Father – Alexander Grant Dallas – of Dunain, Invernesshire", 1948, in "Dallas, Alexander Grant, Miscellaneous Information Relating To," BCA, W/D16, 4.

[122] This line of argument is suggested by John Adams, *Old Square Toes and his Lady: The Life of James and Amelia Douglas* (Victoria: Horsdal and Shubert, 2001), for example, 106.

Canadian histories: Martha and Rebecca were from Douglas' probable maternal line, and Jane, James, Alexander, and Cecilia were names used by Douglas' Scottish family. The Connolly lineage was less visible but still present in given names. One daughter was named after Amelia, and the family's one son to survive early childhood was James William, named for both his father and his maternal grandfather.

The ties of kin and lineage were not just symbolic. Douglas' ties to his sister Cecilia were active enough for him to sponsor her daughter's education, to fold her husband into his network of colonial patronage, to welcome her family into his home, and to include her daughters and their descendants in his will. But the importance of Guyana as a location and a source of meaning slipped farther out of sight as the nineteenth century wore on. Thirteen years after Douglas' grandmother willed his daughters some money, he explained to a solicitor "that, yourself accepted, I have no acquaintances in Demerara."[123] Without the tethers of human ties, with little available language to name his family's history and possible social costs for doing so, Guyana became one of the many locations where relations might be sent on errands of empire. In 1873, Young, who had served as Colonial Secretary under Douglas' administration and was married to Douglas' Demerara-born niece Cecilia, was appointed Colonial Secretary of British Guiana. Douglas was thrilled at this rise in Young's colonial fortunes but had nothing to say about where it would occur. Another relation reported that Cecilia and her children would be staying "home," by which they meant England.[124] This remobilized the distinction between "home" and "away" along predictable imperial lines, and cut the family's histories in Guyana entirely out of the equation.

That the family's Metis history was closer at hand made it more complicated to navigate. Christina McDonald McKenzie Williams recalled Connolly Douglas' joy at hearing "the old language," which she defined as a mixture of French, "Indian," and English, a reasonably good definition of Michif.[125] Another old friend spoke of Connolly Douglas' fondness for the country foods of bison tongue and camas or bitter root. Angus McDonald sent these delicacies to her Victoria home and

---

[123] James Douglas to James Stuart, October 7, 1868, Private Letter Book, 102.

[124] James Douglas to Martha Douglas, September 16, 1873, Letters to Martha; Alexander Grant Dallas to John Sebastian Helmcken, November 15, 1878, Helmcken Papers, Volume 2, File 5. Also see James E. Hendrickson, "Young, Sir William Alexander George," in *Dictionary of Canadian Biography*, Volume XI, University of Toronto/Université Laval, 2003, www.biographi.ca, accessed November 26, 2012.

[125] Christina McDonald McKenzie Williams, "The Daughter of Angus McDonald," *Washington Historical Quarterly*, 13 (1922) 116.

celebrated her preferences: "Roots and buffalo tongues for this lady while she is much bored by the compound dishes which the rank and wealth of civilization offer her table every day." McDonald reported that Connolly Douglas "often expresses a desire to see the Indian country before she died."[126] For the Indigenous people in and around Victoria, the city was of course a kind of "Indian country," but it was not the one that this old fur trader had in mind when he invoked the specific Metis space of the western fur trade as a location of shared memory, yearning, and loss.

The family's Metis kin were both present and absent in settler Victoria. Connolly Douglas' strongest bonds of friendship were to other elite Metis families, but her family of birth was spread out geographically, reshaped by the shifting fortunes of the Indigenous elite in nineteenth-century North America, and marked by their father's high-profile remarriage and the court case that contested it. As for the imperial families analyzed by historian Laura Ishiguro, letters provided a means of maintaining ties of kinship across geographical spaces that were not much more navigable than oceans. Amelia's sister Marguerite was a nun with the Soeur Gris in the largely Metis community of Red River. Their mother, Miyo Nipay, lived in the convent with her daughter, and would die there in 1862. Marguerite wrote a long letter to one of her Victoria nieces in 1858. She complained that she had not heard from her distant kin in four years, assuring them that her "Dear mother" had not forgotten them. She told of an aging mother who brightened when she received news of family, a brother who had died unexpectedly, and a widely scattered set of relations. Their brother John was in Montreal, James was in Peru, and Henry was with the HBC at Esquimaux Bay.[127]

The Connolly family's geographic mobility and elite status did not preclude a kind of Indigenous identity. Marguerite made an application for scrip under Canada's "Half-Breed Land Act" in 1875, claiming herself as the daughter of a Canadian and a Cree. In doing so, this Connolly put

[126] F. W. Howay, William S. Lewis, and Jacob A. Meyers, "Angus McDonald: A Few Items of the West," *Washington Historical Quarterly*, 8:3 (1917) 225.
[127] Marguerite Connolly to Cecilia Douglas Helmcken, May 8, 1858, Helmcken Papers, Volume 14, File 2. See Laura Ishiguro, "Settling Complaints: Discontent and Place in Late-Nineteenth-Century British Columbia," in Karen Dubinsky, Adele Perry, and Henry Yu, eds., *Within and without the Nation: Canadian History as Transnational History* (University of Toronto Press, in press). Also see Lesley Erickson, "Repositioning the Missionary: Sara Riel, the Grey Nuns, and Aboriginal Women in Catholic Missionary Northwest," in Sarah Carter and Lesley Erickson, eds., *Recollecting: Lives of Aboriginal Women of the Canadian Northwest and Borderlands* (Edmonton: Athabasca University Press, 2011).

her identity as a Metis person with a particular claim on the state into the colonial archive.[128] Martha Douglas Harris would use different tools to put her Indigenous history into the written record. In 1901 she published a small book that was in effect a work of salvage ethnography, beginning with a predictable lament for Indigenous society withering in the face of presumably relentless and inevitable White arrival. "Their legends are now fast being forgotten, and as a contribution towards their preservation, I have translated them as a memento of British Columbia," she promised. Her authorial voice shifted when she wrote her own life into the project with a concluding section on "Folk Lore of the Cree Indians." "As a little girl I used to listen to these legends with the greatest delight, and in order not to lose them, I have written down what I remember of them," she wrote. She went on to note the limits of the written word for conveying that which was best expressed in person.[129]

This was a particular and highly precarious kind of Indigenous identity. People with similar backgrounds spoke of their Indigenous histories and distanced themselves from those they named as "Indians" at the same time. In the early twentieth century, a descendant of the Tolmie and Work families criticized a local historian's depiction of her grandparents, asking that the author remove descriptions of children wearing "skins" and references to "papooses" with a firm claim of denial: "They were not Indian."[130] The kind of Indigenous history claimed by people like these had no ready and widely agreed-on language. The Connollys were part of historic Metis communities and all of their most enduring markers: the territories northwest of the Great Lakes, the Roman Catholic Church, the French, Michif, and Cree languages, the fur trade. But their late nineteenth-century lives were not contained within such geography, cultural reference points, or economy. Correspondence maintained kinship ties across geographical space as it did for so many imperial families. In 1869 Douglas wrote to a Connolly nephew who had a "good position" with a San Francisco wine merchant.[131] Marguerite Connolly replied to her widowed sister's letter in 1884, careful to note the

128 Scrip Affidavit for Marguerite Connolly, Library and Archives Canada, RG 15-D-II-8-a, http://collectionscanada.gc.ca, accessed November 29, 2012.
129 Martha Harris Douglas, *History and Folklore of the Cowichan Indians* (Victoria: Colonist Printing and Publishing, 1901) n.p., 7–8, 121.
130 "Copy: From Jean Tolmie, June 25th, 1904. Comments upon the First 15 Chapters (or part of) Mrs. E. E. Dyes Book, Ronald [sic] McDonald," in Edward Huggins, "Huggins Letters Outward 1899–1906 to Mrs. Eva Emery Dye, Joseph Huntsman," typescript, 83–84. Thanks to the Tacoma Public Library for making this available.
131 James Douglas to Edward [Connolly], December 29, 1869, Private Letter Book.

limited access that she as a nun had to letter writing, and that she was grateful for the modern gift of photography. "What a God send is photography," she declared, seeing it as a medium through which God "brought to me the dear faces of those loved ones, from whom I have been parted for so many long years, and others whom I have never seen, otherwise than through the eyes of a loving heart." Marguerite assured her sister that she had not forsaken her worldly kin, passed on news of their brothers, and reiterated that hers was the love of a little sister and aunt.[132]

Correspondence was not always able to maintain the kin ties of people spread across a continent whose histories could be at odds with their claims to bourgeois resources and identities. Marguerite had hoped that she would be among the Roman Catholic sisters sent to Victoria in 1858 and was sad that this opportunity of living near her sister did not materialize. When Connolly Douglas decided to join her siblings in litigating their father's will, arrangements had to be made through intermediaries. Douglas apologized that he had "no opportunity of becoming acquainted with our late friend Connollys relations in Canada."[133] It was only after the railroad cut through western Canada that Amelia's brother Henry visited Victoria in 1887, the visit captured in the image in Figure 6.1.[134] Whatever the affective power and endurance of these Metis kin ties, they remained subcutaneous in settler Victoria. Connolly Douglas' brother's visit was recalled by him and captured in a photograph, but it seems to have gone unmentioned amongst the almost obsessive observation of elite visits and social rituals mapped in Victoria's local newspaper, *The Colonist*.

It was the mechanism of colonial appointments that put members of the Douglas-Connolly family into the most intimate touch with Metis kin and community in Red River. In 1862 Jane's husband, Alexander Grant Dallas, was appointed governor of Red River Colony. Dallas was proud that presumptions of bourgeois White women's incapacity for travel through Indigenous North America did not apply to his wife. He explained that Jane could manage the long trip from Canada to Red River: "She is young, strong & a capital rider & her father sees no difficulty whatever."[135] In Red River, Jane was the governor's wife, giving

---

[132] Sister Marguerite Connolly to Amelia Douglas, April 26, 1884, Box 16, Harris Papers.
[133] James Douglas to T. C. Alwyn, June 8, 1868, Private Letter Book.
[134] Henry Connolly, "Reminiscences, of One of the last descendants of a Bourgeois of the North West Company," manuscript made available by Anne Lindsay, Centre for Rupert's Land Studies, n.d., 14; pagination added.
[135] Alexander Grant Dallas to [Joseph] Berens, March 6, [1862], quoted in "Miscellaneous Information Relating to Alexander Grant Dallas," BCA, w/D16, 3.

balls and receiving visitors. These visitors included Lakota Sioux refugees
fleeing an increasingly aggressive and militarized American settler state to
the south. Douglas Dallas called the Sioux "wretched creatures," but recognized that "We are obliged to treat them with civility as we are entirely
at their mercy just now." Part of Douglas Dallas' diplomacy was to show
a group of visiting Sioux "Papa's likeness," and in doing so link ties of
kinship with the ground politics of empire in different local spaces.[136]
Ties of kin and state made Vancouver Island news in Red River. The Red
River newspaper reported when Douglas was named to the Order of the
Bath, noting that "Mr. Douglas is father of Mrs. Dallas" and reporting
mundane sorts of family news.[137]

In Red River, Douglas Dallas was a Metis daughter as well as the
governor's wife. Her imperial careering ironically returned her to her
mother's Indigenous kin and social networks. Letters home provided
updates on old friends. "I am sure Mama will remember who I mean,"
she wrote about a young Metis doctor who had married into an elite
HBC family. Douglas Dallas aspired to be a good granddaughter and
niece to the grandmother and aunt she found herself proximate to for the
first time. When she first heard of her husband's move, she promised that
"I shall see grandmamma there & I shall do everything in my power to
make her comfortable" and hoped that her grandmother would stay with
her when her husband traveled. When "poor Grandmama" died before
Douglas Dallas could pass on a gift, she assured her mother that she
would honour her grandmother's memory with the bourgeois material
culture of death. "I am going to have a railing put round her grave as I
know you would like it," she wrote home to Victoria.[138]

This particular sort of imperial return produced uncomfortable conflicts as well as heartfelt reunions. In 1863 Marguerite Connolly wrote to
Douglas, reporting that his daughter was spreading stories of Red River's
nuns' "designating their abode as a house of prostitution." Douglas was
horrified by the stories and his daughter's presumed role in relaying them,
explaining to Jane that the news had "excited the most painful emotions
in his mind." Linking the rumours to the stories of Maria Monk that

[136] Jane Dallas to Cecilia Helmcken, January 1, 1862, Volume 14, File 9, Helmcken Papers, Transcript; Jane Dallas to Amelia Connolly Douglas, December 30, 1862, Helmcken Papers, Volume 14, File 9, Transcript.

[137] "Sir James Douglas," *Nor'Wester* (Red River Colony), October 14, 1863; "Accident to Sir James Douglas," *Nor'Wester*, July 2, 1864.

[138] Jane Dallas to Cecilia Helmcken, July 19, 1862; Jane Dallas to Amelia Connolly Douglas, December 19, 1862, Helmcken Papers, Volume 14, File 9; Jane Dallas to Amelia Connolly Douglas, August 9, 1861, and Jane Dallas to Amelia Connolly Douglas, December 19, 1862, Helmcken Papers, Volume 14, File 9, Transcript.

had circulated through Canada, he instructed his daughter to tell the truth if she had been falsely accused, but to apologize if she had "injured those good ladies by giving countenance to such fabrications." In that case, she should "make every reparation in your power – prove that you are above the prejudices of ignorant narrow minded bigots" and "let no false pride restrain you from doing what is honourable and right."[139] Like so many members of her extended family in other colonial places and times, Douglas Dallas had a range of different identities and subjectivities to draw on and be asked to answer for here: Roman Catholic and Protestant, Metis and British, local and imperial, wife, niece, and daughter.

John Sebastian Helmcken was critical in negotiation of the terms by which British Columbia joined the new nation-state of Canada as a province in 1871. His father-in-law called the idea of confederation one of the "ruling manias" of the day, but his interest in the topic was limited. In the 1860s and '70s Douglas described his James Bay house as a fixed and cherished space. He wrote to his half-sister Jane in Paris, explaining why he valued the "quiet pleasur[e]s of my own fireside." "This you know is natural," he explained, "in my case a wanderer as I have been for more than forty years on the face of the earth."[140] Douglas enumerated his travels within North America, counting the seven times he crossed the continent, once by the Peace River and six times by Jasper House.[141] He sometimes admired other geographies in Vancouver Island but found that his "love for dear James Bay" would revive itself. He also wrote the history of his own family into the grid of the city of Victoria. When the city expanded through his considerable property, he not only made a tidy sum but tied his daughters and one son-in-law to the place by naming streets after them: Jane, Alice, Martha, and Bushby Streets, "A monument you see in honour of my dear little daughters."[142]

Douglas loved his family and his house, and perhaps more so he loved the land around it, much of which he owned. He was fascinated with colonial land policy as governor and, in his retirement, was attentive to the various modes of regulating land in different British colonies. In his regular rides he articulated his own, deeply personal, and direct stake in

---

[139] James Douglas to Jane [Douglas Dallas?], March 2, 1863, James Douglas, "Letters," BCA, Reel 246A.

[140] James Douglas to Alexander Grant Dallas, March 22, 1870; James Douglas to Jane Douglas, July 13, 1868, Private Letter Book.

[141] James Douglas, March 19, 1869, untitled notes, in Douglas, Outward Correspondence.

[142] James Douglas to Martha Douglas, October 24, April 26, 1873, Letters to Martha.

colonization and the transformation of North American space into land for non-Indigenous people to claim and enjoy. Like so many settlers, he had intense feelings about the territory he lived in and thought beautiful, and a tendency to discursively empty it of people who might complicate his relationship to it. The intensity and volume of settler affect about Indigenous space speaks not to a secure relationship, but to a pervasive anxiety about a home that can never really be ours.

The land that Douglas rode over and the streets he named as a retired colonial servant and doting father and grandfather had been very different when he was named governor some twenty years before. It was under his watch and authority that this space became an insecure and often violent settler colony. Douglas' career as governor reflected the thick and insurgent histories of both local colonial space and the ties that linked colonies to one another. Observers of his government could celebrate his supposed skill at ruling an Indigenous and polyglot settler society, but they could also criticize his lack of metropolitan credentials and his imbrication in fur-trade, Indigenous, and transimperial networks. Douglas' authority as the highest representative of the local colonial state was secured and maintained alongside his family's ongoing and complicated connections to metropolitan British, elite Metis, and Caribbean networks and identities. The meanings of these peoples, connections, and places complicated the family's claim to what American legal scholar Cheryl Harris calls the "property of Whiteness,"[143] but they did not unseat it.

The Douglas-Connolly family was situated in multiple places in the complicated politics of empire, race, and nation and the places created and re-created by them. By the time of Connolly Douglas' death in 1890, Martha Douglas Harris was the only one of the family's four remaining children who was resident in Victoria. The others lived around the emergent Anglo-American world: two in California, another in Britain.[144] The family's relationship to empire and to race had changed over the course of the long nineteenth century. In different places and in different ways members of the family were both colonizers and colonized, metropolitans and colonials. These locations did not count one another out. They were rarely even in social weight, and one subject position could and routinely did trump the others: Connolly Douglas' Indigeneity and Douglas'

[143] Cheryl I. Harris, "Whiteness as Property," *Harvard Law Review*, 106:8 (June 1993) 1710–1794.
[144] "Death of Lady Douglas: Another of Victoria's Earliest Pioneers Passes Away," *Colonist*, January 9, 1890.

Caribbean background complicated their claims to colonial authority, but they did not unseat them. Identities and histories were lived simultaneously and in conversation, and remind us of how layered and complicated the lived history of colonialism was for this family and for the places they lived in, claimed, and sometimes ruled over.

8   Wealth and descendants

Intimacy changed alongside empire in northern North America in the second half of the nineteenth century and the first decades of the twentieth century. This chapter ties together the analytic threads of the previous two by examining education, sociability, and marriage for James Douglas and Amelia Connolly Douglas' children and some of their grandchildren. It begins in the middle years of the nineteenth century with the marriages of the two eldest Douglas children, Cecilia and Jane, locating them within the evolving fur-trade elite. I then turn to the marriages of Agnes and Alice, partnerships that cemented the family's role in the settler elite that took shape in the colonies of Vancouver Island and British Columbia after 1858. The chapter then examines the family's two youngest children, Martha and James William, examining their metropolitan educations and their marriages at the intersection of a transimperial elite and a local bourgeoisie shaped by British Columbia's new status as a Canadian province. Finally, the chapter reaches into the twentieth century to analyze two of the family's grandchildren, James Andrew and John. They were the primary heirs to the Douglas estate, and their histories map further changes to the lived histories of marriage, race, empire, and class.

Whether they are drawn from the middle of the nineteenth century or the first decades of the twentieth, these histories make clear the importance of education, sociability, and marriage for negotiating and maintaining status and authority for the colonial elite, and sometimes for undoing it. In a range of ways the Douglas-Connolly family worked to marry their descendants into families with particular racial, imperial, and national credentials and in doing so, they shored up their position within a shifting local bourgeoisie. They also ensured that Metis and Creole histories that had produced their family would be hard to register in the settler societies of late nineteenth- and early twentieth-century western Canada. What begins as a history of local elites and the British Empire becomes one about class and status in the modern settler-colonial world. Practices of intimacy were critical to both securing and undoing the family's locations within shifting histories of class and of empire and nation.

The six Douglas children who lived to adulthood each married outside the dense, interconnected Metis world within which they were raised at Fort Vancouver, Fort Victoria, and the small colonial city that grew around it. This suggests the limits to the longstanding and cherished ties that existed between Victoria's elite Metis families, at least for the family that, at mid-century, was the wealthiest and most influential among them. The daughters and sons of Douglas and Connolly Douglas all married spouses who were identified as White. All had secure social and economic places within the local elite, half were British-born, and most of them maintained active connections to Britain. These outcomes reflected the enormous care and strategic labor that Connolly Douglas and Douglas put into their children's intimate relations. Like the fur traders who had mentored him, Douglas wielded his authority to grant his daughters in marriage carefully with an eye to securing their places in a colonial elite and mindful of the privileges that marriage might bring to both sons-in-law and to a father-in-law. When Anglican bishop George Hills visited London's Colonial Office in 1863, he explained that Douglas' sons-in-law had not "found it easy to obtain their wives."[1] Connolly Douglas was also cautious about how her children courted and married. One son-in-law recalled that Connolly Douglas "was awfully particular at home and did not like to lose her daughters and in consequence did not like me over much."[2]

Marriage had always mattered to empire and it continued to do so in ways that speak to the shifting politics of rule in northwestern North America. Jane and Cecilia, the two eldest Douglas children, both made fur-trade marriages reframed by the newly available rites of Christian ceremony and British law. Like many elite fur-trade daughters before them, Cecilia and Jane married Hudson's Bay Company (HBC) men drawn from insecure places within the mobile, nineteenth-century colonial elite. These marriages repositioned Douglas as a father-in-law with obligations to junior men working to establish themselves in the trade's upper echelons. Cecilia and Jane both wed in their late teens, and for them marriage marked a transition from girlhood to womanhood. The men they married were both considerably older, and the gendered inequality between husbands and wives set by British common law and reinforced by both metropolitan culture and fur-trade practice were further buttressed by imbalances in age and experience. Set against this was the Douglas

---

[1] George Hills, Journal, Diocese of New Westminster/Archives of the Ecclesiastical Province of British Columbia, Vancouver School of Theology, Transcript, June 26, 1863 (hereafter Hills, Journal).

[2] Dorothy Blakey Smith, ed., *The Reminiscences of Doctor John Sebastian Helmcken* (Vancouver: UBC Press, 1975) 129 (hereafter Helmcken, *Reminiscences*).

daughters' established location within the dense networks of kinship and alliance that governed fur-trade society, here made especially powerful by their father's authority, wealth, and reputation. Like so many other elite colonial women, the Douglas-Connolly women brought resources of thick local knowledge and connections to their relations with newcomer men.

Cecilia married HBC surgeon John Sebastian Helmcken. He was born in London to a working-class family with German roots. His mother kept a pub and his father was a drunk. As a teenager Helmcken found upward mobility as a physician's "outdoor apprentice" in the hardscrabble East End. After completing his training, he signed on as a physician for a man-of-war bound for Africa and then with the HBC. After stints in York Factory and Fort Rupert, he landed in Victoria in the early 1850s, and began to court Cecilia, Douglas and Connolly Douglas' second eldest daughter. He remembered that "The courtship was a very simple affair – generally in the evening, when we had chocolate and singing and what not – early hours kept." Save for an occasional outing organized by Douglas, their courtship occurred within the protected space of the Douglas household, watched over carefully by Connolly Douglas. The terms of Cecilia and Helmcken's marriage were negotiated around the mobilities and geographic distance of nineteenth-century empire. Douglas insisted that Helmcken prove himself "to be a single man of good character" and the surgeon turned to the mails that laboriously connected Vancouver Island and London to do so.[3] In the spring of 1852 his mother, Catherine, wrote from London: "This is to certify that J. S. Helmcken, my son was a single man when he left England for Van. Couver's Island. I give him my full & willing consent for him to enter into the Matrimonial State." Along with this she included a braided piece of her greying hair, a token of intimacy for the new daughter-in-law she would never meet.[4]

Helmcken and Cecilia's marriage was also arranged on Douglas' terms, ones that were structured by his assessment of patriarchal responsibility and colonial danger. For much of the 1850s and early '60s, vocal settlers in and around Victoria perceived themselves and the colony as an aggregate to be under a military threat from northern Indigenous peoples who came to Victoria for wage-work and trade. In this context, the 1852 expedition that Douglas led in search of an Indigenous man accused of murdering a settler was seen as a risky and portentous endeavor. The possibility of integrating a son-in-law into the family provided Douglas with

---

[3] Helmcken, *Reminiscences*, 120, 129, 142.
[4] Cecilia Helmcken to unknown, July 6, 1852, Helmcken Family Fonds, British Columbia Archives (BCA), Add MSS 505, Volume 14, File 2 (hereafter Helmcken Papers).

a practical means to balance his duties as the head of a martial colonial state with his obligations as a father and husband. He asked Helmcken to consider marrying earlier than planned so Douglas might "go feeling that if anything happened to me my daughter would be in safe hands and Mrs. Douglas would have some one to look to as well as my children."[5]

Twenty-six-year old Helmcken and seventeen-year-old Cecilia were married in Fort Victoria's mess hall in November of 1852, an event that Helmcken would later recall as a "wedding in the high life." In some respects, this wedding was not unlike those negotiated in fur-trade communities for centuries, between an older newcomer man and a younger local woman, and celebrated within the vernacular space of the fur trade. But this ceremony was also very different. A missionary chaplain officiated, written records were kept, and British law was invoked. Indigenous practice was either absent or invisible within the archive. Certainly the wedding mattered to those who bore witness to it. The children from the fort school all attended, and at least one still recalled the celebration as an old woman.[6]

Jane Douglas married Alexander Grant Dallas six years later. Dallas was a son of an imperial family not unlike Douglas', with ties to Scotland, the Caribbean, and beyond. He was born in Berbice in 1816, and worked in Scotland and China as a merchant for a textbook imperial trading company, Jardine, Matheson, and Company. The HBC hired him in 1856 and sent him to Vancouver Island, in part to manage relationships between the Company and Douglas, now a governor. Jane was nineteen when she married forty-two-year-old Dallas in March of 1858. They were the first of the family to wed in Victoria's Christ Church Cathedral, the colony's first church, and the wedding was announced in London's *Times*.[7] Vancouver Island had finally met the demand that British colonies include churches, and was finding its place in a wider imperial world tied together by formal and informal networks of information and exchange.

As a young married woman, Cecilia Douglas Helmcken maintained close ties to her parents and to the fur-trade elite in Victoria. Douglas

---

[5] Helmcken, *Reminiscences*, 130; Kenton Scott Storey, "'What Will They Say in England?': Violence, Anxiety, and the Press in Nineteenth Century New Zealand and Vancouver Island," *Journal of the Canadian Historical Association*, 20:2 (2009) 28–59.

[6] "Fort Vancouver and Fort Victoria Register of Marriages, 1839–1860," BCA, Add MSS 520/3/4, Transcript, no. 27; Helmcken, *Reminiscences*, 296–297; Aurelia Manson, "Reminiscences and Recollections of School Days," BCA, Add MSS E/E/M31, Transcript, 8.

[7] W. Kaye Lamb, "Dallas, Alexander Grant," in *Dictionary of Canadian Biography*, Volume XI, University of Toronto/Université Laval, 2003, www.biographi.ca, accessed July 24, 2010; "Dallas, Alexander Grant, Miscellaneous Information Relating To," BCA, W/D16; "Marriages," *The Times* (London), May 18, 1858.

gave Helmcken an acre of land, and while the doctor considered it a poor location for private practice, he knew that his wife took comfort from being "near her mother and relatives."[8] Letters from Cecilia that were preserved in her husband's archive suggest the extent to which the twinned business of reproduction and respectability governed her experience as a young wife and mother. In 1857, she wrote to a friend in Fort Nisqually, noting that a friend was "round as a puncheon of ale" and hoping that another would bear a child soon after marriage and come to know the womanly approbation she herself had meted out to others. "*I sincerely hope two at once, for she is always turning us all into ridicule for having little* brats so soon," she wrote.[9]

Unlike her sister, Jane Douglas Dallas would not remain within the fur-trade space of her childhood. With her husband and later family, she lived in various parts of northern North America and Britain before settling in Scotland. Alexander Grant Dallas and Jane Douglas Dallas began their married life as a prominent and well-connected couple in Victoria, with Jane's teenaged sisters as regular visitors at their home. In 1861 Jane Franklin and Sophia Cracroft had an enjoyable dinner there, enumerating Dallas' considerable worldly credentials and inspected Jane's body and manners for signs of Indigeneity. Franklin found Douglas Dallas a "very natural, lively & nice looking person" with a face, intonation, and voice characteristic "of her descent."[10] In 1859 Dallas and Douglas Dallas left Vancouver Island. They spent time in the United Kingdom, Canada, and in Red River, where Dallas served as governor, before permanently relocating to Scotland in 1864. Douglas Dallas learned to live with the Red River winters, enjoyed the London fashions, valued her Scottish in-laws, and maintained a bourgeois family life at their Inverness estate. But she still worried about the color of her babies. "The old lady is so glad she has blue eyes like her father," she wrote about her mother-in-law's response to an 1861 birth.[11] Douglas also monitored his grandchildren's complexions. In 1866 he wrote to Jane with congratulations about a new baby and questions about its appearance. "[W]e are one and all longing to know, who baby resembles, is she like papa, Mamma, or does she take after her remoter ancestry, is she stout or thin, dark or

[8] Helmcken, *Reminiscences*, 127.

[9] Cecilia Helmcken to Jane Work Tolmie, March 17, 1857, Helmcken Papers, Volume 2, File 3, Transcript, emphasis original.

[10] Dorothy Blakey Smith, ed., *Lady Franklin Visits the Pacific Northwest: Being extracts from the Letters of Miss Sophia Cracroft, Sir John Franklin's Niece, from February to April 1861 and April to July 1870* (Victoria: Provincial Archives of British Columbia Memoire, No. 11, 1974), February 21, 1861, 12–13.

[11] Jane Dallas to Cecilia Helmcken, October 19, [1861], Helmcken Papers, Volume 14, File 9.

fair – all these and many other questions you are expected to answer," he instructed. As Meghan Vaughan remarks in her fine study of eighteenth-century Mauritius, "New babies pose a challenge to every fantasy of racial fixity."[12]

Cecilia's and Jane's marriages confirmed the family's critical place in the mid-century imperial elite in both its colonial and metropolitan itera-tions. For Cecilia and Jane, marriage meant adult womanhood and a life marked by the labors of child-bearing and rearing and by the politics of bourgeois respectability. But intimacy was not simply about women, and nor was it ever separate from the contentious work of the local colonial state and enterprises. Dallas and Helmcken were Douglas' sons-in-law and his fur-trade cronies, and his political allies and sometimes oppo-nents. Douglas and Helmcken would work together in the HBC and in colonial government throughout the middle years of the nineteenth cen-tury, and their bonds of kinship would survive the trauma of Cecilia's death in childbirth in 1865. Helmcken's children were raised alongside the younger Douglas children, and Helmcken, called "the Doctor" by his father-in-law, was a regular source of knowledge and support. As HBC officials and governors, Dallas and Douglas came into direct conflict on a number of occasions, but the conflicts never undid the ties of kin-ship. Douglas began letters with "my dear Dallas" without any obvious rancour.[13]

The shifting governance and economy of Vancouver Island brought new opportunities and expectations for the colony's elite in the 1850s. A handful of settler families with British wives arrived soon after Vancouver Island was made a colony. "The arrival of such nice people altered matters amazingly," recalled Helmcken. "Visits – little teas – occasional party, or amateur theatricals, or a ball in the mess-room took place."[14] In 1854 the Royal Navy established Esquimalt as a naval station and with that came British men, many of them young, unmarried, and separated from expected networks of sociability. On Vancouver Island they created opportunities for heterosexual performance and Victoria's Metis elite came into sustained contact with a highly mobile transimperial world. The Fraser River gold rush of 1858 brought a sizeable non-Indigenous

---

[12] James Douglas to Jane Dallas, May 8, 1868, "Private Letter Book of Sir James Douglas, Correspondence Outward, March 22, 1867–Oct. 11, 1870," BCA, Add MSS B/40/2, Transcript (hereafter Private Letter Book); Megan Vaughan, *Creating the Creole Island: Slavery in Eighteenth-Century Mauritius* (Durham, NC and London: Duke University Press, 2005) 127.

[13] See, for instance, James Douglas to Martha Douglas, December 5, 1872, in James Douglas, "Letters to Martha Douglas, 30 October 1871 to 27 May 1874," BCA, B/40/4A, Transcript (hereafter Letters to Martha).

[14] Helmcken, "In the Early Fifties," in Helmcken, *Reminiscences*, 293.

population to Victoria. With this came new schools and modest versions of the public spaces of nineteenth-century bourgeois sociability.

This local imperial public sphere included an uneven patchwork of Roman Catholic, Protestant, state-run, and private schools that catered to Victoria's expanding middle class. In 1858, the Sisters of Saint Ann opened a school for girls.[15] In keeping with longstanding elite Metis preference for Roman Catholic education for girls, Agnes and Alice Douglas were enrolled there. But expectations for virtuous Roman Catholic girlhood clashed with expectations for governors' daughters, perhaps especially those who were expected to take on social roles that might elsewhere be fulfilled by their mother. In 1859 after the Sisters learned that the Douglas girls had attended a ball on board a naval ship, Douglas wrote to the Mother Superior in French, assuring her that in general he did not permit "ses chères filles" to frequent balls, but that on some occasions, "quand sa position et un devoi public y demande sa presence da tells occasions n'arrivent pas souvent" and asked that the rules be bent for his daughters.[16] The Sisters were apparently unwilling to bend their policy for the governor, and Alice and Agnes Douglas were among the ten or so girls withdrawn.[17] One observer reported that the convent school was "broken up about some dancing difficulty."[18]

That a school might be shaken by the question of dancing suggests the power of this particular form of heterosexual sociability to elite Victoria in the 1850s and '60s. It was at naval dances that a local and largely Metis elite met and sometimes married into a transimperial British one. "Two or three naval officers have been inveigled into marrying out here," reported one officer. Helmcken saw things differently, recalling that some of the commitments between naval men and local elite women were forgotten by sailors who moved on.[19] Douglas' two Demerara-born nieces each

[15] Shawna Lea Gandy, "Fur Trade Daughters of the Oregon Country: Students of the Sisters of Notre Dame de Namur, 1850," MA thesis, Portland State University, 2004; Edith E. Down, *A Century of Service: A History of the Sisters of Saint Ann and their Contribution to Education in British Columbia, the Yukon, and Alaska* (Victoria: Sisters of Saint Ann, 1966, revised edition, 1999) 38.

[16] James Douglas to Mère Superieur du convent de St Anne, March 17 1859, Sisters of Saint Ann Archives, Victoria, Series 35, Box 3, File 1 (hereafter SSAA).

[17] "Liste des Nomes des Eleves du Convent des Soeurs de Ste Anne a Victoria depuis es mois de June 1858 jusque a Sept 1859," in "Register – Pupils, 1858–1923," SSAA, Series 35, File 11.

[18] Sam Anderson to Janet, April 23, 1860, Samuel Anderson Papers, WA MSS s-1292, Correspondence, 1859–1862, Beinecke Rare Book Room and Manuscript Library, Box 1, Folders 17–20, Transcript (hereafter Anderson Correspondence).

[19] Sam Anderson to Janet and Aunt Harriet, March 28, 1860, in Anderson Correspondence; Helmcken, *Reminiscences*, 172. Also see Phillip Hankin, "Memoirs," BCA, Add MSS E/B/H19A, Transcript, 34.

married navy men. Cecilia Eliza Cowan Cameron married W. A. G. Young in 1858. Young would remain in Vancouver Island as Colonial Secretary before launching a peripatetic colonial career that took him to England, Jamaica, and British Guiana and to the Gold Coast. Another Douglas niece, seventeen-year-old Edith Rebecca Cameron, married eighteen-year-old midshipman Henry Montagu Doughty in 1860. There was "romance connected to the union," and the bride's parents had taken some convincing.[20]

Balls and dances put knowledges as well as bodies and lives into contact, sometimes in unsettling ways. Newcomers accessed elite Metis women through the lenses of global racial languages, and the Douglas daughters were on a special sort of display and subject to a particularly relentless scrutiny. In 1858, one newcomer wrote that Douglas' "daughters are rather nice looking, and seem to have a great deal of attention paid to them by the Officers of the man-of-war ships, two of which have been there this summer."[21] Samuel Anderson, a British officer with the North American Boundary Commission, wrote that "There are 2 Miss Douglas's daughters of the Governour [sic] and of course the greatest flirts on this island."[22] Men passing through were well aware of and attentive to what they registered as race. An American surveyor reported on a naval ball, explaining that "Most of the young ladies are half breeds & have quite as many of the propensities of the savage as the civilized beings." For him, the Douglas girls were especially usable scripts, noted for their supposed practice of head-flattening and lack of familiarity with the cumbersome fashions of bourgeois, imperial femininity. "They had just had some hoops sent out to them & it was most amusing to see their attempts to appear at ease in their new costume."[23] The ideals of racial hierarchy that animated these discussions could clash uncomfortably with the local relations of power and authority. Anderson recalled Alice Douglas being invited to dance, and replying "what my Papa would say if he knew I was going to dance with a midshipman!" and the sailor replying "I wonder what *my* Papa would say if he knew I was going to dance with a 'squaw.'" Here, Alice Douglas' sense of her status as the governor's daughter comes

[20] Martha Harris, "Reminiscences of her early life in Victoria, including notable Victoria Families," BCA, Add MSS 2789, Box 1, File 12 (hereafter Douglas Harris, Reminiscences). Bishop George Hills Journal, 1860, Archives Ecclesiastical Province of British Columbia, UBC, VST, August 21, 1860, 205 (hereafter Hills, Journal).

[21] C. C. Gardiner, "To the Fraser River Mines in 1858," ed. Robie L. Reid, *British Columbia Historical Quarterly*, 1:1 (October 1937) 253.

[22] Sam Anderson to Janet, March 6, 1860, Anderson Correspondence.

[23] George F. G. Stanley, ed., *Mapping the Frontier: Charles Wilson's Diary of the Survey of the 49th Parallel, 1858–1862, while Secretary of the British Boundary Commissions* (Toronto: Macmillan, 1870) 28.

into sharp conflict with the midshipman's reckoning of racial hierarchy and their respective locations within it. Anderson concluded that "The young ladies are very touchy at being reminded that they have Indian blood in them."[24]

The courtships and marriages of the Douglas family's middle daughters reflected these new practices of empire and heterosexual sociability and reinforced the Douglas-Connolly family's centrality to the revamped local colonial state. Charles Good was a British vicar's son with an Oxford education who arrived in Victoria in 1858 and was deemed a "laddy-da government clerk" by one naval officer.[25] Good was a regular visitor to the Douglas house at James Bay, joining in walks, rides, meals, music, and dancing with the family and their guests.[26] These events drew together the old fur-trade elite with the new one tethered to the settler state and gold economy and, at the same time, facilitated courtship opportunities for the family's eligible daughters.

Forms of sociability could complicate and undermine the familial and particularly patriarchal control of courtship and marriage that the Douglas-Connolly family had practiced for some time. In August 1861, Good and Alice eloped to American territory by boat and married there. The Victoria press reported that the rumours were true: "the daughter of a distinguished official had eloped with a clerk in one of the public offices."[27] In his private journal, Hills explained that "the Governors Secretary Mr. Good induced Miss Alice to go off with him to the American territory to get married without consent of her parents. Great distress in consequence to her parents as she is but barely 17."[28] Douglas arranged to have the couple remarried by Anglican ceremony within a day. This did not stop the marriage from becoming a local scandal and fodder for doggerel poetry that Indigenized the governor and his family by calling him "Chief Douglas."[29] Anderson saw the whole affair as another

24 Samuel Anderson to Janet, November 20, 1861, Anderson Correspondence. This story is retold with Agnes Douglas as its focus in Frank Tarbell, "Life and Trade in Victoria during the Fraser River Excitement," Bancroft Collection, P-C 26, Bancroft Library, University of California, Berkeley, 9.

25 John Adams, *Old Square Toes and his Lady: The Life of James and Amelia Douglas* (Victoria: Horsdal and Shubert, 2001) 173; Edmund Hope Verney to Harry Verney, July 20, 1862, in Allen Pritchard, ed., *The Vancouver Island Letters of Edmund Hope Verney, 1862–65* (Vancouver, UBC Press, 1996) 75.

26 Arthur Bushby, "Journal of Arthur T. Bushby," BCA, Add MSS 811, Transcript, for instance May 22, 1859, 104, June 28, 1859, 116 (hereafter Bushby, Journal). I thank Irving House for allowing me to use this version, and Frederike Vespoor and Judy de Root of BCA for their assistance. On this, see Dorothy Blakey Smith, "Introduction," "The Journal of Arthur Thomas Bushby, 1858–1859," *British Columbia Historical Quarterly*, 21 (1957/8) 83–198.

27 "Elopement," *Colonist*, August 30, 1861.   28 Hills, Journal, April 30, 1861, 133.

29 "Married," *Colonist*, September 2, 1861; Benjamin Pitt Griffin, "Chief Douglas' Daughter," BCA, Add MSS 952.

example of a local woman taking advantage of a hapless newcomer, one he deemed "the more innocent of the two."[30] At a distance, Jane Douglas Dallas marshaled her sisters' support for Alice in the face of their father's disapproval. "I do hope most sincerely that all may go well with them do like a good girl, Agnes dear, plead their cause with Papa," she urged. Jane feared losing Alice to the family: "she was always a pet sister on account of her delicate health & although we used to quarrel sometimes I have often felt that if she were taken from us how very sorry we would be & what a bitter trial."[31]

With their marriage confirmed and renegotiated, Alice and Good were sent to the mainland colony, out of Douglas' sightline and away from Victoria's watchful eyes. Within a few years Alice had borne four children, lost one, left her husband, and taken "her own Income in hand."[32] Douglas was distressed by the separation and by Alice's decision to move to England with her young children. "I was greatly opposed to it," he explained, "but the fact is, she hates her husband with a bitter hatred [sic], which amounts almost to insanity, and her going to England is to get away from him, a most unchristian course, only redeemed in a measure by her strong desire to get education for her children." He struggled to reconcile the Alice who was well mannered and industrious with the woman who repeatedly rejected ideals of womanly respectability, and hoped that a Christian God might help Alice reconcile herself to the demands of patriarchal marriage. "I have pointed out the folly and wickedness of ceasing according to her marriage vows to love and obey her husband," Douglas explained, "and I hope through the blessing of God that she will be brought to a better state of mind."[33]

But Douglas supported Alice even when her actions seriously challenged the ideals of wifely dedication that he had come to grips with in the 1830s. "Alice may have stayed with me, and made this her home but she would not, and it was with bitter anguish of heart that I saw her leave," he reported. "She has a strong will and is proud as Lucifer & would rather starve than submit beg [sic]." When his moral and presumed paternal authority failed, Douglas turned to his considerable material resources and wide-ranging connections to control his daughter and her movements. He arranged for her to have £120 a year on his account, and wrote to shipping and customs agents between Victoria and London, trying to smooth and monitor her way. "Mrs. Good is full of courage but an utterly inexperienced traveller or she would not have commenced her

---

[30] Sam Anderson to Janet, November 20, 1861, Anderson Correspondence.
[31] Jane Dallas to Agnes Bushby, October 17, 1861, Helmcken Papers, Volume 14, File 9.
[32] James Douglas to Jane Dallas, April 26, 1869; James Douglas to Jane Dallas, September 5, 1869, both in Private Letter Book.
[33] James Douglas to Jane Douglas Dallas, September 5, 1869;

journey at this time of year," he explained.[34] After a peripatetic couple of years in England, Alice returned to Vancouver Island with her daughter, leaving her two sons in the care of their paternal grandparents in England. Douglas had earlier urged her to return to the family home at James Bay, and it was under these more complicated circumstances that she did so in 1872. Douglas drew on new languages of companionate affection, a sentimental reckoning of family and beliefs in parental authority to explain a turn of events that sat uneasily with his presumed beliefs. He hoped that "God's blessing, and home influence" would counteract "the depressing events of her unhappy married life." Douglas saw these as vindication of paternal management of intimate life, or at least this was the take-away point he drew out for a teenaged Martha: "How carefully young people should eschew mystery and secrecy in all the important steps in life, doing nothing that may compromise their future happiness, without the full knowledge and consent of their parents."[35]

Alice would continue to make choices that confounded and challenged her family, or at least her father. Douglas "would never hear of her getting a Divorce,"[36] but after his death she obtained divorces in both the United States and the United Kingdom. Good hired three barristers to represent his interests in the latter. "The circumstances of the case were peculiar," opined the (London) *Times*, recounting the couple's elopement, remarriage, and separation in three legal jurisdictions.[37] A further complication was Alice's 1879 marriage to a British-born merchant and wheeler-dealer who called himself Baron de Widerhold, General of Brigade and Chief of Staff of the Army of Portugal. The marriage occurred in Victoria after the American divorce but before the British one, and Alice's kin wondered about the status of the divorce, Alice's second marriage, and the child or perhaps children produced by it.[38]

Alice's intimate life demonstrated how new opportunities for heterosexual coupling available for elite daughters in settler British Columbia could challenge patriarchal and familial control. Her younger sister

---

[34] James Douglas to Jane Douglas Dallas, January 22, 1870; James Douglas to Alexander Dallas, January 3, 1870; James Douglas to Mr. Halladay, January 3, 1870; James Douglas to Mr. Sheperd, January 3, 1870, Private Letter Book.

[35] James Douglas to Martha Douglas, May 1, 1873, Letters to Martha.

[36] Alexander Grant Dallas to John Sebastian Helmcken, October 1, 1877, Helmcken Papers, Volume 2, File 4.

[37] "Legal Intelligence," *Daily Alta California*, September 4, 1878. "Good v. Good and De Wiederholt," *The Times* (London), August 3, 1883. See High Court of Justice Divorce Division, "Good v. Good otherwise de Widerholt," 1881, National Archives, J 77/233/6550.

[38] Alexander Grant Dallas to John Sebastian Helmcken, November 15, 1878, Helmcken Papers, Volume 2, File 4. Also see Adams, *Old Square Toes and his Lady*, 208–209.

Agnes' marriage confirmed the Douglas-Connolly family's commitment to using marriage as a means of buttressing bourgeois status and the racial identities that went with it. Arthur Bushby was the son of a London merchant who migrated to Victoria in 1858. Like many men with metropolitan connections and colonial aspirations, one of his first steps was to establish his credentials with the governor, and he was quickly folded into the sociability of the Douglas household. "Tuesday went & presented my letters to the Gov: he recd me very well & before I left he invited me to dine that evng," he explained to his journal. There was a mixture of kin and company at the dinner: unmarried daughters Agnes and Alice, Jane and her husband, a naval official, and a judge. Bushby found it "a most pleasant evng . . . & a good dinner – music & cards. I got on very well with them & the Gov: a jolly brick one of his daughters is pretty – the other I should say bad tempered." Within a week he had set his sights on Agnes, the pretty one. As Bushby established himself within the Douglas household and Agnes' affections, he also found a berth in the local colonial state, appointed as clerk for the colony's first legally trained judge who had finally replaced Douglas' brother-in-law.[39]

The transition from sociability to courtship was a gradual one that brought a range of gendered knowledges into conversation and sometimes confusion. Bushby joined the family for meals, outings, celebrations, and church. From Scotland, Jane Douglas Dallas fondly recalled the convivial social times she, her sisters, and their suitors and husbands shared, recalling them as "*happy happy* days."[40] There were ample opportunities for Bushby and Agnes to pair off and engage in a sort of intimate play that Bushby described in his journal as "tickling" and "romps." Bushby's pleasure in this was haunted by his worry that Agnes subscribed to a different model of sexual decorum, one rooted in what he considered a bodily racial difference. He thought Agnes "lucky in having fallen in with an honourable fellow, as having a tint of Indian blood in them they are not the most capable of controlling their passions." In August 1859 Agnes and Arthur found themselves in a room with no one other than her mother – who played a limited role in their courtship, or at least in Bushby's account of it – and kissed. The terms of their relationship shifted thereafter. Agnes broke up with John Work, the Metis son of longstanding family friends. She explained that she did not love him enough, and "besides my parents wd [*sic*] never consent to John's &

[39] Bushby, Journal, December 29, 1858, 31; January 1, 1859, 36; "Death of Judge A. T. Bushby," *Colonist*, May 20, 1875.
[40] Jane Douglas Dallas to Cecilia Douglas Helmcken, October 19, [1861], Helmcken Papers, File 9, Transcript, emphasis original.

my union."[41] Marriage was a matter of love, but also a process governed by parents and a critical means of upward mobility and race-making, not a way of consolidating even the most enduring of lateral connections.

For all the companionate sociability of their courtship, Bushby and Agnes' marriage was negotiated among men. Bushby first asked Douglas for permission to marry sixteen-year-old Agnes in 1859. Douglas put him off in what the younger man described as "a quiet kind way." Douglas explained that he had "a great regard & esteem" for Bushby, but he was too poor and Agnes too young. Douglas would not grant his permission to marry for at least a year, and in that meantime, Bushby "might visit the house simply as a visitor – that he left it to my honor – neither to engage myself to her nor to pay her any particular attentions." Bushby couldn't help but register this as the response of someone who was both his employer and his prospective father-in-law. If Douglas thought his income too small, then "why the d— does he not make it larger," Bushby asked his journal.[42] From Scotland, Jane Douglas Dallas reframed the matter, arguing that a long courtship was in her teenaged sister's interest. "I think you are very right to wait a while," she wrote to Agnes, "as *courting* is a very pleasant business."[43]

Bushby was a sojourning middle-class British man and Agnes an elite local woman, and as such, they had very different things at stake in these negotiations. Some of Bushby's worries were the pedestrian ones of intimacy and risk: that Agnes loved him more than he loved her, that he was unable to think clearly in the face of her charm and his own desire. His ambivalences were also those of a newcomer and an English man amongst the local, Metis elite. Like imperial men elsewhere, men in settler British Columbia often lived their lives in two phases and on two stages. But if a settler man was to have a short-term relationship with a local woman, it would not be with the governor's daughter. "It would be impossible to reside here except as her fiance," Bushby realistically acknowledged. To pledge himself to Agnes was to associate himself with local places and peoples, and this threatened his English identity in very real ways. "I am a coward – yes I am a coward," he confessed to his journal, "it is the love of home & the thought of leaving for ever the pleasure & enjoyments of my English home which frightens me." As Bushby traveled as court's clerk, his fears of what a local marriage might mean intensified. He could not imagine taking Agnes away from "her home & family," and even

---

[41] Bushby, Journal, June 25, 1859; August 17–21, 1859.

[42] Bushby, Journal, August 30, 1859, 139.

[43] Jane Douglas Dallas to Agnes Douglas Bushby, October 17, 1861, Helmcken Papers, Volume 14, File 9, Transcript, emphasis original.

more so, could not imagine forsaking England. "But I cannot hide from myself the fact that I do not love her sufficiently to leave England home & beauty for her sake & for ever," he wrote.[44]

The twenty-eight-year-old Bushby married the nineteen-year-old Agnes in May of 1862. Their wedding was very different from that of Agnes' parents or those of her sisters and represented the family's commitment to a highly visible practice of bourgeois marriage. "You must have had a grand wedding and am very glad it went off so well," wrote Jane Douglas Dallas to her mother.[45] This was an intimate rite and a highly public one that tied marriage to a military empire. The local newspaper described it as a "wedding in the high life," and a more jaundiced observer termed it "a *very* grand affair."[46] There were eight bridesmaids and eight groomsmen, three of them military men in uniform, including Royal Engineers "in red coats and crooked hats."[47] Material culture and food further associated the wedding with bourgeois metropolitan culture. A younger sister recalled that the bride's "trousseau came from England" and that Douglas would not allow his daughter to accept wedding gifts.[48] The "splendid breakfast" that capped the wedding managed to impress even the most doubting metropolitan observers, including one who commented that "you would be astonished indeed to see how well they do those things in these wild parts, as good and as ornamental as you could see it done in London."[49]

Yet Victoria was not and could not be London. The Bushby–Douglas wedding was a clear display of the family's wealth, status, and centrality to the local state and, by extension, an affirmation of that colonial project in the face of the instabilities encoded within its own tissue. It occurred in the midst of the contested and often violent assertion of British authority over Indigenous peoples, and however loud, the wedding's display of material power and cultural authority could not drown this out. The *Colonist* newspaper fawned over the wedding the same day it reprinted news of anti-slavery meetings in the metropole, detailed

[44] Bushby, Journal, October 21, 1859, 164; September 9, 1859, 143; September 14, 1859, 144.

[45] Jane Dallas to Amelia Douglas, July 19, [1862], Helmcken Papers, Volume 14, File 9, Transcript.

[46] "Marriage in High Life," *Victoria Daily Press*, May 8, 1862. Also see Stanley, ed., *Mapping the Frontier*, May 13, 1862, 175; Mary Moody to dearest Mother, April 3, 1862, Mary Susanna[h] (Hawks) Moody, Correspondence Outward, Transcript, BCA, Add MSS 60, Transcript, 87 (hereafter Moody Correspondence).

[47] Sam Anderson to Janet, May 13, 1862, Anderson Correspondence.

[48] Douglas Harris, Reminiscences, n.p.

[49] Robert Burnaby to My darling Mother, May 22, 1862, in Anne Burnaby McLeod and Pixie McGeachie, eds., *Land of Promise: Robert Burnaby's Letters from Colonial British Columbia* (Burnaby, BC: City of Burnaby, 2002) 169.

a local smallpox epidemic, and demanded that "every Indian, whether male or female" be removed from Victoria, "to some place remote from the Whites, and without a moment's delay."[50] Bourgeois, creole marriages occurred alongside the devastating assertion of settler imperialism within local colonial space and transimperial conversations about humanity, nationhood, and empire.

Bushby and Agnes' marriage spoke to empire and the work of intimacy within it, and to new expectations of heterosexual companionship and the reticulation of patriarchal authority. In a letter to Bushby's English family, Douglas celebrated the match, located it within a rich local network of kin and friends, and subtly praised his own management of the relationship:

seldom have a youthful couple entered upon the serious work of life under happier circumstances than our children. With a comfortable home, an income equal to their support[,] a large circle of warm and devoted friends, fondly attached to each other, we can hardly fancy a happier lot than has fallen to them.[51]

Agnes and Bushby moved to the mainland capital of New Westminster, and seemed happy even there. Douglas was pleased by the mutual affection he saw between Bushby and his daughter, a woman described by a casual observer as "strong-minded."[52] "Agnes," Douglas explained, "has a sunny mind and is not easily damped, as long as Arthur is on hand, so they got on merrily enough stumps notwithstanding."[53]

The Bushby–Douglas marriage may have tied together strains of bourgeois wealth, local political authority, and new expectations for companionate heterosexuality, but it still possessed the power to unsettle expectations of race, gender, and empire. British colonial servant Robert Burnaby was happy to be Bushby's best man, but he was "really sorry" for his friend's choice of mate. Burnaby found Agnes "amiable enough", but "mild and queer, and can never get rid of the taint of Indian Blood; poor fellow it will be long before he gets home again as he has made up his mind that he couldn't take her with him."[54] Here, Agnes' Indigeneity outweighs her individuality and status and fundamentally compromises Bushby's Englishness. The young British observer could not see what a young, elite Metis woman might lose in marrying an older British man, but Jane Douglas Dallas did. The elder sister was living in Red River, and

50 "Small Pox among the Indians," *Colonist*, May 8, 1862.
51 James Douglas to Arthur Bushby, November 24, 1862, in James Douglas, "Letters," BCA, Mflm Reel 246A.
52 Samuel Anderson to Janet, May 13, 1862, Anderson Correspondence.
53 James Douglas to Jane Dallas, February 22, 1869, in Private Letter Book.
54 Robert Burnaby to My dearest Rose, March 14, 1860, in McLeod and McGeachie, eds., *Land of Promise*, 138.

she was shattered when she received a letter announcing "dear Agnes' wedding." Douglas Dallas was a governor's wife and a young mother, and she received this news with the weary eyes alert to what bourgeois imperial marriage could cost women like herself and her sister. "The letters made me feel so nervous and shaky that I cannot write properly," she explained. Jane mustered some routinized good wishes and laced them with fear and concern. "And so Agnes is married at last poor dear girl I know they will be very happy if dear Arthur is not too exacting." This letter resituates the celebrated bride and elite daughter as a "poor dear girl" vulnerable to a man who, though "such a good creature and a perfect gentleman," still possessed the power to demand too much.[55]

Changing practices of rule and economy brought new subjects with new roles to Vancouver Island in the late 1850s and the early 1860s, and changing expectations of marriage introduced new opportunities and pressures for couples and their families. Intimacy continued to do heavy economic and political work in empire and be framed in patriarchal terms. By marrying their daughters to British-born men with secure racial identities and stable metropolitan connections, the Douglas-Connolly family cemented their membership in transimperial circles and provided important cultural glue to their status with Victoria's local elite. By marrying into a colonial family with enormous political authority, local influence, and material wealth, young British men with cultural capital and metropolitan connections accessed colonial opportunities that might have otherwise been unavailable. Marriage knitted newcomer men into dense local networks organized around kinship in the colonial era, just as it had in the fur trade. For Good and Bushby, marriage established a kin relationship with a man who was at once father-in-law, supervisor, and mentor. Like Helmcken and Dallas, Bushby became a trusted and loved member of the family. Douglas called him "my son Bushby,"[56] using language of direct kinship rather than the modified ones usually reserved for in-laws. Marriage made empire in mid-nineteenth-century British Columbia, just as it did earlier in the Caribbean and in fur-trade country.

The marriages of James Douglas and Amelia Connolly Douglas' children changed alongside colonialism in northern North America. Marriage bound the two eldest Douglas daughters to the fur-trade elite, and the middle ones to a settler colonial state under their father's

---

[55] Jane Dallas to Cecilia Helmcken, July 15, 1862, Helmcken Papers, Volume 14, File 9, Transcript. Emphasis original.
[56] See James Douglas to Jane Douglas, December 15, 1866, James Douglas, Correspondence Outward, December 15, 1866 to March 16, 1867, BCA, B/40/3, Transcript (hereafter Douglas Correspondence, 1866–1867).

administration. James William and Martha were the family's youngest children, and they came of age in a different iteration of settler colonialism reworked by British Columbia's new role as a province within what historian Ian McKay calls Canada's liberal project.[57] Martha and James William were both formally educated in Britain, and their metropolitan credentials were brought to local marriages, each to a spouse tied to a British Columbia reconfigured as a Canadian province.

James William and Martha's early schooling was like that of their older siblings, carried out at home and in small nearby institutions. Their experiences in private or public local schools were profoundly shaped by the family's authority and status. The family's only surviving son first attended Victoria's "Colonial School," a state-funded school that a polyglot group of boys and girls attended. But class and status still shaped the schooling Douglas' son received there. James William was able to leave school and spend afternoons riding, and he was withdrawn when the family decided the long walk was too much for his precarious health.[58] After she witnessed a nun make a girl "kneel and kiss the floor," Martha rejected the Roman Catholic school her sisters had attended. She would instead attend the Female Collegiate School, opened in 1860 by Anglicans critical of the monopoly Roman Catholics had on education for girls of "the middle & higher classes."[59]

It was a sign of the family's growing prosperity and the changing politics of race and empire that James William and Martha did not complete their educations in these local schools and were instead sent to England. Sending children to the metropole was a longstanding practice of colonial elites in northern North America, the Caribbean, and beyond, and in both Douglas' and Connolly Douglas' families in particular. But it was still a difficult and divisive choice. Douglas made clear that he found sending James William and Martha away painful, but that the decision to do so was his to make. Connolly Douglas had no such authority, and separation from her two youngest children was an enduring struggle. James William was eleven when he traveled from Vancouver Island to England, a small boy with a large hat in the photograph in Figure 8.1. Connolly Douglas was heartbroken and Douglas worried. "The anxiety

[57] Ian McKay, "The Liberal Order Framework: A Prospectus for a Reconnaissance of Canadian History," *Canadian Historical Review*, 81 (2000) 613–678.
[58] Edgar Fawcett, *Some Reminiscences of Old Victoria* (Toronto: William Briggs, 1912) 29, 33; Charles Good to Mr. J. Burr, November 15, [1860], Douglas Correspondence, 1866–1867.
[59] Douglas Harris Reminiscences, n.p.; George Hills to J. B. Murray, March 27, 1860, Text 57, Box 6, File I, Bishop George Hills Correspondence, Anglican Diocese of British Columbia Archives, Victoria, BC.

Figure 8.1 James William Douglas.

which I naturally feel about the little fellows welfare, is, as you may well imagine, very great, and I shall be much relieved when I hear of his safe arrival at home," he explained.[60] Upon landing, care for him was transferred to metropolitan kin and relations. Caring for colonial children in the metropole for schooling was a heavy and often complicated task, and here it fell to the Doughtys and then to the Dallases, who became the sometimes doting and sometimes exasperated guardians and go-betweens for Jane's two youngest siblings. Douglas took special comfort in this, glad that his son, "alone in a far country," had kin nearby. When James

---

[60] James Douglas to Henry Doughty, April 30, 1862, British Columbia – Governor (Douglas). Correspondence Outward (miscellaneous letters), November 30, 1859– December 8, 1863.

William got in trouble, it was his eldest sister of whom the family asked most. "You my dear Jane must be a mother to him as well as a sister," explained Douglas.[61]

These demanding rearrangements of intimacies and care were undertaken in an effort to ensure children's location in the transimperial elite that could span both metropole and colony. Douglas wanted for his son what so many elite families in the imperial world did: for him to attend university and read law at one of the Inns of Court. For Douglas, these metropolitan credentials were predicates to a life in North America, and he hoped that his son would return and assume his own role as a landowner and legislator in British Columbia. "I had one main object in sending him to England," he wrote to Dallas, "to give him a sound and good education, that he might, in after life be qualified, through his own exertions to occupy a respectable position in society, and perhaps take a distinguished part, in the legislation of his Native country." Here metropolitan education is sought as preparation for a career in what Douglas clearly situates as his son's "Native country." The ironies were not lost on Douglas.

> It is very distressing to have children scattered over the world, abandoned to the care of strangers, who may utterly neglect their moral and mental training. [A]nd what are Colonists to do, who have no facilities for educating their sons at home? They must send them to other countries, where these advantages are found, and their boys have the benifit [sic] of a liberal education.[62]

The lived experience of metropolitan education could produce results different from those intended, imagined, and planned for. James William struggled at two small boarding schools, and then at Rossall, a public school in Lancashire. "In his letters to me he complains of 'ennui'!!!," his father reported, deeming this "a strange expression for a school boy to use." Douglas' letters to his son offer occasional praise and more routine exhortations and criticism. He wrote that the boy's letters were "full of blunders" and reflected "the most inveterate habits of careless indolence which you seem to have fallen into." Douglas felt the disappointment of his son's performance keenly. "I have made many sacrifices to give you a good sound education," he explained, adding that "I wish my Father had been as kind to me." He urged his seventeen-year-old son to study and postpone heterosexual entanglements, explaining that "It will be time enough for you, in 8 or 10 years hence, to think of marrying, when you

---

61 James Douglas to Jane Douglas Dallas, May 15, 1867; James Douglas to Jane Douglas Dallas, June 18, 1868, both in Private Letter Book.

62 James Douglas to Alexander Grant Dallas, July 23, 1867; James Douglas to Alexander Grant Dallas, July 28, 1868, both in Private Letter Book.

have finished your education and made your mark in the world and have wherewith to support a wife in comfort." The goal here was to produce a man fit for local colonial rule. When James William wanted to join the army, Douglas demanded that he "dismiss the idea of being a soldier, and qualify himself for a political career in his native country."[63]

James William returned to Victoria in 1870. He was almost nineteen, in poor health, and with no apparent occupation. His brother-in-law quipped that "It is very difficult to know what to make of him, unless he puts in for the vacant Spanish throne."[64] James William would fulfill at least some of his father's ambitions when he was elected to represent Victoria in British Columbia's provincial legislature from 1876 to 1878. Douglas' reticence to put his wealth under his son's control still sent a strong signal of fatherly disappointment. James William was the only surviving son and presumed heir to the Douglas family wealth and the less tangible but no less important commodity of their reputation, and his ordinary shortcomings took on extraordinary importance.

Gender guaranteed that Martha's metropolitan education would mean something very different. She was a relatively mature eighteen when her father decided that she would accompany her married sister and family to England for "the benefit of finishing her education." Douglas tapped every available metropolitan connection. He placed Martha under Dallas' charge and requested that the Bushby family assist "in placing her at a proper finishing school, where she may have the comforts of a home and a careful training in manners and general knowledge." He explained that his daughter was fairly educated in literature, played and sang well, could draw, wrote a good hand and a "nice letter." What he wanted from an English school were more distinctly metropolitan commodities, most notably "larger & broader views of life, and that expansion of the mind, which may be called the education of the eye, and cannot be acquired out here."[65]

In sending a daughter to England for schooling, the family broke with traditions of keeping girls close to home. Douglas had particular ambitions for his clever youngest daughter, and by the 1870s, the family's financial resources were considerable and their metropolitan

---

[63] James Douglas to Alexander Dallas, May 4, 1868; James Douglas to James William Douglas, May 22, 1868, August 10, 1868, and May 17, 1867; James Douglas to Alexander Grant Dallas, June 8, 1868, all in Private Letter Book. On Rossall, see Peter Bennet, *A Very Desolate Position: The Story of the Birth and Establishment of a Mid-Victorian Public School* (n.p.: Rossall Archives, 1977).

[64] Alexander Grant Dallas to John Sebastian Helmcken, November 5, 1870, Helmcken Papers, Volume 1.

[65] James Douglas to Mr. Bushby, August 10, 1872, Letters to Martha.

connections solid. Maintaining elite status was harder and harder for the Metis elite, and fur-trade daughters who received British educations might have seemed particularly able to weather the storms of a changing North America. The image of the "new woman" was traveling around the imperial world, recalibrating womanhood with youth, mobility, and independence in ways that offered particular opportunities for colonial women who moved around metropolitan space. The possibilities of "new womanhood" were taken up by Indigenous writer and performer E. Pauline Johnson and by the White Australian women analyzed by Angela Woollacott.[66]

Martha spent two years as a "parlour boarder" at a ladies' school near Wimbledon run by two unmarried sisters, the Turks. A decade later the school would promote its ability to provide young women with a suitable moral and physical environment, a set of specific bourgeois social graces, and enough but not too much formal education. The school was in a park and had a large garden. The Turks' school offered a "liberal education" of English, French, music, dancing, the use of globes, ancient and modern history, elocution, writing, arithmetic, chronology and composition, and drawing. Instruction in German, Latin, singing, and Italian cost extra.[67] Douglas was pleased with what the Turk sisters provided. He told Martha that the sisters were "every thing you could wish as kind and experienced Teachers," and their school "in all respects admirably adapted to promote healthy developement [sic] of the body and mind." He was also pleased at the less tangible kinds of metropolitan credentials Martha seemed to be accruing. He dubbed Martha the family's "foreign correspondent," asking that she use her "ears, eyes, and mind" to interlocute between metropolitan and colonial worlds. Martha seemed "quite at home in the metropolis," he noted approvingly, and urged her to see the expected celebrations of and monuments to Britain and, more critically, empire: the houses of Parliament in session, the British Museum, and Kew Gardens. Douglas was happy to report that Martha had shaken off what he called the "cobwebs of colonial training." Connolly Douglas wanted her daughter home, but Douglas declared to Martha that she should not remain "a half learned lady all your life."[68]

---

[66] Veronica Strong-Boag and Carole Gerson, *Paddling her Own Canoe: The Times and Texts of E. Pauline Johnson (Tekahionwake)* (University of Toronto Press, 2000) Chapter 2; Angela Woollacott, *To Try her Fortune in London: Australian Women, Colonialism, and Modernity* (Oxford University Press, 2000).

[67] Captain F. S. Dumaresq de Carteret-Bisson, *Our Schools and Colleges, Volume II: For Girls* (London: Simpkin, Marshall, and Co., 1884) 601.

[68] James Douglas to Martha Douglas, October 31, 1872; for instance, James Douglas to Martha Douglas, August 31, 1872, and October 6, 1873; James Douglas to Martha Douglas, June 9, 1873, May 14, 1874, January 31, 1873, all in Letters to Martha.

Figure 8.2 Jane Douglas Dallas and Martha Douglas. The photograph is marked Collier and Park, a photographer from Inverness, Scotland.

For all of this, metropolitan education and the travel it required remained a risky business for Martha Douglas and for those who cared about her. Douglas worked hard to guard and monitor her womanly reputation by arranging for her to travel with kin whenever possible. Figure 8.2 shows a portrait taken of Martha Douglas and Jane Douglas Dallas by an Inverness photographer and documents the persistence of family ties within metropolitan space. Douglas was disappointed when

Dallas did not chaperone Martha on a train trip, declaring this "neither provident nor kind." When Martha wanted to study in Paris, he fretted about "French morals and sentiment" and demanded a detailed plan and itinerary.[69] He visited Martha and Jane on a trip to England in 1874, the second and much shorter of his two adult journeys to Europe.[70]

Martha's British education also challenged familial languages of race, identity, and home. Douglas was alert to how his daughter might be seen and understood. He instructed Martha to keep quiet that it was her mother who gave her Indigenous knowledge. "I have no objection to your telling the old stories about 'Hyass,'" he explained, "But pray do not tell the world that they are Mammas." He was concerned about how Martha presented herself, and also about whether access to metropolitan resources and wealth would undermine her connection to the colonial place he considered her home. "How did you like London on your first arrival, you have got accustomed by this time; perhaps partial to excitement, and may find your home here, too quiet, when you come back next year," he worried in a letter. He wondered whether her experience of difference might foster her affect rather than unseat it. He asked if "Home will appear dull to you after these exciting travels" or that "dear Victoria, your native land, be cherished as much as ever."[71] Here the usual distinction between "home" and "away" is reversed, but the colonial home, however real and however dear, is still presumed lesser.

Both James William and Martha returned to Victoria and married there. These marriages tied them to the most recent iteration of the local elite, this one reflecting British Columbia's new status as a province within Canada. As the family's primary heir and a man with financial problems that the right match could solve, James William's marital prospects were carefully watched in Victoria.[72] He became engaged to Mary Rachel Elliott. In the colonial period, her father, Andrew Charles Elliott, served as a judge and helped to mark out Indian reserves and impose an enduring spatial logic on colonial dispossession. In 1876 he became premier of the province, and in that role superintended its complicated relationship with the federal government and railway building.[73] The marriage of Douglas' son to Elliott's daughter was thus a

---

[69] James Douglas to Martha Douglas, March 19, 1874, May 27, 1874, both in Letters to Martha.

[70] See Adams, *Old Square Toes*, Chapter 17.

[71] James Douglas to Martha Douglas, May 6, 1873, June 9, 1873, both in Letters to Martha.

[72] See Alexander Grant Dallas to John Sebastian Helmcken, November 15, 1878, February, 22 1878, Helmcken Papers, Volume 2, File 5.

[73] See Margaret A. Ormsby, "Elliott, Andrew Charles," in *Dictionary of Canadian Biography*, Volume XI, University of Toronto/Université Laval, 2003, www.biographi.ca, accessed August 1, 2010.

significant one that forged a kin connection between two different itera-tions of British Columbia's elite.

The 1878 Douglas–Elliott wedding again used careful material cul-ture and social performance to assert the family's location within British Columbia. There were eight bridesmaids, two hundred guests, fashion-able clothing, a sumptuous breakfast, and "numerous and costly" gifts. Elliott did not come from fur-trade stock, but her eight bridesmaids included a Finlayson, a Todd, and a Helmcken. The Metis fur-trade elite thus were folded into a newer, Whiter one more clearly anchored in lib-eral, capitalist modernities. The stories that ran alongside notice of the wedding in the local newspaper speak to the shifting politics of 1870s' British Columbia, including a financial crisis in the embattled provin-cial government led by the bride's father and calls for the restriction of Asian immigration, couched in a language of provincial identity asserted against an unknowing federal state.[74]

The following year, Martha's marriage suggested how practices of the "new woman" could be accommodated within patriarchal marriage. Her mother and sisters had all married in their teens, but Martha was twenty-four, well traveled, and formally educated. She also had her own income, and the family took careful legal steps to protect it from laws that here and through so much else of the British Empire rendered wives legal minors and stripped them of the capacity to control their property and wages. Her mate was Dennis R. Harris, a British-born civil engineer who helped plan the Canadian Pacific Railway's (CPR) route in British Columbia. The railway was a symbolic and tangible instrument of nation-building and Canada's incorporation of western territories, dependent on the related poles of Aboriginal dispossession and brutalized labor of the often racialized men who built it. The Douglas–Harris wedding was documented in the photograph of the party in Figure 8.3. The event tied Victoria's Metis elite to the nation-in-the-making of Canada and to a metropolitan world. Martha was accompanied by ten bridesmaids, many of them with kin ties to the fur trade. But the trappings were those of modernity and a global world. "The bride looked charming in a rich White silk dress, made with the skill and taste of a Parisian *modiste*, beautifully trimmed with White tulle and orange blossoms," the press gushed. A breakfast at the bride's mother's house and a local honeymoon followed.[75] James William and Martha both received the metropolitan

---

[74] "Fashionable Wedding," "The Chinese," "Public Meeting at Cedar Hill," all in *Colonist*, March 21, 1878.

[75] "Fashionable Wedding," *Colonist*, March 21, 1878. On Harris, see the City of Victo-ria Archives List of Private Records (By Number), PR 26, www.victoria.ca, accessed December 18, 2010.

Figure 8.3 The wedding of Martha Douglas and Dennis Harris, with Amelia Connolly Douglas at the right.

educations designed to secure their places in a mobile world, and their weddings both celebrated that status and rearticulated it in local colonial space with thick histories, complicated identities, and multiple layers of nation and empire.

The local context within which these weddings occurred was an increasingly secure settler society and a part of the peculiar hybrid political form of the new Canadian dominion, at once a self-governing nation and a part of the British Empire. Empire, class, nation, and race meant different things in this context, and they meant different things in the lives of James William's two sons. The boys were born soon into their parents' marriage, James Andrew in 1879 and John in 1880, creating the family shown in Figure 8.4. In 1883 James William died after years of poor health and personal struggle. His young widow, described as "a silly woman"[76] by Bishop Hills, separated herself both literally and figuratively from her kin in Victoria and moved to San Francisco and then England. In 1890, Martha Douglas Harris, her husband, and brother-in-law launched a legal challenge to Elliott Douglas' custody of her sons. The putative issue was Elliott Douglas raising her sons as Roman Catholics,

---

[76] "Death of Mr. James W. Douglas," *Colonist*, November 10, 1883; Hills, Journal, January 15, 1890, 3.

Figure 8.4 James William Douglas, Mary Elliott Douglas, and their two sons, c.1882.

but the family was presumably motivated by a desire to establish control over the children who were primary heirs to the Douglas family estate. Making note of the family's long history of Roman Catholic practice, the court dismissed the challenge and confirmed Elliott Douglas' right to raise her children.[77] In 1901 the Douglas estate came into a trust administered for them by a local real estate company, the British Columbia Lands and Investment Agency (BCLIA).

This was a substantial estate based in the critical medium of settler colonialism: land. Map 2 shows exactly how much of central Victoria the Douglas estate owned around the time of James Douglas' death in 1877. Douglas had made strategic land purchases in and around Victoria during Vancouver Island's early days as a colony and helped his friends do the same. The Andersons were another family that was able to parlay their role in the fur-trade bourgeoisie into a role in settler British Columbia's elite and James Robert Anderson recalled another early settler claiming that "'It was Sir James Douglas who made us rich by insisting upon our taking up land.'" Anderson acknowledged that those empowered to make decisions about land were in a unique position to profit from this work of settler colonialism. "It must be remembered that rock and swamp were not considered land and therefore being worthless were thrown in free," he explained, concluding that "It may be surmised that those who had the job of designating the various characters of land were not slow to take advantage of the opportunity."[78] Douglas tended to his landholdings carefully and expanded them over the course of the nineteenth century, and in doing so, ensured that fur-trade wealth was transformed into settler wealth. Two years after his death a substantial amount of land had been transferred to his legatees. The estate still owned undeveloped land, farm lands, and urban properties valued at $34,600 in land and another $16,398 in improvements.[79]

This estate was symbol and substance of the family's class position. Inadvertently, it also produced a revealing archive that speaks to the changing politics of empire and intimacy in the early decades of the twentieth century. Its administration required that the estate's primary heirs, grandsons John and James Andrew, be closely tracked. As young men they led mobile, bohemian lifestyles and relied on Douglas family money. Each made an early marriage that broke down, and in one way or another rejected respectable bourgeois models of manhood and marriage. Invariably, these departures from gendered and familial norms

---

[77] See *Harris v. Douglas*, British Columbia Supreme Court (Victoria District), BCA, GR 1566, 1890, 479; "Harris v. Douglas," *Colonist*, November 19, 1890; "In the Courts," *Colonist*, February 19, 1891.

[78] James Robert Anderson, "Notes and Comments on Early Days and Events in British Columbia, Washington and Oregon, Including an Account of sundry happenings in San Francisco; being the Memoirs of James Robert Anderson, Written by himself," BCA, MS 1912, Box 9, Transcript, 157.

[79] Property Registers, 1879, City of Victoria Archives, PR 150. I thank Chris Hanna for his assistance with these records.

James Douglas Estate Properties, central Victoria, 1879

Properties named in James Douglas' will, c. 1877

GONZALES FARM

City Boundary Line

CADBORO BAY RD

Ross Bay

Clover Pt

BUSHBY ST

MOSS ST

FAIRFIELD ESTATE

FAIRFIELD RD

COOK ST

JOHNSON ST

YATES ST

VIEW ST

FORT ST

PANDORA AVE

VANCOUVER ST

SOUTHGATE ST

WALLACE ST

QUADRA ST

BURDETT AVE

HUMBOLDT ST

PARK RD

Public Park

Beacon Hill

Finlayson Pt

BLANCHARD ST

RAE ST

Douglas Family Home

DOUGLAS ST

GOVERNMENT ST

JAMES BAY

BIRD CAGE WALK

VICTORIA

TORONTO ST

SIMCOE ST

NIAGARA ST

BOYD ST

Holland Pt

MENZIES ST

BELLVILLE ST

ST JOHN ST

WHARF ST

VICTORIA HARBOUR

OSWEGO ST

DALLAS RD

CROSS ST

MONTREAL ST

INDIAN RESERVE

ST LAURECE ST

ERIE ST

ONTARIO ST

Ogden Pt

STRAIT OF FUCA

VICTORIA WEST

Shoal Pt

WEST BAY

1000 feet

Map 2 Map of central Victoria, showing the property named in James Douglas' 1877 will and still owned by the estate in 1879. Based on Dennis Reginald Harris and James Wyld, *Map of the city of Victoria British Columbia revised and corrected from the best authorities by D. R. Harris CE 1884* (London: James Wyld, 1884).

were read primarily through the lens of class rather than race. In correspondence, the Douglas grandsons were figured primarily as flawed or defiant representatives of a moneyed and storied family. While racial language animated the story, it did not structure it. Empire mattered, but in ways that reversed the presumed flows of the nineteenth century and relocated its subjects therein. For John and especially for James Andrew, Victoria was small and conservative, and the metropole a location they might escape to and find both freedom and recognition within.

At the turn of the century James Andrew married Jane Isabella Williams, known as Jennie, in England. They returned to Victoria, began a family, and established a well-appointed home. By naming it Lillooet, "the Indian word for beautiful," James Andrew gestured to elite British practice and inserted it within local and indigenized vernacular. Doing so held little if any risk for this generation of Douglases, whose place within local practices and identities of Whiteness were firm and secure. A local booster reported that James Andrew's home was decorated with "refined and superior taste" and noted that "Mr. Douglas is very highly regarded as a citizen" and as a businessman of "enterprise and energy."[80] Working as a real estate agent and being elected to city government, James Andrew was briefly poised to reclaim his grandfather's social role. These hopeful bourgeois beginnings came asunder when in 1907 he left Victoria for England with a woman named Lucille, with whom he would raise two children and from whom he would later separate. Most of this occurred far away from the watchful eyes of Victoria: James Andrew lived his adult life almost entirely in southern England.[81]

John Douglas also departed from expectations of bourgeois respectability. He seems to have abandoned early on his intentions to train to be a physician. In 1906 he married Jessie Ward in Washington Territory.[82] The Douglas–Ward marriage made formal ties between the Douglas' home of Victoria and Ward's of San Juan Island, places with a long shared history that confounded the border set at the forty-ninth parallel and drawn awkwardly between islands. John and Jessie moved between

---

[80] R. E. Gosnell, *A History: British Columbia* (n.p.: Lewis Company, 1906) 340, 341.

[81] See marriage record for Christchurch, Hampshire, 1900 at http://search.ancestry. ca/cgi-bin/sse.dll?ti=5543&indiv=try&db=freebmdmarriage&h=8221537, accessed November 1, 2013; James Andrew Douglas, "Scrapbook," 1894–1905, BCA, Add MSS 568. Further Information on James Andrew's life and marriage in England come from a "family tree" at http://trees.ancestry.ca/tree/1152584/person/-1986527723, accessed December 20, 2010,

[82] Gosnell, *A History*, 341; State of Washington Marriage Certificate, November 20, 1906, available at www.digitalarchives.wa.gov/ViewRecord.aspx?RID= 80199FD1D1EA753F05FC942CC1C0E7B8, accessed December 20, 2010.

western Canada, the United States, and the United Kingdom, adopting a daughter, Gertrude, along the way. By the 1910s their marriage was foundering, and John began a long and never fully successful effort to outrun Jessie and her claims on his affection, loyalty, and income. This was given legal weight by a formal divorce in 1922. Divorce remained expensive and inaccessible in Canada, but as historian Jamie Snell shows, people like Douglas increasingly availed themselves of it. After the divorce John married Orsa Demetrius Chungranes, arranging a wedding and honeymoon on "love and kisses" rather than family money.[83]

John and James Andrew both rejected the sort of marriages their grand-parents had embraced for themselves and struggled to arrange and main-tain for their own children. Their aunt Alice had made a not dissimilar rejection a half-century ago. The early twentieth century offered different intimate possibilities to bourgeois, mobile subjects. And critically John and James Andrew were both men, and the autonomy they possessed as gendered subjects was both buttressed and compromised by their status as the primary heirs to a family fortune. All this made their rejection of bourgeois marriage both less and more important. They had greater free-dom to challenge normative expectations, but there were notable costs when they did so. For John and James Andrew the context was multiply different. James Andrew's correspondence was oblique about his intimate arrangements, and the London solicitors of the estate would make game references to visits from "Jimmie and his present consort." Certainly James Andrew regularly considered divorcing Jennie, but he never did so, and he made clear that his was a deliberate rejection of marriage. He was baffled by his brother's remarriage and laid claim to the right to be unmarried, situating this in temporal terms as a possibility of modernity. "I think its best not to be married these days," he wrote in 1924; "*Be free be free* is the best."[84]

The intimate histories of John, James Andrew, and their female part-ners occurred within a series of relentlessly gendered expectations that exacted different costs and offered different languages to men and women. Both John and James Andrew formed relationships with women who were not their legal wives, but bristled at the very thought of women

[83] Arthur Wolfenden to James A. Douglas, April 3, 1923, British Columbia Land and Investment Agency Papers, BCA, MS 2880, Series 002, Box 395 (hereafter BCLIA). See also Arthur Wolfenden to James A. Douglas, November 16, 1923, BCLIA, Box 395; marriage record for John Douglas and Orsa Demetrius Chungranes, BCA, 1923–09–257084, Mflm B13745, accessed December 19, 2010, http://bcarchives.gov.bc.ca. James G. Snell, *In the Shadow of the Law: Divorce in Canada, 1900–1939* (Toronto: University of Toronto Press, 1991).
[84] James Andrew Douglas to Arthur Wolfenden, January 8, 1924, BCLIA, Box 395, empha-sis original.

doing the same. When John heard that Jessie might be living with another man, he declared that "I hate to keep up other *men*." Wives could and did access different gendered and class languages. Both Jessie and Jennie claimed their rights as elite wives who were entitled to be supported at a certain level of comfort and to maintain a certain kind of appearance. "Jack must remember I am his wife and it is up to him to look after me," demanded Jessie. The expectations that could compel reluctant men to support their partners also profoundly undermined women's capacity to support themselves. In 1917, Jessie needed to support herself but struggled to do so as a putatively married woman. Even the influence of her married name could not bend this barrier. She was rejected from a nursing training program in Victoria on the grounds that the "rules are to admit no married women or widows to the training school... If an exception *could* be made it would surely be in favour of a *Douglas*." "I guess it is up to the married women to starve," Jessie concluded. She was pleased when she finally found waged work as a hospital nurse. "It is very hard work, but I like it always did," she explained.[85]

The Douglas grandsons' challenge to ideals of bourgeois marriage was paired with a rejection of the professional and occupational identities that had become an anchor of modern middle-class masculinity. John spent much of the early twentieth century traveling through the United States, Europe, Russia, and the Pacific, living in hotels and sometimes in rented accommodation. "It is impossible to keep track of you," the estate's executors wrote, explaining that John was "like a grass-hopper, jumping all over the place." John especially liked Japan, declaring "This is the place to live cheap, you can live in great style for 100 per month including rent and wife."[86] James Andrew was more rooted in urban England, writing plays, operas, and short stories. At least two of his plays were staged in London, including *The Duchess' Necklace* at the Adwych Theatre in 1913. *The Times* was not impressed, noting that "Mr. James A. Douglas is, surely, the most artless playwright."[87] By the 1930s James Andrew was increasingly absorbed in theosophy, boring

---

[85] John Douglas to Arthur Wolfenden, January 22, 1916, BCLIA, Box 393, emphasis original; Jessie Ward Douglas to Arthur Wolfenden, 26 [no month] [1916], BCLIA, Box 393; Drake, Jackson, and Helmcken to BCLIA, August 31, 1909, BCLIA, Box 358; Sister Mary Aura to Jessie Ward Douglas, October 14, 1917, emphasis original; Jessie Douglas to Arthur Wolfenden, October 16, 1917, BCLIA, Box 393; Jessica Douglas to Arthur Wolfenden, August 4, 1921, BCLIA, Box 394.

[86] Arthur Wolfenden to John Douglas, November 23, 1916, BCLIA, Box 393; John Douglas to Arthur Wolfenden, July 19, 1914, BCLIA, Box 381.

[87] "The Duchess's Necklace," *The Times* (London), June 9, 1913.

his correspondents with lengthy reports of conversations with the dead, including his grandfather.[88]

The estate that supported the two grandsons dwindled over the first decades of the twentieth century. This presumably reflected the volatile resource economy and land values in western Canada, but the administrators of the estate were quick to blame James Andrew's and John's personal habits. "It is a great pity that they cannot take care of their money. If they were wise men, they would have been millionaires long ago," they wrote in 1910. In the following years the remaining properties in the estate were placed in a trust to "prevent the Douglas Brothers from becoming absolutely penniless." The brothers and their wives were given modest monthly incomes and regular doses of advice for prudent living. John received the most. The trustees urged him to join the navy during the Great War, explaining to him that he could not "continue to idle away your time as you are doing at present." An Oregon hotel-keeper who would later be stiffed with John Douglas' bill saw him as a cautionary tale of the dangers of a soft bourgeois upbringing. "I sometimes think Mr. Wolfenden that [it] is a crime to raise children either boys or girls, to do nothing – reverses too often come and then, one is helpless."[89]

By the 1920s the class location of this branch of the Douglas-Connolly family was unstable. For all the awareness of the family's elite background and local currency of the Douglas name, the lived present of the family was a working-class one. Don, James Andrew's teenaged son, worked at the CPR machine shops and supported his mother, who was in effect a single parent. The trustee reported that "The young kid is a hard worker" who earned more than $80 a month and had offered to help his uncle get a job threading pipe. The symbolism of this enraged James Andrew, who wrote that he "always thought my son would be a *gentleman*." This was the anger of someone stripped of their rightful place in hierarchies of capitalism. And John Douglas could probably have used the work. By 1923 he was living outside Victoria, keeping chickens, chopping wood, staying away from drink, and trying to avoid people he owed money to. By the end of the 1920s he was "busy with roadwork," the kind of seasonal, manual labor that working-class men in twentieth-century British Columbia routinely did.[90] John Douglas spent his later years in

---

[88] E. H. Cooper to Arthur Wolfenden, August 5, 1931, BCLIA, Box 406.

[89] Arthur Wolfenden to Albert E. Brayde, November 1, 1910, BCLIA, Box 501; Arthur Wolfenden to Coulthard, Suntherland and Co., February 6, 1919, BCLIA, Box 394; Arthur Wolfenden to John Douglas, July 15, 1915, BCLIA, Box 383; K. C. Manion to Arthur Wolfenden, n.d. [1915] BCLIA, Box 383.

[90] Arthur Wolfenden to John Douglas, September 30, 1920, BCLIA, Box 394; James A. Douglas to Arthur Wolfenden, October 20, 1920, BCLIA, Box 394, emphasis original;

Victoria, the city his grandparents had been so connected to. But this Douglas had no celebrated place within local society, and when he died in 1963 his death certificate described him as a retired sea captain.[91]

These stories were ones of class, status, and reputation animated but not determined by ideas of race and nation. Mary Rachel Elliott Douglas blamed her sons' flaws on their lineage, explaining that the Douglases had no "pedigree" but that she hailed from "old Irish family" and had "married beneath" her. Her sons also turned to racialized and gendered language in times of intimate stress. In one misogynistic rage John wrote about Jessie: "Anyhow she is only a damned *Yank* she is not my wife by law, as she had a *husband living* when she supposed to have married me in my drunken state. You know in any sober mind no man would marry a whore." John's correspondents would tire of these cruel tirades. But racial language, and more especially the anti-Asian discourses that were so critical to early twentieth-century Pacific Canada, had special power to express strong and negative affect. James Andrew put part of the blame for the rift between him and Jennie on her "Chinaman lover." John Douglas wrote that Jessie was a "*dirty lying half-bred smelling cow*," but his harshest charge was the same as his brother's, namely that his wife might have had an intimate relationship with a Chinese man. "You know she allowed a chink to govern her & made a home a hell on earth with her *drink* & the *chink*," he raged. Race figures as an arbiter of sexual and marital respectability, but the Creole and Metis heritage of the Douglas grandsons is no longer in question, and the sharpest axis of difference draws on a distinctly early twentieth-century racial lexicon of west-coast Canada, namely the pathologization of the uniquely domestic figure of the Chinese male servant. In this context, John Douglas' getting "*hitched up to Greek's*," as his brother put it, did not occasion much remark.[92]

John Douglas to Arthur Wolfenden, February 14, 1923, BCLIA, Box 395; Arthur Wolfenden to John Douglas, October 10, 1923, Box 395; Arthur Wolfenden to Mary Rachel Douglas, September 25, 1924, BCLIA, Box 395; Arthur Wolfenden to James A. Douglas, October 9, 1929, BCLIA, Box 395.

[91] *British Columbia, Canada, Death Index, 1872–1990*, number 1963–09–003836, BCA B 13260, www.ancestry.ca, accessed February 6, 2013; Province of British Columbia, Registration of Death, 63–09–003836.

[92] John Douglas to Arthur Wolfenden, June 24, 1921, BCLIA, Box 394; Arthur Wolfenden to John Douglas, July 25, 1921, BCLIA, Box 394; James Andrew Douglas to Arthur Wolfenden, January 1, 1924, BCLIA, Box 395; John Douglas to Arthur Wolfenden, October 17, 1919, March 8, 1922, BCLIA, Box 394; James A. Douglas to Arthur Wolfenden, May 1, 1924, BCLIA, Box 395, emphasis original. See Karen Dubinsky and Adam Givertz, "It Was Only a Matter of Passion: Masculinity and Sexual Danger," in Kathryn McPherson, Cecilia Morgan, and Nancy Forestell, eds., *Gendered Pasts: Historical Essays on Femininity and Masculinity in Canada* (Oxford University Press, 1999) 12–28.

Indigenous histories were far enough removed from Douglas and Connolly Douglas' grandsons experience that they could embrace a kind of North American identity and heritage inflected by strategic sorts of Indigenous symbols. James Andrew gave his house a self-consciously indigenous name, and joined the Native Sons of British Columbia, a fraternal organization rooted in a mythic understanding of local history and open to any man who had been born in the province. The Native Sons lobbied against Asian migration and had a limited and predictable sort of idea of Indigenous peoples and history. But Indigenous men did join, some with decisive identities and politics and others like another Douglas grandson, James Douglas Helmcken. James Andrew also paid the Native Sons membership fees and more generally claimed to be a *"real native son"* with "as much right to Victoria as any of these *outsiders,* & *intruders,* who have ruined the place." In this correspondence, British Columbia was figured as a small-minded, parochial place best escaped from. "Personally, I mean to remain in England because, for one thing, the public over in England appreciate a man with certain talents," James Andrew explained in 1912. "In our dear old country, it's a matter of grind, grind, grind."[93]

Cash-strapped and with an irregular local presence, the Douglas grandsons proved unable or uninterested in acting as stewards of the materials deemed symbolic of their grandfather's legacy. In 1921, a carriage they couldn't afford to store was donated to an HBC keen to connect its local history to its new incarnation as a modern department store. The Douglas grandsons claimed to be too poor to pay for the upkeep of the family's plot in the cemetery.[94] Representation of the family at events designed to honor British Columbia's colonial history was left to other relations with more secure locations in the province's elite.[95]

The Douglas family did not disappear. But it did disperse, become eclipsed by practices of patrilineal naming, and lose critical ingredients of its secure bourgeois identity. For this generation of the Douglas-Connolly

---

[93] James A. Douglas to Arthur Wolfenden, January 4, 1909, BCLIA, Box 358; October 20, 1920, BCLIA, Box 394, emphasis original; James Andrew Douglas to Mr. Holland, March 19, 1912, BCLIA, Box 504. See Forrest D. Pass, "The Wondrous Story and Traditions of the Country: The Native Sons of British Columbia and the Role of Myth in the Formation of an Urban Middle Class," *BC Studies,* 155 (Autumn 2006) 3–38.

[94] Mary Rachel Douglas to Arthur Wolfenden, March 23, 1927, BCLIA, Box 395; C. H. French to Arthur Wolfenden, August 8, 1921; James A. Douglas to Arthur Wolfenden, October 5, 1921; John Douglas to Arthur Wolfenden, November 8, 1921, all in BCLIA, Box 394.

[95] See Mrs. W. Fitzherbert Bullen's participation in "Celebration of the Victoria Centenary," *British Columbia Historical Quarterly,* 7:2 (1943) 137–138. Fitzherbert Bullen was Agnes Douglas Bushby's daughter.

family as for those before them, intimacy was a political terrain that derived meaning from the imperial contexts within which they lived. For these Douglas-Connolly grandchildren, imperial intimacies were settler ones tied to an increasingly Canadian British Columbia, within which the Metis and Creole heritage of the family played complicated and modest roles. What did matter was the family's local prestige and material wealth, and the vexed histories of James Andrew and John Douglas make clear that these could diminish as well as shore up the family's location in British Columbia and the British Empire's elite.

What it meant to be a person of Indigenous origin or repute shifted in late nineteenth-century western Canada. In 1876, Canada enacted the Indian Act, an instrument of invasive social regulation and byzantine race-making predicated on a patrilineal sort of blood quantum that worked hard to strip Indigenous women and children of whatever minimal rights they might be able to claim. Historian Heather Devine has shown that who ended up being "Metis" and who ended up being an "Indian" depended on social, economic, and spatial circumstances rather than bloodline. Elite fur-trade families like the Douglas-Connollys were not a direct part of these conversations and histories. As Sarah Carter has explained, they "did not acknowledge, and even took steps to obliterate," their maternal Indigenous heritage, adopting cultural, social, and behavioral codes that built on material privilege to insulate themselves from the most powerful discourses of Indigeneity.[96] None of this stopped the rumors, judgments, and conversations about their Indigenous backgrounds, or the less frequent and always cautious self-identification with Indigenous histories and peoples. Like James Douglas' racial performance some fifty years before, the practice of elite Metis people in modern western Canada was not "passing" but a more complicated and fragile making and remaking of social selves.

This chapter has traced the threaded histories of intimacy, education, and sociability in the lives of James Douglas and Amelia Connolly Douglas' children and some of their grandchildren in the latter half of the nineteenth century and the first part of the twentieth. Education and sociability helped maintain the family's location within the shifting local elite and transimperial circles, and marriage was the mechanism that secured it. Marrying securely racialized men and women drawn from different waves of the local elite maintained the family's status and authority.

---

[96] Heather Devine, *The People who Own Themselves: Aboriginal Ethnogenesis in a Canadian Family, 1660–1900* (University of Calgary Press, 2005); Sarah A. Carter, "The 'Cordial Advocate': Amelia McLean Paget and *The People of the Plains*," in Celia Haig-Brown and David A. Nock, eds., *With Good Intentions: Euro-Canadian and Aboriginal Relations in Colonial Canada* (Vancouver: UBC Press, 2006) 200.

For the two boys destined to inherit much of the family's estate, this was a story of class and material wealth, and its ability to trump certain iterations of race. It was also a story of empire, but one where settler Canada and a reconfigured British metropole played very different roles than they had for much of the family's history. Ultimately class, like race, was far from stable, and it was both made and unmade through the work of intimacy, and more particularly marriage. How marriage and intimacy made colonialism shifted, but their power to do so remained.

9   Conclusion: empire, colonies, and families

James Douglas died in Victoria, British Columbia, in 1877. His death merited a substantial obituary in the London *Times*, with consequent circulation around the imperial world.[1] Douglas' death was much bigger news in the small settler city in what was by then Canada's Pacific province. There, he was a wealthy and powerful man whose authority could be measured in honors, raw material wealth, or reputation. Accordingly, his funeral was a richly symbolic and relentlessly political occasion not wholly unlike the sort of royal tour analyzed by historian Ian Radforth. Douglas' widow consented to a "state funeral." (See Figure 9.1.) Schools in Victoria closed for the day and there was a "general suspension of business." This was a military as well as public event. The British gunboat HMS *Rocket* arrived in the harbor, fired its guns, and a hundred sailors escorted the funeral cortege.[2] Twelve years later, Amelia Connolly Douglas' funeral was a smaller, more domestic, and less official affair, but one that still articulated her location within a local elite. Her coffin was carried by pallbearers who combined British Columbia's fur-trade bourgeoisie with its newer elite tied to provincial and federal Canadian politics.[3]

This book has tracked questions of intimacy, mobility, and power in the lives of Douglas, Connolly Douglas, their family, and peers from the early years of the nineteenth century to the first decades of the twentieth. It has followed these colonial relations around the eastern Caribbean, northern North America, and the United Kingdom. It has drawn out the connections between the intimate life of partners, friends, husbands,

---

[1] "British Columbia," *The Times* (London), September 12, 1877.
[2] Alexander Grant Dallas to John Sebastian Helmcken, October 1, 1877, Helmcken Family Fonds, British Columbia Archives, Add MSS 505, Volume 2, File 4; "The Funeral of Sir James Douglas," *Colonist*, August 7, 1877; Ian Radforth, *Royal Spectacle: The 1860 Visit of the Prince of Wales to Canada and the United States* (University of Toronto Press, 2004).
[3] "The Late Lady Douglas," *Colonist*, January 10, 1890; "Funeral Arrangements," *Colonist*, January 12, 1890; "Borne to the Grave," *Colonist*, January 16, 1890.

Figure 9.1 Funeral of James Douglas, Victoria, 1877.

wives, children, and grandchildren, and the local workings of governance and economy in different configurations of empire. Putting this one family at the center of an analysis of the imperial world confirms and pushes a number of points argued in recent critical scholarship on the history of empire and the places remade by it.

The history of the Douglas-Connolly family prompts us to connect people, places, and histories across the presumed boundaries of empire, nation, and region, and suggests the power of studying empire from its ragged margins. The histories mapped here have most often been told as a British Columbian or, to a lesser extent, Canadian story. Whether as the admirable founder of a settler society, an archetypal colonizer, or a revealing example of a fur-trade wife, both Douglas and Connolly Douglas are familiar figures in the annals of Canadian history, recently offered as a usable history for a pluralist vision of Canada as a Metis nation.[4] But this history cannot be contained within the present-day nation or region projected backwards in time. To approach the history of the Douglas-Connolly family as if it could, to presume that the histories

[4] John Ralton Saul, *A Fair Country: Telling Truths about Canada* (Toronto: Viking, 2008) 15–16.

that occur outside the borders of what is now Canada are curious back-stories, difficult to understand sub-plots, or archives beyond reach truncates and misunderstands the histories of James Douglas, Amelia Connolly Douglas, and their friends and relations. Their lives were mobile ones and our history needs to be the same.

Putting a family at the core of this project provides a revealing window into the imperial world. A hemispheric history goes part of the way toward putting these particular histories into view, but risks minimizing the connections of rule, trade, and migration that tied the Americas to Europe and beyond. Yet these histories aren't best understood as ones contained within the British Empire either, at least not as defined in the usual ways. Demerara, Lower Canada, Rupert's Land, Red River, Oregon Territory, Vancouver Island, British Columbia, and Canada were all parts of the British Empire, but they were tethered to that empire in complicated ways. Colonialism was lived, administered, and conditioned through the layered histories of Dutch and French colonialism, by enduring and powerful Indigenous histories, and by emerging settler nation-states located within and outside the British Empire. Most definitions of the "British world" stress the importance of self-government and while forms of responsible government are part of the histories here, they do not define it, and can risk leaving difficult histories of fur-trade and sugar colonialism out altogether. Oceanic frames also strain to contain this history: the history of the Douglas-Connolly family is a history of both the Pacific and Atlantic worlds, and of the endless lakes and rivers of North America's interior.[5]

These were emphatically colonial relations. The lives of the Douglas-Connolly family link together a series of places that are routinely and revealingly described as "distant." This references a lived history of space and people's and goods' capacity to move through it that historians of the Antipodes have named the "tyranny of distance." Distance was real enough. The space between Guyana and Oregon Territory allowed people to reinvent their social selves, and the distance between Vancouver Island and Britain shaped the possibilities for and limits on imperial rule. But "distant" can also be a shorthand used to describe places that commanded little attention in contemporary Britain and have received a similarly small notice from historians of empire. The Douglas-Connolly

---

[5] See Allan Greer, "National, Transnational, and Hypernational Historiographies: New France Meets Early American History," *Canadian Historical Review*, 91:4 (December 2010) 695–724; Philip Buckner and R. Douglas Francis, "Introduction," to Buckner and Francis, eds., *Rediscovering the British World* (University of Calgary Press, 2005); Alison Games, "Beyond the Atlantic: English Globetrotters and Transoceanic Connections," *William and Mary Quarterly*, 63:4 (October 2006) 675–692.

family points our attention to these ragged margins, and suggests that we might re-read empire from them. Demerara, Rupert's Land, Oregon, Vancouver Island, and British Columbia were poorly funded, geographically distant colonies that never commanded much attention beyond their own borders. In these places, the enduring questions of the nineteenth-century empire – slavery, abolition, trade, dispossession, settlement, and rule – played out differently. Here the normative expectations of what empire was or ought to be fell apart and were reworked in provisional and local ways.

Putting colonial spaces in conversation with one another confirms that we need to consider colony and metropole in one analytic frame, and pushes us to probe the connections that bound different colonial spaces to one another in what Tony Ballantyne has called the "web" of empire. The histories mapped here confirm the germinal arguments made in Alan Lester and David Lambert's collection of essays on imperial biographies and, in different ways, by biographical studies like Linda Colley's biography of Elizabeth Marsh.[6] They also suggest how the frame of the individual might be expanded to that of the family. Scholars of the fur trade have found families useful and compelling frames for good reason.[7] So have historians of eighteenth-century empire like Emma Rothschild, and of American and Caribbean race like Martha Hodes.[8] Moving from the individual to the family makes it easier to put women into the practice of history, and register the complicated ties that bound colonial spaces to one another. Here those ties between the Caribbean and British North America come into especially sharp relief. The available archive does not allow us to definitively connect James Douglas' history as a Caribbean son to his history as a North American husband, son-in-law, and father, but it certainly suggests the connections between these two histories.

Different sorts of imperial intimacies made each other, and so did economies and politics. Slavery and abolition helped to make Indigenous

---

[6] David Lambert and Alan Lester, eds., *Colonial Lives across the British Empire: Imperial Careering in the Long Nineteenth Century* (Cambridge University Press, 2006); Linda Colley, *The Ordeal of Elizabeth Marsh: A Woman in World History* (New York: Harper, 2008).

[7] See, for instance, Nicole St. Onge, Carolyn Podruchny, and Brenda Macdougall, eds., *Contours of a People: Metis Family, Mobility, and History* (Vancouver: UBC Press, 2012); W. Brian Stewart, *The Ermatingers: A 19th-Century Ojibwa-Canadian Family* (Vancouver: UBC Press, 2008); Heather Devine, *The People who Own Themselves: Aboriginal Ethnogenesis in a Canadian Family, 1660–1900* (University of Calgary Press, 2005).

[8] Emma Rothschild, *The Inner Lives of Empires: An Eighteenth-Century History* (Cambridge, MA: Harvard University Press, 2011); Martha Hodes, *The Sea Captain's Wife: A True Story of Love, Race and War in the Nineteenth Century* (New York: Norton, 2006).

dispossession and resettlement. Colonial states borrowed administrative practices and processes from one another and the metropole. To explore how the histories of, say, Red River and Demerara worked to produce each other is not to diminish the enormous and consequential histories of either mode of imperial exploitation, but to explore the connections between the appropriation of labor, the appropriation of land, and the administration of states. The most powerful representative of the British Empire on North America's Pacific coast was of Caribbean origin and maintained active kin ties with the Caribbean. He was not the only colonial official in British Columbia who did. British Columbia's polymath observer and critic, Gilbert Sproat, remarked on the extent to which the colony's officials came from and through the Caribbean, noting that "the majority of the officials, governors, judges, magistrates, with many of their subordinates either were persons with Tropical connections or training, or were Irishmen. All the governors were in this category – Douglas, Kennedy – Seymour, Musgrave." Sproat noted that the only exception was Blanshard, who Sproat dubbed an "Uncaribbean Englishman."[9] Douglas was one of the Caribbean Englishmen, and one who was married into an elite Metis family whose kin networks stretched across the continent and beyond. To examine what these histories and ties meant for governance in Vancouver Island and British Columbia does not mean that we empty our analysis of considerations of power, and more particularly metropolitan and White power. It is, instead, to recall that this power was obtained, secured, and maintained through complicated means, ones that still complicate the present. Douglas was a Caribbean son, an old fur-trade hand, and a Metis husband and in-law. He was also a wealthy landowner and the superintendent of what was, by all accounts, a violent and hungry colonial regime. That he occupied these roles simultaneously does not negate any of them, and suggests the sorts of circuits that sustained empire and made it so durable.

The history of the imperial world told here has the histories of colonized places at its analytic center of gravity. The history of the Douglas-Connolly family played out in Demerara, Barbados, Lower Canada, Oregon, Red River, and British Columbia. It also occurred in England and Scotland, but the importance of these places was more symbolic and political than it was fleshy, material, and quotidian. Britain was omnipresent as a cultural reference point and an imperial authority, but as a site of lived histories and connections it did not matter all that much. Douglas and Connolly Douglas' children reversed the spatial and

---

[9] G. M. Sproat, "James Douglas," in Walter N. Sage Papers, "BC History – James Douglas," Box 35, File 34, Transcript, 18.

domestic language of empire most familiar to historians of empire: Vancouver Island was home, and England was away. A rich literature has convincingly argued that empire made the history of metropolitan Britain, and that historians' seeming willingness to think otherwise is a function of the discipline's radically unequal relationship with empire.[10] Acknowledging this should not mean forgetting the particular stake that the colonial world, and more particularly its Indigenous peoples, had in these histories. In his study of early nineteenth-century colonial scandal around the body of one free woman of color, James Epstein found that "the actual victims of colonial violence slipped into the background as debate centred on Britain's own image as an imperial nation bound by law."[11] Similar slippages can occur in the histories we write about empire. Australian historian Julie Evans points out that recent scholarship on the British Empire can adopt a disconcerting sort of "academic distance" from the troubling legacies of European expansion for colonized peoples and places.[12] As a non-Indigenous historian who lives and works in one of the many shattered spaces of empire, I find this kind of remove neither possible nor desirable. In different ways, we are all products of the brutal, complicated history of empire, and our histories must speak to the present we cannot escape and are obliged by circumstance and conscience to try to change.

In the past two decades feminist scholars have shown us how attending to questions of gender, family, and sexuality prompts us to excavate different histories of empire, ones that tell different stories about imperial power, its authority, and its limits. It also cautions us against invoking the category of family without due attention to the uneven working of power and authority within it and to the historical processes that made and remade ideas of what constituted and might constitute a family. Here I have tried to re-read the history of imperial politics and economies through the lens of what Ann Stoler has prompted us to register as "intimacy."[13] Doing so puts questions of marriage and

---

[10] See, for instance, Antoinette Burton, "Who Needs the Nation? Interrogating 'British' History," *Journal of Historical Sociology*, 10:3 (September 1997) 227–248; Catherine Hall, *Civilizing Subjects: Metropole and Colony in the English Imagination, 1830–1867* (University of Chicago Press, 2002), esp. preface.

[11] James Epstein, *Scandal of Colonial Rule: Power and Subversion in the British Atlantic during the Age of Revolution* (Cambridge University Press, 2012) 271.

[12] Julie Evans, "Biography and Global History: Reflections on Examining Colonial Governance Through the Life of Edward Eyre," in Delsey Deacon, Penny Russell, and Angela Woollacott, eds., *Transnational Ties: Australian Lives in the World* (Acton: ANU EPress, 2008) 22.

[13] Ann Laura Stoler, "Intimations of Empire: Predicaments of the Tactile and Unseen" and "Tense and Tender Ties: The Politics of Comparison in North American History and

sexuality in a wider frame that also includes a range of affective and domestic relations. Exploring the history of intimacy also points to connections between histories of governance, rule, and economy and those of marriage, sexuality, family, kinship, and child-rearing, between slavery and housekeepers, between the fur trade and influential fathers-in-law, between dutiful daughters and settler governance.

Intimacy helped make the imperial world, and the histories and politics of empire in turn helped chart the history of gender and family. The emergence and dissemination of practices and ideologies of separate spheres and domesticity have long concerned historians of the nineteenth century, as the uneven development of ideals of companionate heterosexual marriage has interested scholars of the modern world.[14] The intimate histories of Douglas, Connolly Douglas, and their kin show us how these layered histories played out in colonial spaces. In different ways, the spacialization of men and women in both the early nineteenth-century Caribbean and North American west was explicitly racialized, and preceded the widespread dissemination of sentimental Anglo-American discourse. Later in the nineteenth century, ideals of companionate marriage coexisted and sometimes conflicted with older models that emphasized parental and especially fatherly control in the intimate lives of Douglas and Connolly Douglas' children. In the twentieth-century lives of at least some of their grandchildren, the balance had tipped, and the grandsons of a man who worked to reconcile sentimental ideals of marriage with fur-trade practice would variously reject the strictures of marriage and the ways it limited their sexual and social choices, imagined in distinctly modern terms. In each of these situations, a lived practice of mobility within a far-flung imperial world profoundly condition how men and women lived their intimate lives. Marriages and families could be and regularly were multiple, men could and did reinvent their social selves, and family members easily could and did lose track of one another.

One of feminism's most enduring interventions has been to insist that the personal is political and the political is personal. The most uncooperative colonial archive can be read with a sharp eye for women. We can also take men seriously as gendered subjects. Doing so recalibrates even the

(Post) Colonial Studies," both in Ann Laura Stoler, ed., *Haunted by Empire: Geographies of Intimacy in North American History* (Durham, NC and London: Duke University Press, 2006).

[14] See, for instance, Leonore Davidoff and Catherine Hall, *Family Fortunes: Men and Women of the English Middle Class, 1780–1850* (University of Chicago Press, 1987); A. James Hammerton, *Cruelty and Companionship: Conflict in Nineteenth-Century Married Life* (London: Routledge, 1992).

most iconic figures and topics of imperial and British North American history.[15] Douglas was a fur trader, a governor, and an explorer. Examining him also as a son, a husband, a father, a grandfather, an in-law, and a friend changes the work he does within history and historiography. Beyond Margaret Ormsby's quick reference to Douglas as a "devoted family man" and John Adams' engaging study of Douglas and Connolly Douglas,[16] the scholarship on Douglas' family runs on a separate track from that dealing with his policies and politics. An adequate feminist scholarship must not only find women in the past but produce different histories of men and the economic and political worlds they inhabited.

As critics of Douglas' government knew, the politics of kinship, loyalty, and family were never easily separable from those of trade or rule. As governor, Douglas relied heavily on thick local knowledge and drew on imperial precedent and instruction when it was possible and advantageous to do so. We might make a similar argument of his intimate life. He was born to a colonial family, and created his own in very different circumstances and under Indigenous terms. When in the 1830s it became possible and expedient to renegotiate these terms, Douglas and Connolly Douglas did so, and they went on to walk a series of fine lines between longstanding local practices and increasingly powerful, widely circulating, and sometimes deeply held beliefs about virtuous wives, dutiful husbands, and the sanctity of a very specific kind of marriage. Practices of intimacy and marriage helped secure and maintain the Douglas-Connolly family's colonial authority in the middle decades of the nineteenth century. In very different ways, intimacy and marriage undermined or at least seriously reconditioned their descendants' reputations and authority in the last decades of the nineteenth century and the first decades of the twentieth.

The history of the Douglas-Connolly family also shows the categories of race and nation to be at once powerful, malleable, and local. At different times over the course of the long nineteenth century, members of the family identified with and were assigned a shifting range of national and racial designations – Colored, Mulatto, Cree, Half-Breed, French-Canadian, British, Scottish, and native-born. It is also a history of a certain and distinctly elite kind of imperial Blackness lived within a part of North America where histories of Blackness run their own track. It is

---

[15] On this, see Gail Cuthbert Brandt, "National Unity and the Politics of Political History," *Journal of the Canadian Historical Association*, 3 (1992) 3–11.
[16] Margaret A. Ormsby, "Douglas, Sir James," in *Dictionary of Canadian Biography*, Volume X, University of Toronto/Université Laval, 2003, www.biographi.ca, accessed September 6, 2008; John Adams, *Old Square Toes and his Lady: The Life of James and Amelia Douglas* (Victoria: Horsdal and Shubert, 2001).

for all of this that poet and cultural critic Wayde Compton sees Douglas as an ambivalent figure for Black British Columbians. "O James Douglas / did you ever see yourself / in us? / did you ever stop / in your war versus the wilderness / and think / we?"[17] This history is also that of Indigenous people who were mobile, both geographically and socially. In the latter part of the nineteenth century and the first part of the twentieth, they circulated among a transnational elite and Canada's settler society, and had a very small part in the regulation of Indigenous identity and life that would come to define Indigenous peoples' relationship with the Canadian state. This does not place the story of the Douglas-Connolly family outside Indigenous history, but reminds us that this history was and continues to be diverse and layered.

The history of the Douglas-Connolly family is a history of mobile elites who worked on behalf of Britain and of local elites produced within the tissue of empire. The complicated economic spaces they occupied in Guyanese cities, fur-trade posts, and Scottish schools suggest some of the particular locations occupied by the local colonial elite around the imperial world. Stories of local elites becoming delegated authority over colonial societies in which they lived and to which they were tied genealogically or intimately are a relatively familiar part of the seventeenth- and eighteenth-century imperial world. Thomas "Indian" Warner, Carib war chief and the British governor of Dominica from 1664 to his death in 1674, the "White moguls" of British India, and Superintendent of Northern Indian Affairs in Canada, William Johnson, partnered with Haudenosaunee clan-mother Molly Konwatsiatsiainni or Molly Brant (1736–1796), are some enduring examples.[18] These intimate connections between colonial governance of colonial peoples and networks lost authority in the nineteenth century as British territorial claims solidified, racial discourses hardened, and the colonial service professionalized. In some respects, we might read the story of James Douglas as an eighteenth-century story that played out in the nineteenth century. But that it did so necessarily shifts the story and how it may be read. That Douglas served as the highest representative of the British imperial state on North America's west coast and possessed significant material wealth

---

[17] Wayde Compton, "JD," in *Bluespring: Black British Columbian Literature and Orature* (Vancouver: Arsenal Pulp, 2001) 273.

[18] Chris Taylor, *The Black Carib Wars: Freedom, Survival, and the Making of Garifuna* (Jackson, MS: University of Mississippi Press, 2012) 36–39; William Dalyrymple, *White Moghuls: Love and Betrayal in Eighteenth Century India* (New York: Viking Penguin, 2003); Elizabeth Elbourne, "Family Politics in Anglo-Mohawk Diplomacy: The Brant Family in Imperial Context," *Journal of Colonialism and Colonial History*, 6 (Winter 2005).

and cultural gravitas is evidence that the authority of mixed-race elites within the British Empire persisted longer than historians usually assume it did, especially beyond the better-known and higher-profile colonies of Britain's far-flung empire. Douglas was a Creole governor married into an elite Metis family, and while this certainly complicated his career as a colonial administrator, it did not halt it.

The story of Douglas, Connolly Douglas, and their extended family and friends confirms the basic outlines of this narrative of decline and erasure, but reminds us that it occurred in uneven ways. Class and material wealth framed questions of race and nation and what they meant to individual lives. This was clear during Douglas' lifetime, and it became clearer after it. Race and class worked variably at different times over the course of the long nineteenth century, and differently in different spaces within the imperial world within which the Douglas-Connolly family moved. As people moved between metropole and colony and between different colonized spaces, they showed how the meanings grafted to different racial categories did not travel easily with the bodies with which they were associated.

In the past decade histories of lives lived across presumed boundaries of race, nation, and empire have proliferated. Stories like those of the Douglas-Connolly family are no longer much of a novelty. The value of this family's history is not that it is exceptional but that it is revelatory about the very prosaic and very consequential business of empire. We cannot separate this history from the colonial archives through which it may be narrated and analyzed and that helped to produce it. The readings these archives prompt are not ones best framed within the rubric of region or of nation. They show us that we can put gender, family, and intimacy into the mainstream of imperial histories, and register histories of marriages, children, and love as political and historical. At the ragged margins of the nineteenth-century empire, these colonial relations helped to make and remake the empire that produced them.

Select bibliography

ARCHIVES

ANGLICAN CHURCH OF CANADA, DIOCESE OF NEW WESTMINSTER/
ECCLESIASTICAL PROVINCE OF BRITISH COLUMBIA ARCHIVES (DNW/EPBCA),
VANCOUVER SCHOOL OF THEOLOGY

Good, John Booth. The Utmost Bounds of the West: Pioneer jottings of forty
  years missionary reminiscences of the Out West Pacific Coast AD 1861–AD
  1900. PSA 52, File 9.
Hills, George. Journal, 1859–90. Transcript.

BANCROFT LIBRARY (BL), BERKELEY, UNIVERSITY OF CALIFORNIA, USA

Bancroft, Hubert Howe. Bancroft Reference Notes for British Columbia and
  Alaska, c. 1870s–1890s. MSS B-C 11, Carton 1.
Cooper, James. Maritime Matters on the North West Coast and Affairs of the
  Hudson's Bay Company in early Times. P-C 6, Mflm 1.
Cridge, E. Characteristics of James Douglas. P-C 8, Mflm 1.
De Cosmos, Amor. The Governments of Vancouver Island & British Columbia.
  P-C 10.
Douglas, James. Journals. British Columbia Manuscripts, P-C 11–15, Mflm Reel
  2. Private Papers. Banc P-C 12, Mflm 2
Finlayson, Roderick. The History of Vancouver Island and the North West Coast.
  P-C 15.
Good, John B. British Columbia. P-C 19, Mlfm Reel 3.
Harvey, Eloise. Life of John McLoughlin, Governor, of the Hudson's Bay Com-
  pany's Possessions on the Pacific Slope at Fort Vancouver. P-P 12, Mlfm Reel
  2.
McKay, Joseph William. Recollection of a Chief Trader in the Hudson's Bay
  Company. P-C 24, Mflm Reel 4.
McKinlay, Archibald. Narrative of a Chief Factor of the Hudson's Bay Company.
  P-C 25, Mflm Reel 5.
Oregon Sketches, 1878. Bank MSS P-A 59–68.
Roberts, George B. Recollections of George B. Roberts. P-A 83, Mflm 2.
Swan, John M. The Colonisation around Puget Sound. P-B 21, Mflm 3.
John M. Swan & the Olympia Club Conversazione. P-B 15, Mflm Reel 3.

Tarbell, Frank. Life and Trade in Victoria during the Fraser River Excitement. P-C 26.

Tarbell, Frank. Territorial Treasurer of Washington. P-C 26.

Tod, John. History of New Caledonia and the Northwest-Coast. P-C 27.

Tolmie, William Fraser. History of Puget Sound and the North West Coast. Bancroft Collection, P-B 25, Mflm 3.

BEINECKE RARE BOOK ROOM AND MANUSCRIPT LIBRARY, YALE UNIVERSITY, NEW HAVEN, CONNECTICUT, USA

Anderson, Samuel. "Correspondence, 1859–1862," WA MSS S-1292, Box 1, Folders 17–20.

BRITISH COLUMBIA ARCHIVES (BCA), VICTORIA, BRITISH COLUMBIA, CANADA

Alston, Edward Graham. Extracts from Diary. 2/B/AL 7.1.

Anderson, James Robert. Notes and Comments on Early Days and Events in British Columbia, Washington and Oregon, Including an Account of sundry happenings in San Francisco; being the Memoirs of James Robert Anderson, Written by himself. Transcript. MS 1912.

Archives of British Columbia Correspondence, 1923–1948, GR 1738, Box 68, File 18.

Ball, Henry Maynard. Journal. Transcript, MS 0750.

Bayley, Charles. Early Life on Vancouver Island. E/B/B34.2.

Briscoe, Doreen Sybil Grant (Dallas). Notes on the late Major General Alister Grant Dallas CB, CMG. Transcript. Add MSS W/A/D168.

British Columbia – Governor (Douglas). Correspondence Outward (miscellaneous letters), November 30, 1859–December 8, 1863. C/AB/10.4/2.

British Columbia, Department of Provincial Secretary. Trustees of the Estate of Sir James Douglas, Deceased, Journal, from 2nd August 1877 to 31st July 1891. MS 1344, Mflm A7.

British Columbia Land and Investment Agency (BCLIA) Fonds, MS 2880.

British Columbia Provincial Archives Correspondence (BCPAC), BCA, GR 1738, Box 68, File 18.

Bushby, Arthur T. Journal. Transcript from original lent by Irving House, New Westminster, British Columbia, MS 811.

Christ Church Cathedral Collection. Proceedings of the Ladies' Committee re the restoration of the Parish Church and Cathedral, 1869–71, 1876–85. Add MSS 520, Box 1, Folder 7.

Crease Family Papers. Add MSS 55.

Dallas, Alexander Grant. Miscellaneous Information Relating To. W/D16.

Deans, Annie. Correspondence. E/13/D343.

Deans, James. Settlement of Vancouver Island. P-C 9, Mflm 1.

Douglas Family Correspondence, Add MSS 2164.

Douglas, James. British Columbia – Governor (Douglas). Correspondence Outward (miscellaneous letters), November 30, 1859–December 8, 1863. C/AB/10.4/2.

Douglas, James. Correspondence Outward, October 11, 1855–July 8, 1859. Mflm Reel 246.

Douglas, James. Correspondence Outward, December 15, 1866 to March 16, 1867. Transcript. B/40/3.

Douglas, James. Correspondence Outward, 1874. F/52/D74.

Douglas, James. Journal of Sir James Douglas' Trip to Europe, May 14, 1864 to May 16, 1865. Transcript. B/20/1864.

Douglas, James. Journals, notebooks and clipping books, etc., 1835–1873. MS 0678, Mflm A00792.

Douglas, James. Letters, 1858–1869. Mflm 246 A.

Douglas, James. Letters to Martha Douglas, October 30, 1871 to May 27, 1874. Transcript. BCA B/40/4 A.

Douglas, James. Miscellaneous Honours. Add MSS 112.

Douglas, James. Papers. Add MSS 1112.

Douglas, James. Private Account. Add MSS B/90/1.

Douglas, James. Private Letter Book, March 22, 1867–October 11, 1870. Transcript. Add MSS B/40/2.

Douglas, James. Will of James Douglas. 1806.

Douglas, James and Joseph William McKay. Nanaimo Correspondence, August 1852–September 1853. Transcript, Add MSS A/C/20.1/N15.

Douglas, James Andrew. Scrapbook, 1894–1905. Add MSS 568.

Douglas, James William. Correspondence Outward, 1863. E/B/D74.

Douglas, Martha. Diary, January 1 1866–April 3, 1869. Transcript. E/B/H24 A.

Fort Vancouver and Fort Victoria Register of Marriages, 1839–1860. Transcript. Add MSS 520/3/4.

Griffin, Benjamin Pitt. Chief Douglas' Daughter. Add MSS 952.

Hankin, Phillip. Memoirs. Transcript. Add MSS E/B/H19 A.

Harris, Martha (Douglas). Collection, Diaries, etc. Add MSS 2789.

Helmcken, John Sebastian. Papers. Add MSS 505.

Lamb, Kaye W. Ancestry of Sir James Douglas, KCB. Transcript. B/90/D741.

McLeod, John. Correspondence, A 1656, MS 2715.

Manson, Aurelia. Recollections. Transcript. EE M31.

Moody, Mary Susanna[h] (Hawks). Correspondence Outward. Transcript. Add MSS 60.

Muir, Andrew Muir. Private Diary, November 9, 1848–August 5, 1850. Transcript, Add MSS E/B/M91 A.

Pearse, Benjamin William. Early Settlement of Vancouver Island, 1900. Transcript. Add MSS E/B/P31.

Tod, John. History of New Caledonia and the North West Coast. E/A/T56, Box 34.

Vancouver Island, Governor. Naval Letters, 1862–4. GR 1308.

Yale, J. M. Correspondence. Transcript, MS 0182.

HUDSON'S BAY COMPANY ARCHIVES, WINNIPEG, MANITOBA, CANADA

Anderson, Alexander Caulfield. History of the Northwest Coast. E 294/1.

Dallas, Alexander Grant. Journal, 1862. E 36/2.

Douglas, James. Journal of J. Douglas, 1840–1841. Transcript. E 243/6.

Douglas, James. Correspondence, 1843–1862. Transcript. E 243/8.

Douglas, James. Correspondence Book, 1850–1855. Transcript. E 243/9.

Douglas, James to John McLoughlin. Correspondence, October 1, 1840. Transcript. E 243/11,

Ermatinger Papers, Volume I. Letters to Edward Ermatinger from John Tod, 1826–1862. Transcript. E 94/1.

Ermatinger Papers, Volume II. Letters of John Tod to Edward Ermatinger, 1864–1874. Transcript. E 94/2.

Ermatinger Papers, Volume III. Miscellaneous Correspondence, 1829–1872. Transcript. E 94/3.

Fort St. James Post Journals. Mflm 1M129.

Fort Vancouver Account Books. B 223d, Mflm 1M616.

Fort William Post Journals. 1817–1851, Mflm 1M152–1M153.

Île-à-la-Crosse Correspondence. B 89/b11.

North West Company – Ledger, 1811–1821. F 4/32, Mflm 5M8.

Register Book of Wills and Administrations of Proprietors, etc., 1841–1858. Mflm A 44/3.

Ross, Donald. Fonds. MG 1, D 20, Mflm 310.

Servants Characters & Staff Records. A 34/1.

Simpson, George. Inward Correspondence. D 5/13.

Will of Dame Julia Woolrich, PP 1865–1, PP 2109.

LIBRARY AND ARCHIVES CANADA, OTTAWA, ONTARIO, CANADA

Hargrave Collection, MG 19 A21.

NATIONAL ARCHIVES, UNITED KINGDOM

Colonial Office Correspondence, British Guiana, CO 111, File 5, Demerary and Essequibo, 1803–1812.

Colonial Office Correspondence, Vancouver Island, CO 305, 1846–1863, accessed on microfilm at British Columbia Archives, Library and Archives Canada, University of British Columbia Special Collections and online at http://bcgenesis.uvic.ca/index.htm.

Colonial Office Correspondence, British Columbia, CO 60, 1858–1871, accessed on microfilm at British Columbia Archives, Library and Archives Canada, University of British Columbia Special Collections and online at http://bcgenesis.uvic.ca/index.htm.

High Court of Justice Divorce Division. Good vs. Good otherwise de Widerholt. J 77/233/6550.

Slave Compensation Valuers' Returns, T71/757.

Slave Registers, T71/391–436.

NATIONAL ARCHIVES OF SCOTLAND, EDINBURGH

Will of John Douglas, April 16, 1841, SC70/1/60.

NATIONAL MARITIME MUSEUM (NMM), GREENWICH, UNITED KINGDOM

Corbett, Sir Julian Stafford Papers, CBT/29/s.
Hornby, Sir Phipps Admiral Papers, PH1/3/5

OREGON HISTORICAL SOCIETY (OHS), PORTLAND, OREGON, USA

Eve Emery Dye Papers, MS 1089.
Sisters of St. Ann Archives (SSAA), Victoria, BC, Canada.
St. Ann's Academy, Victoria series, Series 35, Box 3, File 1.
St. Boniface Museum Collection.
Dossier de Sr Connolly, Srs Gris de Montreal, Mais Porv.

UNIVERSITY OF BRITISH COLUMBIA (UBC), SPECIAL COLLECTIONS

Walter N. Sage Papers.

WALTER RODNEY NATIONAL ARCHIVES (WRNA), GEORGETOWN, GUYANA

Petitions, March 1820 to October 1821.
Population of St. Mary's Parish, Demerara, 1839, AK 1/2B.
Population of St. Mary's Parish, East Demerary, 1841, AK 1, 12.
Population of St. Paul's Parish, East Coast Demerara, 1839, AK 1, 3.

PRIVATE COLLECTION

Connolly, Henry. "Reminiscences of One of the Last Descendants of a Bourgeois
of the North West Company," undated manuscript made available by Anne
Lindsay and Jennifer S. H. Brown.

NEWSPAPERS, PERIODICALS, AND DATABASES

Ancestry.ca.
British Columbian (New Westminster, British Columbia).
British Guiana Colonist Index: www.vc.id.au/th/bgcolonistsD.html.
California Digital Newspaper Collection: http://cdnc.ucr.edu/cgi-bin/cdnc.
Colonist (Victoria, British Columbia).
Dictionary of Canadian Biography: www.biographi.ca.
Fort Victoria Journal, accessed at http://fortvictoriajournal.ca/.
Guyana Colonial Newspapers, including the *Essequebo and Demerary Gazette*:
www.vc.id.au/edg/index.html.
Historic Oregon Newspapers: http://oregonnews.uoregon.edu/.
Index of Historical Victoria Newspapers: www.victoriasvictoria.ca.
Manitobia.ca, including the *Nor'Wester* (Red River Colony): http://manitobia.ca/
content/en/newspapers.
Metis Scrip Database: www.collectionscanada.gc.ca/metis-scrip/005005–1000-
e.html.
Royal Gazette of British Guiana (Georgetown, Guyana).

The Times (London).
Vancouver Island censuses and maps: http://vihistory.ca/index.php.
Voyageurs database: http://voyageurs.shsb.mb.ca/.

PRINTED SOURCES

A Landowner, *British Guiana: Demerara after Fifteen Years of Freedom* (London: T. Bosworth, 1853).

Baker, William. *The Local Guide Conducting to Whatever is Worthy of Notice, in the Colonies of Demerary and Essequebo* (Georgetown: Demerary, 1819).

Baker, William. *The Local Guide Conducting to Whatever is Worthy of Notice in the Colonies of Demerary and Essequebo, for 1821* (Georgetown: Royal Gazette, n.d. [1821]).

Ballantyne, Robert Michael. *Hudson Bay: Everyday Life in the Wilds of North America, 4th edition* (London: Thomas Nelson and Sons: 1879).

Bancroft, Hubert Howe. *History of the Northwest Coast*, Volume II (San Francisco: A. L. Bancroft and Co., 1884).

Bancroft, Hubert Howe. *Literary Industries: A Memoir* (New York: Harper and Brothers, 1891).

Bancroft, Hubert Howe. *The Works of Hubert Howe Bancroft: Volume 27, History of British Columbia, 1792–1887* (San Francisco: The History Company, 1887).

Barker, Burt Brown, ed. *The McLoughlin Empire and its Rulers: An account of their personal lives, and of their parents, relatives and children; in Canada's Quebec Province, in Paris, France, and in the West of the Hudson's Bay Company* (Glendale, CA: The Arthur Clark Company, 1959).

Bouchenroeder, Friedrich von. *Map of British Guyana containing the colonies of Esequebo, Demerary & Berbice in which are Described all the Lands granted under the Batavian Government, Surveyed in 1798 and 1802, by Major Bouchenroeder with Additions* (London: James Wyld, 1824).

Bowsfield, Hartwell, ed. *Fort Victoria Letters, 1846–51* (Winnipeg: Hudson's Bay Company Record Society, 1979).

British Anti-Slavery Society, *General Anti-Slavery Convention, Called by the Committee of the British and Foreign Anti-Slavery Society Held in London on the 12th of June, 1840, and Continued by Adjournments to the 23rd of the Same Month* (London: Johnston and Barrett, 1840).

British Anti-Slavery Society, *Proceedings of the General Anti-Slavery Convention, Called by the Committee of the British and Foreign Anti-Slavery Society, and Held in London, from Friday, June 12th, to Tuesday, June 23rd, 1840* (London: British and Foreign Anti-Slavery Society, 1841).

British Guiana, *Report of the Titles to Land Commissioners on Claims to Land in the County of Berbice* (Demerara: C. K. Jardine, 1893).

Burnell, John. *British Guiana and Demerara after Fifteen Years of Freedom by a Landowner* (London: T. Bosworth, 1853).

Cameron, Malcolm. *Lecture Delivered by the Hon. Malcolm Cameron to the Young Men's Mutual Improvement Association* (Quebec: G. E. Desbartes, 1865).

Cole, Jean M., ed. *This Blessed Wilderness: Archibald McDonald's Letters from the Columbia, 1822–44* (Vancouver: UBC Press, 2001).

Connolly vs. Woolrich and Johnson *et al.*, Superior Court, Montreal, July 9, 1867, *The Lower Canada Jurist: Collection de Decisions du bas Canada*, Volume XI, (Montreal: John Lovell, 1867).

Cox, Ross. *The Columbia River, Or scenes and adventures during a residence of six years on the western side of the Rocky Mountains among various tribes of Indians hitherto unknown; together with "A Journey across the American Continent"*, ed. Edgar I. Stewart and Jane R. Stewart (Norman, OK: University of Oklahoma Press, 1957 [1831].

Dalton, Henry G. *The History of British Guiana Comprising a General Description of the Colony*, Volume I (London: Brown, Green and Longmans, 1855).

Davis, N. Darnell. "The Records of British Guiana," *Timehri*, Volume 2, new series (1888), 339–357.

Douglas, Martha Harris. *History and Folklore of the Cowichan Indians* (Victoria: Colonist Printing and Publishing, 1901).

Dumaresq de Carteret-Bisson, F. S. *Our Schools and Colleges, Volume II: For Girls* (London: Simpkin, Marshall, and Co., 1884).

Dunn, John. *History of Oregon Territory: The British North American Fur Trade; with an Account of the Habits and Customs of the Principal Native Tribes of the Northern Continent* (London: Edwards and Hughes, 1844).

Drury, Clifford Merill, ed. *First White Women over the Rockies: Diaries, Letters, and Biographical Sketches of the Six Women of the Oregon Mission who made the Overland Journey in 1836 and 1838*, Volume I (Glendale, CA: Arthur H. Clark, 1963).

Dye, Eva Emery. *Stories of Oregon* (San Francisco: Whitaker and Ray, 1900).

Emmerson, John. *Voyages, Travels, & Adventures by John Emmerson of Wolsingham* (Durham, UK: William Ainsley, 1865).

Ens, Gerhard J., ed. *A Son of the Fur Trade: The Memoirs of Johnny Grant* (Edmonton: University of Alberta Press, 2008).

Farnham, Thomas J. *Travels in the Great Western Prairies, the Anuhuac and Rocky Mountains, and in the Oregon Territory* (New York: Da Capo Press, 1973 [1843]).

Fawcett, Edgar. *Some Reminiscences of Old Victoria* (Toronto: William Briggs, 1912).

Fleming, R. Harvey, ed. *Minutes of Council Northern Department of Rupert Land, 1821–31* (London: Champlain Society for the Hudson's Bay Record Society, 1940).

Forsyth, John and W. A. Slacum. "Slacum's Report on Oregon, 1836–7," *Quarterly of the Oregon Historical Society*, 13:2 (June 1912) 175–224.

Franchère, Gabriel. *Narrative of a Voyage to the Northwest Coast of America in the Years 1811, 1813, and 1814; or, The first American settlement on the Pacific*, trans. and ed. J. V. Huntington, 2nd edition (New York: Redfield, 1854).

Franklin, John. *Narrative of a Journey to the Shores of the Polar Sea, in the Years 1819, 20, 21 and 22* (Edmonton: M. G. Hurtig, 1969 [1824]).

Gardiner, C. C. "To the Fraser River Mines in 1858," ed. Robie L Reid, *British Columbia Historical Quarterly* 1:1 (October 1937) 243–253.

Gay, Theresa, ed. *Life and Letters of Mrs. Jason Lee, First Wife of Rev. Jason Lee of the Oregon Mission* (Portland, OR: Metropolitan Press Publishers, 1936).

Gibbs, Mifflin Winstar. *Shadow and Light: An Autobiography with Reminiscences of the Last and Present Century* (Washington, DC: n.p. [1902]).

Glazebrook, G. P. de T., ed., *The Hargrave Correspondence, 1821–1843* (Toronto: The Champlain Society, 1938).

Gough, Barry M., ed. *The Journal of Alexander Henry the Younger, 1799–1814* (Toronto: The Champlain Society, 1992).

Great Britain. "Further Papers relating to Slaves in the West Indies (Berbice)," in *Papers and Correspondence Relating to New South Wales Magistrates; The West Indies; Liberated Africans; Colonial and Slave Population; Slaves; The Slave Trade; &c.*, Session 2, Volume 16 (1826).

Great Britain. *Report from the Select Committee on the Hudson's Bay Company; Together with the Proceedings of the Committee, Minutes of Evidence, Appendix and Index* (London: House of Commons, 1857).

Hale, Horatio. *An International Idiom: A Manual of the Oregon Trade Language or "Chinook Jargon."* (London: Whittaker and Co., 1890).

Harmon, Daniel. *Harmon's Journal, 1800–1819*, with a foreword by Jennifer S. H. Brown (Victoria: Touchwood Editions, 2006).

Harris, Dennis Reginald and James Wyld. *Map of the City of Victoria British Columbia revised and corrected from the best authorities by D. R. Harris CE 1884* (London: James Wyld, 1884).

Hendrickson, James E., ed. *Journals of the Colonial Legislatures of the Colonies of Vancouver Island and British Columbia, 1851–1871*, 5 volumes (Victoria: Provincial Archives of British Columbia, 1980).

Howay, F. W., William S. Lewis and Jacob A. Meyers. "Angus McDonald: A Few Items of the West," *Washington Historical Quarterly*, 8:3 (1917), 188–229.

Huntsman, Joseph, ed. Huggins Letters Outward 1899–1906 to Mrs. Eva Emery Dye (n.p., n.d., typescript).

Isbister, Alexander Kennedy. *A Few Words on the Hudson's Bay Company; With a Statement of the Grievances of the Native and Half-Caste Indians, Addressed to the British Government through their Delegates in London* (London: C. Gilpin, 1846 (?)).

Jesset, Thomas E., ed. *Reports and Letters of Herbert Beaver, 1836–1838, Chaplain to the Hudson's Bay Company and Missionary to the Indians of Fort Vancouver* (Portland: Champoeg Press, 1959).

Keith, Mrs. J. C. "Fort Victoria in Pioneer Days, 70 Years Ago," *The Daily Province* (Vancouver), January 24, 1925.

Kerr, J. B. *Biographical Dictionary of Well-known British Columbians with a Historical Sketch* (Vancouver: Kerr and Begg, 1890).

Kirke, Henry. *Twenty Five Years in British Guiana* (London: Sampson Low, Marston and Co., 1898).

Labonte, Louis. "Louis Labonte's Recollections of Men," *Oregon Historical Quarterly*, 5:3 (September 1903) 264–266.

Lamb, W. K., ed. "The Diary of Robert Melrose," *British Columbia Historical Quarterly*, 7:2 (1943) 119–134.

Lamb, W. Kaye, ed. "Five Letters of Charles Ross, 1842–44," *British Columbia Historical Quarterly*, 7:2 (1943) 103–118.

Leighton, Caroline C. "Diary of Caroline C. Leighton, December 1868," in *Life at Puget Sound, with Sketches of Travel in Washington Territory, British Columbia, Oregon & California* (Boston, MA: Lee and Sheppard, 1884).

Lewis, William S. and Naojiro Murakami, eds. *Ranald MacDonald: The Narrative of his Early Life on the Columbia under the Hudson's Bay Company's Regime; of his Experiences in the Pacific Whale Fishery; and of his Great Adventure to Japan; with a Sketch of his Later Life on the Western Frontier, 1824–1894* (Spokane: Eastern Washington State Historical Society, 1923).

Lugrin, N. de Bertrand. *The Pioneer Women of Vancouver Island, 1843–1866* (Victoria: Women's Canadian Club, 1928).

McDonald, Lois Halliday, ed. *Fur Trade Letters of Francis Ermatinger, Written to his brother Edward during his service with the Hudson's Bay Company 1818–1853* (Glendale, CA: The Arthur H. Clarke Company, 1980).

McDonnell, Alexander. *Considerations on Negro Slavery with Authentic Reports Illustrative of the Actual Condition of the Negroes in Demerara* (London: Longman, Hurst, Rees, Orme, Brown, and Green, 1824).

Macfie, Matthew. *Vancouver Island and British Columbia: Their History, Resources, and Prospects* (London: Longman, Green, Longman, Roberts, and Green, 1865).

McLeod, Margaret Arnett, ed. *The Letters of Letitia Hargrave* (Toronto: The Champlain Society, 1947).

McKelvie, B. A. *1843–1943* (n.p. [Victoria]: The Sir James and Lady Douglas Chapter of the IODE, 1943).

Mayne, Richard Charles. *Four Years in British Columbia and Vancouver Island* (Toronto: S. R. Publishers, 1969 [London: John Murray, 1862]).

Meany, Edmond S., ed. "Diary of Wilkes in the Northwest," *Washington Historical Quarterly*, 16 (1925) 49–61, 137–145, 206–223.

Menezes, M. N. *An Annotated Bibliography of Governors' Dispatches (British Guiana), Selected Years 1781–1871 (CO 111/1 (1781)–CO 384 (1781) and CO 884/1–19)* (Georgetown: Department of History, University of Guyana, 1978).

Moresby, John. *Two Admirals: Admiral of the Fleet Sir Fairfax Moresby, GCB, K MT, DCL (1786–1877) and his Son, John Moresby* (London: John Murray, 1909).

Morice, A. G. *The History of the Northern Interior of British Columbia, Formerly New Caledonia, 1660–1880*, 2nd edition (Toronto: William Briggs, 1904).

Munnick, Harriet Duncan, ed., and Mickell de Lores Wormell Warner, trans. *Catholic Church Records of the Pacific Northwest: Vancouver, Volumes I & II, and Stellamaris Mission* (St Paul, OR: French Prairie Press, 1972).

Nelson, George. *My First Years in the Fur Trade: The Journals of 1802–1804*, ed. Laura Peers and Theresa Schenck (Montreal: McGill-Queen's University Press, 2002).

Ogden, Peter Skene. *Traits of American Indian Life and Character, by a Fur Trader* (New York: Cosimo, 2009 [1933]).

Palmer, Joel. "Journal of Travels over the Rocky Mountains, 1845–6," in Rueben Gold Thwaites, ed., *Early Western Travels, 1748–1846*, Volume XXX (Cleveland, OH: Arthur H. Clark, 1906).

Pambrum, Andrew Dominique. *Sixty Years on the Frontier in the Pacific Northwest* (Fairfield, WA: Ye Galleon Press, 1978).

Parker, Samuel. *Journal of an Exploring Tour Beyond the Rocky Mountains, under the Direction of the A.B. C. F. M. Performed in the Years of 1835, '36, and '37* (Minneapolis: Ross and Haines, 1968 [1937]).

Phillips, Paul C. and John W. Hakola, eds. "Family Letters of Two Oregon Fur Traders, 1828–1856," in *Frontier Omnibus* (Missoula: Montana State University Press, 1962).

Pinckard, George. *Notes on the West Indies: written during the expedition under the command of the late General Sir Ralph Abercromby* . . . Volume III (London: Longman, Hurst, Rees, and Orme, 1806).

Pinckard, George. *Notes on the West Indies Including Observations Relative to the Creoles and Slaves of the Western Colonies and the Indians of South America Interspersed with Remarks upon the Seasoning or Yellow Fever of Hot Climates*, 2nd edition, Volumes I and II (London: Baldwin, Cradock and Joy, 1816).

Pipes, Nellie Bowden. "Extract from Exploration of the Oregon Territory, the Californias, and the Gulf of California, Undertaken during the Years 1840, 1841, and 1842 by Eugene Duflot de Mofras," *Quarterly of the Oregon Historical Society*, 26:2 (June 1925) 151–190.

Powers, Kate N. B. "Across the Continent Seventy Years Ago: Extracts from the Journal of John Ball of his Trip across the Rocky Mountains and his Life in Oregon, Compiled by his Daughter," *Quarterly of the Oregon Historical Society*, 3:1 (March 1902) 83–106.

Premium, Barton. *Eight Years in British Guiana; Being the Journal of a Residence in that Province, from 1840 to 1848, Inclusive* (London: Longman, Brown, Green and Longmans, 1850).

Pritchard, Allan, ed. *Vancouver Island Letters of Edmund Hope Verney, 1862–1865* (Vancouver: UBC Press, 1996).

Ramsey, L. F., ed. "With an Eagle's Quill: The Journal of Joseph Thomas Heath 1845–1849" (n.p., n.d., typescript).

Reese, Gary Fuller, ed. "Reminiscences of Puget Sound: Writings of Edward Huggins as Published in Pacific Northwest Newspapers and other Locations" (unpublished MS, Tacoma, 1984, held at Washington State Library, Olympia, WA).

Rich, E. E., ed. *The Letters of John McLoughlin from Fort Vancouver to the Governor and Committee, First Series, 1825–38* (London: Hudson's Bay Company Record Society, 1941).

Rich, E. E. and William Kaye Lamb, eds. *The Letters of John McLoughlin from Fort Vancouver to the Governor and Committee, Second Series, 1839–44* (London: Hudson's Bay Company Record Society, 1943).

Rich, E. E., ed. *The Letters of John McLoughlin from Fort Vancouver to the Governor and Committee, Third Series, 1844–46* (London: Hudson's Bay Company Record Society, 1944).

Rich, E. E., ed., *London Correspondence Inward from Eden Colville, 1849–1852* (London: Hudson's Bay Company Record Society, 1956).

Roberts, George. "Letters to Mrs. F. F. Victor, 1878–83," *Oregon Historical Quarterly*, 63:2/3 (June–September 1962) 175–236.

Ross, Helen E., ed. *Letters from Rupert's Land, 1826–1840* (Montreal: McGill-Queen's University Press, 2009).

Roth, Walter E., ed. and trans., *Richard Schomburgk's Travels in British Guiana, 1840–1844*, Volume I (Georgetown: Daily Chronicle, 1922).

Seemann, Berthold. *Narrative of the Voyage of the HMS Herald, during the Years 1845–51, Under the Command of Captain Henry Kellett, RN, CB* (London: Reeve and Co., 1853).

Simpson, Alexander. *The Life and Travels of Thomas Simpson: The Arctic Discoverer* (London: Richard Bentley, 1845).

Simpson, Frances Ramsay. "Diary, British North America, 1830," in Kathryn Carter, ed., *The Small Details of Life: 20 Diaries by Women in Canada, 1830–1996* (University of Toronto Press, 2002).

Simpson, George. "George Simpson's Journal, Entitled Remarks Connected with the Fur Trade in the Course of a Voyage from York Factory to Fort George and Back to York Factory 1824–25" in Frederick Merk, ed., *Fur Trade and Empire* (Cambridge, MA: Harvard University Press, 1968).

Simpson, George. "The 'Character Book' of George Simpson," in Glyndwr Williams, ed., *Hudson's Bay Miscellany, 1670–1870* (Winnipeg: Hudson's Bay Company Record Society, 1975).

Rich, E. E., ed., *Simpson's 1828 Journey to the Columbia* (London: Hudson's Bay Company Record Society, 1947).

Simpson, George. *Journal of Occurrences in the Athabasca Department, 1820 and 1821, and Report 1*, ed. E. E. Rich (Toronto: The Champlain Society, 1938).

Smith, Dorothy Blakey, ed. "The Journal of Arthur Thomas Bushby, 1858–1859," *British Columbia Historical Quarterly*, 21 (1957–1958) 83–198.

Smith, Dorothy Blakey, ed. *Lady Franklin Visits the Pacific Northwest: Being Extracts from the Letters of Miss Sophia Cracroft, Sir John Franklin's Niece, February to April 1861 and April to July 1870* (Victoria: Provincial Archives of British Columbia Memoire, No. 11, 1974).

Smith, Dorothy Blakey, ed. *The Reminiscences of Doctor John Sebastian Helmcken*, (Vancouver: UBC Press, 1975).

Smith, Marion B. "The Lady Nobody Knows," in Reginald Eyre Watters, ed., *British Columbia: A Centennial Anthology* (Toronto: McClelland and Stewart, 1958) 472–481.

Stanley, George F. G., ed. *Mapping the Frontier: Charles Wilson's Diary of the Survey of the 49th Parallel, 1858–1862, while Secretary of the British Boundary Commissions* (Toronto: Macmillan, 1870).

St. Clair, [Thomas Staunton]. *A Soldier's Recollection of the West Indies and America with a Narrative of the Expedition to the Island of Walcherrn* (London: Richard Bentley, 1834).

Tolmie, William Fraser. *The Journals of William Fraser Tolmie, Physician and Fur Trader* (Vancouver: Mitchell Press, 1963).

Walker, Thomas. *A Chart on the Coast of Guyana, Comprehending the Colonies of Berbice, Demerary & Essequebo* (London: C. G. Playter, 1799).

Wallace, W. Stewart, ed. *Documents Relating to the North West Company* (Toronto: The Champlain Society, 1934).

Warre, H. J. *Overland to Oregon in 1845: Impressions of a Journey across North America by H. J. Warre*, ed. Madeline Major-Frégeau (Ottawa: Public Archives of Canada, 1976).

Whitman, Narcissa. "Diaries and Journals of Narcissa Whitman, 1836," accessed at www.isu.edu/~trinmich/00.ar.whitman1.html.

Williams, Christina McDonald McKenzie. "The Daughter of Angus McDonald," *Washington Historical Quarterly*, 13 (1922) 107–117.

Wyeth, John B. *Oregon; or a Short History of a Long Journey from the Atlantic Ocean to the Region of the Pacific by Land, Drawn up from their Notes and Oral Information of John Wyeth . . .* (Cambridge, MA: John B. Wyeth, 1833).

SECONDARY SOURCES

Adams, John. *Old Square Toes and his Lady: The Life of James and Amelia Douglas* (Victoria: Horsdal and Shubert, 2001).

Adamson, Alan H. *Sugar without Slaves: The Political Economy of British Guiana* (New Haven and London: Yale University Press, 1972).

Alston, David. "'Very Rapid and Splendid Fortunes?': Highland Scots in Berbice (Guyana) in the Early Nineteenth century," *The Gaelic Society of Inverness*, 8 (November 2002) 208–236.

Andersen, Chris. "'I'm Métis, What's Your Excuse?': On the Optics and Ethics of the Misrecognition of Métis in Canada," *Aboriginal Policy Studies*, 1:2 (2011) 161–165.

Anderson, Clare. *Subaltern Lives: Biographies of Colonialism in the Indian Ocean World, 1790–1920* (Cambridge University Press, 2012).

Anderson, Nancy Marguerite. *The Pathfinder: A. C. Anderson's Journey in the West* (Victoria: Heritage House, 2011).

Appadurai, Arjun. *Modernity at Large: Cultural Dimensions of Globalization* (Minneapolis: University of Minnesota Press, 1996).

Arondekar, Anjali. "Without a Trace: Sexuality and the Colonial Archive," *Journal of the History of Sexuality*, 14:1/2 (January/April 2005) 10–27.

Backhouse, Constance. *Petticoats and Prejudice: Women and Law in Nineteenth-Century Canada* (Toronto: Osgoode Society and the Women's Press, 1991).

Bannister, Jerry. *The Rule of the Admirals: Law, Custom, and Naval Government in Newfoundland, 1699–1832* (University of Toronto Press, 2003).

Barman, Jean. "Invisible Women: Aboriginal Mothers and Mixed-Race Daughters in Rural Pioneer British Columbia," in Ruth Sandwell, ed., *Beyond the City Limits: Rural History in British Columbia* (Vancouver: UBC Press, 2000) 159–179.

Barman, Jean. "Taking Everyday People Seriously: How French Canadians Saved British Columbia for Canada," 2007, available at www.sfu.ca/humanities-institute-old/Taking%20Everyday%20People%20Seriously.pdf (access October 6, 2014).

Barman, Jean. "What a Difference a Border Makes: Aboriginal Racial Inter-Mixture in the Pacific Northwest," *Journal of the West*, 38:3 (July 1999) 14–24.

Barman, Jean and Bruce McIntrye Watson. *Leaving Paradise: Indigenous Hawaiians in the Pacific Northwest, 1787–1898* (Honolulu: University of Hawai'i Press, 2006).

Brandt, Gail Cuthbert. "National Unity and the Politics of Political History," *Journal of the Canadian Historical Association*, 3 (1992) 3–11.

Beckles, Hilary McD. "Freedom without Liberty: Free Blacks in the Barbados Slave System," in Verene A. Shepherd, ed., *Slavery without Sugar: Diversity in Caribbean Economy and Society since the 17th Century* (Gainsville, FL: University Press of Florida, 2002) 201–209.

Bennet, Peter. *A Very Desolate Position: The Story of the Birth and Establishment of a Mid-Victorian Public School* (n.p.: Rossall Archives, 1977).

Bonin, Marie. "The Grey Nuns and the Red River Settlement," *Manitoba History*, 11 (Spring 1986) 12–14.

Bosher, J. F. "Vancouver Island in the Empire," *Journal of Imperial and Commonwealth History*, 33:3 (September 2005) 349–368.

Bourgeault, Ron. "The Indians, the Metis and the Fur Trade: Class, Sexism and Racism in the Transition from 'Communism' to Capitalism," *Studies in Political Economy*, 12 (1983) 45–79.

Bourgeault, Ron. "Race, Class and Gender: Colonial Domination of Indian Women," *Socialist Studies: A Canadian Annual*, 5 (1989) 87–115.

Bradbury, Bettina. "Colonial Comparisons: Rethinking Marriage, Civilization and Nation in 19th Century White-Settler Societies," in Phillip Buckner and R. Douglas Francis, eds., *Rediscovering the British World* (University of Calgary Press, 2005) 135–158.

Bradbury, Bettina. *Wife to Widow: Lives, Laws, and Politics in Nineteenth-Century Montreal* (Vancouver: UBC Press, 2011).

Brown, Jennifer S. H. "Partial Truths: A Closer Look at Fur-Trade Marriage," in Ted Binnema, Gerhard Ens, and R. C. McLeod, eds., *From Rupert's Land to Canada: Essays in Honour of John E. Foster* (Edmonton: University of Alberta Press, 2002) 59–80.

Brown, Jennifer S. H. *Strangers in Blood: Fur Trade Company Families in Indian Country* (Vancouver: UBC Press, 1980).

Brown, Jennifer S. H. "Women as Centre and Symbol in the Emergence of Metis Communities," *Canadian Journal of Native Studies*, 1 (1983) 39–86.

Buettner, Elizabeth. *Empire Families: Britons and Late Imperial India* (Oxford University Press, 2004).

Burley, Edith I. *Servants of the Honourable Company: Work, Discipline, and Conflict in the Hudson's Bay Company, 1770–1879* (Oxford University Press, 1997).

Burnett, D. Graham. *Masters of All They Surveyed: Exploration, Geography, and a British El Dorado* (University of Chicago, 2000).

Burton, Antoinette, ed. *Archive Stories: Facts, Fictions, and the Writing of History* (Durham, NC: Duke University Press, 2004).

Burton, Antoinette. *Dwelling in the Archive: Women Writing House, Home, and History in late Colonial India* (Oxford University Press, 2003).

Burton, Antoinette and Jean Allman. "Gender, Colonialism, and Feminist Collaboration," *Radical History Review*, 101 (Spring 2008) 198–210.

Cail, Robert E. *Land, Man, and the Law: The Disposal of Crown Lands in British Columbia, 1871–1913* (Vancouver: UBC Press, 1974).

Campbell, Carl. "Black Testators; Fragments of the Lives of Free Africans and Free Creole Blacks in Trinidad, 1813–1877," in Bridget Bereton and Kevin A. Yelvington, eds., *The Colonial Caribbean in Transition: Essays on Post-emancipation Social and Cultural History* (Kingston, Jamaica: UWI Press, 1999) 44–54.

Carter, Sarah. *Capturing Women: The Manipulation of Cultural Imagery in the Prairie West* (Montreal: McGill-Queen's University Press, 1996).

Carter, Sarah. *The Importance of Being Monogamous: Marriage and the Politics of Nation-Building in Western Canada to 1915* (Edmonton: Athabasca University Press, 2008).

Carter, Sarah A. "The 'Cordial Advocate': Amelia McLean Paget and *The People of the Plains*," in Celia Haig-Brown and David A. Nock, eds., *With Good Intentions: Euro-Canadian and Aboriginal Relations in Colonial Canada* (Vancouver: UBC Press, 2006) 129–228.

Cavanagh, Edward. "A Company with Sovereignty and Subjects of its Own: The Case of the Hudson's Bay Company, 1670–1783," *Canadian Journal of Law and Society*, 26:1 (2011) 25–50.

Chilton, Lisa. "Canada and the British Empire: A Review Essay," *Canadian Historical Review*, 89:1 (March 2008) 89–95.

Clarke, R. C. "Editorial Comment: Reverend Herbert Beaver," *Oregon Historical Quarterly*, 39:1 (March 1938) 65–73.

Clarkson, Chris. *Domestic Reforms, Political Visions and Family Regulation in British Columbia, 1862–1940* (Vancouver: UBC Press, 2007).

Clayton, Daniel. *Islands of Truth: The Imperial Fashioning of Vancouver Island* (Vancouver: UBC Press, 2000).

Coats, Robert Hamilton and R. E. Gosnell. *Sir James Douglas: The Makers of Canada* (Toronto: Morang and Co., 1908).

Colley, Linda. *The Ordeal of Elizabeth Marsh: A Woman in World History* (New York: Harper, 2008).

Compton, Wayde. *Bluesprint: Black British Columbian Literature and Orature* (Vancouver: Arsenal Pulp Press, 2001).

Craton, Michael. 'Reluctant Creoles: The Planters' World in the British West Indies," in Bernard Bailyn and Philip D. Morgan, eds., *Strangers within the Realm: Cultural Margins of the First British Empire* (Chapel Hill: University of North Carolina Press, 1991) 314–362.

da Costa, Emilia Viotti. *Crowns of Glory, Tears of Blood: The Demerara Slave Rebellion of 1823* (Oxford University Press, 1994).

Dallas, James. *The History of the Family of Dallas, and their Connections and Descendants from the Twelfth Century* (Edinburgh: T. and A. Constable, 1921).

Davidoff, Leonore. "Kinship as a Categorical Concept: A Case Study of Nineteenth-Century English Siblings," *Journal of Social History*, 39:2 (2005) 411–428.

Davidoff, Leonore and Catherine Hall. *Family Fortunes: Men and Women of the English Middle Class, 1780–1850* (University of Chicago Press, 1987).

De Barros, Juanita. *Order and Place in a Colonial City: Patterns of Struggle and Resistance in Georgetown, British Guiana, 1889–1924* (Montreal: McGill-Queen's University Press, 2003).

Devine, Heather. *The People Who Own Themselves: Aboriginal Ethnogenesis in One Canadian Family* (University of Calgary Press, 2004).

Devine, Thomas. *Scotland's Empire: 1600–1815* (London: Penguin, 2003).

Donald, Leland. *Aboriginal Slavery and the Northwest Coast of North America* (Berkeley: University of California Press, 1997).

Down, Edith E. *A Century of Service: A History of the Sisters of Saint Ann and their Contribution to Education in British Columbia, the Yukon, and Alaska* (Victoria: Sisters of Saint Ann, 1966; revised edition, 1999).

Draper, Nicholas. *The Price of Emancipation: Slave Ownership, Compensation, and British Society at the End of Slavery* (Cambridge University Press, 2010).

Duff, Wilson. "The Fort Victoria treaties," *BC Studies*, 3 (Fall 1969) 3–57.

Elbourne, Elizabeth. "Family Politics in Anglo-Mohawk Diplomacy: The Brant Family in Imperial Context," *Journal of Colonialism and Colonial History*, 6 (Winter 2005).

Elbourne, Elizabeth. "The Sin of the Settler: The 1835–36 Select Committee on Aborigines and Debates over Virtue and Conquest in the Early Nineteenth-Century British White Settler Empire," *Journal of Colonialism and Colonial History*, 4:3 (Winter 2003).

Elliot, T. C. "Marguerite Wadin McKay McLoughlin," *Oregon Historical Quarterly*, 36 (1936) 338–347.

Emberley, Julia V. "'A Gift for Languages': Native Women and the Textual Economy of the Colonial Archives," *Cultural Critique*, 17 (1990–1) 21–50.

Epstein, James. *Scandal of Colonial Rule: Power and Subversion in the British Atlantic during the Age of Revolution* (Cambridge University Press, 2012).

Erickson, Lesley. "Repositioning the Missionary: Sara Riel, the Grey Nuns, and Aboriginal Women in Catholic Missionary Northwest," in Sarah Carter and Lesley Erickson, eds., *Recollecting: Lives of Aboriginal Women of the Canadian Northwest and Borderlands* (Edmonton: Athabasca University Press, 2011) 115–134.

Evans, Julie. "Biography and Global History: Reflections on Examining Colonial Governance through the Life of Edward Eyre," in Desley Deacon, Penny Russell, and Angela Woollacott, eds., *Transnational Ties: Australian Lives in the World* (Canberra: ANU EPress, 2009) 21–40.

Evans, Julie. *Edward Eyre: Race and Colonial Governance* (Dunedin: Otago University Press, 2005).

Eyford, Ryan. "Slave Owner, Missionary, and Colonization Agent: The Transnational Life of John Taylor, 1813–1884," in Karen Dubinsky, Adele Perry, and Henry Yu, eds., *Within and Without the Nation: Canadian History as Transnational History* (University of Toronto Press, in press).

Finlay, K. A., ed. *"A Woman's Place": Art and the Role of Women in the Cultural Formation of Victoria, BC 1850s–1920s* (Victoria: Maltwood Art Museum and Gallery, 2004).

FitzGerald, Sharron A. and Alicja Muszynski. "Negotiating Female Morality: Place, Ideology and Agency in Red River Colony," *Women's History Review*, 16:5 (November 2007) 661–680.

Foner, Philip S. "The Colored Inhabitants of Vancouver Island," *BC Studies*, 8 (Winter 1970/1) 29–33.

Foster, Hamar. "Letting Go the Bone: The Idea of Indian Title in British Columbia, 1849–1927," in Hamar Foster and John McLaren, eds., *Essays in the History of Canadian Law: British Columbia and the Yukon* (Toronto: Osgoode Society, 1995) 28–86.

Foster, Hamar. "Long-Distance Justice: The Criminal Jurisdiction of Canadian Courts West of the Canadas, 1763–1859," *American Journal of Legal History*, 34:1 (January 1990) 1–48.

Foster, John L. "Wintering, the Outsider Adult Male and Ethnogenesis of the Western Plains Métis," *Prairie Forum*, 19:1 (Spring 1994) 1–13.

Francis, Mark. *Governors and Settlers: Images of Authority in the British Colonies, 1820–60* (London: Macmillan, 1992).

Friesen, Jean. "Magnificent Gifts: The Treaties of Canada and the Indians of the Northwest, 1869–1876," *Transactions of the Royal Society of Canada*, 5:1 (1986) 41–51.

Frogner, Raymond. "'Innocent Legal Fictions': Archival Convention and the North Saanich Treaty of 1852," *Archivaria*, 70 (Fall 2010) 45–94.

Fuchs, Denise. "Embattled Notions: Constructions of Rupert's Land's Native Sons, 1760 to 1860," *Manitoba History*, 44 (Autumn/Winter 2002/3) 10–17.

Fuchs, Denise. "Native Sons of Rupert's Land 1760 to the 1860s," Ph.D. dissertation, University of Manitoba, 2000.

Galbraith, John S. *The Hudson's Bay Company as an Imperial Factor, 1821–1869* (University of Toronto Press, 1957).

Games, Alison. "Beyond the Atlantic: English Globetrotters and Transoceanic Connections," *William and Mary Quarterly*, 63:4 (October 2006) 675–692.

Gandy, Shawna Lee. "Fur Trade Daughters of the Oregon Country: Students of the Sisters of Notre Dame de Namur, 1850," MA thesis, Portland State University, 2004.

Ghosh, Durba. "Decoding the Nameless: Gender, Subjectivity, and Historical Methodologies in Reading the Archives of Colonial India," in Kathleen Wilson, ed., *A New Imperial History: Culture, Identity, Modernity, 1660–1840* (Cambridge University Press, 2004) 297–316.

Ghosh, Durba. *Sex and the Family in Colonial India: The Making of Empire* (Cambridge University Press, 2006).

Girard, Charlotte. "The Guiana World of Sir James Douglas' Childhood," unpublished MS.

Girard, Charlotte S. M. "Sir James Douglas' Mother and Grandmother," *BC Studies* 44 (Winter 1979/80) 25–31.

Girard, Charlotte S. M. "Sir James Douglas' School Days," *BC Studies* 35 (Autumn 1977) 56–63.

Girard, Charlotte S. M. "Some Further Notes on the Douglas Family," *BC Studies*, 72 (Winter 1986/7) 3–27.

Gosnell, R. E. *A History; British Columbia* (Victoria(?): Lewis Publishing, 1906).

Gough, Barry. *Gunboat Diplomacy: British Maritime Authority and Northwest Coast Indians, 1846–1890* (Vancouver: UBC Press, 1984).

Gough, Barry M. "Sir James Douglas as Seen by his Contemporaries, a Preliminary List," *BC Studies*, 44 (Winter 1979) 32–40.

Green, Cecilia A. "'A Civil Inconvenience'? The Vexed Question of Slave Marriage in the British West Indies," *Law and History Review*, 25:1 (2007) 1–59.

Green, Cecilia A. "Hierarchies of Whiteness in the Geographies of Empire: Thomas Thistlewood and the Barretts of Jamaica," *New West Indian Guide/Nieuwe West-Indische Gids*, 80: 1/2 (2006) 4–53.

Greer, Allan. "National, Transnational, and Hypernational Historiographies: New France Meets Early American History," *Canadian Historical Review*, 91:4 (December 2010) 695–724.

Greer, Allan. *The Patriots and the People: The Rebellion of 1837 in Rural Lower Canada* (University of Toronto Press, 1993).

Hall, Catherine. *Civilizing Subjects: Metropole and Colony in the English Imagination, 1830–1867* (University of Chicago Press, 2002).

Hall, Catherine. *Macaulay and Son: Architects of Imperial Britain* (New Haven: Yale University Press, 2012).

Hall, Lizette. *The Carrier, My People* (Cloverdale, BC: Friesens Printers, 1992).

Hall, Norma J. "Northern Arc: The Significance of the Shipping Seafarers of Hudson Bay, 1508–1920," Ph.D. thesis, Memorial University of Newfoundland, 2009.

Hamilton, Douglas J. *Scotland, the Caribbean, and the Atlantic World, 1750–1820* (Manchester University Press, 2005).

Harring, Sidney L. *White Man's Law: Native People in Nineteenth-Century Canadian Jurisprudence* (University of Toronto Press, 1998).

Harris, Cheryl I. "Whiteness as Property," *Harvard Law Review*, 106:8 (June 1993) 1710–1794.

Harris, Cole. *Making Native Space: Colonialism, Resistance, and Reserves in British Columbia* (Vancouver: UBC Press, 2002).

Harris, Cole. *The Reluctant Land: Society, Space, and Environment in Canada before Confederation* (Vancouver: UBC Press, 2008).

Harris, Cole. *The Resettlement of British Columbia: Essays on Colonialism and Geographical Change* (Vancouver: UBC Press, 1997).

Henderson, Jarett. "'I am Pleased with the Lambton Loot': Arthur George Doughty and the Making of the Durham Papers," *Archivaria*, 70 (Fall 2010) 153–176.

Hendrickson, James E. "The Retirement of Governor James Douglas: The View from the Colonial Office," unpublished paper, 1984.

Henry, Natasha I. *Emancipation Day: Celebrating Freedom in Canada* (Toronto: Dundurn, 2010).

Higman, B. W. *Slave Populations in the British Caribbean, 1807–1834* (Baltimore and London: Johns Hopkins University Press, 1984).

Hodes, Martha. "The Mercurial Nature and Abiding Power of Race: A Transnational Family Story," *American Historical Review*, 108:1 (February 2003) 64–118.

Hodes, Martha. *The Sea Captain's Wife: A True Story of Love, Race and War in the Nineteenth Century* (New York: Norton, 2006).

Hussey, John A. "The Women of Fort Vancouver," *Oregon Historical Quarterly*, 92:3 (Fall 1991) 265–308.

Hyde, Anne F. *Empires, Nations and Families: A History of the North American West, 1800–1860* (Lincoln: University of Nebraska Press, 2011).

Innes, Robert Alexander. "Multicultural Bands on the Northern Plains and the Notion of 'Tribal' Histories," in Jarvis Brownlie and Valerie Korinek, eds., *Finding a Way to the Heart: Feminist Writings on Aboriginal and Women's History in Canada* (Winnipeg: University of Manitoba Press, 2012) 122–145.

Ishiguro, Laura. "Settling Complaints: Discontent and Place in Late-Nineteenth-Century British Columbia," in Karen Dubinsky, Adele Perry, and Henry Yu, eds., *Within and Without the Nation: Canadian History as Transnational History* (University of Toronto Press, in press).

Jette, Melinda Marie. "'We Have Almost Every Religion but Our Own': French-Indian Community Initiatives and Social Relations in French Prairie, Oregon, 1834–1837," *Oregon Historical Quarterly* 108:2 (2007) 222–245.

Joseph, Betty. "Proxies of Power: Women in the Colonial Archive," in Felicity Nussbaum, ed., *The Global Eighteenth-Century* (Baltimore: Johns Hopkins University Press, 2003) 123–137.

Joseph, Betty. *Reading the East India Company, 1720–1840: Colonial Currencies of Gender* (University of Chicago, 2003).

Judd, Carol M. "Native Labour and Social Stratification in the Hudson's Bay Company's Northern Department, 1770–1870," *Canadian Review of Sociology and Anthropology* 17:4 (November 1980) 305–314.

Killian, Crawford. *Go Do Some Great Thing: The Black Pioneers of British Columbia* (Vancouver: Douglas and McIntyre, 1978).

Klippenstein, Frieda E. "The Challenge of James Douglas and Carrier Chief Kwah," in Jennifer S. H. Brown and Elizabeth Vibert, eds., *Reading Beyond Words: Contexts for Native History* (Peterborough, Ontario: Broadview Press, 1996) 163–192.

Koenig-Sheridan, Erika. "'Gentlemen, This is no Ordinary Trial': Sexual Narratives in the Trial of Reverend Corbett, Red River, 1863," in Jennifer S. H. Brown and Elizabeth Vibert, eds., *Reading Beyond Words: Contexts for Native History*, 2nd edition (University of Toronto Press, 2003) 365–384.

Laidlaw, Zoe. "'Aunt Anna's Report': The Buxton Women and the Aborigines Select Committee, 1835–1837," *Journal of Imperial and Commonwealth History*, 32:2 (May 2004) 1–28.

Laidlaw, Zoë. *Colonial Connections, 1815–1845: Patronage, the Information Revolution, and Colonial Government* (Manchester University Press, 2005).

Lake, Marilyn and Henry Reynolds, *Drawing the Global Colour-Line: White Men's Countries and the International Challenge of Racial Equality* (Cambridge University Press, 2008).

Lamb, W. Kaye. "The James Douglas Report on the 'Beaver Affair,'" *Oregon Historical Quarterly*, 18 (March 1946) 19–28.

Lamb, W. Kaye. "Letters to Martha." *British Columbia Historical Quarterly*, 1 (1937) 33–44.

Lamb, W. Kaye. "Some Notes on the Douglas Family," *British Columbia Historical Quarterly*, 17:1/2 (1953) 41–51.

Lambert, David and Alan Lester, eds., *Colonial Lives across the British Empire: Imperial Careering in the Long Nineteenth Century* (Cambridge University Press, 2006).

Lange, Erwin F. "Oregon City Private Schools, 1843–59," *Oregon Historical Quarterly*, 37:4 (December 1936) 308–328.

Lepore, Jill. "Historians who Love too Much: Reflections on Microhistory and Biography," *Journal of American History* 88:1 (2001) 129–144.

Lester, Alan. *Imperial Networks: Creating Identities in Nineteenth-Century South Africa and Britain* (London: Routledge, 2001).

Lindsay, Anne. "Children," unpublished research on Connolly family.

Little, Jack. "The Foundations of Government," in Hugh J. M. Johnson, ed., *The Pacific Province* (Vancouver: Douglas and McIntyre, 1996) 6–96.

Livesay, Daniel. "Extended Families: Mixed-Race Children and Scottish Experience, 1770–1820," *International Journal of Scottish Literature* 4 (Summer 2008) 1–17.

Loo, Tina. *Making Law, Order, and Authority in British Columbia, 1821–1871* (University of Toronto Press, 1994).

Lutz, John Sutton. *Makúk: A New History of Aboriginal–White Relations* (Vancouver: UBC Press, 2008).

McCallum, Mary Jane Logan. "Indigenous Labor and Indigenous History," *American Indian Quarterly* 33:4 (Fall 2009) 523–44.

McCormack, Patricia A. "Lost Women: Native Wives in Orkney and Lewis," in Sarah Carter and Patricia McCormack, eds., *Recollecting: Lives of Aboriginal Women of the Canadian Northwest and Borderlands* (Edmonton: Athabasca University Press, 2011) 61–88.

Macdonald, Charlotte. "Between Religion and Empire: Sarah Selwyn's Aotearoa/New Zealand, Eton and Lichfield, England, *c.*1840s–1900," *Journal of the Canadian Historical Association*, 19:2 (2008) 43–75.

Macdougall, Brenda. *One of the Family: Metis Culture in Nineteenth-Century North-western Saskatchewan* (Vancouver: UBC Press, 2009).

Macdougall, Brenda. "The Myth of Metis Cultural Ambivalence," in Nicole St-Onge, Carolyn Podruchny, and Brenda Macdougall, eds., *Contours of a People: Metis Family, Mobility, and History* (Vancouver: UBC Press, 2010) 422–464.

McKay, Ian. "The Liberal Order Framework: A Prospectus for a Reconnaissance of Canadian History," *Canadian Historical Review*, 81 (2000) 613–678.

McKenzie, Kirsten. *Scandal in the Colonies: Sydney and Cape Town, 1800–1850* (University of Melbourne Press, 2004).

Mackie, Richard. "The Colonization of Vancouver Island, 1849–1858," *BC Studies*, 96 (Winter 1992/3) 3–40.

Mackie, Richard. *Trading Beyond the Mountains: The British Fur-Trade on the Pacific* (Vancouver: UBC Press, 1997).

Marshall, Daniel. "Mapping the New El Dorado: The Fraser River Gold Rush and the Appropriation of Native Space," in Ted Binnema and Susan Neylan, eds., *New Histories for Old: Changing Perspectives on Canada's Native Pasts* (Vancouver: UBC Press, 2007) 119–144.

Mawani, Renisa. *Colonial Proximities: Crossracial Encounters and Judicial Truths in British Columbia, 1871–1921* (Vancouver: UBC Press, 2009).

Mehta, Uday Singh. *Liberalism in Empire: A Study in Nineteenth-Century British Liberal Thought* (University of Chicago Press, 1999).

Menezes, Mary Noel. *British Policy towards the Amerindians in British Guiana, 1803–1873* (Oxford: Clarendon Press, 1977).

Miller, Robert J. "American Indians, the Doctrine of Discovery, and Manifest Destiny," *Wyoming Law Review*, 11:2 (2011) 329–348.

Mills, Charles W. *The Racial Contract* (Ithaca and London: Cornell University Press, 1997).

Moore, Brian L. *Cultural Power, Resistance, and Pluralism: Colonial Guyana, 1838–1900* (Montreal: McGill-Queen's University Press, 1995).

Moore, Brian L. *Race, Power, and Social Segmentation in Colonial Society: Guyana after Slavery* (New York: Gordon and Breach, 1987).

Morgan, Cecilia. "'When Bad Men Conspire, Good Men Must Unite!': Gender and Political Discourse in Upper Canada, 1820s–1830s," in Kathryn M. McPherson, Nancy Forstell, and Cecilia Morgan, eds., *Gendered Pasts: Historical Essays in Femininity and Masculinity in Canada* (Oxford University Press, 1999) 12–28.

Mouat, Jeremy. "Situating Vancouver Island in the British World, 1846–49," *BC Studies*, 145 (Spring 2005) 5–30.

Nelson, Jay. "'A Strange Revolution in the Manners of the Country': Aboriginal–Settler Intermarriage in Nineteenth-Century British Columbia," in John McLaren, Robert Menzies and Dorothy E. Chunn, eds., *Regulating Lives: Historical Essays on the State, Society, the Individual and the Law* (Vancouver: UBC Press, 2002) 23–62.

Newton, Melanie. "Geographies of the Indigenous: Hemispheric Perspectives on the Early Modern Caribbean," paper presented at the University of Manitoba, March 23, 2012.

Newton, Melanie J. *The Children of Africa in the Colonies: Free People of Color in Barbados in the Age of Emancipation* (Baton Rouge: Louisiana State University Press, 2008).

Noel, Jan. *Canada Dry: Temperance Crusades before Confederation* (University of Toronto Press, 1995).

Orsmby, Margaret A. "Douglas, Sir James," in *Dictionary of Canadian Biography*, Volume X, University of Toronto/Université Laval, 2003, accessed June 9, 2008.

Pannekoek, Frits. *A Snug Little Flock: The Social Origins of the Riel Resistance, 1869–70* (Winnipeg: Watson and Dwyer, 1990).

Pascoe, Peggy. *What Comes Naturally: Miscegenation Law and the Making of Race in America* (Oxford University Press, 1991).

Pass, Forrest D. "The Wondrous Story and Traditions of the Country: The Native Sons of British Columbia and the Role of Myth in the Formation of an Urban Middle Class," *BC Studies*, 155 (Autumn 2006) 3–38.

Pateman, Carole. *The Sexual Contract* (Stanford University Press, 1988).

Peake, Linda and D. Alissa Trotz. *Gender, Ethnicity, and Place: Women and Identities in Guyana* (London: Routledge, 1999).

Penson, L. M. "The Making of a Crown Colony: British Guiana, 1803–33," *Transactions of the Royal Historical Society*, 4th series, 9 (1926) 107–134.

Perry, Adele. *On the Edge of Empire: Gender, Race, and the Making of British Columbia, 1849–1871* (University of Toronto Press, 2001).

Peterson, Jacqueline. "Many Roads to Red River: Métis Genesis in the Great Lakes Region, 1680–1815," in Jacqueline Peterson and Jennifer S. H. Brown, eds., *The New People: Being and Becoming Métis in North America* (Winnipeg: University of Manitoba Press, 1985) 37–72.

Pethick, Derek. *Victoria: The Fort* (Vancouver: Mitchell, 1968).

Pethick, Derek. *James Douglas: Servant of Two Empires* (Vancouver: Mitchell, 1969).

Petley, Christer. "'Legitimacy' and Social Boundaries; Free People of Colour and the Social Order in Jamaican Slave Society," *Social History* 30:4 (November 2005) 481–498.

Phillips, Lisa. "Transitional Identities: Negotiating Social Transitions in the Pacific NW 1825–1860s," *Canadian Political Science Review* 2:2 (2008) 21–40.

Pickles, Katie. *Female Imperialism and National Identity: The Imperial Order of the Daughters of the Empire* (Manchester University Press, 2002).

Pilon, James W. "Negro Settlement in British Columbia, 1858–71," MA thesis, University of British Columbia, 1951.

Podruchny, Carolyn. *Making the Voyageur World: Travelers and Traders in the North American Fur Trade* (University of Toronto Press, 2006).

Pollard, Juliet. "The Making of the Metis in the Pacific Northwest Fur Trade Children: Race, Class, and Gender," Ph.D. dissertation, University of British Columbia, 1990.

Porter, Kenneth W. "Negroes and the Fur Trade," *Minnesota History*, 15:4 (December 1934) 421–433.

Pybus, Cassandra. "Tense and Tender Ties: Reflections on Lives Recovered from the Intimate Frontier of Empire and Slavery," *Life Writing*, 8:1 (2011) 5–17.

Racette, Sherry Farrell. "Sewing for a Living: The Commodification of Métis Women's Artistic Production," in Katie Pickles and Myra Rutherdale, ed., *Contact Zones: Aboriginal and Settler Women in Canada's Colonial Past* (Vancouver: UBC Press, 2005) 17–46.

Radforth, Ian. *Royal Spectacle: The 1860 Visit of the Prince of Wales to Canada and the United States* (University of Toronto Press, 2004).

Reimer, Chad. *Writing British Columbia History, 1784–1958* (Vancouver: University of British Columbia Press, 2009).

Robertson, A. D. and Thomas Harvey. *Lanark Grammar School (1183–1983): The First 800 Years* (Lanark: Strathclyde Regional Council, 1983).

Robinson, Gemma and Carla Sassi. "Editorial: Caribbean–Scottish Passages," *International Journal of Scottish Literature* 4 (Spring/Summer 2008) 1–8.

Rodney, Walter. *A History of the Guyanese Working People, 1881–1905* (Baltimore: The Johns Hopkins University Press, 1981).

Rothschild, Emma. *The Inner Lives of Empires: An Eighteenth-Century History* (Cambridge, MA: Harvard University Press, 2011).

Royle, Stephen. *Company, Crown, and Colony: The Hudson's Bay Company and Territorial Endeavour in Western Canada* (London: Macmillan, 2011).

Rushford, Brett. *Bonds of Alliance: Indigenous and Atlantic Slaveries in New France* (Chapel Hill: University of North Carolina Press, 2012).

Russell, Penny. *Savage or Civilised? Manners in Colonial Australia* (Sydney: New South Books, 2010).

Sage, Walter N. *Sir James Douglas and British Columbia* (University of Toronto Press, 1930).

Salesa, Damon Ieremia. *Racial Crossings: Race, Intermarriage, and the Victorian British Empire* (Oxford University Press, 2011).

Scheper-Hughes, Nancy. *Death without Weeping: The Violence of Everyday Life in Brazil* (Berkeley: University of California Press, 1993).

Schuler, Monica. "Liberated Africans in Nineteenth-Century Guyana," in Brian L. Moore *et al.*, eds., *Slavery, Freedom, and Gender: The Dynamics of Caribbean Society* (Kingston, Jamaica: University of West Indies Press, 2001) 133–160.

Simmons, Deidre. *Keepers of the Record: The History of the Hudson's Bay Company Archives* (Montreal: McGill-Queens University Press, 2009).

Slater, G. Hollis. "New Light on Herbert Beaver," *British Columbia Historical Quarterly*, 6:1 (January 1942) 24–26.

Sleeper-Smith, Susan. *Indian Women and French Men: Rethinking Cultural Encounter in the Western Great Lakes* (Boston: University of Massachusetts Press, 2001).

Sleeper-Smith, Susan. "Women, Kin, and Catholicism: New Perspectives on the Fur-Trade," *Ethnohistory* 47:2 (Spring 2000) 423–452.

Smith, Donald B. *Honore Jaxon: Prairie Visionary* (Regina: Coteau Books, 2007).

Smith, Dorothy Blakey. *James Douglas: Father of British Columbia* (Oxford University Press, 1971).

Smith, Raymond T. "Hierarchy and the Dual Marriage System in West Indian Society," in Jane Fishburne Collier and Sylvia Junko Yanagisako, eds., *Gender and Kinship: Essays toward a Unified Analysis* (Stanford University Press, 1987).

Smith, Raymond T. *The Matrifocal Family: Power, Pluralism, and Politics* (New York: Routledge, 1996).

Smith, Raymond T. *The Negro Family in British Guiana: Family, Structure, and Social Status in Two Villages* (London: Routledge and Kegan Paul, 1956).

Snell, James G. *In the Shadow of the Law: Divorce in Canada, 1900–1939* (University of Toronto Press, 1991).

Stewart, Brian W. *The Ermatingers: A 19th-Century Ojibwa-Canadian Family* (Vancouver: UBC Press, 2008).

Stoler, Ann Laura. *Along the Archival Grain: Epistemic Anxieties and Colonial Common Sense* (Princeton University Press, 2009).

Stoler, Ann Laura, ed., *Haunted by Empire: Geographies of Intimacy in North American History* (Durham, NC and London: Duke University Press, 2006).

Storey, Kenton Scott. "'What Will They Say in England?': Violence, Anxiety, and the Press in Nineteenth Century New Zealand and Vancouver Island," *Journal of the Canadian Historical Association*, 20:2 (2009) 28–59.

Strong-Boag, Veronica and Carole Gerson. *Paddling Her Own Canoe: The Times and Texts of E. Pauline Johnson (Tekahionwake)* (University of Toronto Press, 2000).

Tennant, Paul. *Aboriginal Peoples and Politics: The Indian Land Question in British Columbia, 1849–1989* (Vancouver: UBC Press, 1990).

Thompson, Alvin O. *Unprofitable Servants: Crown Slaves in Berbice, Guyana, 1803–1831* (Kingston, Jamaica: University of West Indies Press, 2002).

Tosh, John. *A Man's Place: Masculinity and the Middle-Class Home in Victorian England* (New Haven and London: Yale University Press 1999).

Twiman, Ann. *Public Lives, Private Secrets: Gender, Honor, Sexuality and Illegitimacy in Colonial Spanish America* (Stanford University Press, 1999).

Van Kirk, Sylvia. "Colonised Lives: The Native Wives and Daughters of Five Founding Families of Victoria," in Alan Drost and Jane Samson, eds., *Pacific Empire: Essays in Honour of Glyndwr Williams* (Melbourne University Press, 1997) 215–236.

Van Kirk, Sylvia. *"Many Tender Ties": Women and Fur Trade Society, 1670–1870* (Winnipeg: Watson and Dwyer, 1980).

Van Kirk, Sylvia. "Tracing the Fortunes of Five Founding Families of Victoria," *BC Studies*, 115/116 (Autumn/Winter 1997/8) 148–179.

Van Kirk, Sylvia. "A Transnational Family in the Pacific North West: Reflecting on Race and Gender in Women's History," in Elizabeth Jameson and Shelia McManus, eds., *One Step over the Line: Toward a History of Women in the North American Wests* (Edmonton: University of Alberta Press, 2008) 81–93.

Vaughan, Meghan. *Creating the Creole Island: Slavery in Eighteenth-Century Mauritius* (Durham, NC and London: Duke University Press, 2005).

Vibert, Elizabeth. "The Contours of Everyday Life: Food and Identity in the Plateau Fur Trade," in Carolyn Podruchny and Laura Peers, eds., *Gathering Places: Aboriginal and Fur-Trade Histories* (Vancouver: UBC Press, 2010).

Vibert, Elizabeth. *Traders' Tales: Narratives of Cultural Encounter in the Columbia Plateau* (Norman, OK: University of Oklahoma Press, 1997).

Vibert, Elizabeth. "Writing 'Home': Sibling Intimacy and Mobility in a Scottish Colonial Memoir," in Antoinette Burton and Tony Ballantynne, eds., *Moving Subjects: Gender, Mobility, and Intimacy in the Age of Global Empire* (Chicago: University of Illinois Press, 2009) 67–88.

Wanhalla, Angela. "Women 'Living across the Line': Intermarriage on the Canadian Prairies and Southern New Zealand, 1870–1900," *Ethnohistory*, 55:1 (Winter 2008) 29–49.

Wanhalla, Angela. *In/Visible Sight: The Mixed Descent Families of Southern New Zealand* (Edmonton: Athabasca University Press, 2010).

Watson, Bruce McIntyre. *Lives Lived West of the Divide: A Biographical Dictionary of Fur Traders Working West of the Rockies, 1793–1858*, 3 volumes (Kelowna: Centre for Social, Spatial, and Economic Justice, 2010).

Welch, Pedro L. V. "'Unhappy and Afflicted Women?': Free Colored Women in Barbados: 1780–1834," *Revists/Review Interamericana* 29:1–4 (1999).

Welch, Pedro and Richard Goodridge. *Red and Black over White: Free Coloured Women in Pre-emancipation Barbados* (Bridgetown: Carib, 2000).

Whaley, Gray H. *Oregon and the Collapse of Illahee: US Empire and the Transformation of an Indigenous World, 1792–1859* (Chapel Hill: University of North Carolina Press, 2010).

Williams, Carol J. *Framing the West: Race, Gender, and the Photographic Frontier in the Pacific Northwest* (Oxford University Press, 2003).

Williams, James. *Dutch Plantations on the Banks of the Berbice and Canje Rivers in the Country Known since 1831 as the Colony of British Guiana and the Village Evolved from the Plantation* (Georgetown: The Daily Chronicle, 1940).

Wolfe, Patrick. "Land, Labor, and Difference," *American Historical Review*, 106:3 (June 2011) 865–906.

Woollacott, Angela. *To Try her Fortune in London: Australian Women, Colonialism, and Modernity* (Oxford University Press, 2000).

Woolworth, Stephen. "'The School is under My Direction: The Politics of Education at Vancouver: 1835–1838," *Oregon Historical Quarterly*, 104:2 (2003) 228–251.

Wright, Donald. *The Professionalization of History in English Canada* (University of Toronto Press, 2005).

Index